Homoeroticism in Classical Arabic Literature

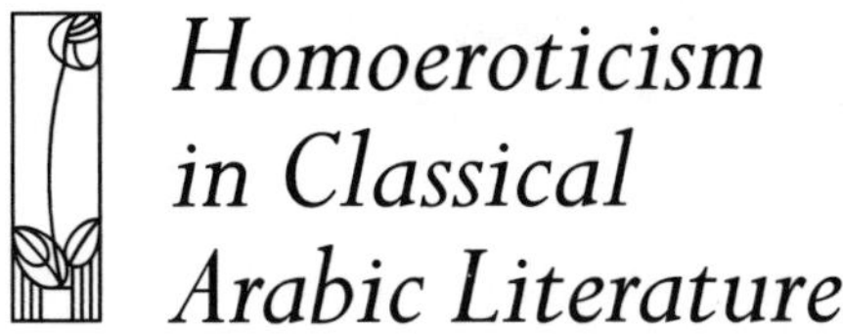

Homoeroticism in Classical Arabic Literature

EDITED BY J. W. WRIGHT JR.
AND EVERETT K. ROWSON

Columbia University Press
NEW YORK

Columbia University Press
Publishers Since 1893
New York Chichester, West Sussex

Library of Congress Cataloging-in-Publication Data

Homoeroticism in classical Arabic literature / edited by J.W. Wright Jr. and Everett K. Rowson.

p. cm.

Includes bibliographical references and index.

ISBN 0-231-10506-1. — ISBN 0-231-10507-X (pbk).

1. Erotic literature, Arabic—History and criticism. 2. Homosexuality in literature. 3. Men in literature. 4. Sex in literature. I. Wright, J.W. (Jerry W.) II. Rowson, Everett K.

PJ7519.E76H66 1997
892'.7093538—dc20 96-9565
CIP

♾

Casebound editions of Columbia University Press books are printed on permanent and durable acid-free paper.

Designed by Linda Secondari

Printed in the United States of America

c 10 9 8 7 6 5 4 3 2 1
p 10 9 8 7 6 5 4 3 2 1

To the memory

of John Boswell

CONTENTS

ABOUT THE CONTRIBUTORS

James T. Monroe was born in Dallas, Texas, and brought up in Chile, where he received a bilingual education in English and Spanish. His undergraduate years at the University of Houston were inspired by the teachings of the Spanish historian Americo Castro, who impressed upon him the importance of the Arab contribution to Spanish civilization. He received a Ph.D. in Romance languages and literatures from Harvard University, while concurrently studying Arabic with Sir Hamilton Gibb. He has published numerous books and articles in the field of Arabic literature, with special emphasis on its Hispano-Arabic component. He is currently Professor of Arabic and Comparative Literature at the University of California, Berkeley, where he has taught since 1970.

Steven M. Oberhelman is Professor of Classics and Head of the Department of Modern and Classical Languages at Texas A & M University. He has published *Rhetoric and Homiletics in Fourth-Century Christian Literature: Prose Rhythm, Oratorical Style, and Preaching in the Works of Ambrose, Jerome, and Augustine* (1991), *The Oneirocriticon of Achmet: A Medieval Greek and Arabic Treatise on the Interpretation of Dreams* (1991), and *Epic and Epoch: Essays on the Interpretation and History of a Genre,* edited with Richard Golsan and Van Kelly (1994), as well as numerous articles in journals and edited books. His monograph *Prose Rhythm in Latin Literature of the Empire: First Century* B.C. *to Fourth Century* A.D. is forthcoming in the series *Aufstieg und Niedergang der römischen Welt*. He has been editor since 1983 of the journal *Helios,* which publishes literary critical and feminist analyses of Greek and Roman literature, culture, and society.

Franz Rosenthal is Sterling Professor Emeritus of Near Eastern Languages at Yale University. Born in Berlin in 1914, he studied Semitic Languages and

Classics with H. H. Schaeder at the University of Berlin. He is the author of dozens of books and hundreds of articles in Arabic and Islamic studies, Aramaic studies, and Semitics. Many of his publications are concerned with the conflicts arising in medieval Muslim society from the clash between universal human urges and the dictates of religion, including *The Herb: Hashish versus Medieval Muslim Society* (1971), *Gambling in Islam* (1975), and *The Muslim Concept of Freedom Prior to the Nineteenth Century* (1960).

Everett K. Rowson obtained his Ph.D. in Arabic Studies from Yale University, where he studied with Franz Rosenthal. He has taught at the University of California at Berkeley and Harvard University, and is currently Associate Professor of Arabic and Islamic Studies and Director of the Middle East Center at the University of Pennsylvania. His publications include *A Muslim Philosopher on the Soul and Its Fate: Al-ʿĀmirī's Kitāb al-Amad ʿalā l-abad* (1988), *The History of al-Ṭabarī, volume XXII: The Marwānid Restoration* (1989), *Homosexuality in Traditional Islamic Culture* (forthcoming from Columbia), and a number of articles on Islamic philosophy and Arabic literature.

Richard Serrano holds a Ph.D. in Comparative Literature from the University of California at Berkeley, and is currently a Mellon Fellow at the Society of Fellows at Columbia University. He has published articles and presented conference papers on topics as diverse as psychoanalysis, ancient Chinese literary criticism, medieval French poetry, film theory, French orientalism, and medieval Arabic poetry. He is currently working on a book about Francophone poetry, tentatively titled *The Dream of a Common Language.*

Paul Sprachman's first encounter with Arabic came in Bisbee, Arizona, where he trained as a Libyan-bound Peace Corps volunteer. He acquired Persian while teaching English and trigonometry in Ghazni, Afghanistan. He studied Persian language and literature at the University of Chicago and the University of Tehran. Sprachman has translated Jalal Al-e Ahmad's *Plagued by the West* (1982) and, with Heshmat Moayyad, M. A. Jamalzadeh's *Once Upon a Time* (1985) from Persian to English. Most recently, he has edited, introduced, and translated *Suppressed Persian: An Anthology of Forbidden Literature* (1995).

Suzanne Pinckney Stetkevych received an A.B. in art history from Wellesley College and a Ph.D. in classical Arabic literature from the University of Chicago. She is currently Professor of Arabic Literature and Ruth N. Halls Professor of Near Eastern Languages and Cultures at Indiana University. In addition to her numerous articles in English and Arabic, she has published *Abū Tammām and the Poetics of the ʿAbbāsid Age* (1991) and *The Mute Immortals Speak: Pre-Islamic Poetry and the Poetics of Ritual* (1993), and has edited *Reorientations: Arabic and Persian Poetry* (1994). She has recently been appointed classical Arabic literature editor of the *Journal of Arabic Literature*.

J. W. Wright Jr. began working on this project while in graduate school at Indiana University, where he studied classical Arabic texts with Suzanne Pinckney Stetkevych. He has lived in Jordan, Saudi Arabia, and the United Arab Emirates, and traveled throughout the Middle and Near East regions. Wright is currently pursuing research as a Fulbright Scholar in Jordan. He has published numerous articles on a broad range of subjects, including an essay on the role of the female martyr motif in classical and modern Arabic literature and a chapter on political themes in Tawfiq Al-Hakim's plays and movie scripts.

PREFACE

Nearly all classical Arabic literature extant today involves stories and studies by men and about men—or so it seems, since medieval Arab scriptors almost always used masculine gender markers and related male motifs when they wrote about pleasure, politics, or power. For example, in classical Arabic literature the stallion and other hunting images represent masculine bravery and valor, and sometimes majestic beauty, while the fawn commonly symbolizes a prophetically beautiful male youth. Such male images are very often erotic, almost always provocative, and found in Arabic writings as diverse as serious and artistic poetry, comic and political satire, mystical and religious lamentation, and interpretations of the dreams of kings and princes. From pre-Islamic poems to the *Thousands and One Nights,* masculine beauty and the youthful grace of beardless boys are glorified.

Male homoeroticism (unfortunately, little survives concerning female homoeroticism) is as pervasive in classical Arabic writing as it is under-studied and misunderstood. While masculine allusion and homoerotic imagery have been noted as significant elements of classical Arabic literature—most often for polemical purposes by Western writers from medieval to modern times—they have not received sustained analysis from specialists who have the combined philological, linguistic, and cultural knowledge necessary to advance real understanding of this topic. For these reasons, our essays will prove useful not only to scholars of classical Arabic literature but also to readers in the related fields of Islamic studies, gender studies, medieval studies, and religious studies. Perhaps our essays will help break the divide that separates Eastern and Western literary and critical studies.

Although the articles in this collection are linked by their shared focus on homoeroticism in classical Arabic writing, it is as important to define at the outset what this collection is not about as to define what it is. None of the essays are about homosexuality in Arab or predominantly Islamic societies. The authors do not make suppositions about the sexual orientations or preferences of the writers whose works we address. We neither study how sexual minorities may have been treated in medieval Arab society nor regard homoeroticism as expressed by the Arab scriptors as in any way resembling modern conceptions of homosexuality. There was certainly a segment of medieval Arab society that pursued same-sex sexual interaction, as is true in all societies, but this is not the focus of our research. Nor do we present polemical statements about either homophobia or homophilia in Islam or in Arab or Muslim societies.

Instead, this collection addresses homoeroticism in classical Arabic writing by viewing the literature through diverse analytical lenses. Although our interests range from Arabic legal texts to Persian philology, this is the first systematic attempt by any group of scholars to understand the Arab scriptors' use of male motifs, masculine allusion, and phallic symbols and metaphors. Yet the collection is broader than either its title or this introduction have so far suggested, for the essays address diverse literary areas, geographical territories, and temporal periods. The authors explore homoerotic motifs in early ʿAbbāsid poetry, courtly letters, political satire, shadow plays, and dreambooks, from the eighth to the fourteenth centuries and from Persia to Andalusia.

Moreover, our essays reflect a multiplicity of approaches to the study of classical Arabic homoeroticism. Our diverse methodological styles reflect both the complexity and the pervasiveness of the homoerotic in Arabic writing, even if this collection may seem at first glance to be as schizophrenic as the Arabic texts we explore must have seemed to earlier polemical writers who rested content with superficial readings. Our essays attempt not only to delve into the sublime meaning of the texts under consideration but also to explore their connections to political conventions, social mores, and subversive theology. We hope that our fractured uses of many critical theories reveal new depths and provide new understanding of classical Arabic letters, poems, prose, and scripts.

While the contributors believe that methodological diversity is intellectually stimulating, we are not of one mind about where to go next in the study of Arabic homoeroticism. On theoretical points, for example, and even on such specific questions as whether a given symbol is homoerotic, we have sometimes disagreed. Nonetheless, the authors have worked hard to develop in our essays a cohesiveness that reflects our firm and shared belief that homoerotic symbolism plays a vital role in classical Arabic literature.

We have also reached general agreement that serious scholarly, gender-conscious, and culture-conscious readings of homoerotic texts reveal levels of meaning far beyond the titillation enjoyed by polemical readers; they reveal complex parody and satire through which artists and writers metaphorically strengthen their social and moral positions vis-à-vis the dominant Islamic polity. By viewing homoeroticism as a reflection of sublime and often subversive ideals, our studies offer new insights into a powerful literary tradition that has been plagued by centuries of misreadings. This collection constitutes the first real attempt to correct these misreadings.

Homoeroticism in Classical Arabic Literature will reach the market during a period of rising excitement about Arabic literary studies that has brought the field closer to the limelight. The authors seek to increase this enthusiasm and recognition by bringing together specialists to consider what may be the two most pervasive themes in classical Arabic literature: homoeroticism and masculine allusion.

Moreover, we prove the importance of these themes by writing from both long-established and new traditions of Arabic literary criticism. For example, my essay takes the relatively new approach to Arabic literary criticism that has been set out by Jaroslav Stetkevych and the "Chicago School." In my review of Abū Nuwās's *khamrīya* and *mujūn* writings, I develop the idea that he goes far beyond the buffoonery for which he is famous; his works present a brilliant array of political satire and social parody. My chapter and the final two essays in the collection, by Paul Sprachman and Suzanne Pinckney Stetkevych, also take the Chicago approach.

In contrast, a more traditional method of studying Arabic texts is provided by Franz Rosenthal, one of the most prolific scholars in the field. He applies in his essay the well-known critical approach that he has perfected over many years of scholarship. In a way reminiscent of his study of medieval debates over the use of cannabis in *The Herb: Hashish versus Medieval Muslim Society,* Rosenthal's article offers a meticulous study of ʿAbbāsid "*Rangstreit*" literature, presents an overview of the development of the genre, and provides an exposition of the epigrammatic context of homoerotic symbolism.

Steven Oberhelman, a classicist by training, presents an analysis of the dreambook collections recorded by Achmet ibn Sereim. Oberhelman provides a compendium of Greek, Byzantine, and Arab dream interpretation literature, and in doing so offers valuable cultural information about social hierarchies and sexual norms among the ruling elites during this period. Moreover, he shows how Achmet's analysis of dreams illustrates medieval men's perceptions of masculine authority and homoerotic beauty.

James Monroe and Richard Serrano represent the "Berkeley Camp" in this collection. Their essays look at homoeroticism in Andalusian Arabic literature. Monroe analyzes the way the poet Ibn Quzmān used ambiguous but explicitly vulgar language and sexual innuendo to form mock panegyrics aimed at subverting courtly etiquette, and, in the end, at challenging the entire social order. Serrano employs a Lacanian psychoanalytic approach to investigate al-Sharīf al-Ṭalīq's uses of homoeroticism in his poetry. Rather than view the poet's use of masculine allusions as a method of subversion, Serrano tries to uncover the motive force of the poem and its imagery. He identifies the homoerotic motifs as part of a circle of mystery that surrounds al-Ṭalīq's poems.

Everett Rowson's essay, like Rosenthal's, combines meticulous linguistic analysis with a deep knowledge of medieval Arabic texts. In addition, Rowson includes a cutting-edge discussion of gender symbolism in general and homoerotic allusion in particular as reflections of social ideals. The result is an article, written in a classicist's style, that yields new insights into the Mamlūk tradition's use of homoeroticism. Rowson analyzes two pieces of homoerotic literature from fourteenth-century Egypt, Ibn Dāniyāl's shadow play *al-Mutayyam wal-Ḍāʾiʿ al-Yutayyim,* which is written in the *mujūn* style, and al-Ṣafadī's prose text *Lawʿat al-shākī wa-damʿat al-bākī,* which is an idyllic romance written in the *sajʿ* style. These texts illustrate two entirely different but standard uses of homoerotic themes in Mamlūk texts.

Paul Sprachman's essay appears next and explores the long-standing literary and social traditions pertaining to the growing of beards in medieval Arab society. By tracing the notion of the beardless beauty in both Arabic and Persian texts, he compares the way homoerotic allusion is reflected in poetic traditions and in legal and political texts. Thus Sprachman helps us contextualize the social meaning of beardedness. He also shows that many Arabic texts cannot be analyzed in isolation from the broader Persian traditions that existed during the medieval period, and uses both Arabic and Persian linguistic analysis to reveal the connections between texts and traditions.

The concluding article in this collection is Suzanne Pinckney Stetkevych's "Intoxication and Immortality: Wine and Associated Imagery in al-Maʿarrī's Garden." One of this article's key contributions is the identification of a circular process Arab scriptors used to morally and socially trap the prevailing political organization. This circular process can be seen in a wide variety of texts in which a writer wants to raise his position in society above that of his foe or courtly patron. This volume thus begins with an article that relies heavily on Suzanne Pinckney Stetkevych's work, presents essays that reflect variant approaches to the study of Arabic homoerotic motifs, and then returns to the Stetkevych article that helped to shape the first essay. Stetkevych's short reintroduction, "Old Wine in a New Bottle," discusses the next steps we need to take to uncover meaning in Arabic texts.

This book will provide much material for debate and intellectual inquiry to scholars in many fields of study. At the same time, the authors' sense of curiosity and the roguish nature of the texts being examined make the collection interesting reading for a wider audience. We hope that you will enjoy reading our book as much as we enjoyed writing it.

J. W. Wright Jr.

ACKNOWLEDGMENTS

Many people have helped us during the long process that has culminated in the publication of this collection of essays. Professor John Boswell of Yale University was an early and ardent supporter of the project. He was, in fact, planning to write the introduction to the collection, but declining health prevented him from doing so. With his death in late 1994 the world lost a prodigious scholar and a dedicated humanitarian. We dedicate this book to his memory.

The editors wish to thank the contributors to this volume for their patience and hard work. It has been a pleasure working with them. We are especially grateful to Suzanne Pinckney Stetkevych for her invaluable support in the initial stages of this project and in the review process. We also thank Lida Daves Baldwin, Fedwa Malti-Douglas, Allen Douglas, Allen M. Omoto, and Jaroslav Stetkevych for assistance and advice. Dawn Baker deserves thanks for her help in preparing the manuscript. We also would like to express our gratitude to our editor, Ann Miller and copyeditor, Leslie Kriesel; to the production staff at Columbia University Press; and to our anonymous readers, whose comments helped us in shaping and refining our articles.

Homoeroticism in Classical Arabic Literature

CHAPTER ONE

Masculine Allusion and the Structure of Satire in Early ʿAbbāsid Poetry

J. W. Wright Jr.

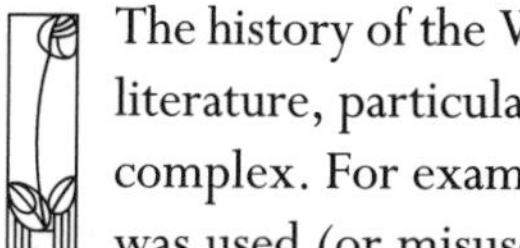

The history of the West's misunderstanding of classical Arabic literature, particularly the use of masculine erotica, is old and complex. For example, homoerotic imagery in Arabic poetry was used (or misused) by conspirators to vilify Arab-Muslim culture and motivate European governments and peoples to participate in the medieval Christian crusades to Jerusalem,[1] and later by politicians and writers intent on establishing European moral and social superiority over the Andalusians, Arabs, Persians, and Ottomans.[2]

In modern times, analysis of classical Arabic literature has too often been limited to readings of medieval rhetorical works that fail to identify the derivation of motifs and symbols.[3] In the case of homoerotic poetry and prose the texts have largely been ignored. For example, even Edward Said's *Orientalism*—a formidable piece of comparative literature—is problematic in its analysis of gender precisely because it fails to discuss readings of homoerotic texts.[4] And while Arabic poetry is increasingly recognized as a vital genre for study in fields ranging from the classics to semiotics, its structure and use of metalanguage and double entendre are notoriously difficult to decipher.[5]

It is understandable, then, that popular readings of Arabic homoerotic literature are usually misreadings marked by the inability to recognize sociocultural twists and taboos unknown in Western writing. Sir Richard Burton's rendition of *The Thousand Nights and a Night* is the classic case in which a

---

Several people have helped me develop the ideas put forth in this paper. I want to thank David Adams, Scott Alexander, Alan Douglas, Audrey Fessler, Lee Irwin, Fedwa Malti-Douglas, John Hartley, Louis Malamud, James Monroe, Everett Rowson, Martha Robertson, Jean Simonian, Jaroslav Stetkevych, Suzanne Pinckney Stetkevych, Jefford B. Vahlbush, and Beverley Wolff for their comments. Early versions of this essay have been presented as lectures at Indiana University, The University of Chicago, and The University of California at Berkeley. I want to thank the organizers of those lectures.

Western translator has assumed surface-level readings to be true.[6] It is not unusual for homoerotic allusions that create political and social satire to be mistaken as evidence of "sexual culture of the Muslim societies"[7] or as "dimensions of gay religious history."[8] James Cleugh's *A History of Oriental Orgies* is supposed to provide "An Account of Erotic Practices Among Peoples of the East and Near East,"[9] but actually offers a catalogue of Western conjecture about Muslim literature. As far back as the thirteenth century, Jacques de Vitry's claim that "Muḥammad, the enemy of nature, popularized the vice of sodomy"[10] shows how preposterous Western assertions have been.

At the other extreme, sympathizers with "gay causes" have tried to attack Western homophobia by projecting homophilia onto classical Arabic texts[11] like those found in al-Jāḥiẓ's treatises, but in the process they fail to recognize the rhetorical depth and complexity of al-Jāḥiẓ's work.[12] This situation has also added to the perceived inability of Occidentals to understand sexual culture in the Arab world. Indeed, such an interpretation literally reproduces the Western fantasy about the "pan-sexualized Middle East, a place of liminality and change . . . the exotic, feminized Eastern Other."[13]

In fact, ʿAbbāsid poetry played "a complex social and political role"[14] as a structure in which to express factionalism, parody, and satire. In many cases, the use of symbols and metaphors such as the "glorifying of wine" and "profane songs" became "a living protest."[15] In other cases, poets used these symbols to recall pre-Islamic tribal mores or to challenge political mandates and theological edicts. In just as many cases, poems about wine and boys were written as entertainment for the courts of elites. But even here this *mujūn* literature, writing that used profligacy motifs or allusions to sexual deviations to flout social and religious norms, succeeded only because basic assumptions surrounding poets' jokes were widely shared by the members of their audiences.[16] Over time, famous poets' styles of jests were extended through *muʿāraḍa,* the writing of poems as responses to poems with the intention of outdoing rival courtiers.[17] It is this common frame of social reference, not the poet's personal behavior, his sincerity or his insincerity, that makes social and political satire humorous. That the poet entertains wealthy clients only serves to make his jokes' satirical sting worse.

In this essay, I explore homoerotic imagery in early ʿAbbāsid *khamrīya* or wine poetry, mainly that of Abū Nuwās,[18] a leading poet in the early years of the ʿAbbāsid empire, to illustrate how Arabic poets used illicit symbolism contained in sacred texts and religious commentaries to create parody and satire about political and spiritual leaders. I also propose carrying on Jaroslav Stetkevych's examination of "Arabic Hermeneutical Terminology"[19] and Suzanne P. Stetkevych's "experiment in literary-critical method"[20] in order to show how homoerotic satirical works written by medieval Arabic scriptors represent a metonymical complex of beliefs and reactions.

The advent of Islam mandated Arab society's transition from a predominantly tribal community to an urban one, and from a diverse community tolerant of many traditions and religions to a single order led by a Muslim Arab ruling elite. This transition did not come easily for Arabs or non-Arabs, and not even for true believers. Expansion of the Islamic Empire forced Arabs to allow peoples from many cultures and tribes to be assimilated into their communities. In addition, the urban-Arab political hierarchy was imposing increasingly strict interpretations of socioreligious mores. Mandates for change were often very unappealing to non-Arabs, particularly Berbers, Greeks, and Persians who felt their subjugation to the Arabs disgraced their grand ancestries. When public protest met militant reprisals, new methods of expressing discontent developed. An increasingly popular genre of poetry exploited structural and literary conceits in a way that marginalized the new polity's authority; it relied on "innovation in the realm of religion and theology"[21] as a means to set reflective textual and theological ambiguities against each other in satirical panegyric. Primary motifs in this poetry include the drinking of wine, the admiration of heavenly-looking ephebes, and the metaphorical sexual subjugation of heroes and religious leaders.

Discussion of the mythopoetic implications of homoerotic symbolism in the *khamrīya* requires an etymological and hermeneutical base allowing a full philological introduction to the texts' semantic complexity and paradox. Jaroslav Stetkevych's article, "Arabic Hermeneutical Terminology: Paradox and the Production of Meaning," is ultimately concerned with literary devices Arab writers in the classical period used to draw scriptural texts into circular-satirical traps. The article begins by recognizing that the origin of hermeneutics is found in attempts to access sacred words and meanings in religious texts. Mortal endeavors to understand these texts often end with the realization that divine meaning is intellectually inaccessible. In response, philosophers and priests create means of making sacred words understandable to humans. In Greek mythical-religious traditions, various messengers appear who can deliver and interpret sacred texts. Hermes, messenger for Olympian gods, is the prototypical "mediator between gods and men."[22] He is between the prescribed positions for gods and men, or, more correctly, his state is liminal. His association with the gods makes him immortal, but his palimpsestic consortium with humans makes his work profane.

Yet Hermes' station gives him control over the gods who must have their messages delivered and over mortals who are damned if he does not interpret sacred edicts. The master patriarch of this paradox is "Hermes Trismegistos, the thrice-great god, one half the archaic Hermes and the other half the equally archaic Egyptian god Thoth; the inventor of the hieroglyphic and the one who measures the true weight, and worth, of the human heart [and who holds] the key to unlocking the significance of the sacred message [written in hieroglyphic]."[23] Thothic-hieroglyphic, then, is thrice-great, but it is also thrice-removed from its sacred origin. This is where scripture fails and religious factionalism begins. The occult and denominational movements form around tensions between the scriptural need for secrecy and the communicability necessary for revelation. As sacred texts are interpreted they form antitexts. As scripture is recited by mortals it becomes dogmatic and perhaps even profane. In time, rituals replace meaning. Control over this circular pattern lies with the "liminal herm" who carries the message but who also bastardizes sacred texts to make them understandable.

Many examples of this self-defeating pattern exist in scriptural texts. The Old Testament condemns sorcery and magic as tricks of the devil. However, when asked by the magicians to prove the divinity of his message, Moses counters their legerdemain by creating snakes from sticks, blood from water, etc. While the Hebrews record Moses' feats as miracles, the court magicians interpret them as sorcery. In the Qur'ān, verses 26:224–226 vilify poets as antagonists, leaders of "those likely to be led into error." The Qur'ān also refutes the idea that Muḥammad is a poet (21:5, 36:69, 37:36, 52:30, 64:41). But when asked to prove that his revelations are sacred, Muḥammad recites verse 52:30–34 and challenges the poets to create anything more beautiful; the scripture's authority is both confirmed in its beauty and subverted by its need to compete with poetry.

Accordingly, says J. Stetkevych, such dialectic tension becomes the basis of an all-pervading cognitive paradox that operates within the texts' structural polarity. The closure of interpretation makes one's position an anti-position, the texts antitexts. The Muʿtazila used this cognitive paradox to escape the anthropomorphist entrapment of literal readings of revelation; the Shīʿa used it, albeit only for a short time, to see imaginative rather than dogmatic meaning in Qu'rānic verses; the Ismāʿīlīs used textual ambiguity to justify their militarism; the Ṣūfīs used the paradox when forming allegorical and anagogical mystical notions and rituals.

The key elements are the mediator's "betweenness," the "inter" of interpretation, and the way marginality and liminality connect the messenger to the realm of eternity. Suzanne P. Stetkevych's article "Intoxication and

Immortality: Wine and Associated Imagery in al-Maʿarrī's Garden," which is reprinted in this volume, makes the link between textual ambiguity and symbols of liminal immortality. Stetkevych shows how scriptural Qur'ānic quotation, poetic quotations, and political prose are interwoven in many texts so that licit and illicit imagery seem to merge. For example, in al-Maʿarrī's version of the heavenly garden the *aqua vitae* is mixed with wine, honey, and milk. Wine, the "eternal liquor," is not only a delightful reward, it is both immortal and immortalizing. In the Qur'ānic garden, too, there are "rivers of wine" (47:15) and "sealed wine" (83:22), wine served to the Lord (12:41), and wine that "causes no throbbing brows, no intoxication" (56:18). The pious are told they will receive the youthful pleasures they desire, including "wide-eyed houris [heavenly virgins], like hidden pearls, . . . [and] immortal youths with goblets" (56:10–38). As for these youths who serve the wine, "when you see them you think them scattered pearls" (76:5–21).

While the sacredness of wine is sustained in the Qur'ān and in many epistles like al-Maʿarrī's, most jurists are eager to point out that the Qur'ān makes drinking real wine strictly illicit (5:90–91, 2:219). When not referred to as one of the delights of heaven, wine is condemned and associated with forbidden pre-Islamic cultic rituals. The message is clear: "Whatever the benefits of mortal wine, immortal wine is better. To forego the latter to indulge in the former is foolhardy."[24] By the same token, what are false pleasures in mortality are true pleasures in immortality. By intertwining illicit this-side-of-life imagery with other-side-of-life texts, the panegyric gives the poet theological, ritual, or mythic power. The poetic outcomes were often comic or satiric paradigms, illustrating social or political hypocrisies.

Determining the sources of these motifs is problematic. Wine is the immortalizing liquid in the Dionysian cult, which has its roots in Egyptian mythology,[25] and al-Maʿarrī's notion of heaven is strikingly close to that found in Euripides' *Bacchae.* The Islamic *sāqī,* for example, dresses in flowing robes, wears scented ringlets, bears wine, and has eyes more beautiful than those of the houris.[26] Ephebes also play key roles in medieval Hebrew poetry, which likewise have their roots in a broader Semitic poetry's homoerotic motifs.[27] Similar allusions to wine and its cupbearers are made in Persian cosmological/religious writings,[28] giving Islamic symbols counterparts in Zoroastrian paradisiacal lore: "the most important of these symbols is the wine of the Magi [served by a beautiful male cupbearer, which] suggested deliverance from the commandments of orthodoxy, as well as a means of ecstasy."[29] Similarities are also found in Manichaean religious texts, some of which are suggestive of ecstatic, possibly orgasmic, ultimate unions with the immortals.[30]

In ancient mythology, Inana (Ishtar), the goddess of sexual love and protector of prostitutes, gains immortality by serving wine to Enki and then seducing him.[31] Gilgamesh searches for immortality by consorting with the barmaid-goddess Siduri, who also tries to seduce him. Gilgamesh's attachment to male lovers certainly ties the quest for immortality to wine drinking and homoerotic love.[32] Palmyrene inscriptions and decorative motifs reveal ritual symbolism resembling that found in the cults of Dionysus.[33] Canaanite traditions include visions of the banquets of the gods, where wine is served by young brothers who are unblemished in their beauty and whose lips a deity can expect to kiss.[34] Hieroglyphic texts indicate that wine drinking followed by homosexual penetration may have been included in religious rituals honoring Seth and Horus.[35] We should not be surprised at the popularity of these motifs, since owning handsome eunuchs and slave boys for sexual gratification was fashionable at Andalusian, Arab, Egyptian, Greek, Hebrew, Hindu, and Persian courts, among others.[36]

In short, the use of hermeneutic-homoerotic motifs is based in long-established Semitic literatures, religions, and rituals. The use of wine and homoerotic symbolism by the ʿAbbāsid poets simply plays into a hermeneutic cycle that interpolates and often juxtaposes pre-Islamic poetic structures and pagan religious motifs into interpretations of Islamic texts. In these ancient traditions, men who associate with, gain control over, or subvert the authority of the "liminal" bearer of the message/liquid (Hermes, Thoth, the *sāqī,* Siduri, or Enki) conquer the vicissitudes of time. As will be seen later, this gives pursuit of the handsome male *sāqī* the utmost textual importance.

One other argument, based on Victor Turner's anthropological-cultural criticism, should be raised about how heterogeneous social constructs prevailing at the time became reflected in literature.[37] Islam called for transition from an endogenous tribal network to a social fabric tied by the more ambiguous concept of Umma. In addition, the new Arab ruling elite began to issue mandates, supposedly furthering Arabization, that became edicts for urbanization. Opponents of these policies included powerful bedouin tribesmen who scoffed at the effeminacy (and Persian-ness) of city life, believing the hardships of the desert produced noble character.[38] When the ʿAbbāsid poet Abū Tammām wrote "You are not you, the abodes are not abodes, desires have turned away. The dwelling nearby the ruins and their folk, that once was sweet to drink at, now tastes of salt,"[39] he was expressing nostalgia for nomadic mores and traditions. Many Arabs, especially those from powerful or militant bedouin tribes, believed social urbanization mocked family and tribal values. In response, tribal poets portrayed urban leaders or their sons as being effeminate, beautiful, smooth-skinned, or promiscuous boys, with dominant male lovers.

It is interesting that the ganymedean myth and other homoerotic Greek stories have been called into question to some extent as sociopolitical rather than religious texts. Bernard Sargeant, for example, asserts that homoerotic symbolism in Greek writing was a means of subversion as it was, he claims, in Arabia.[40] Patricia Springborg points out in her chapter on "Hesiod and the Oriental Cosmologies" that Semitic mythical traditions became motifs, if not methodologies, for subverting the Greek cosmological order following Alexander's campaigns to Persia.[41] Eva C. Keuls supports this notion by illustrating the political aspects of the effeminization of leaders through erotica in Greek political writing.[42]

It is not surprising, then, that the literary styles and structures chosen to create parody and satire were drawn from the *Jāhilīya,* a pre-Islamic age famous for, among other things, distinctly Arabo-nomadic poetry.[43] The poetic genre of this period had a rich history of wine symbolism and some use of homoerotic imagery.[44] More important, it was a literature that used gender-based double entendre to express criticism and satire.[45] The eyes of the gazelle, for example, do not simply describe beautiful women, but represent motifs for hierarchical subversion. Poems that metaphorically emasculated or feminized enemy armies often formed conceits for military rhetoric. This genre allowed poets to interweave theological and textual ambiguities, pagan religious symbolism, and pre-Islamic literary structures into a *tropos* in which the poet's social derelictions/predispositions make him "a member of a caste of advanced standing."[46] Poets earn this station through their control of Islam's "liminal herm," the wine-bearing *sāqī.*

Before turning to works by Abū Nuwās and others, it is important to consider further the tension that exists in Islamic texts between homoerotic beauty and homosexual activities. Clearly, there is recognition that men can be inspired by masculine beauty and homoerotic intimacy. Later Ṣūfī poets claimed that Muḥammad's love for Muʿādh represented a paradigm condoning chaste love between men.[47] There is also evidence that the Prophet understood the lure of pedophilia, although he forbade the act. In one *ḥadīth* he reportedly said, "Keep not company with the sons of Kings, for verily souls desire them."[48] Another *ḥadīth* reads, "Do not gaze at the beardless youths, for verily they have eyes more tempting than the houris."[49] Certainly he was not seen as being socially at odds with effeminate men, for in another commentary it is claimed Muḥammad let transvestites (*mukhannath,* effeminate men who often served as entertainers for the Arab elite) see the faces of his unveiled wives.

Some Muslim writers, like P. D. Nahum, claim these traditions show that Islam views homosexuality with "philosophical indifference."[50] This might seem to be the case when verses like Sura 4:16 are viewed in isolation:

> If two of you have committed an unchastity,
> then punish you both.
> If they repent and amend
> leave them alone, for God
> is oft-returning, and merciful.

More striking is Muslim texts' use of masculine beauty as a measure of divinity. The story of Joseph is a primary example of the way the Qur'ān promotes the notion of masculine beauty, and descriptions of the heavenly *sāqīs* give them a beautiful, homoerotic, and greater-than-mortal quality. In other texts written by ʿAbbāsid caliphs and Islamic jurists, and in some *ḥadīth,* Allah is presented in the form of a beautiful male youth. As used in these contexts, male beauty marks Allah's divinity and Joseph's prophet role. Richard Serrano discusses the image of Joseph's beauty in greater detail in his essay in this volume, as does Suzanne Pinckney Stetkevych.

However, just as some traditions of the Prophet display tolerance for homoerotic desires, Muslim men are clearly forbidden to have sex with each other, primarily because it distracts them from propagating the faith.[51] The sins of the people of Lot are mentioned twelve times in the Qur'ān, which explicitly links homosexual activities to the destruction of Lot's tribe. The legality of two men having sexual relations is also addressed in Sura 26:165–173: "Of all creatures do you come unto the males and leave the wives the Lord has created for you? . . . dreadful is the rain on those who have been warned," and in Sura 7:81: "Lo! Ye who come with lust unto men instead of women. Nay you are wanton folk." In a *ḥadīth* the Prophet is reported to have said, "Whenever a male mounts another male the throne of God trembles, the angels look down in loathing and say, Lord, why do you not command the earth to punish them and the heavens to rain stones upon them?"[52]

Given the weight of these traditions, the level of homosexual tolerance among the general population in early Islamic society is difficult to determine, beyond the fact that homosexual copulation was widely known to be considered unproductive and self-indulgent by the religious polity. It is just this sort of textual tension, however, that ʿAbbāsid poets used to turn scriptural conflicts into exegetical tools for trapping the ruling elite in satirical panegyrics in which the authority of Islamic rituals is undercut, theological chaos ensues, and rebellion begins.[53] A favorite ploy of Abū Nuwās was to impose homoerotica onto descriptons of Islamic rituals. In one poem he claims that Islamic rhetoric on submission (*islām*) means that he and other pious men should assume an active sexual position with Christian, Jewish, and Zoroastrian boys, thereby making them submit to Muslim pleasure. He asserts that it is the "duty of every Muslim to sleep with them [boys of other faiths]."[54]

On a social level, too, the poets' choice of homoerotic motifs is clever. Various medieval texts indicate that Arab males followed a progression of initiatory stages from boyhood into manhood. These included a prepubescent period when the dominant adult figure was the mother, a stage between puberty and manhood when a homosocial male environment was introduced (much like the stage of the Greek and Roman ephebes), and attainment of the age of majority when a boy should prove his willingness to defend the faith. In the second stage, a beardless youth's station was somewhat liminal. At this age, he moved from being female-dominated to male-dominated. In short, he existed, like the *sāqī*, to serve men who had earned their positions, but at this stage in life boys were not held accountable for manly ventures such as propagating sons or proving military valor; their beauty and sexual activities were not condemnable on socioreligious pretexts.

It should be noted that Abū Nuwās uses heteroerotic motifs as well, such as comparing a virgin's blood to flowing wine, although references to male youths are more common. However, there is substantial reason to believe that sexual references to women were more scandalous than sexual references to boys. For example, wine in feminine allusion usually refers to flowing virgin blood, while in references to boys it implies drunkenness. In cultural context, the stealing of a bride's virginity was a much more serious offense than penetrating a boy. In fact, pederastic penetration does not imply the loss of personal or family honor, as I discuss with reference to al-Jurjānī later in this essay.

Several poets are famous for metaphorical religious and social justifications of their sexually initiating young male infidels into the Muslim fold, claiming their predilection was their form of *jihād*.[55] Obviously, Islam neither encourages nor rationalizes sexual domination of boys by men as a legitimate form of *jihād*, and the word *islām* does not imply sexual subjugation. Rather, the poets are imposing sexual proclivities onto theological mandates about submission. In appropriating the community's social/religious initiatory stages, the poets create satire and parody in which faithful submission means pursuing illicit homoerotic activities.

In a parody of Islam's obligatory prayers, Abū Nuwās describes two boys who are in love and who want to thank Allah for bringing them together. Instead of performing the regular *ṣalāt* at the mosque, the two decide to replace their five-times-daily prayers with fornication at each prayer call. The poet concludes that the boys have "brought the religion to perfection, and even increased the laws of Islam."[56] The poem attacks the very heart of Islam, but it does so from within the religion. The boys are fulfilling their obligation to praise God, they are obeying orders against celibacy, and they are submitting to the religion's rituals in the most intense way possible. Their method, of course, is scandalous and subversive, and the poet uses vulgarity to reduce ritual *ṣalāt* to nothing more than a joke in which homosexual intimacy becomes a pun for prayer.

A later Andalusian poet, Ibn Sahl, one of Abū Nuwās's disciples, wrote a poem about his decision to leave a Jewish lover named Mūsā (Moses) for the passion of a new, younger lover named Muḥammad:

> I abandoned the love of Moses to adore Muḥammad;
> thus without the direction opened up by the merciful one,
> I would have not discovered the right path.
> This change is not inspired by aversion;
> but the law of Moses has been abrogated by that of
> Muḥammad.[57]

Once again this outrageous jest identifies the religion with homoeroticism. This time the poet accuses male lovers of prophets of being whimsical, and the stages of God's relevations to humanity are depicted as akin to the emotions of immature lovers. The poet's perspective also equates religious faith with youthful infatuation and by extension makes men's attachment to any religion at best temporary. This sentiment also plays into a common "lament over the inevitable brevity of one's passion for a boy."[58] Abū Nuwās's objection was to the mandated cessation of desire, but by the eleventh century this mandate was commonly addressed in debates over the continued passion for the bearded in both Arabic and Persian texts.[59]

The ʿAbbāsid poets thrived on symbiotic textual relationships equating text with antitext and scripture with antiscripture, the licit with the illicit, and immoral with immortal. For example, the Garden's immortalizing wine is found in the cupbearer's glass and the pearls of heaven glimmer in a drunken boy's eyes. Compare the following verses from the Qur'ān,

56:17 Surrounding them will be (male) youths to serve them in their perpetual freshness, with goblets, shining beakers, and cups filled from flowing fountains.

56:22 And they (the male cupbearers) will be with beautiful, big, and lustrous eyes; like well-guarded pearls. A reward for the deeds of life.

71:20 Upon them will be green robes of fine silk and they will be adorned with bracelets of silver and their lord will give them to drink wine which is pure and holy.

and verses from two of Abū Nuwās's poems:

A beautiful lad came carrying the wine
with smooth hands and fingers dyed with henna,
and with long hair of golden curls around his cheeks.
Whenever he approached he made a promise with his eyes
and he addressed us with alluring eyelashes.
If you had seen them,
you would have thought them more than human;
as if they were instead concealed pearls.[60]

I have a lad who is like the beautiful lads of paradise
and his eyes are big and beautiful . . .
his face is as the moon in its full perfection
and you think he is mysteriously struck by a magician
because he is so tender and pretty.
We spent that night together as if we were in paradise
doing nothing except making love and pleasure.[61]

And:

A beautiful lad carries this wine in his beautiful hands.
He walks in a tempting way like the fawns in the Garden.[62]

Abū Nuwās's contentious use of imagery equates the heavenly *sāqī* with the earthly server of the wine. He suggests he has indeed found the rewards of paradise on earth, hidden in the cupbearer/waiter's heavenly eyes and prophetic beauty. Just as the *sāqī*/ephebe is between man and god, the youthful cupbearer/waiter is between boyhood and manhood. By seducing the cupbearer, the poet dominates the messenger and asserts his right of refusal of common religious rituals and rites of passage. He has, at least symbolically, tasted immortality by seducing and controlling the bearer of the wine, the liminal character on earth and in heaven.

In other poems, the level of satire is raised. For example.

> Oh Sulayman, sing to me
> and give me a cup of wine . . .
> So if the wine comes round
> seize it and give it to me!
> Give me a cup of distraction
> from the Mu'adhdhin's call
> Give me wine to drink publicly
> and bugger and fuck me now.[63]

In this poem the imam, Sulayman, becomes the wine-bearing *sāqī,* deliverer of distraction from the day's prayer calls. Given the choice between the mosque's call to prayer and drunken, passive sodomy, Abū Nuwās asks for the latter. In his sexual role the poet's position is submissive to that of the imam, making his disobedience virtuous and superior; he has shown a passionate willingness to submit to the religious polity's messenger. At the same time, his defiance of the *mu'adhdhin*'s call has made him superior to his Islamic patron and gained him power.

In the following poem Abū Nuwās inverts prescribed Islamic burdens into mandates for pursuing heavenly pleasures on earth.

> Don't worry when people say
> "That is not allowed and that is not permitted."
> Obey your passion and, in the early morning, bring it a yellow
> wine spraying fire.
> Make love to boys in their youth, when their beards begin to
> sprout, and in ripe old age.
> Sit down in every tavern, where wine and lovemaking are
> offered . . .
> When the month of the fast comes, make out like you are sick.
> And if you are asked: "Is pederasty permitted at this time?"
> Say: "Of course!"
> To keep souls away from what they love is a great sin . . .
> In this way you will carry out the holy war.
> A share of the booty and paradise will then be your right . . .

> This is the testament of Abū Nuwās, the polemicist since his youth,
> He made it his testament after facing the changes of fate.[64]

The poet's challenge to the community of believers becomes clear. His soul and heart, he claims, love drinking wine and consorting with boys, the pursuit of which is the burden of his life. To fail to bear this fateful plight would be a sin. From this position, his detractors receive the blame if he is damned, and it is his critics who become the object of a holy war. Once again, Abū Nuwās parodies the prescribed burdens of Islam, and he makes his position and approach to religion morally and virtuously superior.

Satirical panegyric is commonly found in later ʿAbbāsid poetry. Al-Badrī, for example, attaches himself to those who follow the choices made by Abū Nuwās, saying that if God were to grant him his choice between earthly pleasures and the pleasures of heaven, he would choose to have each day of his life a "handful of hashish, a pound of meat, a kilo of bread, and the company of a willing boy."[65]

Al-Jawbarī asserts that a poet's position allows him to operate above the law and commit "acts of immorality involving married women and boys from good families":

> Drunkenness is kind to lovers, not unkind
> I accomplished what I wanted from him and thanked him . . .
> To those of lewd inclinations the method [is] fivefold . . .
> Leave the killjoys and let me be
> Among those who hide from the good opinion of the people.[66]

The poet is taking a poke at the idea that Muslims are the people of good opinion. They are also the very people who commit lewdness with the poets when they need to escape the torrent of Islamic edicts. Rather than use wine to seduce women and boys, the poet uses five-leafed hemp, which is not banned. Or is the "fivefold" also a reference to the *ṣalāt*? Whether the seduction comes via inebriation or prayer, the result is that the poet, like the goddess Inana, achieves control over the drunken messenger, in this case the boy/*sāqī* from a good family or the wife/*houri* of a wealthy man.

In other cases, the poet seduces warriors and heroes into sexual subjugation as a means of dominating society, fate, and time. In the following poem Abū Nuwās uses homoeroticism to stab at the heart of the Muslim community, making warriors effeminate and self-indulgent on the night before battle. At the same time, the poet becomes the dominant figure, or, more correctly, "Adonis the seducer . . . the perfect antithesis of a warrior hero."[67]

And many are the brave burning bright
  like lamps in blackish night
  ones among the proud and penetrating men!
They overpower time (*dahr*)
  with the pleasure they embrace
  so their rope is never sundered (by time)!
Time came round with lucky stars for them
  and it turned aside bowing a loving neck before them!

Most important here is the strategic use of "penetration" and "pleasure." It is clear in this poem that the soldiers are not only penetrating and being penetrated, presumably along with the poet, but also that this is a pleasant experience. According to al-Jurjānī's vice lists, there are different levels of admonition due to homosexual offenders.[68] In general the penetrating partner is seen as wasteful, but he is not considered perverted; he even gains an enhanced masculinity because the penetrator has assumed a position of power over another male. A male prostitute who sells use of his anus for profit commits the act for rational reasons, although as the receiving partner he is obviously the economically or socially weaker party. However, it is the bearded man who seeks passive sex for pleasure (*ubna*) that is derelict and culpable for vice. In this poem Abū Nuwās turns the "proud and penetrating men" into men overpowered by the "pleasure they embrace." By following Abū Nuwās's libertine morality, the warriors not only ascend to the pleasures of heaven, but also conquer time; they taste immortality, and martyrdom becomes superfluous because they have already won the moral battle.

The structure of the poem is also important. In this poem and many others Abū Nuwās employs a mock-heroic panegyric that turns battle poetry into love poetry. The style is equivalent to raid or battle poems, but here sexual adventure replaces heroic metaphors drawn from warfare or hunting motifs. These sorts of poems are often enhanced by visions of butting rams, fighting stallions, or racing camels; or references to military arms or equipment. Another example of this is found in the following stanza:

I rose up and made for him,
  swaggering and erect,
  having prepared my ram for butting.
When I had fixed my lance in him, he woke
  like one prostrated by wounds.[69]

Again, the success of the poet's phallus/lance makes him the victor/conqueror. His position is active and masculine while his victim/soldier is passive and effeminate. Abū Nuwās is a warrior too, using different weapons and reveling in hyperbole about wine's ability to make him master, prostrator, and subjugator of the community's heroes. What must also be recognized here is the implicit pain of the victim, because it is the "wound" that places the poet in a dominant position over an honorable, not dishonorable, man. In this case Abū Nuwās has turned another trick for entrapping his patron. His ramming has not hurt a prostitute who should know his trade, or an effeminate pervert who might enjoy this situation; instead he has butted a masculine, virile soldier: "his retribution frequently comes in the form of homosexual rape."[70] One could also read these lines as referring to *dabīb*, or the practice of initiating anal intercourse with a sleeping boy; however, one would expect that a warrior could fend off this attack. The soldier's pain is Abū Nuwās's celebration of his brutal superiority.

It should be pointed out that the poets of this era did not confine their critiques and jokes to the Muslim social order. Another common target was the Christian monastic orders, which were notorious in some areas for being little more than bars and brothels for male prostitutes. For example, al-Jurjānī's list of euphemisms about anal intercourse includes terms like a "monk in his monastery," and insults like "more devoted to *liwāṭ* than a [Christian] monk."[71] It was common even to call a *lūṭī,* a pederast, a monk. The phrase used to describe being forced to take a woman instead of a boy was "drinking water when you want wine," another Muslim-Christian comparison. (See Sprachman, this volume, for examples.)

J. C. Bürgel translates a story in which a pair of brothers are traveling. One is bearded and one is not.[72] Unable to escape a torrent of sexual offers from people on the street, they decide to spend the night in a monastery. Afraid of *dabīb,* the younger brother goes to the extreme of building a wall around his buttocks so that he will not be sodomized in his sleep. However, a tricky guest/monk succeeds in stealing away the bricks and begins his sexual act. The boy exclaims, "Where can I go? For wherever I go, [I am] persecuted [by] their eyes, horny for semen, and their hands, greedy for testicles." The main point here is that if Muslims cannot be trusted with boys, Christians are worse. Moreover, if the reference to their hunger for semen and greed for testicles implies a taste for performing oral sex, the insult in the poem is worse because oral sex was likely considered to be even more perverted than *ubna*.[73]

It should also be admitted that there is much buffoonery going on in *mujūn* literature, wherein the poet serves as a "ritual clown."[74] In a good public contest tribal poets tried to outdo one another through bawdy verbal aggression and numerous responses. For example, when the comic poet Hishām b. Hudayj, in a public contest, accuses the men of a rival tribe of having small penises, Abū Nuwās replies,

> He complained of the paltriness [thinness] of cocks to us
> So we answered with this reply prepared in advance:
> "Cocks would not be so paltry, Ibn Hudayj,
> If your arse was not so terribly wide."[75]

The comic element in these poems and responses is clear. Here too, however, readers must be careful not to take this jest and buffoonery at face value, for they will miss the poet's clever entrapment of his patron (see Monroe's chapter). If the insult is so public and so ridiculous that it could only be made by a fool, then who would punish the fool but a bigger fool? By creating this trap, rival poets leave their patrons few options. As the heat of the verbal aggression rises and the comic responses intensify, the patron is rapidly left unable to respond without also compromising his personal integrity, without removing his veil of etiquette or proper social demeanor.[76]

In the end we see that Abū Nuwās and his contemporaries used homoerotic conventions, symbols, and motifs to create satirical chaos in the early ʿAbbāsid courts. Speculating about the poets' personal proclivities may be of interest to some, but it is time poorly spent. We do not know the poets' sexual needs or preferences, and even if we did, Western detractors' fascination with the East's supposed attachment to pederasty is beside the point and lacks cultural context. The titillation Burton and other Orientalist writers find in these texts is more likely a reflection of attitudes that prevailed in European, not Arab, cultures. As Malti-Douglas comments, "In the Arabo-Islamic cultural sphere, true homosexuality, while certainly present, poses less of a psychological problem [than it does in Western culture]."[77]

The early ʿAbbāsid poets like Abū Nuwās successfully deconstruct textual, theological, and social-hierarchical barriers dominating Arabic literature, politics, and society. The wine, the *sāqī,* and the mock panegyric are all satirical devices used to confine the polity within its own claims of religious devotion. It is true that most of this poetry was written to entertain paying patrons, but this does not lessen the sublime power of the work because the poets seem to go beyond courtly jest by undermining canonical texts and making textual interpretations weak, if not ridiculous. Such parody makes the prevailing political structure nothing more than a cruel hoax; it allows the poets to dominate their foes with a discourse that is simultaneously penetrating and pleasant.

NOTES

1. John Boswell, *Christianity, Social Tolerance and Homosexuality: Gay People in Western Europe from the Beginning of the Christian Era to the Fourteenth Century* (Chicago: University of Chicago Press, 1980), pp. 278–83, especially notes 32–36.

2. See Edward Said, *Orientalism* (New York: Vintage, 1978) for a discussion of the need of the European community to establish superiority over the Ottomans, and *Culture and Imperialism* (New York: Vintage Books, 1993) for broader discussions of Western justifications for colonialism. Arab homoerotic practices are negatively cited in texts ranging from Aristophanes' *The Birds* to Evelyn Waugh's *Brideshead Revisited.*

3. Suzanne P. Stetkevych, "Intoxication and Immortality: Wine and Associated Imagery in al Maʿarrī's Garden" (see this volume).

4. The only allusion to homoeroticism in the book is a strong one, because it is reflected visually. On the cover of the first paperback edition of the book is a naked boy involved in a snake-charming exercise before a hoard of villainous older Arab and African men and a group of anxious-looking warrior types. One presumes that Said's point in putting Jean-Léon Gérôme's "The Snake Charmer" on the cover of his book is to point out the outrageous way Western art has promoted an image of the Arab as exotic and morally corrupt. The picture indeed displays the naked male/homoerotic image. But Said never discusses the cover or the image, although it is clear that he sees how misunderstood the image is. An anonymous reader of a draft of this essay deserves thanks for pointing out Said's and others' omissions of homoerotic texts. Similar comments are found in Marjorie Garber, "The Chic of Araby: Transvestitism, Transsexualism and the Erotics of Cultural Appropriation" in Julia Epstein and Kristina Straub, eds., *Body Guards: The Cultural Politics of Gender Ambiguity* (New York: Routledge, 1991), pp. 223–47; and Joseph A. Boone, "Mappings of Male Desire in Durrell's *Alexandria Quartet,*" *South Atlantic Quarterly* 88 (1989): 81–95.

5. See Alan Jones, ed., *Early Arabic Poetry: Marathi and Suʿluk Poems,* vol. 1 (Reading, England: Ithaca Press, 1992); and Michael Sell's *Desert Tracings: Six Classical Arabian Odes* (Hanover, N.H.: Wesleyan University Press, 1989), which is a good source on meaning in Arabic odes. Still, Arabic poetry and prose have rarely been understood by comparative literary critics in the West. On the tension this situation causes see Michael Sells, "The Qasida and the West," *Al-Arabiyya* 20 (1987): 307–57.

6. See Richard F. Burton, trans. *The Book of the Thousand Nights and a Night,* L. C. Smithers, ed., vol. 10 (London: H. S. Nichols & Co., 1886). In his "Terminal Essay," pp. 205–53, Burton expresses his theory that among the people who live east of the Mediterranean all the way to Japan, pederasty "is popular and endemic, held at worst a peccadillo." Also see Everett K. Rowson, "The Categorization of Gender and Sexual Irregularity in Medieval Arabic Vice Lists," in Epstein and Straub, *Body Guards,* pp. 50–79.

7. Jeffrey Weeks in Arno Schmitt and Jehoeda Sofer, eds., *Sexuality and Eroticism Among Males in Moslem Societies* (New York: Harrington Park Press, 1992), xi. The essays in this book are primary examples of the assertions I make in this paragraph. With one exception, an article by Maartin Schild, these essays show little philological background and do not exhibit cultural sensitivity or in-depth knowledge of Middle Eastern social traditions or mores.

8. James Wafer, "Sacred and Profane Love in Islam: Dimensions of Gay Religious History," M. A. thesis, Indiana University, 1986. I find this thesis interesting and use several of Wafer's translations and comments later in this article. However, I do not agree with his use of a Western definition of "gay" as it is often applied to medieval (or even modern) Arabic and Persian poetry.

9. James Cleugh, *A History of Oriental Orgies: An Account of Erotic Practices Among Peoples of the East and Near East* (New York: Crown Publishers, 1968).

10. As quoted by Boswell, *Christianity, Social Tolerance and Homosexuality,* p. 281.

11. This is the main fault of Asʿad Abu Khalil's "A Note on the Study of Homosexuality in Arab/Islamic Civilization," *Arab Studies Journal* 1 (Fall 1993): 32–34. The articles in Schmidt and Sofer also tend to make this mistake. A much better approach to the study of homosexuality in Middle Eastern communities is found in Bruce W. Dunne's "Homosexuality in the Middle East: An Agenda for Historical Research," *Arab Studies Quarterly* 12/3 & 4 (1990): 55–82. This article also, unfortunately, tends to assume that homoerotic elements of Arabic and Persian literature can be defined as "gay." Still, Dunne's work appropriately underscores the need to continue research on this aspect of Arab culture.

12. Suzanne P. Stetkevych properly discusses Al-Jāḥiẓ's exegetical method in "Toward a Redefinition of 'Badiʿ' Poetry," *Journal of Arabic Literature* 12 (1981): 1–29. David Ayalon also presents key arguments supporting my assertions on al-Jāḥiẓ's writings in "On the Term *Khādim* in the Sense of 'Eunuch' in the Early Muslim Sources," *Arabica* 32 (1985): 289–308.

More important, see al-Jāḥiẓ's own work for illustrations of his mastery of classical Arabic's ambiguity. For example, in *Kitāb Mufākharat al-jawārī wa-l-ghilmān,* in *Rasāʾil al-Jāḥiẓ,* ed. ʿAbd as-Salām M. Hārūn (Cairo, 1384/1964–1965), II, 92–94, al-Jāḥiẓ "found it advisable to apologize for [his] outspokenness," but in his apology he inverts usage of verbal statements and references to proper places in a way that makes men of the past irreproachable and men of the present worth less than the value of a regular verb. See Franz Rosenthal, "Fiction and Reality: Sources for the Role of Sex in Medieval Muslim Society," in Afaf Lutfi al-Sayyid-Marsot, ed., *Society and the Sexes in Medieval Islam* (Malibu, Calif.: Undena Publishers), p. 18.

13. Garber, "The Chic of Araby," pp. 225, 228. The "Arab-Islamic East" is also portrayed as "fantasies of sword and sorcery . . . dictated by a legacy of suspicion and fear," in most twentieth-century literature. This situation adds to the Western reader's view of Arabs as exotic deviates and unnatural human figures. These quotes come from M. Riad Atef Nourallah, "Sorcerers, Straight Swords, and Sorcery," *International Journal of Islamic and Arabic Studies* 7(2): 1–41, but readers should also see *Orientalism* and, more important, Edward Said's discussion of Victorian and modern literary references to Arabia in *Culture and Imperialism*.

14. Suzanne P. Stetkevych, "The ʿAbbāsid Poet Interprets History: Three Qaṣīdahs by Abū Tammām," *Journal of Arabic Literature* 10 (1979): 49–64. While the complex social functions in the ʿAbbāsid period should not be overlooked, it is also true that the connection between politics and poetry, as well as the connection between biblical textual ambiguities and poetic puns, has much more ancient origins. Reference has been made to this issue in my earlier discussion of Jaroslav Stetkevych's work. However, see Suzanne Pinckney Stetkevych's "Sarah and the Hyena: Laughter, Menstruation, and the Genesis of a Double Entendre," *History of Religions* 35 (5): 13–41 for a more thorough discussion of this issue.

15. Ignaz Goldziher, *Muslim Studies*, S. M. Stern, ed., 2 vols. (New York: Aldene Publishing Company, 1967), I, 35. Goldziher was probably the first Middle East Studies scholar to link classical Arabic poetry to the politics of the time, and he deserves credit for doing so. But serious work on this poet-politics connection is relatively new. Reference should be made to two recent articles by Suzanne Pinckney Stetkevych, "ʿAbbāsid Panegyric and the Poetics of Political Allegiance: Two Poems of al-Mutanabbī on Kāfūr" in Stefan Sperl and Christopher Shackle, eds., *Qasida Poetry in Islamic Asia and Africa* (Leiden: E. J. Brill, 1996), I, 35–63: and "ʿAbbāsid Panegyric: The Politics and Poetics of Ceremony in Al-Mutanabbi's Id-Poem to Sayf al-Dawlah," in J. R. Smart, ed., *Tradition and Modernity in Arabic Language and Literature* (London: Curzon), pp. 119–43.

16. The essential point of *mujūn* literature is that it be entertaining, and usually satirical. See Rowson, "Arabic Vice Lists," p. 52.

17. Paul E. Losensky, "The Allusive Field of Drunkenness: The Safavid-Moghul Responses to a Lyric," in Suzanne Pinkney Stetkevych, ed., *Reorientations/Arabic and Persian Poetry* (Bloomington: Indiana University Press, 1994), pp. 227–62.

18. Abū Nuwās, *Dīwān Abī Nuwās,* recension of Abū Bakr al-Ṣūlī, B. al-Ḥadīthī, ed. (Baghdad: Dār al-Risāla, 1980).

19. Jaroslav Stetkevych, "Arabic Hermeneutic Terminology: Paradox and Production of Meaning," *Journal of Near Eastern Studies* 48 (1989): 84–87. This argument is further explored in Suzanne Pinckney Stetkevych, "Sarah and the Hyena: Laughter, Menstruation, and the Genesis of a Double Entendre."

20. Suzanne P. Stetkevych, "Intoxication and Immortality" (this volume).

21. Suzanne P. Stetkevych, "Toward a Redefinition of Badīʿ Poetry," *Journal of Arabic Literature* 12 (1981): 1–29.

22. E. D. Hirsh, *The Aims of Interpretation* (Chicago and London: University of Chicago Press, 1974), 19.

23. Jaroslav Stetkevych, "Arabic Hermeneutic Terminology," p. 82.

24. Suzanne P. Stetkevych, "Intoxication and Immortality" (this volume).

25. Sami A. Hanna and Rebecca Salti, "Ahmad Shauqi: A Pioneer of Modern Arabic Literature," *American Journal of Islamic Literature* 1 (1973): 81–117.

26. James A. Bellamy, "Sex and Society in Islamic Popular Literature," in Afaf Lutfi al-Sayyid-Marsot, ed., *Society and the Sexes in Medieval Islam* (Malibu, Calif.: Undena, 1979), pp. 23–42.

27. See, first, Ross Brann, *The Compunctious Poet: Cultural Ambiguity in Muslim Spain* (Baltimore: Johns Hopkins University Press, 1991), although his later critiques of Monroe are unfounded. J. Schirman, in "The Ephebe in Medieval Hebrew Poetry," *Sefarad* 15 (1955): 55–68, discusses these dynamics in Hebrew poetry; unfortunately, he does not make sufficient reference to the roots of this poetry, which are found in Arabic and Persian poetry. Also see Norman Roth's articles, "Fawn for My Delights: Boy-Love in Hebrew and Arabic Verse," in Joyce E. Salisbury, ed., *Sex in the Middle Ages* (New York: Garland Publishing, 1991), and "Deal Gently with the Young Man: Love of Boys in the Medieval Hebrew Poetry of Spain," *Speculum* 57 (1982). Short references to homoerotic "fashions" at the Andalusian courts are found in Elmer Bendiner, *The Rise and Fall of Paradise* (New York: The Scholars Press, 1983). For discussions of homosexuality in the context of Hebrew sacred texts, see T. M. Horner, *Jonathan Loved David: Homosexuality in Biblical Times* (Philadelphia: Westminster Press, 1978).

28. E. Westermarck, *Early Religious Beliefs* (Cambridge: Cambridge University Press, 1948). For the interdependence of Arabic and Persian poetry see Edward G. Brown, *A Literary History of Persia,* 4 vols. (Cambridge: Cambridge University Press, 1956).

29. Jacques Duchesne-Guillemin, *Symbols and Values in Zoroastrianism: Their Survival and Renewal* (New York: Harper and Row, 1966), p. 166. Important, more recent discussions of Zoroastrianism are in Jamsheed K. Choksy, *Purity and Pollution in Zoroastrianism: Triumph Over Evil* (Austin: University of Texas Press, 1989), and in Janet Amighi, *The Zoroastrians of Iran: Conversion, Assimilation or Persistence* (New York: AMS Press, 1990). Readers should also see Mary Boyce, *Zoroastrians: Their Religious Beliefs and Practices* (London: Routledge and Kegan Paul, 1979), and *A Persian Stronghold of Zoroastrianism* (Oxford: Oxford University Press, 1977).

30. Mary Boyce, *Manichaean Hymn-Cycles in Parthian* (London: Oxford University Press, 1954).

31. Jeremy Black and Anthony Green, *Gods, Demons and Symbols of Ancient Mesopotamia* (London: British Museum Press, 1992), p. 28, 89–91, 150.

32. David M. Halperin, *One Hundred Years of Homosexuality* (New York: Routledge, 1990), 81.

33. Javier Teixidor, *The Pantheon of Palmyra* (Leiden: E. J. Brill, 1979), pp. 144–45.

34. Conrad E. L'Heureux, *Rank Among the Canaanite Gods: El, Baal, and the Repha'im,* Harvard Semitic Studies Monograph no. 21 (Atlanta: Scholars Press, 1979).

35. On Seth and Horus see D. B. Redford, *Akhenaten: The Heretic King* (Princeton: Princeton University Press, 1984), p. 193. For other discussions of homoerotic rituals in ancient Egyptian religions see J. Collier, *King Sun: In Search of Akhenaten* (London: Ward Lock, 1970).

36. It should also be noted that eunuchs, in particular, and slave boys often amassed great power in royal houses. See Alayon, cited above, and Karl A. Wittfogel, *Oriental Despotism: A Comparative Study of Total Power* (New Haven: Yale University Press, 1957), pp. 354–58. For an excellent historical-fictional depiction of this dynamic in both Macedonian and Persian courts, see Mary Renault's *The Persian Boy* (New York: Vintage, 1988).

37. Clifford Flanigan, "Liminality, Carnival, and Social Structure: The Case of Late Medieval Biblical Drama," in *Victor Turner and the Construction of Criticism* (Bloomington: Indiana University Press, 1990), pp. 42–63.

38. Suzanne P. Stetkevych, "The ʿAbbāsid Poet Interprets History," pp. 49–65. See also Felicitias D. Goodman, *Ecstasy, Ritual and Alternative Reality: Religion in a Pluralistic World* (Bloomington: Indiana University Press, 1988), p. 148.

39. See the discussion "The Tragacanth's Fruit" in chapter 6 of Suzanne P. Stetkevych, *Abū Tammām and the Poetics of the ʿAbbāsid Age* (Leiden: E. J. Brill, 1991), p. 133.

40. Bernard Sargeant, *Homosexuality in Greek Myth* (Boston: Beacon Press, 1984), pp. 205–13.

41. Patricia Springborg, *Western Republicanism and the Oriental Prince* (Austin, Tex.: University of Texas Press, 1992).

42. Eva C. Keuls, *The Reign of the Phallus: Sexual Politics in Ancient Athens* (New York: Harper and Row, 1985).

43. For the best discussion of pre-Islamic poetry, see Suzanne P. Stetkevych, *The Mute Immortals Speak: Pre-Islamic Poetry and the Poetics of Ritual* (Ithaca: Cornell University Press, 1993).

44. On wine symbolism see Mohammed Birairy, "The Symbol of Wine in Pre-Islamic Poetry," M. A. thesis, American University in Cairo, 1980 (unpublished). Discussions in published texts about *mujūn* homoeroticism in research on pre-Islamic writings are more difficult to find and are usually hidden in footnotes or ignored. However, examples of homoerotic symbolism are found in the *dīwāns* of al-Aʿshā, al-Nuʿmān b. Mundhir, ʿAdī b. Zayd, and Imru' al-Qays. The degree to which homoerotic imagery is rebellious has not been studied, but the fact that these poems are to a degree satirical or political is not in question.

45. See Suzanne P. Stetkevych, "Pre-Islamic Panegyric and the Poetics of Redemption," pp. 1–57.

46. Franz Rosenthal, *The Herb: Hashish versus Medieval Muslim Society,* p. 157.

47. A. J. Arberry, trans. *The Mystical Poems of Ibn al-Farid* (New York: Emery Walker, 1956), p. 53, n. 24.

48. Joseph Bell, *Love Theory in Later Ḥanbalite Islam* (Albany: The State University of New York Press, 1979), p. 31.

49. Bellamy, "Sex and Society," p. 39. *Mukhannath* is sometimes translated as inverts or effeminates, but transvestite is appropriate here.

50. Pinus Ben Nahum, *The Turkish Art of Love* (New York: Panurge Press, 1933), p. 88.

51. Madelain Farah, *Marriage and Sexuality in Islam: A Translation of al-Ghazali's Book on*

the Etiquette of Marriage from the Ihyā' (Salt Lake City: University of Utah Press, 1984), pp. 160–61.

52. Bellamy, "Sex and Society," p. 37.

53. James Monroe discusses this methodological trap in his essay in this collection. However, the technique's origins are likely attributable to the early ʿAbbāsid poets. For example, Abū Nuwās's mastery of the ambiguous language in Islamic texts saved his life during his heresy trials.

54. As quoted by Wafer, "Sacred and Profane Love in Islam," p. 50.

55. Annemarie Schimmel, "Eros—Heavenly and Not So Heavenly–in Sufi Literature and Life," in Lutfi al-Sayyid-Marsot, *Society and the Sexes*, 37. In this case *jihād* refers only to the process of proselytizing a youth into the religion.

56. Wafer, "Sacred and Profane Love in Islam," p. 71.

57. Ibid., p. 73.

58. Rowson, "Vice Lists," p. 58.

59. Paul R. Sprachman, "The Comic Works of ʿUbayd-i Zākānī: A Study of Medieval Persian Bawdy, Verbal Aggression, and Satire," Ph.D. diss., University of Chicago, 1981, pp. 122–47.

60. *Dīwān Abī Nuwās*, pp. 218–19. The translations are mine.

61. Ibid, p. 142.

62. Ibid, p. 102.

63. Abū Nuwās, trans. by Th. Emil Homerin in "Filled With a Burning Desire," Ph.D. diss., University of Chicago, 1989.

64. Wafer, "The Sacred and Profane Love in Islam," p. 70.

65. Rosenthal, *The Herb,* p. 83, n. 3.

66. Ibid., p. 157.

67. Marcel Detienne, *Gardens of Adonis: Spices in Greek Mythology*, trans. Janet Lloyd (Atlantic Highlands, N.J.: 1977), p. 67, as quoted by Suzanne Pinckney Stetkevych, "Structuralist Interpretations of Pre-Islamic Poetry: Critique and New Directions," *Journal of Near Eastern Studies* 42 (1983): 85–107.

68. Rowson, "Vice Lists," discussing al-Qāḍī Abū l-ʿAbbās Aḥmad b. Muḥammad al-Jurjānī (d. 1089), *al-Muntakhab min kināyāt al-udabā' wa-ishārāt al-bulaghā'* (published together with al-Thaʿālibī, *Kitāb al-kināyāt*), Hyderabad, 1983. This is an anonymous abridgment of the original work, which apparently has not survived. Rowson's is a brilliant review of this and other vice lists.

69. Abū Nawās, "no. 170," in Aḥmad ʿAbd al-Majīd al-Ghazālī, ed., *Dīwān Abī Nuwās* (Cairo: 1953), as translated by John N. Mattock, "Description and Genre in Abū Nuwās," *Quaderni di Studi Arabi* 5.5 (1987–88), but forwarded to me in its prepublication, revised format for the forthcoming *Abu Nuwas Newsletter.*

70. Sprachman, "The Comic Works of ʿUbayd-i Zākānī," p. 173.

71. Rowson, "Vice Lists," p. 60.

72. This comes to me from "The Reflection of God or Satan's Snare?: The Homoerotic Element in Medieval Islamic Literature," an unpublished translation by Lida Daves Baldwin of J. C. Bürgel's lecture "Abglanz Gottes oder Schlinge des Teufels?" See also

the translations in M. Glünz and J. C. Bürgel, eds., *Intoxication, Heavenly and Earthly* (Bern: University of Mannheim Press, 1991).

73. Oral sex is rarely mentioned in Arabic literary texts, and for that matter it is rare in Persian and Turkish texts. Its nonexistence seems to imply that the act was truly considered a social taboo, if not a sickness. Rowson notices this deletion in his review of vice lists, as does Rosenthal in *The Herb.* However, Sprachman refers to a Persian manuscript that deals specifically with the benefits of both oral and anal sex: *Essay on the Superiority of the Rectum over the Mouth*, which is attributed by al-Nadīm to Abū l-ʿAnbas in Bayard Dodge, ed. and trans., *The Fihrist of Al-Nadīm* (New York: Columbia University Press, 1970), vol. 1, p. 333. See Sprachman, "The Comic Works of ʿUbayd-i Zākānī."

74. See the chapter on "The Poet as Ritual Clown" in Andras Hamori, *On the Art of Medieval Arabic Literature* (Princeton: Princeton University Press, 1974), pp. 31–77.

75. Sprachman, "The Comic Works of ʿUbayd-i Zākānī," p. 84.

76. This pattern of entrapment was pointed out to me by James Monroe after I gave a lecture on Abū Nuwās at the University of California at Berkeley. His comments and those of his colleagues and students are greatly appreciated.

77. Fedwa Malti-Douglas, *Woman's Body, Woman's Word: Gender and Discourse in Arabo-Islamic Writing* (Princeton: Princeton University Press, 1991), p. 15.

CHAPTER TWO

Male and Female: Described and Compared

Franz Rosenthal

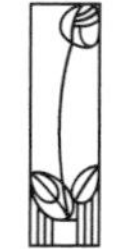

An age-old intellectual game cherished by people of diverse educational and social status was the comparison of the meaning and value of two objects or concepts, either as seen by their advocates or, in a clever literary refinement, as depicted by the two sides personified, fighting it out between themselves. In the Muslim tradition, such *Rangstreit* literature became significant during the early heyday of ʿAbbāsid rule,[1] and it continued to command attention throughout the Muslim Middle Ages. Together with the widespread preference of secular moralists for pointing out the dichotomy of good and bad inherent in almost everything, it appears to have furnished a much-needed outlet for a relativist view of life contrasting with the dominant absolutism of religious dogma and practice.

It was recognized that comparison has to stay within certain limits in order to remain credible. One of the many insights of al-Ṣafadī in the fourteenth century was expressed in this concise survey of a few of the relevant topics pursued by Muslim littérateurs:

> Some have written works comparing the virtues of the rose and the narcissus, because poets were fond of the subject and spoke at length about it (so that there was much material available for compiling essays on it. They were able to do so) since such a comparison is possible. In the same way, excellent authors have written on debates between the sword and the pen concerning their respective merits, between *dirham* and *dīnār* (silver coins and gold coins), between stinginess and generosity, between Egypt (Cairo) and Syria (Damascus), between the East and the West (of the Muslim world), between Arabs and non-Arabs (Persians), between poetry and prose, and between girls and beardless boys, for in all these cases

> arguments in favor of either side are possible. On the other hand, a debate between musk and ashes on their respective merits would be irrational, and a gifted littérateur would hardly speak about ashes when debating the virtues of musk. Al-Jāḥiẓ has written an original essay on the subject.[2]

Although al-Ṣafadī's reference to al-Jāḥiẓ could aim at the latter's total oeuvre, which includes a number of comparison essays, it would seem likely from the context that the reference is to his *Kitāb Mufākharat al-jawārī wa-l-ghilmān*, "The mutual rivalry of maidens and young men."[3] By good fortune, this essay is preserved; it was first edited by Charles Pellat in 1958.[4] Al-Jāḥiẓ may have introduced the subject into the mainstream literature. The timeliness of his effort is evident from the fact that it was soon imitated. Already from the next generation a treatment of the subject by two famous intellectuals is known, having been preserved in a later quotation. Both were outstanding representatives of the general culture of the age. One of them was better known as a littérateur, and the other as a philosopher. The littérateur, Aḥmad b. Abī Ṭāhir Ṭayfūr, lived from 204/819–20 to 280/893; he was credited with essays on "the mutual rivalry of the rose and the narcissus" and on "the greater merit of the Arabs as compared to the non-Arabs."[5] The philosopher and all-around scholar, Aḥmad b. al-Ṭayyib al-Sarakhsī, may have been born around 835, and he died in 286/899.[6] It is true that al-Jāḥiẓ (ca. 160–225/776–869) was much older than either of them, but as he happened upon the literary scene at a relatively advanced age, we are justified in speaking of a one-generation difference.

The work that has preserved the discussion between the male homosexual (*lūṭī*) who takes the part of (*ṣāḥib*) the boys and the fornicator (*zānī*) who takes the part of the girls is an exhaustive and highly informative treatise on all aspects of sexuality, entitled *Jawāmiʿ al-ladhdha,* approximately "Synopsis of all that is known about pleasure." The author was a certain Abū l-Ḥasan ʿAlī b. Naṣr al-Kātib, who is possibly the man of the same name who lived from 428/1036 to 518/1124.[7] It is not clear whether the discussion was taken from one of al-Sarakhsī's published works or, more likely, was derived from oral transmission, but this makes hardly any substantive difference. It would agree with the assumption of oral transmission that any dependence on al-Jāḥiẓ's treatise is not expressly acknowledged. Such dependence is obvious, however, from the striking use of identical quotations and particularly from the fact that both al-Jāḥiẓ's and al-Sarakhsī's discussions begin with references to the *ghulāmīyāt,* girls dressed as boys in an erotic fashion of the early ninth century,[8] and later happen to include references to eunuchs, who are rather marginal to the subject. The author of the *Jawāmiʿ* mentions the humorist Abū l-ʿAnbas al-Ṣaymarī (213–275/828–888), who wrote an apparently rather coarse essay on the same subject.[9] He has also preserved many precious fragments of other old treatises.[10]

An English translation of *Jawāmiʿ* has been published in typescript by Salah Addin Khawwam with the title *Encyclopedia of Pleasure*.[11] The title page seems to suggest that the Arabic text was published simultaneously; if so, it has remained inaccessible to me. This is all the more regrettable since the two manuscripts, of which I have copies, show a good deal of textual divergence and are not of a consistently high quality.[12] The English translation has been an exceedingly difficult effort and deserves credit for being reasonably successful. Though it has not been published in a more accessible format, the translation's existence makes detailed information on the discussion unnecessary at this juncture. The beginning and the end of the discussion are clearly marked, but this does not necessarily mean that everything in between originally belonged there. However, in the absence of firm evidence to the contrary, we may assume that the text is basically intact as transmitted.[13]

Al-Sarakhsī is well known as the star student of al-Kindī, whose interests, including a deep concern with the love phenomenon on the theoretical level, he shared.[14] This concern was widespread in that period, apparently as a result of attempts by the intellectual theologians lumped together as "Muʿtazilites" to fuse Greek philosophy with Muslim religious thought. The inclusion in al-Sarakhsī's bibliography of a work called *fī l-ʿishq*, "On [Sensual] Love," is poorly attested, but a passage from his pen on the subject is preserved, and it clearly shows his fascination with the Platonic tradition.[15] As a littérateur, he was also much interested in the more down-to-earth love affairs and escapades of singers and other entertainers. In the text discussed here, it was natural for sensitive and explicit material to appear side by side. Other Sarakhsī quotations in the *Jawāmiʿ* include a description of ideal female beauty noteworthy for its exceptional length, put in the mouth of his patron, the caliph al-Muʿtaḍid, and followed by al-Sarakhsī's comment that only caliphs and persons of high rank are capable of such a refined description. Ordinary people would use less refined ones, which he goes on to quote.[16] Elsewhere, he is quoted for a sex-based recipe he was given for curing the shortness and thinness of his beard,[17] and in the chapter on the common belief that greater hairiness meant greater sexual power he expressed scientific criticism of al-Jāḥiẓ and argued that, contrary to al-Jāḥiẓ's opinion, compensatory effects among bodily functions do not apply to sexuality.[18]

Notwithstanding the general tendency among authors to deal with all aspects of sexuality, then as well as in later times a clear distinction was often made between serious emotional love and obscene facetiousness (*mujūn*), particularly as it affected the work of poets.[19] Al-Jāḥiẓ made a much-quoted defense of the use of sexually explicit terminology, arguing that the words considered objectionable by some would not have been allowed to enter the language if they were not intended to be used. Soon after, Ibn Qutayba expressed himself in a similar vein.[20] Al-Jāḥiẓ, however, found it necessary to apologize in his essay for dealing with a subject that some might find offensive. This apology may not have been as much for the particular subject as in defense against the general aversion to all lighthearted and frivolous occupations resulting from religious concerns. This attitude was no doubt shared by al-Sarakhsī, at least in his public stance.

The tone set by the introduction of the discussion (translated incompletely by Khawwam) points in the same direction. It alludes to the problem of why in early Muslim society poets could have composed love poetry addressed to identifiable living women of high rank when in the later view accepted morality made this definitely improper and unlikely to occur:

> Aḥmad b. al-Ṭayyib said: I said to Aḥmad b. Abī Ṭāhir: It is easy for real men[21] to recite love poetry directed at women and describe their yearning for them, although they do not have the close relationship that would legally allow contact with them. This was done, for instance, by Abū Dahbal al-Jumaḥī and ʿAbd al-Raḥmān b. Ḥassān b. Thābit[22] in connection with a daughter of Muʿāwiya b. Abī Sufyān, who was a caliph!—He mentioned the story and quoted the poems.—(Ibn Abī Ṭāhir) said:[23] You talk so much (about the subject) as if you were someone who does not know (*qad aktharta ikthār man lam yaʿlam*) that discussions and debates have taken place among the partisans of males and the partisans of women. I replied: So, I would like you to tell me about that debate and discussion and how and where the victorious outcome based on firm proof was established. He said: Yes, I shall report to you what I remember. I came to a gathering that included some refined persons (*ẓurrāf*) who were friends with youths and other refined persons who were friends with women. These persons were engaged in an acrimonious dispute before I entered, (even) calling the

> friend of youths *lūṭī* and the friend of women *zānī*.[24] In the ensuing debate they mentioned what I am going to tell you.

The choppiness of the first half of this statement does not, it seems, reflect any textual distortions or omissions; rather, it is due to al-Sarakhsī's desire to get to his subject without the delay of detailing the implications of the initial problem, that is, how to explain the daring of earlier poets in dealing with identifiable women instead of using generic female names or none at all. After about the end of the first century of Islam, the accepted social order that had evolved officially made contact with unrelated free women unusual and suspect, whereas contact with other males, regardless of differences in age and status, was the natural order of social interaction.

The discussion reported by al-Sarakhsī occurs in the *Jawāmiʿ* in the chapter devoted to homoerotic male love, entitled "on young men (*fityān*)," another term of many meanings, designating in males youthful age, nobility of young adults, even something like knighthood, but also serving in other situations as a polite indication of unfree status. The discussion might thus be assumed to be favorable to the male side. In fact, the *lūṭī* has the first word, and he starts out with the observation (derived from al-Jāḥiẓ) that "when one wants to describe a girl as beautiful, one says that she is like a boy." He goes on to quote verses on the *ghulāmīya* that appear to give preference to the boy, such as those ascribed to Abū Nuwās's mentor Wāliba b. al-Ḥubāb:

> A girl (?)[25] who walks proudly and with disdain and speaks
> boldly—
> She is dressed like a boy,[26] though I would not compare
> her to him and did not mean to disparage the boy.

At the end, however—as already hinted at in the initial equation of male and female beauty—the discussion concludes with what might be called a draw:

> When Ibn Abī Ṭāhir had finished with the description, I (al-Sarakhsī) said to him: What is your opinion about what these two (the partisans of boys and the partisans of girls) have to say? He replied: A boy's jealousy of his lover is more refined than a woman's jealousy of a man because of her fellow wife. I said: But what do you say about the remarks made by either party? Tell me something that I can report on your authority with attribution to you. He said: Where they slandered each other I think they went too far,[27] and where they praised they made untrue and unseemly statements.

> However, among animals, the females are rarely more beautiful than the males. It is only the face of the human male that changes[28] with the growing of the first hair on his cheek, when his coloring has been infused with life and youth and the surface of his skin polished to a shining glow, his figure and whole being having reached perfection and his proportions (true) beauty. Nature then has produced the following bloom and mark (?) of young manhood.[29]

It is not quite certain whether the final three sentences, with their affirmation of the superiority of adolescent male beauty, go back to the original discussion or are editorial comment. Assuming them to be part of the discussion, the overall judgment expressed can be summarized as follows: An attempt is first made to evade a direct answer by merely referring to the supposed greater refinement of male jealousy compared to the coarseness of female jealousy. Jealousy was much debated, also in the religious tradition, as a sort of touchstone for genuine feeling in the relation of the sexes,[30] and since refinement was so highly valued in the intellectual climate of the times a slight tilt toward male eroticism is implied. But then, both sides are blamed for too much partisanship, with the apparent implication that their claims are equivalent. This again is modified by an acknowledgment of nature's assumed gift of greater beauty in the adolescent male. Thus, on the whole, no forceful and exclusive endorsement of any one point of view seems intended.

The material presented by either side is not arranged in a strictly logical progression, and such haphazard raising of various points would seem natural in a disputation. Prose portions are used by the debaters to bolster their respective cases with arguments from Qur'ān and *ḥadīth* and a few statements on the alleged attitude of early Muslims. Most of this material condemned homosexuality. An interesting defense advanced by the *lūṭī* against hostile traditions is a denial of their authenticity. He says that he "does not know those *ḥadīth*s" and thus reduces them to the status of unknown or little-known traditions that are of no value as legal arguments.

As befits a work not meant to be an earnest debate on moot points of religion or philosophy but a literary entertainment that nonetheless had fundamental implications for societal morals and behavior, the stress is on how poets, as the secular keepers of the Muslim social conscience, expressed themselves on those points. Poetry therefore dominates the discussion. Much of it is anonymous; verses are often introduced as authored by "the poet" or "our poet" (or "our friend," *ṣāḥibunā*), meaning a poet favorable to the side quoting him, or merely by "another." Few names of poets are given. Not surprisingly, Abū Nuwās's name appears most frequently, again attesting to his role as the principal originator of homoerotic poetry in the Muslim environment. With the exception of the twice-quoted ʿUkkāsha, all poets from the early ʿAbbāsid period, among them Wāliba b. al-Ḥubāb, al-Raqāshī,[31] and an unidentified al-Zawwānī (reading?), are represented but once, and (following al-Jāḥiẓ), there is a sprinkling of pre-Islamic poets such as Imruʾulqays, al-Aʿshā, and ʿAlqama b. ʿAbada. Some of the individuals remain practically unidentified, as, for instance, Abū Salīṭ al-Aʿrābī and al-Ṭarsūsī.[32] As is usually the case in poetry of this kind, the authenticity of an attribution can rarely be confirmed; formal collections of a poet's work, when they are preserved, often seem to disregard such minor products.

Among the individuals addressed in verses, two early ʿAbbāsid judges stand out as examples of the supposed inclination of judges toward forbidden homosexuality, a topic that endured through the centuries. Al-ʿAwfī (d. 201/816–7)[33] served as judge of the East Side and al-Ruṣāfa (ʿAskar Mahdī) in Baghdad under al-Rashīd, while Yaḥyā b. Aktham (d. 242/857) held a dominant position as al-Maʾmūn's chief justice. Little is said in the biographical sources about the reputation of al-ʿAwfī, except that he was considered a weak transmitter of *ḥadīth*. A generation later, when the prevailing attitudes had changed, Yaḥyā b. Aktham could already during his lifetime become an open target for scurrilous attacks on his supposed homosexuality, and the verses and anecdotes about him continued to be standard fare in literature.[34]

The distinction between facetiousness and serious purpose is obscured in the discussion, and this lack of distinction blurs the picture. This seems to be characteristic of the literary genre; occasionally, some particular argument may intrude rather improperly. Thus the *lūṭī* contends that the heterosexual lover needs material possessions to be successful in his search for a partner:

> When I asked the girls to have intercourse with me on credit,
> They turned away from me without agreeing to my quest for making love.
> If I had money, they would have agreed to it,
> But I have no access to money.[35]

The idea that a woman's love must be won with wealth and youth was an old one;[36] thus it is not really surprising that it turns up in the debate. What may at first glance seem surprising is the failure of the champion of girls to make use of the reputed venality of male lovers, which is repeated in many variations throughout the literature. Famous, for instance, was the reply attributed to the poet Abū Tammām when he was taunted with the remark that his *ghulām* was more accommodating to the high government official al-Ḥasan b. Wahb than the latter's *ghulām* was to him: "That is indeed so because he gives my *ghulām* money, whereas I give his *ghulām* idle chatter."[37] An ancient antecedent of this witticism exists, ascribed in Greek literature to the poet Anacreon and the tyrant Polycrates: "Smerdies received from Polycrates gold and silver and all that is customary for a pretty boy to get from a tyrant in love, but from Anacreon he received songs and praising poems and all that is customary for one to get from a lover who is a poet."[38] The missed opportunity of making a case here from male venality is explained by the connection of this literature with prostitution. Dwelling on that subject unnecessarily was not tolerated in the refined climate of the discussion and repeatedly rejected as inappropriate even by the author of the *Jawāmiʿ*.[39]

The most important question for us to consider is the aesthetic quality of the material presented, as this leads to the heart of the matter: its emotional content or apparent lack of it. Cleverness and wit are present and combined with a bluntness often aimed at provoking laughter rather than proving some point of sexual preference. Technical perfection in the use of language and literary artistry that for native critics were the hallmark of poetry are foremost throughout, although not explicit issues. Feeling and emotion, however, appear to have very little place. Admittedly, poetry can be appreciated fully only by native speakers of a language, and even their objectivity is open to doubt and their supposed criteria, as expressed by the analysis of literary figures or as unstated preferences, often seem to lack intrinsic force. Therefore, an evaluation by non-native speakers of poetry for artistic and, above all, emotional impact is nearly impossible. However, it can safely be contended that the poetry here seems to lack felt emotion, unless emotion rests in sexuality as such.

It has often been remarked that emotion and feeling take second place even in the work of as gifted a poet as Abū Nuwās, and may often be sought in vain. This is more obvious in a related poetical genre, the epigrammatical description in verse (*waṣf*) of boys or girls. Comparison is implicit here. In the sexological literature as in the *Jawāmiʿ*, the chapters dealing with the characteristic features of maleness and femininity are also for the most part kept separate. Those chapters may, however, contain comparisons or have comparative chapter headings referring to the "greater excellence (*tafḍīl*)" of homosexuality as against heterosexuality, as is the case in Ibn Falīta's *Rushd al-labīb ilā muʿāsharat al-ḥabīb.*[40]

The *waṣf*[41] of boys and girls adopted as its most poetical form the ancient vehicle of four lines (corresponding to two Arabic verses).[42] Rarely one, quite frequently three, or in exceptional cases four verses may also serve the purpose. In the homoerotic setting, the epigram describes not an individual as such but a "pretty (*malīḥ*)" representative of a certain occupation or someone engaged in a special activity or having noteworthy personal characteristics, including name or origin. "Handsome" may often serve as a better translation for *malīḥ* but does not capture its full meaning, which is important for the proper understanding of the word's possible sexual connotation. At times, *malīḥ* may even be used for something as vague and impersonal as the English all-purpose word "nice," for instance, in connection with objects such as books. In the corresponding Greek literature (see below, n. 52), the term *kalos*, which would not ordinarily appear as *malīḥ* in Arabic translation, is used.

In Muslim civilization, the epigram's popularity increased in the urban climate of the tenth century. Already in the early post-classical period, epigrams achieved that pinnacle of prominence that is marked by collections in monograph form. Al-Thaʿālibī, whose lifetime straddled the transition from the tenth to the eleventh century, may have been the first to make such a collection (this requires confirmation from the *Kitāb Alf ghulām* preserved in manuscript but to my knowledge not yet published). In the following centuries, the body of material available to a potential collector grew steadily larger. The natural consequence was that it became more and more difficult for a poet or hopeful versifier to be original. The topics and situations chosen for "description" became more contrived; the sort of encyclopedic all-inclusiveness that generally characterized the development of Muslim literary activity was soon attempted. Compilers of collections not only had an increasing amount of material at their disposal but also added to it with verses of their own composition. Practically every poet, it would seem, felt obliged to try his hand on the subject; as minor occasional poetry, however, such epigrams were not always included in a poet's collected works (see above, p. 30), although in the course of time they were more and more. *Adab* works, such as al-Ṣafadī's commentary on the famous *Lāmīyat al-ʿajam*, reveled in these epigrams.[43] The biographies of individual poets did not fail to include many specimens.

The eventual result may be exemplified here by two fifteenth-century monographs that constitute the final stage of the collectors' zeal. The authors are Shibāb al-Dīn al-Ḥijāzī (790–875/1388–1471) and Abū l-Tuqā al-Badrī (847–894/1443–1489). Among his many works, the former wrote two brief treatises. One of them is entitled *Jannat al-wildān fī l-ḥisān min al-ghilmān*, "The Paradise (peopled by) Youths: On Beautiful Males," and the other *al-Kunnas al-jawārī fī l-ḥisān min al-jawārī*, "The Retrograde Running Stars (Qur'ān 81:16): On Beautiful Maidens."[44] Al-Ḥijāzī began his first treatise with the customary fictitious reference to popular demand ("as demanded by my contemporaries") and with what must be taken as an apology for writing on the subject. As he states, all of the epigrams are of his own composition. Thus, the more than 160 entries for males is quite a respectable number; typically, the verses addressed to females add up to considerably less than half of that.

Al-Badrī's vastly larger monograph is entitled *Ghurrat al-ṣabāḥ fī waṣf al-wujūh al-ṣibāḥ*, "The Shining Dawn: On the Description of Fair Faces."[45] The *Ghurra* will serve as the source for the quotations on the following pages. It is noteworthy that al-Badrī appears to have aimed at collecting verses different from those in al-Ḥijāzī's treatise. That the latter was written earlier seems clear from the biographical data. The possibility that al-Ḥijāzī could have conceived the idea for his work upon hearing about al-Badrī's project can safely be excluded; more likely, it was he who suggested the project to al-Badrī.

Al-Ḥijāzī was born in Egypt, al-Badrī in Damascus, but the intellectual center for both was Cairo, which only in the next century was fated to lose its political independence and with it much of its cultural dominance. The poets' backgrounds were as different as could be. Al-Ḥijāzī was the precocious son of a well-established family of scholars and had all the educational advantages going with this status. Al-Badrī apparently was responsible for his own education and lived his life at the lower end of the intellectual establishment in minor positions, occasionally making a living as a merchant and at one time having the good fortune of inheriting from one of his wives. Their lives crossed in a significant manner: al-Ḥijāzī transmitted a considerable number of epigrams to al-Badrī orally as well as, occasionally, in writing, and when al-Badrī published his *Ghurra* (also referred to as *al-Majmūʿ*), al-Ḥijāzī was one of those he solicited to write an endorsement (*taqrīẓ*, "blurb") to accompany the publication. Al-Ḥijāzī obliged by contributing a rather lengthy statement of praise in the customary flowery fashion. Like the other *taqrīẓ*es, it was dated in 871/1467; his, precisely, on Friday, 16 Jumādā II 871/23 January 1467. Al-Ḥijāzī was close to eighty at the time. Only one other of the preserved *taqrīẓ*es was written by an old man, (Ibn) al-Hā'im al-Manṣūrī (798 or 799 to 887/1396(7)–1482), then about seventy.[46] Two were written by young men who were more or less contemporaries of al-Badrī: ʿAbd al-Barr Ibn al-Shiḥna (b. 9 Dhū l-Qaʿda 851/16 January 1448, d. 921/1515) was not yet twenty at the time of writing,[47] and Abū Bakr Muḥammad b. ʿUmar Ibn al-Naṣībī (b. Rabīʿ I 851/May–June 1447) was but a few months older.[48] No dates are known for the fifth and last of the preserved blurbists, Aḥmad b. Muḥammad al-Awtārī.[49] The choice of a mixture of beginners and accomplished authors was hardly accidental but served to advertise the appeal of the work for both the older generation and those destined to keep the flame burning in the future. Al-Ḥijāzī, in particular, was a natural choice. Having reached the end of a prolific career, he could well afford to be generous in his praise of the much younger man whom he may have inspired and who was ready to perpetuate his literary interests. Other blurbists whose statements are not preserved are also represented in the *Ghurra* by verses of their own composition (see below, n. 56), if fewer than those of al-Ḥijāzī. The ready availability of prominent endorsers is a further testimony to the great popularity of the work's subject.

Al-Badrī's principal achievement was his attempt to classify the vast material he collected (and to which, as expected, he contributed some epigrams of his own). He arranged it in a number of chapters, seventeen altogether; the decision as to where to put some of the epigrams seems at times to have caused a small problem for him. A striking difference between al-Ḥijāzī and al-Badrī is that the former, having begun with caliphs and officials, placed verses on bearers of certain names close to the end, while al-Badrī started out with them. The first epigram he quotes is appropriately on the name Muḥammad, and its author was Saʿd al-Dīn Muḥammad, the son of a famous father, the great mystical writer Ibn ʿArabī:

> O Muḥammad! Your eyes testify in my behalf
> That I am one likely to be killed by beautiful eyes.
> You have surpassed all the pretty ones, thus being their seal,
> Just like your namesake (the Prophet), the seal of the Messengers.
>
> *(A-Muḥammadun*[50] *ʿaynāka tashhadu lī*
> *annī l-qatīlu l-aʿyuni l-nujlī*
> *Fuqta l-milāḥa fa-anta khātamuhum*
> *wa-kadhā samīyuka khātamu l-ruslī)*

The *dīwān* of Saʿd al-Dīn b. ʿArabī contains a large number of epigrams on the topics found in the *Ghurra*, but only a few of those quoted by al-Badrī appear to have been included in it.[51] Among sons of famous fathers in medieval Islam, Saʿd al-Dīn stands out as one of those who represented a totally divergent outlook: his interest in love poetry seems entirely secular and artistic, in contrast to the mystical bent so all-consuming and deep in his father's works.

From this appropriately religious beginning, the *Ghurra* goes on to present, according to a rough count, well over 2,500 items, an astonishing number keeping in mind that all deal with one overall subject; moreover, al-Badrī was selective and could have included very much more pertinent material. The large Greek collection of epigrams known as the *Anthologia Graeca* is estimated to contain about fifty percent more entries,[52] but it deals with a large variety of different topics. As in the case of the *Rangstreit* literature, it is obvious that the Arabic erotic epigrams stand in line of succession to their Greek antecedents as well as such ancient materials as the "love-name" inscriptions. However, as in the case of the *Rangstreit* literature, the line of succession, tortuous and underground as it was, cannot be traced by us. An in-depth comparison of the Arabic with the Greek material might yield interesting contrasts.

Many poets are represented in the *Ghurra*. The vast majority of the collection dates from Ayyūbid and Mamlūk times and thus reflects the cultural climate of the author's own period. Poets of the golden age of the ʿAbbāsids, most notably Ibn al-Muʿtazz as well as (with hardly more than two entries each) Abū Nuwās and Ibn al-Rūmī, make sporadic appearances, but all the pre-Ayyūbid material is too sparse to disrupt the essential chronological unity of the most valuable aspect of the collection: it draws a detailed and well-rounded picture of life in medieval Muslim society, and this picture, despite its occasional baroque traits, reflects concrete reality. We could, of course, glean all the data of al-Badrī (and al-Ḥijāzī) from the works of individual poets, but it is instructive to find the information here together in one place. The concentration on the male component—only very rarely are women expressly mentioned[53]—gives the appearance of one-sidedness, but with respect to many situations poets would have had little occasion to speak of females.

The variety of component parts of proper names was characteristic of Muslim onomastics.[54] It is tempting to assume that verses on names came in handy as quotations for anyone who wanted to display his wit in communicating with someone of a given name. Such a practical purpose, however, could hardly have motivated the profusion of epigrams on gentilics dealing with localities and religious groups such as Christians, Jews, Samaritans, Zoroastrians, even polytheists. A Shīʿite could thus be addressed as rejecting his lover, just as the Khārijites rejected ʿAlī:

> A Shīʿite with a figure like the branch of a ben tree,
> In whose eyelid is ensheathed and glitters the sword of the Legatee (ʿAlī),
> A youth whose face is a luminous full moon,
> Whose breath is fragrant musk,
> To the one who wants to get intimate with him
> He says what the Khārijites said about ʿAlī.
>
> (*Wa-shīʿīyun ka-ghuṣni l-bāni qaddan*
> *yalūḥu bi-jafnihī sayfu l-Waṣīyī*
> *Ghulāmun wajhuhū badrun munīrun*
> *wa-nakhatuhū min al-miski l-dhakīyī*
> *Yaqūlu li-man yarūmu l-waṣla minhū*
> *kamā qāla l-khawāriju fī ʿAlīyī* [fol. 37b])

A Christian reading the Gospels suggests to the poet the famous metaphor of love union being as close as the ligature of the letters *lām* and *alif:*

> O (you) who, when you are reading the Gospel,
> Always turn away my unhappy heart from the Torah!
> "I have seen you in my sleep embracing me,
> As the *lām* of the scribe embraces the *alif.*"[55]
>
> (*Yā man idhā qaraʾa l-injīla ẓalla lahū*
> *qalbī l-shaqīyu ʿani l-tawrāti munḥarifā*
> *Innī raʾaytuka fī nawmī tuʿāniqunī*
> *kamā yuʿāniqu lāmu l-kātibi l-alifā* [fol. 39b])

A pretty Jew was reminded by Saʿd al-Dīn b. ʿArabī of his humble social status as a member of a protected religious community and a non-Muslim:

> This Jew who may belong to the
> People of Hell but whose face is Paradise for me,
> Shows himself always haughty and proud toward his lover,
> Although (as a Jew) he bears the mark of humiliation.
>
> (*Hādhā l-Yahūdīyu lladhī kāna min*
> *ahli l-jaḥīmi fa-wajhuhū lī jannatū*

Abadan yatīhu ʿalā l-muḥibbi taʿazzuzan
hādhā wa-qad ḍuribat ʿalayhi l-dhillatū [fol. 40b])

In the social context, an individual's dress was almost as important as his name. Thus, the next, third chapter of the *Ghurra* is entirely devoted to garments of various kinds and accessories like jewelry. A garment's color most notably added to its wearer's attractiveness, as did the complexion of the individual himself (which is a different subject and treated in another chapter [13]). There follow the epigrams addressed to *malīḥ*s of various social status, beginning with caliphs (it is doubtful, however, whether the existence of a "caliph" in contemporary Cairo was the reason for the retention of such verses), statesmen, all kinds of military and civilian officials, and then on down the entire scale of socially useful occupations and not-so-useful occupations, such as those of robbers and thieves. Slaves are also included in the scheme. Such rather lowly jobs as, for instance, that of courier (*sāʿī*) are not forgotten:

I'd give my life for a courier
Whose beauty has captured mankind.
I must become intimate with him,
Come what may.[56]

(*Bi-l-rūḥi afdī sāʿiyan*
jamāluhū sabā l-warā
Lā budda lī min waṣlihī
wa-law jarā mahmā jarā [fol. 53a])

Hunting, shooting, riding, traveling to near or far places—each activity has its own chapter. A returning traveler, his face weathered by his journey, may thus be greeted with this epigram:

The friend whom I love has returned from a trip
With sunburn on his face.
I wonder about the sun's impression on a moon
When the sun must not reach the moon.[57]

(*Jāʾa l-ḥabību lladhī ahwāhu min safarin*
wa-l-shamsu qad aththarat fī wajhihī atharā
ʿAjibtu min atharin li-l-shamsi fī qamarin
wa-l-shamsu lā yanbaghī an tudrika l-qamarā [fol. 65b])

The merchant traveler occurs again in chapter 8, dedicated to merchants and jewelers, in verses playing on the similarity in sound and writing of the words for camels, loads, and beauty:

A merchant who did not stay put in a land—
It is the moon's custom to move from place to place.
He became so exceedingly beautiful that
Beauty turned out to be his camels' loads.[58]

(*Wa-tājirin lam yuqim bi-arḍin*
wa-ʿādatu l-badri l-intiqālū
Afraṭa fī ḥusnihī fa-aḍḥā
Aḥmāla ajmālihī jamālū [fol. 85b])

Polo and ball games are included here, as are other activities of children such as playing with pigeons and small birds. An imagined specific situation such as a *malīḥ* feeding a small bird (*zurzūr*) from his mouth is transformed into an erotic play on words:

O (you) who is carrying (his pet) sparrow in his hand
You commit a grave sin among humankind!
Would you forbid lovers to kiss (your) red lips,
While you allow the sparrow to feed from your mouth?
For your sparrow's sake, spare just a single visit,
And you will quench the thirst in the breast of your friends.

(*Yā ḥāmila l-zurzūri fī kaffihī*
aktharta fī l-nāsi tajannīkā
A-tamnaʿu l-ʿushshāqa lathma l-lamā
wa-tuṭʿima l-zurzūra min fīkā
Bi-ḥaqqi zurzūrika zur zawratan
tashfī ṣadā ṣadri muḥibbīkā [fol. 64a])

Verses on military and civilian officials are combined with those on legal administrators; on the representatives of artistic and scholarly disciplines such as poetry, prosody, and *ḥadīth;* on scientists such as astronomers and what are seen as related activities—prayer leader, muezzin, and astronomical/religious timekeeper (*muwaqqit*); on teachers, ascetics, and even philosophers and logicians. On a pretty student of logic, al-Ṣafadī composed this epigram:

O you beautiful gazelle of a logician whose love
Has made (my) eyelids unable to meet for slumber,
When it covered my body with wasting disease.
"Affliction may come from talk/logic."[59]

(*Yā ḥusna ẓabyin manṭiqīyin ḥubbuhū*
jaʿala l-jufūna ʿalā l-karā lā taltaqī
Wa-adhāba qalbī idh kasā jismī l-ḍanā
inna l-balāʾa muwakkalun bi-l-manṭiqī [fol. 72a])

Details of a central profession in a manuscript society, that of copyist, are not overlooked. The obligatory manuscript "collation" (*muqābala*) elicits several epigrams playing with various meanings of the Arabic word such as "opposition," "facing (punishment)," and "algebra":

My beloved collated his books,
And my heart became covered with apprehension.
Lord, keep him safe, for
The full moon that he is is in opposition.[60]

(*Qābala l-ḥibbu kutbah*
fa-fuʾādī ktasā walah
Rabbi sallimhu innah
badruhū fī l-muqābalah [fol. 84a])

Or:

I plucked a fresh rose that is
Your cheek from you with the slender figure.
So, all the time, I commit
A crime while you are collating/facing punishment.[61]

(*Janaytu khaddaka wardan*
ghaḍḍan wa-qadduka dhābil
Fa-hā anā kulla waqtin
ajnī wa-anta tuqābil [fol. 84a])

Or:

I have collated books with an (otherwise) aloof friend
Who thereby gave joy to a heart about to perish from fear.

I said: O you who inherits my heart in passion,
You have combined between restoration-and-collation/algebra.[62]

(*Qābaltu kutban maʿ ḥabībin hājirin*
fa-sarra qalban kāda an yafnā walah
Fa-qultu yā wāritha qalbī fī l-hawā
jamaʿta bayna l-jabri wa-l-muqābalah [fol. 84b])

The playing with the endless variety of human activities goes on and on. Large merchants and small shopkeepers; jewelers; craftsmen employed in the production of different kinds of weapons; workers in wood, stone, and metal; builders; buyers and sellers of flowers and fruits; gardeners—all had epigrams dedicated to the *malīḥ*s among them. A salesman of drawer strings (*tikka*) evokes a couplet of a type that is comparatively rare here in that it suggests explicit sexuality:

O seller of drawer strings in his shop
Well braided and tied!
I don't need but a drawer string
That you untie when we are alone in my house.

(*Yā bāʾiʿa l-tikkati fī sūqihī*
muḥkamatan bi-l-ḍafri wa-l-ʿaqdī
Mā ḥājatī illā ilā tikkatin
taḥulluhā fī khalwatin ʿindī [fol. 97a])

The only thing a skillful painter (*muṣawwir*) cannot capture in his work is his own beauty.

In the craft of painting has risen a moon
Who matches every(thing) created with its like.
He paints all that is beautiful on earth,
Yet is unable to paint something like his face.

(*Samā fī ṣanʿati l-taṣwīri badrun*
yuqābilu kulla makhlūqin bi-shibhih
Yuṣawwiru kulla mā fī l-arḍi ḥusnan
wa-yaʿjizu an yuṣawwira mithla wajhih [fol. 101b]

Players of various instruments, singers, dancers, singers who also play an instrument while dancing, shadow players, all find the attention they deserve because of their central position in the entertainment industry of their civilization. Even the sweating of a dancer is grist for the poet's mill:

One with intoxicating, bewitching eyes,
With sweet red lips and a well-proportioned figure,
Danced till he sweated, producing something like
Dewdrops as on a rose on his cheek.[63]

(*Wa-sāḥiri l-alḥāẓi nashwāniha*
ʿadhbi l-lamā muʿtadili l-qaddī
ʿArraqahū l-raqṣu fa-fī khaddihī
mithlu saqīṭi l-ṭalli fī l-wardī [fol. 132b])

The eating of hashish was common in the time of al-Badrī. It is documented by no less than three epigrams in this context (fols. 127a–130b); four more are quoted under varia (fol. 188a). Players of various games also have their epigrams; in the case of chess, there are twelve entries. The concluding chapters, 16 and 17, are devoted to the traditional themes of the beauty mole and the first growth of hair on the face of the beloved. The interest in these chapters is thus confined to specialists in these standard conceits of amatory poetry. But chapter 15 on varia offers again many observations on daily life. *Malīḥ*s are depicted as laughing, crying, walking arm in arm, walking slowly. There are Ṣūfīs and Qalandarīs among them. They go on the pilgrimage and perform its various rites. They swim, engage in nautical pursuits, and, in particular, participate in the many activities of the public bath. They look into mirrors, thus offering an opportunity for the poet to expand on an ancient and favorite subject. From another practitioner of the homoerotic epigram, Mujīr al-Dīn Ibn Tamīm (d. 684/1285), comes a variant on the mirror metaphor that has intrigued people since mirrors were discovered and that is so commonly employed in Arabic literature. In Mujīr al-Dīn's case, the metaphor is the double enjoyment of an individual's beauty caused by its reflection in the mirror:

A blessing upon the friend's mirror for being carried
In the hand of (someone as straight as) a branch of a fully grown
  ben tree!
It faced the moon in heaven with its (sur)face,
"Thus showing me two moons together at one time."[64]

(*Ṭūbā li-mirʾāti l-ḥabībi fa-innahā*
ḥumilat bi-rāḥati ghuṣni bānin aynaʿā

Wa-staqbalat qamara l-samāʾi bi-wajhihā
fa-aratniya l-qamarayni fī waqtin maʿā [fol. 185a])

An entire chapter (14) deals with physical imperfections and defects that are viewed as not being obstacles to true love. It starts out with epigrams on the medical profession, physicians, oculists, barbers, and bloodletters. The comparison of physical ailments with the potential psychic harm caused by unfulfilled love was a favorite subject of love theory. Verses of (Ibn) Daftarkhwān, for instance, address an unfeeling physician:

A physician, with whose glances passion toyed
So that his eyes became his eyelids' arrows,
Cures the sick but does not cure a lover
And turns away from his moans and sighs.
How can someone passionately in love be healed
When the physician is no help for him against passion?

(*Mutaṭabbibun ʿabatha l-hawā bi-liḥāẓihī*
fa-ghadat lawāḥiẓuhū sihāma jufūnihī
Yubrī l-saqīma wa-laysa yubrī ʿāshiqan
wa-yaḥīdu ʿan zafarātihī wa-anīnihī
Kayfa l-sabīlu ilā shifāʾi mutayyamin
laysa l-ṭabību ʿalā l-hawā bi-muʿīnihī [fol. 152b])

Professions of love for *malīḥ*s affected by malformations or diseases, often of a kind considered loathsome, and the defense of such love against public censure are touching, even if they degenerate into scurrilous verses on such an insignificant flaw as bad breath, and play on the common theme of the beloved's enjoyable saliva:

You people attack me for being deeply in love with someone with bad breath.
I'll tell you frankly what my situation is:
My friend is chary with (his) saliva, so the mouth water
Just changed because it stayed (in the mouth) for too long.[65]

(*Wa-ʿannaftumūnī idh kaliftu bi-abkharin*
sa-ukhbirukum ʿan sharḥi ḥālī wa-baththihī
Ḥabībī ḍanīnun bi-l-ruḍābi wa-innamā
taghayyara māʾu l-thaghri min ṭūli makthihī [fol. 157a]

True love is not dependent on physical characteristics, and real beauty lies in the mind and soul rather than the eye of the beholder. Verses by Ibn al-Muʿtazz as quoted in the *Jawāmiʿ al-ladhdha* are the most eloquent expression of love as a universal feeling that does not discriminate:

> My heart jumps constantly at this and that.
> Whatever it is that it sees, it does not reject it.
> It falls deeply in love with beauty as is fitting,
> And taking pity on ugliness, it loves it.[66]

The few examples here, selected from thousands, may not be the best of their kind, and the literal translations do not do justice to the literary artistry, the lilting rhythm, and the allusive power of words and meanings that most of them share. The poetic imagery is standard and worn out by common use; it is much too repetitive and unoriginal to be great poetry. True feeling is obviously absent from the genre as such, just as we have contended it is at our starting point, the *Rangstreit* discussion. Epigrams are usually exercises in technical skill, and these Arabic epigrams are so perhaps to an even greater degree since composing them had become a test that anyone aspiring to be called a cultured individual, let alone a poet, had to pass. Above all, love had developed into a routine subject of versemaking that could dispense with felt emotion; the erotic vocabulary had all but lost its original meaning and could even be applied as a form of flattery. Sexuality gives way to a cult of beauty sought in every aspect of daily life and in all the manifestations of higher civilization; sexual distinctions are reduced to a minor role. Whether homoerotic or heteroerotic elements prevail in direct comparisons or are analyzed in separate chapters or separate essays, these collections present a shimmering, albeit solid and encompassing, picture of a society in which a significant segment of the intellectual leadership tried to teach that seeing love as beauty was the indispensable means for its true fulfillment.

NOTES

1. M. Steinschneider's bibliographical approach, which popularized the word *Rangstreit* in the scholarly literature, remains very informative; see "Rangstreit-Literatur" in *Sitzungsberichte der kaiserlichen Akademie der Wissenschaften in Wien, Philosophisch-Historische Klasse* 155(4) (Vienna, 1908). The most comprehensive survey of the subject from the Arabist point of view is Ewald Wagner's *Die arabische Rangstreitdichtung und ihre Einordnung in die allgemeine Literaturgeschichte* (Wiesbaden: Akademie der Wissenschaften und

der Literatur, Abhandlungen der Geistes- und Sozialwissenschaftlichen Klasse, no. 8, 1962). Wagner makes sharp distinctions between different forms and types of *Rangstreit* and the Arabic words used to characterize it. This seems, indeed, the only way to attempt to bring order to an enormous amount of varied material. For the purpose of this brief paper, however, no such effort seemed necessary and any consistent distinction between the Arabic words would have been cumbersome. See also Wagner's contributions to *The Encyclopaedia of Islam,* 2nd ed. (Leiden: E. J. Brill, 1960–) under Mufākhara and especially Munāẓara.

Another important problem is that of interdependence among the civilizations that cultivated the genre; it has been much discussed but is unlikely to find a generally acceptable solution. A. Mez was convinced that "the extension of the *mufāḍalah* to objects and concepts, for which the first evidence is found in the ninth century . . . can be explained only as resulting from the influence of the Greek *syncrisis*"; see al-Azdī, *Ḥikāyat Abī l-Qāsim,* ed. A. Mez, *Abulḳâsim, ein bagdâder Sittenbild* (Heidelberg: Carl Winter's Universitätsbuchhandlung, 1902), p. xix. Such influence would seem highly plausible in view of the historical circumstances but cannot be proved, and Wagner's cautious attitude is preferable for now, but see also below, p. 32 and n. 52. The problem of the existence and direction of influence here is in a way similar to that of the medieval troubadour poetry of western Europe.

For a combined effort to deal with the phenomenon of comparative debate, as well as a rich source for the scholarly literature on the subject, see G. J. Reinink and H. L. J. Vanstiphout, eds., *Dispute Poems and Dialogues in the Ancient and Medieval Near East* (Leuven: Departement Orientalistiek, 1991. *Orientalia Lovaniensia Analecta* 42). Contributions on the Arabic side are by J. N. Mattock, F. Leemhuis, W. Heinrichs, and C. J. Van Gelder.

2. Al-Ṣafadī, *al-Ghayth al-musajjam fī sharḥ Lāmīyat al-ʿajam,* 2 vols. (Cairo, 1305 [1888]), 2:158.

3. It must be stressed here again that English terms usually have ranges of meaning and subconscious connotations quite different from the Arabic terms they try to translate. This causes particular problems in the sociosexual context. Moreover, the Arabic words for males and females, which are more varied for the former in the texts under consideration here, have implications of age, physical development, and social status in the minds of native speakers; when encountered on the written page, these often can no longer precisely be determined and even less precisely captured by seemingly equivalent English words. The institution of slavery as practiced in medieval Islam furthermore infused the terms *jāriya* (pl. *jawārī*) and *ghulām* (pl. *ghilmān*) with the notion of unfree status, probably more so for the former than the latter. In the famous description of Baghdadi cabarets, the entertainers are counted as *al-rijāl wa-l-ṣibyān wa-l-jawārī wa-l-ḥarāʾir,* presumably understood as free men and unfree boys, unfree girls and free women. See al-Tawḥīdī, *al-Imtāʿ wa-l-muʾānasa,* Aḥmad Amīn and Aḥmad al-Zayn, eds., 3 vols. (Cairo: Lajnat al-Taʾlīf wa-l-Tarjama wa-l-Nashr, 1939–44), 2:183; al-Azdī, *Ḥikāyat Abī l-Qāsim,* p. 87. For the related problem of *malīḥ,* see below, p. 32.

4. The Arabic text is cited here according to the edition of ʿAbd al-Salām Muḥammad Hārūn, *Rasāʾil al-Jāḥiẓ,* 4 vols. in 2 (Cairo: Maktabat al-Khānjī, 1384 [1964–65]), 2:87–137.

5. See *The Encyclopaedia of Islam,* 2nd ed., s. v. Ibn Abī Ṭāhir Ṭayfūr; Fuat Sezgin, *Geschichte des arabischen Schrifttums* (Leiden: E. J. Brill, 1967–) 1:348–49, 2:614.

6. See Franz Rosenthal, *Aḥmad b. aṭ-Ṭayyib as-Saraḫsī* (New Haven: American Oriental Society, American Oriental Series no. 26, 1943). Reference to Sarakhsī quotations in the *Jawāmiʿ* (see below) is made in Franz Rosenthal, "From Arabic Books and Manuscripts VI: Istanbul Materials for al-Kindî and as-Saraḫsî," *Journal of the American Oriental Society* 76 (1956): 31.

7. The quotations to be found in the *Jawāmiʿ* would allow for it a date no earlier than the end of the tenth century. H. Ritter, *Das Meer der Seele* (Leiden: E. J. Brill, 1955), p. 457, may be correct in identifying the author of the "*ars amandi*" with the Iraqi Shīʿite of the same name who is further described as "secretary" (al-Kātib) in Yāqūt, *Irshād al-arīb,* D. S. Margoliouth, ed., 7 vols. (Leiden: Gibb Memorial Series no. 6, 1907–27), 5:433, and Aḥmad Farīd Rifāʿī, ed., 20 vols. (Cairo: Maktabat ʿĪsā al-Bābī al-Ḥalabī, n. d. [1938]), 15:97–98, but this identification remains so far as unprovable as the one with a tenth-century namesake suggested by Rosenthal, "From Arabic Books and Manuscripts VI: Istanbul Materials for al-Kindî and as-Saraḫsî," p. 31.

8. The most complete, if somewhat too inclusive, treatment of the phenomenon remains Ḥabīb Zayyāt, "al-Marʾa al-ghulāmīya fī l-Islām," in *al-Machriq* 50 (1956): 153–92. It is, of course, commented upon in all works dealing with ʿAbbāsid cultural history.

9. Quoted in the edition of Abū Nuwās's *Dīwān* by Ḥamza al-Iṣfahānī (first half of the tenth century) and made known first by E. Mittwoch, "Die literarische Tätigkeit Ḥamza al-Iṣbahanis," in *Mittheilungen des Seminars für Orientalische Sprachen, Westasiatische Studien* 12 (1909): 126. The last part of the *Dīwān,* on *mujūn,* where it appears (Istanbul MS Fatih 3775, fols. 55b–56b), has not yet been published. My thanks to Professors E. Wagner and G. Schoeler for kindly giving me detailed information on the passage.

The title of the work is given by Ḥamza al-Iṣfahānī as *Kitāb (tafḍīl) al-satihayn ʿalā l-ḥariḥayn.* Another title (for the same work?) appears among the works of Abū l-ʿAnbas (*sic leg.,* instead of Abū l-ʿbs) in Ibn al-Nadīm, *Fihrist,* G. Flügel, ed. (Leipzig: F. C. W. Vogel, 1871–72), p. 314, l. 5; the Persian tanslation of M. Reza Tajaddod (Tehran: Ibn Sīnā, 1965), p. 557, and the English translation by Bayard Dodge (New York: Columbia University Press, 1970), p. 736, have nothing on the author. The title *Kitāb al-Saḥḥāqāt wa-l-baghghāʾīn,* "On Lesbians and homosexual offenders," appears with the inversion of the two components in *Jawāmiʿ* with the authorship of Abū-l-ʿAnbas (as correctly stated in MS Chester Beatty, whereas in MS Fatih it looks as if the author was the one of the *Jawāmiʿ* himself). *Baghghāʾ* is often used as a word for male prostitute, but this may here be too specific; see Everett K. Rowson, "The Effeminates of Early Medina," *Journal of the American Oriental Society* 111 (1991): 685–86. It cannot be determined whether the other references to Abū l-ʿAnbas in the *Jawāmiʿ* go back to this work, which is possible but need not be.

10. See, at the end of the discussion treated here, the remarks on Ibrāhīm b. Hilāl (b. Ibrāhīm) b. Zahrūn al-Ṣābī (313–384/925–994) and a certain Abū Naṣr Bishr b. Hārūn. The latter remains to be identified; his namesake mentioned in Miskawayh in 311/923 (H. F. Amedroz and D. S. Margoliouth, *The Eclipse of the ʿAbbasid Caliphate,* 7 vols. [Oxford: Basil Blackwell, 1920–21], 1:112) seems too early, but another more likely—if unconfirmed—candidate appears in al-Tanūkhī, *Nishwār al-muḥāḍara,* Abood Shalchy, ed., 8 vols. (Beirut, 1971–73), 1:93–94, 3:114.

The *Jawāmiʿ* (MS Fatih, fols. 205a–208b; MS Chester Beatty, fols. 217a–220b) quotes the work of a certain Yazdjard b. (?, corrupted from Mahbundād?) on the greater merit of no-longer-virginal women as compared to virgins.

11. *Encyclopedia of Pleasure by Abul Hasan ʿAli Ibn Nasr al-Katib,* Salah Addin Khawwam, B. Sc., ed. and annotator, ʿAdnan Jarkas and Salah Addin Khawwam, translators (Toronto: Aleppo Publishing, 1977). Copy in the Library of Congress.

12. The manuscripts are Istanbul MS Fatih 4729, dated in Rabīʿ II 582/June–July 1186, fols. 65a–70a, and Dublin MS Chester Beatty 4635, dated Sunday, 15 Ṣafar 724/12 February 1324, fols. 62a–70b. See A. J. Arberry, *A Handlist of the Arabic Manuscripts, The Chester Beatty Library,* 8 vols. (Dublin: E. Walker, 1955–66), 6:42. A fuller description is needed but cannot be given here.

The discussion was quoted, no doubt from the *Jawāmiʿ*, by the historian al-ʿAynī (762–855/1361–1451) in his *Ḥikāyāt,* MS Bursa Hüseyyin Çelebi 890, fols. 7a (—10a? I did not take down the full text and thus am unable to say how much was copied). As indicated by ʿAbd al-Salām Muḥammad Hārūn in his introductory remark to the Jāḥiẓ essay, the Bursa manuscript was known to Ṣalāḥ al-Dīn al-Munajjid, who referred to it briefly in a review of Pellat's edition of al-Jāḥiẓ's *Mufākhara* in *Majallat Maʿhad al-Makhtūṭāt al-ʿArabīya* 3 (1957): 335, n. 5.

13. In connection with other Sarakhsī quotations the same problem shows up; for instance, in al-Tawḥīdī, *al-Baṣāʾir wa-l-dhakhāʾir,* Wadād al-Qāḍī, ed., 10 vols. (Beirut: Dār Ṣādir, 1408/1988), 8:10–13.

14. Another aspect of this relationship is illuminated by a text discovered by Matti Moosa that deals with a religious disputation between a Christian church dignitary and various Muslims, whose group also included Jews. See "A New Source on Aḥmad ibn al-Ṭayyib al-Sarakhsī," *Journal of the American Oriental Society* 92 (1972): 19–24; Arabic text in *al-Majalla al-Baṭrīrakīya* (Damascus) 7 (1969): 189–97, 244–52.

15. Franz Rosenthal, *The Classical Heritage in Islam* (London: Routledge and Kegan Paul, 1975), pp. 106–7. For a brief excerpt form Mughulṭāy, see Rosenthal, "From Arabic Books and Manuscripts IV: New Fragments of as-Saraḫsî," *Journal of the American Oriental Society* 71 (1951): 135–36.

16. MS Fatih, fols. 96a–100a, MS Chester Beatty, fols. 100a–103b, trans. Khawwam, pp. 207–9.

17. MS Fatih, fol. 73a, MS Chester Beatty, fol. 74a, apparently omitted in trans. Khawwam, where it should appear on p. 173. The reading of the text and thus the point of the remark are not quite clear to me.

18. MS Fatih, fols. 8a–9a, MS Chester Beatty, fols. 8b–9a, trans. Khawwam, pp.

54–55. MS Fatih, fols. 82b–83a, and MS Chester Beatty, fol. 85a–b, lack the chain of transmitters beginning with al-Sarakhsī from al-Kindī that appears in trans. Khawwam, p. 107, introducing a story about a woman being asked by a man to use an artificial penis (*kīrbanaj*) on him. For a related anecdote, see al-Jāḥiẓ, *Rasāʾil,* 2:187, and Manfred Ullmann, *Wörterbuch der klassischen arabischen Sprache,* vol. K (Wiesbaden: Otto Harrassowitz, 1970), p. 489.

19. Compare the comment in Ḥamza al-Iṣfahānī's edition of the *Dīwān* of Abū Nuwās that he preferred keeping this material distinct; see Abū Nuwās, *Dīwān,* vol. 4, Gregor Schoeler, ed. (Wiesbaden: Franz Steiner, 1402/1982. *Bibliotheca Islamica* 20d), pp. 8 and 144. Serious homoerotic or heteroerotic love poetry (which in the case of Abū Nuwās was kept separate) was not affected by that distinction.

20. The Jāḥiẓ passage, for instance, was translated by Charles Pellat in *Arabische Geisteswelt* (Zürich and Stuttgart: Artemis Verlag, 1967), pp. 434–35, and by James A. Bellamy in "Sex and Society in Islamic Popular Literature," as well as J. C. Bürgel in "Love, Lust, and Longing: Eroticism in Early Islam As Reflected in Literary Sources," both in *Society and the Sexes in Medieval Islam,* Afaf Lutfi al-Sayyid-Marsot, ed. (Malibu, Calif.: Undena, 1979. *Sixth Giorgio Levi Della Vida Biennial Conference*), pp. 29 and 81, respectively. For the Ibn Qutayba passage, see Franz Rosenthal, "Fiction and Realty: Sources for the Role of Sex in Medieval Muslim Society," in *Society and the Sexes,* p. 19, and reprinted in idem, *Muslim Intellectual and Social History* (Aldershot: Variorum, 1990). For al-Sarakhsī's aversion to inappropriateness in thought and language, see the quotation from his *Marāḥ al-rūḥ* in al-Tawḥīdī, *Baṣāʾir,* 6:106–7; al-Ābī, *Nathr al-durr,* 7 vols. (Cairo: al-Hay'a al-Miṣrīya al-ʿĀmma lil-Kitāb, 1981–91), 3:312–13.

21. This translates *ahl al-murūwāt,* as in MS Fatih. The reading *ahl al-mawaddāt* in MS Chester Beatty is unlikely.

22. For information on these two seventh-century poets, the latter the son of a more famous father, see Sezgin, *Geschichte,* 2:149–50 and 422–23. The name of Muʿāwiya's daughter is said to be ʿĀtika.

23. MS Chester Beatty: *fa-qāla* seems more correct than MS Fatih: *fa-qul.*

24. This sentence is missing in MS Fatih. It seems that the use of *lūṭī* and *zānī,* which were also the legal terms, was considered inappropriate under the circumstances. "Friends with" renders *aṣḥāb.*

On the *ẓurrāf,* see M. F. Ghazi, "Un groupe social: 'Les Raffinés' (Ẓurafāʾ)," *Studia Islamica* 11 (1959): 39–71.

25. MS Fatih simplifies by reading an unmetrical *wa-fatātu/in.* The unreadable word in MS Chester Beatty may reflect *wa-mīrāthīyatu/in* found in al-Jāḥiẓ, *Rasāʾil,* 2:96. The unexplained *mīrāthīya* could perhaps mean a legally married woman since inheritance rights are a condition of legal marriage, in contrast to a temporary *mutʿa* marriage as explained at length in the *Jawāmiʿ*, but without further confirmation this is no more than a fanciful guess. E. K. Rowson plausibly suggests that the word might refer to an inherited slave girl.

26. This translates the text as found in al-Jāḥiẓ: *wa-lahā zīyu l-ghulāmi.* MS Fatih: *tahādā* (for *tatahādā*) *ka-l-ghulāmi,* "she struts"; MS Chester Beatty, slightly against the

meter: *tamshī mashya l-ghulāmi,* "she walks as boys walk." *Tahādā* looks sufficiently similar to *lahā zīyu* to be a corruption of it: *tahādā* is defined as "walking (unsteadily) with someone's support" or, generally, as *tamāyul,* "swaying (in walking)"; see, for example, al-Azharī, *Tahdhīb al-lugha,* ʿAbd al-Salām Muḥammad Hārūn, ed., 15 vols. (Cairo: al-Dār al-Miṣrīya li-l-Ta'lıf wa-l-Tarjama, 1964–67), 6:383; also, with the addition of "slowly" (*al-tamāyul fī l-mashy al-baṭī*ʾ), see Ibn Ḥajar, *Fatḥ al-bārī,* 17 vols. (Cairo: Muṣṭafā al-Bābī al-Ḥalabī, 1378–83/1959–63), 2:294–95. Al-Jāḥiẓ may have the more correct text; however, the situation is far from clear.

27. The available manuscripts differ as to whether the statement is intended to be positive or negative. The positive statement adopted here appears in MS Fatih: *fa-mā arāhumā illā abʿadā fīhi.* The negative version in MS Chester Beatty (*fa-mā abʿadā fīhi*) appears to be also in the text used by Khawwam. Either would be suitable, but until further evidence I would prefer the above, possibly more weakly attested, rendering.

28. A word seems to be missing in the text. "Changes, becomes changed" seems a good guess.

29. The manuscripts seem to have: *fa-innamā abdat al-ṭabīʿatu zahra[ta] l-shabābi wa-nawrahū wa-shīʾ(at)ahū,* but the textual problems are many. Khawwam's translation is too paraphrastic to be of help.

We may add to the preceding discussion that even as late a text as the *Arabian Nights* could maintain that "if boys were not more excellent and more handsome, girls would not be compared to them." See *Arabian Nights,* 421st night, of the Calcutta text (*Alf layla wa-layla,* 4 vols. [Calcutta: Thacker, 1839–42], 2:459); 3:582–83 of Enno Littmann's masterful German translation, *Die Erzählungen aus den Tausendundein Nächten,* 6 vols. (Leipzig: Insel, 1924).

30. For one convenient collection of statements on jealousy among many, see, for instance, al-Nuwayrī, *al-Ilmām bi-l-iʿlām fīmā jarat bihi l-aḥkām wa-l-umūr al-maqḍīya fī waqʿat al-Iskandarīya,* Aziz Surial Atiyya, ed., 6 vols. (Hyderabad: Maṭbaʿat Majlis Dāʾirat al-Maʿārif al-ʿUthmānīya, 1388–96/1968–76), 6:221ff.

31. Al-Raqāshī (Sezgin, *Geschichte,* 2:516) is credited with a poem in which he recommends homosexuality, wine drinking, gambling, cockfights, and dogfights as the familiar catalogue of fashionable misbehavior in his time; see Ibn al-Muʿtazz, *Ṭabaqāt al-shuʿarā*ʾ, ʿAbd al-Sattār A. Farrāj, ed. (Cairo: Dār al-Maʿārif, n. d. [1375/1956]), p.226.

32. Khawwam, p. 167, shows some confusion, involving the omission of al-Ṭarsūsī. He is no doubt the Abū Ayyūb al-Ṭarsūsī mentioned several times in the edition of Abū Nuwās's *Dīwān;* see for example 4:75. Professors Wagner and Schoeler kindly answered my question concerning him.

33. For al-Ḥusayn b. al-Ḥasan b. ʿAṭīya al-ʿAwfī, see, for instance, Ibn Saʿd, *Kitāb al-Ṭabaqāt al-kabīr,* Eduard Sachau et al., eds., 8 vols. (Leiden: E. J. Brill, 1904–40), 7, 2:74; Wakīʿ, *Akhbār al-quḍāt,* ʿAbd al-ʿAzīz Muṣṭafā al-Marāghī, ed., 3 vols. (Cairo: Maṭbaʿat al-Istiqāma, 1366–69/1947–50), 1:53, 3:265ff.; al-Muʿāfā, *al-Jalīs al-ṣāliḥ,* Muḥammad Mursī al-Khawlī, ed., 4 vols. (Beirut: ʿĀlam al-Kutub, 1981), 1:489–90; al-Khaṭīb al-Baghdādī, *Taʾrīkh Baghdād,* 14 vols. (Cairo: Maktabat al-Khānjī, 1349/1931),

8:29–32; Ibn Ḥajar, *Lisān al-Mīzān,* 6 vols. (Hyderabad: Maṭbaʿat Majlis Dāʾirat al-Maʿārif al-Niẓāmīya, 1329–31/1911–13), 2:278. Most of the sources cited by Ibn Ḥajar are now in print.

34. Yaḥyā b. Aktham needs no documentation here. For an example, see al-Masʿūdī, *Murūj al-dhahab,* C. A. C. Barbier de Meynard and B. M. M. Paret de Courteille, eds., 9 vols. (Paris: Imprimerie Impériale, 1861–77), 7:43–48. The Aḥmad b. Abī Nuʿaym quoted there is suggested, without further justification, by the editor of Ibn al-Muʿtazz, *Ṭabaqāt al-shuʿarāʾ*, p. 523, to be possibly identical with Jaḥshōyah, who belonged to the circle of Yaḥyā b. Aktham and who is also frequently quoted in the *Jawāmiʿ*. See the references in the edition of Ibn al-Muʿtazz, *Ṭabaqāt al-shuʿarāʾ*, pp. 522–23; C. E. Bosworth, *The Mediaeval Islamic Underworld* (Leiden: E. J. Brill, 1976), p. 63; Abū Nuwās, *Dīwān,* 4:8. In the statement quoted by Ibn al-Muʿtazz, *Ṭabaqāt al-shuʿarāʾ*, p. 226, he appears among a number of intellectuals who are claimed to have practiced a more conservative lifestyle than the one they vaunted in their poetry. The statement reappears in Ibn Falīta (see below, n. 40); compare Rosenthal, "Fiction and Reality," p. 11, n. 19.

35. Regrettably, the poet is not known to me. He is unlikely to have been pre- or early Islamic.

36. The verses by Imruʾulqays and ʿAlqama quoted in the discussion also speak of the need for money, in addition to youth, to be able to attract women. See also Ibn Qutayba, *ʿUyūn al-akhbār,* 4 vols. (Cairo: al-Muʾassasa al-Miṣrīya al-ʿĀmma li-l-Taʾlīf wa-l-Tarjama wa-l-Ṭibāʿa wa-l-Nashr, 1963–64), 4:44–45.

37. The anecdote is translated here from al-Kutubī, *Fawāt al-Wafayāt,* M. Muḥyī al-Dīn ʿAbd al-Ḥamīd, ed., 2 vols. (Cairo: Maktabat al-Nahḍa al-Miṣrīya, 1951), 1:268. As stated by al-Ṣūlī, *Akhbār Abī Tammām,* Khalīl Maḥmūd ʿAsākir et al., eds. (Beirut: al-Maktab al-Tijārī lil-Ṭibāʿa wa-l-Tawzīʿ wa-l-Nashr, n. d [1965?]), p. 196, it circulated with many minor variations. It clearly is a distillation of longer stories on the subject, in which Abū Tammām and al-Ḥasan b. Wahb are the supposed actors.

38. Maximus Tyrius, *Philosophoumena,* Hermann Hobein, ed. (Leipzig: Teubner, 1910), 1 (p. 243). It needs to be stressed that no direct relationship can be established.

39. MS Fatih, fols. 42a, 71b: MS Chester Beatty, fols. 49b, 72a.

40. The once-popular work is preserved in many manuscripts. I used the two manuscripts in the Yale Library, MS Landberg 114 (Catalogue Nemoy 1609), fols. 52a–67a (fols. 64 and 65a are blank), and MS Arabic 490, fols. 44b–60b (the manuscript is dated on Thursday, 18 Rabīʿ I 1067/4 January 1657, and for those interested in the history of Arabic scholarship in Europe, bears the stamp of the library of Barbier de Meynard).

I have not seen the Erlangen dissertation by Mohamed Zouher Djabri (1968) that is a translation of the relevant chapters 9–11 of the work, nor do I know whether an edition of the Arabic text was actually published in New York in recent years (?). An English translation by the translator(s) of the *Jawāmiʿ* supposedly appeared in Toronto in 1977, according to the *National Union Catalogue* for 1981, vol. 7, p. 265a, but the Library of Congress was unable to trace its copy, and the entry may be a mistake.

41. An instructive discussion of *waṣf* in general at its tenth-century stage is that of

Alma Giese, *Waṣf bei Kušāǧim* (Berlin: Klaus Schwarz Verlag, 1981. *Islamkundliche Untersuchungen* 62). As an example of how Kushājim handled erotic verses of this type, we may quote from his *Dīwān*, Khayrīya Muḥammad Maḥfūẓ, ed. (Baghdad: Mudīrīyat al-Thaqāfa al-ʿĀmma, 1390/1970), p. 70:

> He passed by us with a falcon in his hand.
> He and the falcon have something wonderful in common.
>
> The falcon hunts birds swooping down from on high,
> while he hunts the hearts with the glances of his eyes.

42. On this type of poetry, see, most recently, the contributions of Benedikt Reinert in *Neues Handbuch der Literaturwissenschaft*, Band 5 (*Orientalisches Mittelalter*), Wolfhart Heinrichs, ed. (Wiesbaden: AULA–Verlag, 1990), pp. 284–300, 366–408.

43. See above, n. 2. Al-Ṣafadī's *al-Ḥusn al-ṣarīḥ fī miʾat malīḥ* has not been available to me.

44. The two treatises, together with a third one on specimens of the Arabic meters, were printed in al-Ḥijāzī, *Majmūʿat thalāth rasāʾil* (Cairo: Maṭbaʿat al-Saʿāda, 1326/1908 [copy in the New York Public Library]), pp. 2–40 and 41–58. I am not aware of a more recent printing. For al-Ḥijāzī, see Carl Brockelmann, *Geschichte der arabischen Litteratur, Supplementbände* 1–3 (Leiden: E. J. Brill, 1937–42), 2:11–12, 3:1248; al-Sakhāwī, *al-Ḍawʾ al-lāmiʿ*, Ḥusām al-Dīn al-Qudsī, ed., 12 vols. (Cairo: Maktabat al-Quds, 1353–55/1934–36), 2:147–49. Al-Sakhāwī, as usual, has much interesting information; he also states that he had published longer biographies of al-Ḥijāzī elsewhere.

45. MS British Museum 1423 (add. 23,445). The British Library kindly provided me with a microfilm. The well-written manuscript is dated on 5 Dhū l-Ḥijja 875/25 May 1471. The old catalogue (*Catalogus codicum manuscriptorum orientalium qui in Museo Britannico asservantur, Pars secunda, codices arabicos amplectens* [London, 1871)], 2:654–55), has a reasonably complete description, indicating the chapter headings and referring to the *taqrīẓ*es, and also mentioning some of the poets quoted. It states correctly that the chapter headings for chapters 5 and 17 are missing in the text. However, it indicates fol. 28 as the place where the chapter heading of chapter 2 (dealing with adjectives formed from the names of localities, religions, and the like, designated in the table of contents quite interestingly by the word *mutajannisūn*) is to be found. This, however, is not the case; the custos on fol. 27b indicates a gap. After fol. 177a there seems to be another gap. Thus, a number of folios are missing; how many is hard to say. An inspection of the original manuscript may be useful. On the basis of notes I took in 1973, I quote some verses in my *Gambling in Islam* (Leiden: E. J. Brill, 1975); see the index under al-Badrī.

On al-Badrī, see Brockelmann, *Geschichte*, 2:132; Brockelmann, *Geschichte der arabischen Litteratur, Supplementbände* 1–3, 2:163; Franz Rosenthal, *The Herb: Hashish versus Medieval Muslim Society* (Leiden: E. J. Brill, 1971), pp. 13–15; al-Sakhāwī, *al-Ḍawʾ al-lāmiʿ*, 11:41–42. Al-Sakhāwī states that al-Badrī wrote the *Ghurar* [*sic*] in Damascus in 865/1460–61. Like the title, the date is no doubt incorrect. Ibn Sūdūn, who died in

868/1464, is listed on fol. 176a as deceased, and the endorsements are dated in 871/1467. Admittedly, the *Ghurra* could have been written and published in stages, but this remains to be proved. The problem is similar to that posed by his work on hashish and wine, as discussed in *The Herb,* pp. 13–15.

For endorsements such as are preserved on the first six folios of the manuscript, see Franz Rosenthal, "'Blurbs' (*Taqrīẓ*) from Fourteenth-Century Egypt," *Oriens* 27–28 (1981): 177–96, reprinted in idem, *Muslim Intellectual and Social History.* Al-Sakhāwī expressly refers to *taqrīẓ*es of the work but mentions only two (al-Ḥijāzī and al-Ḥā'im al-Manṣūrī) of the five authors quoted in the manuscript. However, he adds five other well-known names. Possibly, different endorsers were solicited for different "editions" (see also below, n. 49), or different selections were made from the original corpus of "blurbs."

46. Brockelmann, *Geschichte*, 2:22, Brockelmann, *Supplementbände,* 2:12; al-Sakhāwī, *al-Ḍaw' al-lāmi',* 2:150–51.

47. Brockelman, *Supplementbände,* 2:94; al-Sakhāwī, *al-Ḍaw' al-lāmi'*, 4:33–35.

48. See al-Sakhāwī, *al-Ḍaw' al-lāmi',* 8:259–60, and, for his father, 6:123. He was very proud of his maternal grandfather, Muḥibb al-Dīn Abū l-Faḍl Muḥammad b. Muḥammad Ibn al-Shiḥna (804–890/1402–1485), a historian of Aleppo from a prominent family of scholars; see Brockelmann, *Supplementbände* 2:40–41.

49. Al-Sakhāwī, *al-Ḍaw' al-lāmi',* 2:214. Al-Sakhāwī knew that he was one of those who wrote blurbs for the *Majmū'* of al-Badrī and that he wrote his in 878/1473–74. He indeed quotes the verses we find in the *Ghurra* manuscript. That manuscript was written before 878, but some *taqrīẓ*es may have been written and attached at a later date, so that the 878 date is not entirely ruled out but very likely a simple mistake rather than an indication that endorsements may have been solicited at different times. See above, n. 45.

50. For the not-uncommon use in poetry of the nunation in the vocative, see W. Wright, *A Grammar of the Arabic Language,* 2 vols. (Cambridge: Cambridge University Press, 1962), 2:387–88. The epigram also appears in the beginning of the treatise *fī asmā' al-ghilmān al-ḥisān* in MS Berlin We. 1786 according to Ahlwardt's *Verzeichnis der arabischen Handschriften der Königlichen Bibliothek zu Berlin*, 10 vols. (Berlin: A. W. Schade, 1887–99), no. 8334. Its author could certainly not have been al-Tha'ālibī, *Alf ghilmān;* and Ibn Daftarkhwān (see n. 54 below), *Alf ghulām wa-ghulām,* raises chronological problems. The manuscript needs to be studied for any possible dependence on al-Badrī (?).

51. Sa'd al-Dīn was born in Malatya in 618/1221 during the stay there of his father, then in his middle fifties; see Brockelmann, *Supplementbände*, 1:802–3; al-Kutubī, *Fawāt al-Wafayāt,* 2:325–29; al-Ṣafadī, *al-Wāfī bi-l-wafayāt,* H. Ritter et al., eds., (Wiesbaden, 1935–), 1:186–88; Claude Addas, *Ibn 'Arabī ou La quête du Soufre Rouge* (Paris: Gallimard, 1989), index, pp. 398–99. The geographical/cultural environment he grew up in was different, but he attended his father's classes on his works. Regrettably, we do not know what Sa'd al-Dīn thought about his father's teachings. He is stated to have died in 656/1258.

His *dīwān* seems to be his only preserved work. Another title listed in Brockelmann is not by him; compare H. Ritter, "Philologika IX. Die vier Suhrawardī," *Der Islam* 25 (1939): 46, 73–79. I have used the Yale manuscript of the *dīwan,* MS Landberg 34 (Catalogue Nemoy, no. 294), a modern copy.

52. According to H. Beckby's introduction to his edition and German translation, 2nd ed. (4 vols., Munich: Heimeran, 1965–68; first published 1957), 1:77. On the "love-names," see David M. Robinson and Edward J. Fluck, *A Study of the Greek Love-names* (Baltimore: The Johns Hopkins Press, 1937), and Konrat Ziegler et al., eds., *Der Kleine Pauly,* 5 vols. (Stuttgart and München: A. Druckenmüller, 1964–75), s. v. Lieblings-Inschriften.

53. As, for instance, in a bisexual context (fols. 125b–126b), on *malīḥ*s consorting with women, or on a *malīḥ* having a son born to him:

> An adolescent married prematurely, so that he gave birth to a son.
> The one a star grown, the other a full moon appearing.
> The lovers shared in him a father with the child.
>
> *(Murāhiqun ʿujila bi-l-nikāḥi ḥattā awladā*
> *Fa-dhāka najmun qad namā wa-dhāka badrun qad badā*
> *Wa-qtasama l-ʿushshāqu minhu wālidan [*MS *waladan] wa-l-waladā)*

The correction suggested for the last line may not be necessary but seems to make better sense.

54. On the basis of a collection devoted to maidens that was compiled in the mid-thirteenth century by Ibn Daftarkhwān al-ʿĀdilī, the topic has been studied in detail by Jürgen W. Weil, *Mädchennamen verrätselt: Hundert Rätsel-Epigramme aus dem Adab-Werk Alf ǧāriya wa-ǧāriya* (Berlin: Karl Schwarz, 1984. *Islamkundliche Untersuchungen* no. 85); see pp. 179–80 for a listing of Weil's other publications on the subject. (Ibn) Daftarkhwān is quoted a number of times in the *Ghurra.* It may be an additional matter of interest that al-Badrī devotes a special section to Turkish names of the ruling establishment of his time.

55. The incorporation of quotations in verses (*taḍmīn*) contributed to their appeal for educated readers. The often-quoted second verse is ascribed to different authors; see Franz Rosenthal, *Four Essays on Art and Literature in Islam* (Leiden: E. J. Brill, 1971), p. 56.

56. The author is Burhān al-Dīn (Ibn) al-Bāʿūnī (777–870/1376–1465), one of the grand old men of the contemporary scholarly establishment. According to al-Sakhāwī (see above, n. 45), he as well as his brothers Shams al-Dīn (b. in the 780s/1378–87, d. 871/1467) and Jamāl al-Dīn (805–880/1403–1475) wrote endorsements for the *Ghurra.* Burhān al-Dīn and Shams al-Dīn died close to the presumptive date of the *Ghurra*'s composition. See the entry al-Bāʿūnī in *The Encyclopaedia of Islam,* 2nd ed., 1:1109–10.

57. The author is Ibn Nubāta (686–768/1287–1366), who is often quoted in the *Ghurra.*

58. The author is al-Ṣafadī, who quotes the epigram in his *Jinān al-jinās fī ʿilm al-badīʿ* (Constantinople, 1299), p. 75; Samīr Ḥusayn Ḥalabī, ed. (Beirut: Dār al-Kutub al-ʿIlmīya, 1407/1987), p. 129.

59. On the proverb and the play on the double meaning of *manṭiq* as "talk" and "logic," see Franz Rosenthal, "The History of an Arabic Proverb," *Journal of the American Oriental Society* 109 (1989): 376–78.

60. Al-Badrī's source is al-Ṣafadī. On the technical meanings of *muqābala,* see *The Encyclopaedia of Islam*, 2nd ed., s. v. Muḳābala. *Qābala* was, of course, also used in its basic meaning of "facing," as in the epigram ascribed to Abū Ḥayyān al-Gharnāṭī, *Dīwān,* Aḥmad Maṭlūb and Khadīja al-Ḥadīthī, eds. (Baghdad: Maṭbaʿat al-ʿĀnī, 1388/1969), pp. 442–43:

> In class, I was faced (*qābalanī*) by a soft white
> And a slim black (*asmar*), who both made my body an heir to perdition.
> The one shaking a straight lance—his upper torso.
> The other drawing a sharp sword—his eyelids.

61. Al-Ṣafadī, *al-Ghayth al-musajjam,* 2:45, explains the double meaning of the *j-n-y* he had in mind ("plucking [fruits, etc.]" and "committing crimes") and of the root *q-b-l* in the third conjugation ("collating" and "a sinner's facing punishment for his crime"). Without his explanation, the reader might have a hard time figuring out the intended sense of *tuqābil.* For the much-used topos of "plucking a rose from the cheek by kissing," see, for instance, Ibn Nubāta, *Dīwān* (Cairo: Maṭbaʿat al-Tamaddun, 1905), p. 174.

62. The author again is al-Ṣafadī. *Walah* apparently represents *walahan.* The two components of the word for "algebra" probably refer to joy and fear.

63. The poet is Najm al-Dīn (Muḥammad b. Sawwār) b. Isrāʾīl (603–677/1206[7]–1278); see al-Kutubī, *Fawāt al-Wafayāt,* 2:431–38; al-Ṣafadī, *Wāfī,* 3:143–45.

64. The last line (or the last two lines?) is said to be a quotation. The same text is given in the biography of Mujīr al-Dīn in al-Kutubī, *Fawāt al-Wafayāt*, 2:541. It is preceded there by verses on a *malīḥ* drinking from a pond that have the same last line. The text in al-Ṣafadī, *al-Ghayth al-musajjam,* 1:73, differs slightly, reading *juliyat,* "polished," for *ḥumilat,* and substituting a metrically impossible synonym (*kaffi*!) for *rāḥati.* Another different first verse appears in one of the biographies of his contemporaries by al-Ṣafadī, *Aʿyān al-ʿaṣr* (Frankfurt am Main: Institute for the History of Arabic-Islamic Science, 1410/1990. Facsimile prepared by Fuat Sezgin), 3:348. See Manfred Ullmann, *Das Motif des Spiegels in der arabischen Literatur des Mittelalters* (Göttingen: Vandenhoeck & Ruprecht, 1992. *Abhandlungen der Akademie der Wissenschaften in Göttingen,* philologisch-historische Klasse, Dritte Folge, no. 198).

65. Contrast the Greek saying in Ibn Abī ʿAwn, *al-Ajwiba al-muskita,* May A. Yousef, ed. (Berlin: Klaus Schwarz, 1988), p. 116, no. 701; Franz Rosenthal, "Witty Retorts of the Philosophers and Sages from the *Kitāb al-Ajwibah al-muskitah* of Ibn Abī ʿAwn," *Graeco-Arabica* 4 (1991): pp. 201–2.

66. *Jawāmiʿ*, MS Fatih, fol. 49b; MS Chester Beatty, fol. 60b. The translation of Khawwam, 123, deserves quoting:

My heart has love for everybody.
It would reject nobody.

It adores beauty
And, having pity on ugliness, loves it.

The Arabic text, as indicated by Khawwam, occurs in al-ʿAbbāsī, *Maʿāhid al-tanṣīṣ,* Muḥammad Muḥyī al-Dīn ʿAbd al-Ḥamīd, ed., 4 vols. (Cairo: Maṭbaʿat al-Saʿāda, 1367/1947, reprint Beirut: ʿĀlam al-Kutub, ca. 1980), 2:41. See also Zayyāt, "al-Marʾa al-ghulāmīya," p. 164. I have as yet no confirmation of the attribution of Ibn al-Muʿtazz.

CHAPTER THREE

Hierarchies of Gender, Ideology, and Power in Ancient and Medieval Greek and Arabic Dream Literature

Steven M. Oberhelman

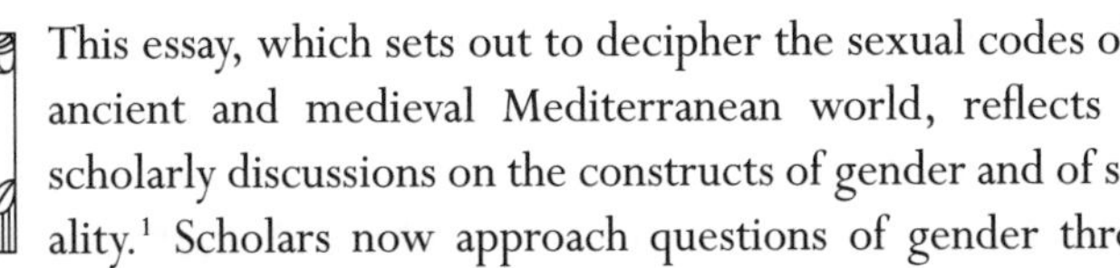

This essay, which sets out to decipher the sexual codes of the ancient and medieval Mediterranean world, reflects new scholarly discussions on the constructs of gender and of sexuality.[1] Scholars now approach questions of gender through one of three theoretical models. Social constructionism insists that sexuality is a modern construct of defining sexual characteristics and desires and argues that sexual taxonomies, identities, and categories are historically specific and socially created.[2] Thus the forms, content, and context of sexuality will always differ according to culture and historical period, with no abstract and universal category of the erotic or the sexual applicable to all societies.[3] The categories and the significance of sexual activity vary according to culture and even subculture, and as members of the society create sexual categories and roles to define themselves and their actions.[4]

Contrasting views are put forth by the essentialists, who assert that social constructs *reflect,* rather than *determine,* sexual phenomena, which are generic to all individuals in all places and times.[5] Essentialists stress that heterosexuals, homosexuals, and bisexuals have existed throughout history, since transcultural generalizations can be made about preferences and behavior and since written records, even in earlier societies, show an awareness of specifically heterosexual and homosexual orientation.[6] The essentialist would insist on, say, a history of gay people;[7] the social constructionist would reject any such history, since only in certain cultures, at certain times, and because of a society's created sexual categories have gay people existed.[8]

The social constructionist–essentialist debate has been waged primarily by scholars of gay history; as feminists rightly claim, the concentration on the phallus and on the experiences of the active male sexual partner is nothing more than patriarchy in new clothing—a discussion of sexuality that removes gender from consideration and replaces it with questions of male status, male age, and male social class.[9] Any conceptualization of sexuality as a hierarchy of power predicated on male social activity is therefore incomplete and insufficient: sexuality must also be seen as gendered—that is, as sexual activity enacting *gendered hierarchies of power.*[10] Many feminist historians also oppose the social constructionists' argument that there is no essential female or male nature and that gender is a product of social conditioning. For if there is no male or female, then there is no explanation for crimes continually and constantly committed against women by men, or for the recurrence of misogyny in cultures unrelated by space and time; one cannot even say that misogyny exists. Feminist history is ethical; it rejects a Foucauldian history of the privilege of the male penis and tries to take gender into account and to create consciousness of the material reality of oppression.[11]

In this paper, I will attempt to synthesize these various theoretical approaches by examining the social signification of sexual activity in three different cultures: Greece of the second century C.E., Byzantine Greece of the fifth through thirteenth centuries, and medieval Islam. The texts on which I base this study will not be canonical sources. What privileged aristocratic males write to and about each other tells us about their social constructs and their ideologies of gender and power,[12] but we should not assume that the sexual codes of the literate male elite were shared by people of lower socioeconomic classes and by others perceived as socially insignificant (women, slaves, and children). Whether these people were willing or unwilling actors in the social discourse fashioned by the upper-class males, they may well have defined themselves and their actions in ways ignored or not understood by their superiors.

The texts I will examine are ancient and medieval *oneirocritica,* or treatises on the interpretation and analysis of dreams.[13] Two types of *oneirocritica* were most popular: those written by professional dream interpreters, who practiced their trade for people of all classes and genders; and short—often five to twenty codex pages in length—do-it-yourself dream manuals, so to speak, of the sort still available in the marketplaces of Athens. Because these dreambooks cover the entire social hierarchy, they are valuable sources of information on cultural ideology, sexual categories, and sexual consciousness. For example, the second-century C.E. dreambook of Artemidorus was not intended for a wide audience; books 4 and 5 were clearly meant for his son's eyes only, while books 1–3 are a highly complex and rhetorical polemic against fellow dream interpreters and critics as well as a self-congratulatory apologia of his own philosophical and methodological principles of interpretation. The dreambook of Achmet ibn Sereim—a product of the encyclopedic craze of tenth-century C.E. Byzantium that was spurred on to a great extent by an influx of Arab learning[14]—mirrors the interests of a new group of nonclerical, middle-class intellectuals. And finally, the short dream manuals, composed in the crudest of iambic hexameters, with repeated references to poor people and laborers and preoccupied with good wages, good health, and an easier way of life, reflect the lives of Byzantine nonaristocratic men and women. All these texts demonstrate the simple fact that in the ancient and medieval worlds a polymorphous sexuality existed, in which the participants were expected to adhere to social constructs of gender and hierarchies of status.[15] The texts also support John Boswell's thesis that the practice of homoeroticism was not affected by the new monotheistic religions of the Mediterranean and did not become the object of full-scale repression, at least in the West, until the thirteenth and fourteenth centuries C.E.[16]

Sexual activity and sex codes in the ancient world have been the focus of much recent research. Scholars like Amy Richlin, Judith Hallett, Marilyn Skinner, Eva Keuls, John Boswell, Peter Brown, David Halperin, and Jack Winkler, to mention but a few, have demonstrated that sex in the ancient world was a unidirectional, nonreciprocal, polarizing action[17]—a sociosexual discourse that was structured by hierarchies of gender, ideology, and power.[18] Sex, to borrow from Halperin, divided, classified, and distributed its participants into distinct and radically opposed categories because it was defined by a single criterion: the penetration of a body by a penis;[19] sexual activity consisted of an active, insertive male penetrating a passive receptor.[20] But penetration was much more than biological process; it was a microcosm of power relations in society.[21] To be the active penetrator was to be dominant, male; to be penetrated, whether one was male or female, meant assuming the subordinate role, servicing the male's desire.[22] To take pleasure, to take the initiative, to insert, to dominate, was virility; to yield, to accept all of this was servility. Thus an adult male citizen of Athens, as the penetrating dominator, could have sexual relations with those inferior to him in status—women, boys, foreigners (male and female), prostitutes (male and female), and slaves (male and female).[23] Sex was not categorized into heterosexuality, homosexuality, bisexuality, prostitution, concubinage, and the like; it was simply insertion and domination by privileged males, and reception and submission by their subordinates. This model explains the anxiety caused by, and the antagonism shown to, the freeborn male who offered himself for penetration.[24] Noncitizen adults and citizen youths could engage in such behavior, for they were excluded from the power structure,[25] but the penetrated adult male abdicated, as it were, the power and responsibility of citizenship; he rejected virility itself.[26] Such passive male citizens threatened the social hierarchy by obscuring gender expectations and, more important, eliminating sexual differentiation by reversals of penetration and reception.[27] Little wonder, therefore, that ancient medical and philosophical writers devised theories of physiological and mental abnormalities to explain the bizarre and shocking behavior of such males.[28] As Winkler has noted in his essay on the *kinaidos* (pathic male), a penetrated male citizen was a sexual but not a social possibility.

The dreambook of Artemidorus, dated to the mid-second century C.E., has long been used by historians of popular culture and by neo-Freudians.[29] But as Winkler has shown, it is invaluable for demonstrating how sexual activity was a social discourse controlled by and devised for males, and for describing in the clearest terms a hierarchy of prestige and power in which the social signification of sex was based on male penetration and domination of subordinate inferiors, male and female.[30]

In his dreambook Artemidorus discusses thousands of dreams and their outcomes that he observed or learned of firsthand. Artemidorus divides all dreams into two distributive categories, the predictive and the nonpredictive. In other words, dreams are considered important only insofar as they prognosticate the future for the dreamer: the past is irrelevant, and the present has value only as an auxiliary tool for deciphering the symbolic future. Nonpredictive dreams are caused by physiological, emotional, or psychological factors and are not treated by Artemidorus and other interpreters; predictive dreams are typically symbolic, and as such require, not surprisingly, the paid services of a professional. The difference between Artemidorean dream science and modern theory is obvious. For Artemidorus, the dream has value only in terms of external circumstances: it forecasts impending changes in a dreamer's social status, wealth, marital and family relations, health, and so forth. As Suzanne MacAlister notes,

> It is the interpreter's function both to determine the dream's outcome in accordance with the individual's situation, experience, role, and status in society and to ascertain the ways in which these social phenomena might have contributed to the actual content of the dream. In order to predict the outcome of a dream, then, the interpreter must translate back and forth between the individual's private dream realm and his or her public waking realm, but can only carry out the process by making use of elements belonging to the social world. The social world therefore imposes upon the pri-

> vate and individual world: it not only serves to identify both dream and outcome, but also emerges as the integrating force between the two. (142)

How the dream related to the dreamer's mental or psychological state was of no concern to Artemidorus.

Methodological guidelines for interpreting symbolic dreams center on one basic principle: the soul draws from a person's cultural experiences and social conditioning when painting the symbolic images of a dream.[31] Six categories for analyzing these images are used: nature, convention, habit, occupation, name, and time, each of which is qualified by *kata* ("in accordance with") and *para* ("in opposition to"). Their definitions are determined by the interpreter through personal interviews with the dreamer about her or his wealth, health, place of birth or residence, family background, job, personal habits and beliefs, and the like.

The two principal categories are *physis* and *nomos,* "nature" and "convention," with convention subdivided into unwritten rules and written rules. Generally speaking, dream images that are *kata physin* ("in accordance with nature") and *kata nomon* ("in accordance with convention") signify something good; those *para physin* ("in opposition to nature") and *para nomon* ("in opposition to convention"), something evil. In his discussion of sexual intercourse, Artemidorus uses these very terms: "The best set of categories for the analysis of intercourse is, first, intercourse according to nature and convention and habit, then intercourse against convention, and third, intercourse against nature." In his three chapters on sex, Artemidorus preserves, with little bias except his decided male-centeredness, a descriptive catalog of sexual and gender relations and how they reflect social status in Greece under the Roman empire.[32]

As the pertinent passages in the Appendix make clear, Artemidorus considers as in accordance with nature (*kata physin*) and convention (*kata nomon*) all actions in which a male penetrates a person socially lower than himself or in which one is penetrated by a socially superior male.[33] Typically, when position in the actual social hierarchy agrees with position in the sexual hierarchy of the dream act, the dreamer can expect a good result; otherwise, he or she can expect a change for the worse.[34] Several points must be made. First, in the matter of partners the social status of the penetrator is of prime concern: whether the passive partner is male or female, free or servile, adult or young, Artemidorus considers of little or no importance.[35] Second, the sexual acts themselves and the associative meanings attached to the dreams are perceived in terms of domination and submission, profit and loss, pleasure and injury, honor and humiliation.[36] These contrasting pairs are replicated in the Byzantine Greek and medieval Arabic dreambooks under discussion here. They may, in fact, appear in any society in which the insertive penis is the determinant of social and sexual codes—a society that Eva Keuls labels "phallocracy," a society dominated by men who sequester their wives and daughters, denigrate the female role in all aspects, erect monuments to the male genitalia, have sex with the sons of their peers, sponsor public whorehouses, create a mythology of rape, and engage in rampant saber-rattling.[37]

Artemidorus calls oral-genital sex and incest "sexual actions *para nomon* ("in opposition to convention")."[38] Dreams involving oral sex are not good, even for the person being fellated, since they foretell hatred and punishment.[39] In the case of incest with a family member (either male or female), the dream results generally are unfavorable, although not if, for example, the male penetrator derives pleasure or profit from the intercourse.

The final category is sexual acts *para physin*. Although the phrase usually means in Greek "in opposition to nature," here it could also be translated as "in opposition to culture," since acts *para physin* include penetration of a woman by a woman.[40] A woman who assumes the penetrator's role usurps the role of the dominating, active, insertive man, violating the sexual and, by extension, social hierarchy. As John Winkler has noted:

> Sexual relations between women are here classed as "unnatural" because "nature" assumes that what are significant in sexual activity are (i) men, (ii) penises that penetrate, and (iii) the articulation thereby of relative statuses through relations of dominance. These three protocols determine the field of significance. Woman–woman intercourse is "unnatural" only and exactly insofar as it lies outside that determinate field of meaning.[41]

A similar attitude is revealed by George Chauncey's research on female homoerotic relations as they were discussed in Victorian medical literature; the label "sexual deviant" was applied to the active partner only, since the so-called passive, by performing her socially mandated subordinate role, did not violate gender expectations.[42] In Spanish and French legal cases of early modern Europe, also, the most severe penalties were reserved for women who cross-dressed or used insertive devices on other women; passive partners were ignored or punished by much less repressive measures.[43]

A number of dreambooks from the Byzantine centuries of Greece have survived.[44] Some are written in iambic verse, ranging from 100 to 450 lines; others are short treatises written in prose. Interpretations of dream symbols are either cosmic—that is, they fit all dreamers—or variable according to the dreamers' social classes, genders, age, health, and so forth. These dreambooks date between the seventh and thirteenth centuries, and are falsely ascribed to famous people like the Persian *magos* Astrampsychus, the patriarch Nicephorus I, the Hebrew prophet Daniel, and the emperor Manuel II Palaeologus. The authors show little reliance on Artemidorus, earlier Greek dream traditions, or Arabic oneirocriticism, and therefore have preserved their own social and sexual codes.

In the Byzantine dreambooks (see Appendix), sex is defined as male penetration of a submissive male or female in a discourse of dominance and power. As a dream symbol, the erect penis represents power in all activities and strength over enemies, while the flaccid penis denotes powerlessness, defeat, and humiliation. All dreams involving penetration of prostitutes, wives, concubines, foreign women, and children portend some kind of profit, goodness, or happiness. The only sexual activity subject to condemnation is seduction of a married woman or holy woman. Regarding male homoeroticism, if a man dreams of being the insertive partner, great goodness and profit will come his way; but if he dreams of being penetrated, he will soon be overpowered and subjected to great humiliation. Only penetration of the vagina and anus is mentioned; oral sex and masturbation are neglected completely.

These types of approved and disapproved sexual relations beg the question: Does not this model of phallocentrism and penetration of non-gender-specific objects conflict with the monogamous heterosexual morality commonly associated with Byzantine religion and legal texts? A number of religious and legal injunctions against homoerotic activity were instituted, beginning in the fourth century,[45] but on closer examination we find that these laws, as well as Byzantine religious texts, are of little value in recovering the morality of the great majority of people living in Byzantium.[46]

First, the Christian attitudes.[47] The Hebrew Bible and the New Testament have very little to say about homoerotic relations;[48] I leave it to John Boswell and to his detractors and supporters to debate and resolve whether or not homosexuality is proscribed by Christianity;[49] whether the antihomoerotic legislation in Leviticus is pre-exile or post-exile or influenced by Zoroastrian religion;[50] whether the story of Sodom deals with rape (homosexual and heterosexual) or hospitality or actual homosexual practices;[51] and whether or not "homosexual" is an accurate translation of *arsenokoitês* and *malakos* in the Pauline and pseudo-Pauline letters.[52] My concern here is the official position of the orthodox Christian church, the power group entrenched in Constantinople. I say "power group," because many forms of Christianity existed in the Byzantine empire, and each had its own sexual codes.[53] I pass over the attitudes of Christians who turned to the most radical renunciation of the body and sex, perpetual virginity, as well as the opinions of church fathers like Gregory of Nyssa, John Chrysostom, and Clement, all of whom either looked on sex with horror and as equivalent to death or preached that sex was permissible only for married couples for the purpose of procreation; anyone who could categorically reject human erotic experiences even between monogamous spouses would not hesitate to strike from the lives of their congregations and audiences other erotic actions and feelings.[54]

If we forsake for the moment the basilica and the patristic text and move instead into the marketplaces and the bedrooms of the Byzantine world, a different picture of sexual codes emerges.[55] Here public ceremonials remained profane, erotic, and carnal even into the eleventh century. The pagan festival of the Lupercalia was still going strong in the sixth century. In sixth-century Palestine, Christian noblemen still sponsored teams of nude girls in water festivals, and prostitutes appeared at the circus in Constantinople dressed in G-strings and with geese pecking at seeds between their thighs.[56] Concubinage was not only tolerated but given legal, religious, and social approval.[57] Byzantine celebrations of saints' days became so lewd that women no longer attended them because of the immense number of rapes, and pagan oracles using virgins flourished until the twelfth century.[58] Even the clergy rejected the strictures of patristic writers: clerics rioted and attacked archbishops when calls for celibacy went out; the bishop of Syracuse was the imperial inspector of brothels; and as John Boswell has demonstrated so extensively, clerics were a major source of homoerotic poetry in the West until the repression of the thirteenth century.[59] In the East, monks like Dorotheos of Gaza (d. 560) chronicled their love for fellow monks; in Egypt monks habitually courted young boys from the villages; and in Greece, in order to eliminate such sexual relations, no male under the age of 18 was allowed to visit or join a monastery.[60] The great saint Basil recommended at first that to keep young monks from same-sex activity an older monk should sleep between them; he revised this rule later, however, because of subsequent scandal and abuse. Ultimately he decreed that all monks were to have separate quarters, a rule that other monastic orders, male and female, adopted.[61] While these facts may not be so important in themselves, we must consider that specific antihomoerotic injunctions in canon law and penitentials were rare until the late Middle Ages.[62] What injunctions there were classified same-sex relations with certain heteroerotic actions like vaginal intercourse from behind. Punishments for people engaged in homoerotic activity were in fact much less severe than those for adulterers: the Byzantine world was much more concerned with the chastity and reputation of wives and daughters.[63]

Some antihomoerotic laws were passed in Byzantium, but enactment of laws is one thing; enforcement, support, and observation, quite another.[64] Byzantine emperors often issued edicts pertaining to morality, often in terms of traditional Christian theology, but these were failures simply because the vast majority of people refused to obey them. For example, despite certain laws regulating prostitution, concubinage, and castration, prostitutes thronged to Constantinople, where their activity was widely supported and encouraged.[65] Concubines were so prevalent that they ultimately achieved legal protection from the emperors. Males, both those self-castrated and those castrated by their parents at a young age, controlled the civil and military bureaucracies of Byzantium to such an extent that the Byzantine empire has been called "the eunuch's paradise."[66] Regarding male homoeroticism, however, same-sex marriages were outlawed in 342,[67] and in 390 the death penalty was instituted for forcing or selling males into prostitution, although the state continued to collect taxes from male prostitution well into the sixth century.[68] In 533, Justinian became the first emperor to subject all homoerotic relations to civil sanctions, and he issued further *novellae* in 538 and 544.[69] Scholars agree that Justinian instituted these laws either to attack his enemies or because of his rural conservatism. No church official seems to have supported or encouraged him; in fact, the only well-known individuals punished under these laws were bishops. The contemporary historian Procopius informs us that Justinian passed these laws to get money, to attack members of the Green faction of the circus, and to avenge himself on anyone who might have done something to offend the emperor or empress.[70] We are at liberty to accept or reject Procopius as a historian, but we cannot neglect the facts that the population did not support these laws (in some instances, they vocally and physically came to the aid of some accused people), that persecutions stopped after Justinian, and that subsequent antihomoerotic legislation was rare—which would be natural given the many emperors who were gay or bisexual[71] and the ready availability of eunuchs and male slaves for sexual pleasure.[72]

It is clear, therefore, that regarding homoeroticism scholars and historians have been misled by a few legal codes, the vitriolic and hysterical rhetoric of the early church fathers, and the rarity of erotic literature in Byzantium, although we must note in the latter case that many of our extant sources are centered around the imperial court, where authors were cautious.[73] Yet there were dreambook writers in the provinces and from the nonaristocratic classes who flourished in an uncensored environment and thus preserved a better picture of the sexual codes of the Byzantine empire.

Sometime in the tenth or eleventh century, a Christian Greek living in Syria or Turkey composed the longest and greatest dreambook of the Byzantine era.[74] The author—writing under the pseudonym Achmet, the son of Sîrîm, the dream interpreter for Ma'mûn, caliph of Babylon—used a variety of sources: Arabic dream traditions, Artemidorus, and Byzantine Greek materials.[75]

The science of dreams had a deep and rich heritage in the Arabo-Islamic world. Dream traditions exist from the pre-Islamic period,[76] but the accounts are not very trustworthy since they were recorded in later centuries. In the Qur'ān there are many references to dreams, oneiromancy, and the interpretation of dreams. Dreams could be sent directly from God in a vision, or from Satan; dreams could also arise from a dreamer's psychological or physiological state.[77]

Many of the great events in Muḥammad's life were prognosticated by dreams. This induced the Prophet to interpret his own dreams and those of his companions.[78] The Prophet's successors solidified their position and justified their decrees through dreams. Interpreters became advisors to caliphs and nobles and wrote up collections of their dream accounts, fragments of which have survived in later treatises. In these early accounts we see evidence of an oral tradition, with interpretations often based upon associations derived from a desert life: Islam-shadow-freshness and infidelity-sun-fire. The dream interpretations by the interpreter Ibn al-Musayyab influenced later writers, particularly Achmet, who wrote of several subjects in the Muslim's treatise, including a caliph who dreamed of urinating four times in a religious shrine, and a noble who tried to deceive a dream interpreter through a slave substitute in a consultation. Achmet also used many of Ibn al-Musayyab's interpretations: urination symbolizes sexual intercourse; teeth, family members; the grapevine, faith; dates, one's livelihood.

Oneirocriticism blossomed in the ninth century C.E. While some Muslim scholars discussed dreams in scientific treatises (many inspired by Greek texts),[79] most dream authorities became interpreters to caliphs and nobles and set down their interpretations in popular dreambooks. One of our earliest sources is in the *Ṭabaqāt* of Ibn Saʿd (d. 845 C.E.), who listed those dreams of the caliph ʿAbd al-Malik (685–705 C.E.) that were interpreted by Ibn al-Musayyab. Somewhat later than this work was the *Taʿbīr al-ruʾyā* of Ibn Qutayba, which Achmet certainly consulted and drew from.[80] With the subsequent appearance of the Arabic translation of Artemidorus's *oneirocriticon,* the number of Arabic dreambooks proliferated;[81] by Achmet's time (c. 1000 C.E.), many were already very famous (*Kitāb al-Jawāmiʿ li-Muḥammad b. Sīrīn; Kanz al-ru ʾyā al-Maʾmūnī; Kitāb al-Uṣūl li-Dāniyāl al-Ḥakīm; Kitāb al-Taqsīm li-Jaʿfar al-Ṣādiq*). Achmet doubtless used these texts for many of his dream interpretations—he certainly used the *Kitāb al-Taʿbīr,* assigned to Ibn Shāhīn, to draw up his compendia and schematic outline of topics.[82]

Achmet also consulted the dreambook of Artemidorus, which had been translated just a century or so earlier into Arabic, as well as Byzantine Christian materials.[83] He designates his various sources by different chapter headings: interpretations of dream symbols that he found in Byzantine materials are in chapters headed "from the account of the Indians," while Arabic materials are in chapters headed "from the accounts of the Persians and Egyptians."[84] The result is a cross-cultural case study, as Achmet discusses specific dream symbols and how they were interpreted, first in Byzantine culture, then in medieval Islamic culture.

Several words about hetero- and homoeroticism in medieval Islam are in order, however. Sex, as well as society, was based on a strict and patriarchal hierarchy of social relations, which consisted of bipolarities of male and female, conquering and conquered, Muslim and non-Muslim.[85] Medieval Islamic scholars constructed a world view of bivalence and dual relations, with the union of the sexes affirming and complementing creation and procreation.[86] This bipolarity of gender did not offer equality, however, only oppression, for the primacy of man over woman was absolute: the woman existed for man's pleasure, his fulfillment, his use.[87] The macrocosm of the medieval Islamic world and the microcosm of the family were both male-worshipping. Even paradise was phallocentric, for exegetes and even verses in the Qurʾān painted it as a place of sexual pleasure for men, an eternity of carnal happiness.[88] A male is said to be married to seventy beautiful young virgins (*houri*) and to the lawful wives he had on earth, every one of whom provides "appetizing sex."[89] Erections are eternal and an orgasm lasts for twenty-four hours. Male and female servants wait upon and provide for the male; although the Qurʾān does not speak of sexual services, Islamic commentators have assumed them to be included. This "heavenly paradise," however, removes real women from the afterlife. As one scholar describes it, man performs sexual acts on imagined virgins, on heavenly dolls; paradise, in other words, is a patriarchal *absurdus,* with sacred sex an activity created by and for the male.[90] One need not take a feminist stance to see how this promised paradise of sex could limit the depth of intimacy between males and females on earth.[91]

Sex in the medieval Islamic world was constructed for the pleasure and domination of the male.[92] A man was limited by the Qur'ān to four wives but was granted an unlimited number of concubines.[93] In medieval Islam, wives were placed into isolated seclusion, jealously guarded as bearers of legitimate children;[94] concubines and slaves (male and female) serviced the sexual pleasure and desires of the master.[95] Social segregation was the most visible expression of the boundary between male and female, which existed not only in the cosmos (as we have seen) but also in social structures.[96] Segregation was an especially concrete demonstration of the notion that male and female are opposites, and that an ordered society depends on maintaining the boundaries established by God. Directly related to this belief was the medieval Islamic view that men can control their nature and are therefore associated with the divine, which they are able to approach.[97] Women, on the other hand, are said to be connected with humanness and the natural world and therefore unable to overcome human desires, especially sexual impulses;[98] thus, females require male supervision, even to the point of mandatory clitoridectomies, as currently in some African countries. Medieval Islamic life was a quest to construct the male as active, central, and public and the female as passive, marginal, and private.[99]

Medieval Islam was not unique in such opinions, however. The late Roman empire and the Christian church also associated man with spirit (or soul) formed directly by God and partaking of his divinity, and associated woman with the body, a fleshly incarnation of lust. Christian literature strove to feminize the flesh, to associate, according to the metaphor of mind and body, man with *mens* or *ratio* ("rational thought") and woman with the corporeal;[100] it also strove to estheticize the feminine, to associate woman with the cosmetic, the superfluous, and the decorative.[101] Augustine wrote:

> The subjugation of woman is in the order of things; she must be dominated and governed by man, just as the soul should regulate the body and virile reason should dominate the animal part of the being. If a woman dominates man, and the animal part dominates reason, the house is turned upside down.[102]

Thomas Aquinas offered an analogy of gender with social hierarchy: "The ruler manages his subjects for their own benefit. . . . Such is the subjection in which woman is by nature subordinate to man because the power of rational discernment is by nature stronger in man."[103] A later theologian stated that man, who has the rational soul, possesses the "germ" of genius. Children, eunuchs, and women (the very people the ancients, Byzantines, and medieval Muslims abused and sodomized) are devoid of ideas: "[Woman] does not generalize at all, does not synthesize. Her mind is anti-metaphysical. . . . Woman does not philosophize."[104] Carolyn Bynum captures this gendering: "*Male* and *female* were constructed and symmetrically valued as intellect/body, active/passive, rational/irrational, reason/emotion, self-control/lust, judgement/mercy, and order/disorder."[105]

Common to all the societies under discussion here is the view that woman is simultaneously good and evil. She is relegated to a role that is passive, subordinate, and controlled, symbolic of domesticity and nurturing; this is the chaste, virginal "bride of Christ," the good mother, the good wife. Yet she can be an evil, active agent whose sexuality is dangerous if not controlled; this is the *fitna,* the devil's handmaiden, the symbol of social and private unrest, turmoil, and peril.[106] Men created their religion, societies, and cultures to perpetuate this conflicting model of the female nature. One need only read the Yahwist myths in Genesis of creation and the origin of evil, and consider the evolution of the Christian cults of virginity and Mariology, study the *ḥadīth* and Ṣūfī literature, or examine historical chronicles from Byzantium.[107]

Medieval Islamic men controlled not only access to God, society, and culture, but also sexuality. According to the Qur'ān, the unity of the world can be achieved only by the man assuming his masculinity and the woman her femininity; thus any sexual behavior that opposes this bipolarity is a deviation, a revolt against God. Divine curses are laid on male and female homoeroticism, bestiality, and autoeroticism, and on female assumption of masculine dress or behavior.[108]

Theory is not practice, however.[109] The Qur'ān calls for a hierarchy of relations based on broad categories of male and female, but medieval Islamic society operated on a hierarchy headed by the privileged male elite.[110] The provenance of the medieval suppression of women and the corresponding exaltation of men has been the subject of much recent scholarly debate.[111] Some modern male, and even a few female, Islamic scholars defend the Qur'ān as advocating complete equality of the sexes and assert its compatibility with the emancipation of women.[112] Most contemporary Muslim feminists disagree with such a view; however, many would agree that later Qur'ānic interpretations and traditions fostered an ever-restrictive patriarchal control of women, and would point to the important role played by women in early Islam.[113] In fact, the debate among Muslim feminists today is whether they should continue trying to interpret Islam in reformist ways, or should stand completely behind secularization and relegate Islam only to private belief and worship.[114]

In medieval Islam a person's sexuality was defined according to the domination by or reception of the penis in the sex act; moreover, one's position in the social hierarchy also localized her or him in a predetermined sexual role.[115] Slaves (male and female), war captives, boys, concubines, wives, and effeminate men were used and sometimes abused by the male elite, despite religious and legal sanctions against this.[116] A popular trend among medieval Muslim men was to have their concubines depilated, dressed as boys, and with hair cut short.[117] Prostitution, male and female, though forbidden by the Qur'ān, was so popular that it was classified into categories and taxed accordingly; taverns, inns, and monasteries offered servants for use by male travelers, and the bathhouses (which in tenth-century C.E. Baghdad, for example, numbered about 27,000) offered young boys and servants to their patrons.[118] Women were subjected to clitoridectomies and depilation, with strict guidelines on when pubic hair did not need to be shaved.[119] Erotological handbooks were written on the sizes of the holes of boys and women,[120] with volumes more devoted to the shape and beauty of male and female buttocks and to the sexual activity that seems to have been most popular, anal intercourse with boys and women.[121] The amount of homoerotic poetry is staggering, and such poetry was composed by people of all socioeconomic classes, from rulers to religious clerics to middle-class poets and tavern singers.[122] Pederasty was cultivated; in fact, much of the love poetry written throughout the medieval Islamic world, from Spain to Baghdad, was by adult males to preteen or teenaged boys.[123] As in Greek and Roman literature, we have scant erotic love poetry addressed by an adult male to a male equal in both age and status; this implies that a stigma was placed on this sort of relationship, preventing men from expressing these feelings in verse.[124]

As stated above, medieval Arabic sources define sexuality as a matter of a male assuming the active role and penetrating a submissive social inferior of either gender.[125] This model of social status and power replayed in sex acts is affirmed by attitudes toward fellatio and male passive partners. In the ancient and Christian worlds, fellatio was condemned in the harshest terms as an illicit, immoral, and loathsome activity. Artemidorus classified it as *para nomon,* and although the Hebrew Bible and Christian Bible do not mention it, oral-genital contact was severely proscribed by Eastern and Western theologians alike. As Amy Richlin has shown, oral rape was the worst possible degradation, especially for an adult male, and represented the ultimate threat in political and literary invective since it was the strongest assertion of the satisfied one's dominance over the one doing the satisfying.[126] If we can accept almost virtual silence on the subject in medieval Islam as proof, then the same attitude prevailed in medieval Islam. When Artemidorus's dreambook was translated into Arabic, the section on fellatio was removed from the chapters on sex.[127] The passive male in homoerotic relations destroyed the definition of masculinity by betraying not only his own privileged status but also the overall hierarchy of privileged males.[128] He therefore required an explanation, so medieval Islamic writers ascribed this condition to the smoking of hashish, genetics, or the deflection of semen to the rectum.[129]

Female homoeroticism was given little or no attention in medieval Greece and Islam[130] except, as in early modern Europe, when the "active" partner effected penetration or when one partner assumed the costume and appearance of an adult male. In these cases the hierarchy regarding sexual boundaries was violated or eliminated. Gender, therefore, was not a biological definition of sex, but a concept embedded in the social understanding, implications, and consequences of maleness and femaleness. In this context, it is interesting to note medieval Islam's treatment of hermaphrodites. In a brilliant essay entitled "Gendering the Ungendered Body: Hermaphrodites in Medieval Islamic Law," Paula Sanders discusses how the hermaphrodite, because s/he was considered unsexed and ungendered, was completely outside the social hierarchy; in fact, a hermaphrodite could remove any other person from that hierarchy through contact, since contact eliminated or completely muddled social and sexual boundaries. An ungendered person caused anxiety for the most important gendered body, namely, the social body.[131]

Achmet's chapters on sexual acts and relations affirm that hierarchies of gender and status in medieval Islam parallel those in Byzantium.[132] Women are insignificant nonpersons throughout Achmet's dreambook;[133] symbolized in dreams by male pubic hairs, penises, mattresses, bedclothes, household vessels and containers—any receptacle that receives fluids—and associated with death and funerals, women have dreams that foretell the future for their husbands, fathers, or sons.[134] If any dream pertains to their own futures, it denotes a change in their beauty or their biological functions, i.e., bearing children.[135] Rarely are female genitalia mentioned, and then in terms of disgust; indeed, one of the more auspicious dreams for a man is of his wife being transformed anatomically into a man (section 127). The penis, on the other hand, is celebrated on page after page in minute detail; it is interpreted, just as in the pagan and Byzantine Greek dreambooks, as power, strength, reputation, dominion, and victory. Sexual relations, as is apparent from the relevant sections in the Appendix, are cast in the framework of penetration and reception, domination and submission, profit and loss, taking and giving pleasure. Generally, the receptor of the penis can expect some profit from the penetrator; the penetrator, if he received pleasure from the act, will do good to that person or someone else, or will trample down and beat his enemy into submission.[136] Any dream involving anal or vaginal sex—no other type is mentioned—is a good sign, but only insofar as the male penetrator experiences pleasure and in direct proportion to the submissive person's beauty, youth, and most important, willingness to be dominated and to obey the male's directions.

Male homoeroticism is frequently referred to in both the Byzantine and Arabic sections.[137] In every instance, the dream is a good sign if the dreamer is the penetrator. Submissive partners are males of a lower social class, eunuchs, young boys, or slaves. Sex between males of equal social rank is not even mentioned. Submission to a social superior, e.g., a religious leader, king, or nobleman, is a very auspicious sign, since it foretells something good for the penetrated. This pattern of domination and submission, of sex as a relation between a male and an inferior (boy, woman, or "pathic" male), of penetration as a manifestation of manhood and male domination, has been well stated by E. Rowson:

> Free adult men virtually defined the public world, sharing it with subordinate adolescent boys, male slaves, and, to a degree, female slaves. In the private world, they dominated their secluded wives and female relations. . . . In sexual terms, he dominated as penetrator. Beardless non-men—women and boys—were his natural sexual partners. Official morality restricted a man's penetrative options to his wives and female slaves, but if he chose to become a "profligate," he could expand these options and seek penetrative satisfaction with other women or boys. Such a course made him a sinner, but did not imperil the status and honor due him as a man. . . . For a man to seek sexual subordination was inexplicable, and could only be attributed to pathology. Boys, being not yet men, could be penetrated without losing their potential manliness, so long as they did not register pleasure in the act, which would suggest a pathology liable to continue into adulthood; the quasi-femininity of their

> appearance, a condition for their desirability as penetratees, was a natural but temporary condition whose end marked their entry into the world of the dominant adult male.[138]

In conclusion, Artemidorus, Achmet, and the Byzantine dreambook writers are valuable culture observers of and culture informants for ancient Greek, Byzantine, and medieval Islamic sexual codes. The Byzantine and Arabic sources show that sexual codes had not changed substantially since Artemidorus's lifetime. While Islam and Christianity did change the spiritual lives of many men and women, neither eliminated certain social and cultural constructs: for example, that a person could claim possession of the bodies of male and female slaves; that males owned the top rungs of the ladder of social hierarchy, with women, children, and noncitizens relegated to subordinate status; that sex is a simple formulation of gain and loss—males receive pleasure from penetrating and dominating whomever they perceive as inferior; that human worth is measured in terms of a masculinity predicated on power and male superiority; and that males may choose for their pleasure from a wide variety of sources—adolescents, wives, concubines, male and female prostitutes, male and female slaves, and subordinate males—even while denying them social and political power.

In 1985, Eva Keuls published *Reign of the Phallus: Sexual Relations in Ancient Athens,* in which she insisted that the sexual privileges Athenian men gave themselves came at the expense of women, children, and marginalized people, and that Athenian men tightly controlled and manipulated women's sexuality for their own pleasure as they revoked women's social and sexual independence. As the pagan Greek, Byzantine, and medieval Arabic dreambooks—if not Western history through today—have shown, the applicability of Keuls' title is, most regrettably, not limited to classical Athens.[139]

Appendix

Selections from Ancient, Byzantine, and Arabic Dream Manuals

Dreambook of Artemidorus:

The best set of categories for the analysis of sexual intercourse is, first, intercourse *kata physin* ("in accordance with nature"), *kata nomon* ("in accordance with convention"), and *kata ethos* ("in accordance with habit"); then intercourse *para nomon* ("in opposition to convention"); and third, intercourse *para physin* ("in opposition to nature").

First, sex *kata physin te kai nomon:* To have sex with one's own female slave or male slave is good, for slaves are the dreamer's possessions; thus, to take pleasure in them signifies the dreamer's being pleased with his own possessions. To be penetrated by one's house slave is not good; this signifies being despised or injured by the slave. The same applies to being penetrated by one's brother, whether older or younger, or *a fortiori* by one's enemy. To be penetrated by a friend is profitable for a woman, depending on what sort of man enters her. For a man to be penetrated by a richer and older man is good, for the custom is to receive things from such men. To be penetrated by a younger and poorer man is bad, for it is the custom to give to such. The same interpretation applies if the penetrator is older but poorer.

Sex *para nomon:* To penetrate a son under five years of age signifies that the child will die; if the child is over five but under ten, he will become ill and the dreamer will be foolishly involved in some business and will take a loss; if the son is a young adolescent and the father is poor, he will send his son to a teacher and the tuition he pays for his son will be a kind of expenditure for him; but if the dreamer is rich, he will give his son many gifts and transfer property to his name, undergoing a loss of substance. To penetrate one's brother, whether older or younger, is good for the dreamer, for he will be above the brother and will look down on him. It is good for a poor man with a wealthy daughter to have sex with her, for he will receive many benefits from her and so will have taken his pleasure.

The most awful dream of all, I have observed, is to be fellated (*arrêtopoieisthai*) by one's mother. If one dreams of being fellated by his own wife or mistress, there will be bad feeling or a divorce or, if the woman is pregnant, a loss of the fetus because of the unnatural reception of the seed. If someone dreams of being fellated by a friend or a relative or a child other than an infant, he will develop an enmity with the fellator; if by an infant, he will bury the infant, for it is no longer possible to kiss such a one. He who is fellated by an unknown person will suffer some penalty or other, because of the useless ejaculation of seed. If someone dreams of performing oral sex (*arrêtopoiêsai*) on someone who is an acquaintance, whether male or female, he will develop an enmity with that person, because it is no longer possible to share mouths.

Sex *para physin:* If a woman penetrates a woman, she will share her secrets (*mystêria*) with her. If she does not know the woman, she will undertake useless projects. If a woman is penetrated by a woman, she will be separated from her husband by divorce or his death; however, she will learn the secrets of the other woman.

Byzantine Dreambooks:

Dreambook of Astrampsychus:

To dream of performing intercourse on a male whom you like is a profitable sign.

Dreambook of Nicephorus I:

To possess a male lover is a useful symbol for the dreamer.

Dreambook of Manuel II Palaeologus:

A penis that is powerful and erect symbolizes a dreamer's domination over his enemies and strength in all his activities. On the other hand, a flaccid penis denotes for a dreamer humiliation at the hands of enemies and a lack of strength in all his actions.

Dreambook of Daniel the Prophet:

If someone dreams of being possessed by a male, he will be completely overpowered by someone.

To dream of being a *kinaidos* ("pathic male") means that your wife will incur a medical disease.

If you dream of having sex with a prostitute, this means considerable profit.

If you dream of having sex with someone else's wife, this means good gain.

If you dream of having sex with your concubine, this signifies goodness.

Dreambook (Anonymous) in the codex Paris.2511:

If you dream that your penis is erect, this means that you will acquire honor and children.

Dreambook of Achmet ibn Sereim:

If someone dreams that he performs intercourse with the Pharaoh as though the Pharaoh were a woman or that the Pharaoh performs intercourse with him as though he were a woman, he will become the Pharaoh's private secretary and be the first man privy to his secrets (*krypta*). [*Krypta,* by punning, also means "genitals."]

The penis is judged as a man's reputation, power, and children. If someone dreams that his penis is large and erect, his reputation will be widespread and he will beget sons; and if the dreamer is a king, first of all he will be long-lived, and then he may see his son succeed him. If the king dreams that his penis is sticking way out and that someone comes along and grabs hold of it, his dominion will be increased, while the person who grabs his penis will come to know his secrets (*krypta*) and become his co-regent; if the dreamer is a commoner, he will grow in his way of life. If a woman dreams that she has a penis, she will bear a son who will honor her family. If someone dreams that his penis is cut off, his son will die and then he will die soon afterward; but if the penis is not completely cut off, his wife will bear a son who will die, and he will grieve, although his sorrow will later turn [into happiness]. If someone dreams that his penis has reached a fantastic length, he will be great and famous and will see happiness in his son. But if he dreams that his penis is small and withered, he will fall from honor and become a beggar, while his children will have disease and lack of power.

If someone dreams that his penis is large, if he is a head of people, his subjects will be wealthy, strong, and great; if a commoner or a poor man is the dreamer, he will find profit in his way of life; and if he dreams that the length of the penis is exceedingly great, he will get honor, glory, and wealth from a woman. If someone dreams that his penis is cut off, he will be severely punished and become poor. If someone dreams that he has two penises, he will soon have a wife and children. If someone dreams that his wife has a penis, he will have an illustrious son.

If someone dreams that his testicles are cut off, if he is a warrior, he will be delivered into the hands of his enemies; if he is a head of people, his people will be destroyed and he will become poor. If someone dreams that his testicles are crushed, he will be beaten by his enemies. If the king dreams that his testicles are large and powerful, he will be strong and masterful over his enemies and be fearless of all; if a commoner has this dream, he too will be fearless, and he will increase the amount of his property. If someone dreams that the skin covering his testicles becomes ripped so that they fall out, his wife will conceive a child who, as will become known, will be from someone else's sperm.

If someone dreams that he performs intercourse on a eunuch he knows, he will entrust his wealth and secrets to that eunuch; but if the eunuch is a stranger, he will do good to his enemy.

If someone dreams that he has sex with an old woman, he will get power from an ancient source of power. If he dreams that he has sex with a beautiful woman, if he has fields, he will rejoice in them many times over; if not, he will own exceedingly beautiful land. If someone dreams that he has sex with a virgin, he will discover the fulfillment of his chief joy and desire; if he dreams that he has sex with a teenaged girl, he will find in that very year joy and wealth, and if the girl is a stranger to him, the joy and wealth will be even more substantial. If someone dreams that he has sex with a prostitute he knows, if he is the king, he will find happiness but conceal it; if he is a commoner, he will be quite happy and wealthy. If a king or nobleman dreams that he has sex with a married woman, he will honor and enrich her family and exalt her husband in proportion to how talked about and discussed was the intercourse; if a commoner has this dream, he too will cause the woman's family to be happy; if a poor man is the dreamer, the woman will give him money. If someone dreams that his wife has been caught in fornication, she will become sickly and will be hated by him; and if the person having sex with her is a friend of his, the dreamer will beg a favor of him and be listened to; but if the person is a stranger, that man is an enemy whom he will be forced to serve. If someone dreams of his daughter being seduced by an adulterer he knows, that man will treacherously take from his wealth; if the man is a stranger, the dreamer's personal enemy will take of his goods. If someone dreams that a friend has sex with his (the dreamer's) wife, the dreamer, his wife, and relatives will all receive from that man wealth and every kind of useful support; but if he dreams that his friend only kisses or speaks with her and does not have sex, they will find his support to be in words only. If someone dreams that a priest enters his (the dreamer's) house and falls asleep on his bed, he will become friends with that man; however, that priest will deal treacherously with him by mounting his wife and the priest will become his heir.

If someone dreams that while having sex with a woman he discovers that she has a penis and testicles, he will have happiness during that year and beget a son who will ennoble the entire family.

If someone dreams of performing intercourse on a young male friend, he will entrust his secret (*mystêrion*) to that man and do him good. But if he dreams that he is penetrated by that friend with violence and pain, the secret will be held up to shame.

If someone dreams of performing sex on a dead man whom he knows, he will do good to that man's heirs; but if the man is a stranger, he will trample down a very powerful enemy ruler. If someone dreams that a dead man is performing sex on his (the dreamer's) wife or daughter, he will receive profit and kindness from that man's heirs.

If someone dreams that he has sex with a [tamed] animal he recognizes, he will show kindness to a worthless man, for which action there will be no gratitude, praise, or reward from God; if he does not recognize the animal, he will trample down an enemy ruler to whom he will later show kindness; however, that man will not show any gratitude. If he dreams that he has sex with a wild animal, he will totally subject himself to a very powerful enemy in proportion to the animal's size and strength. If someone dreams that a wild animal performs sex on him, he will receive great goodness from an enemy in proportion to the animal's size and strength. Likewise, if someone dreams that he has sex with anyone or anything apart from wild animals, he will do good to that person or thing.

If someone dreams that he has sex with some animal, he will rise up against an unreasoning, lawless, and foreign man and humble him. Likewise, if he has sex with a bird, if the bird is one that we eat, he will receive joy from someone with an evil reputation; but if the bird is inedible and has a crooked beak, for example, an eagle, he will become friends with a very great man who will be analogous to the bird and who will aid him with his wealth.

NOTES

1. See E. Stein, ed., Introduction to *Forms of Desire: Sexual Orientation and the Social Constructionist Controversy* (New York: Garland, 1990), pp. 4–5, on the status of the debate; see his bibliography on pp. 355–65 and, in the same volume, J. Weinrich, "Reality or Social Construction?," pp. 176–77, on why the debate is important.

2. D. M. Halperin, *One Hundred Years of Homosexuality and Other Essays on Greek Love* (New York: Routledge, 1990), p. 25: "Sexuality . . . is not . . . a universal feature of human life in every society. . . . Unlike sex, which is a natural fact, sexuality is a cultural production: it represents the *appropriation* of the human body and of its erogenous zones by an ideological discourse." See D. M. Halperin, J. J. Winkler, and F. I. Zeitlin, eds., Introduction to *Before Sexuality: The Construction of Erotic Experience in the Ancient Greek World* (Princeton: Princeton University Press, 1990), p. 3; G. Chauncey, Introduction to *Hidden from History: Reclaiming the Gay and Lesbian Past,* M. B. Duberman, M. Vicinus, and G. Chauncey, eds. (New York: New American Library, 1989), p. 5; and the numerous studies cited in J. Boswell, *Same-Sex Unions in Premodern Europe* (New York: Villard Books, 1994), p. xxvinn17–25. See E. Stein, "Conclusion: The Essentials of Constructionism and the Construction of Essentialism," in *Forms of Desire,* pp. 340–43, on the different types of social constructionism. On the meaning of the phrase "social constructionism," see A. Richlin, *The Garden of Priapus: Sexuality and Aggression in Roman Humor,* rev. ed. (New York: Oxford University Press, 1992), pp. xviii–ix.

3. R. Padgug, "Sexual Matters: Rethinking Sexuality in History," in *Hidden from History,* pp. 54–55, and D. M. Halperin, "Sex Before Sexuality: Pederasty, Politics, and Power in Classical Athens," in ibid., p. 48.

4. Padgug, "Sexual Matters," p. 60; Halperin, *One Hundred Years,* p. 29. Compare the sexual practices described in G. H. Herdt, ed., "Ritualized Homosexual Behavior in the Male Cults of Melanesia, 1862–1983: An Introduction," in *Ritualized Homosexuality in Melanesia* (Berkeley: University of California Press, 1984), pp. 1–82, esp. pp. 17, 21–29, 56, 60–73.

5. J. Boswell, "Concepts, Experience, and Sexuality," in *Forms of Desire,* p. 135; see

also Boswell, "Revolutions, Universals, and Sexual Categories," in *Hidden from History,* p. 18. Social constructionists often cite Boswell as an example of an essentialist scholar, although he himself refused the label; see his "Concepts," p. 136, on the different types of social constructionists and essentialists, and p. 148 on why social constructionists are viewed better.

6. Boswell, "Revolutions," pp. 29–30; but see Halperin, *One Hundred Years,* pp. 18–24, for his refutation of Boswell.

7. Boswell, "Revolutions," pp. 19–20; see p. 35 for his redefinition of "gay" people, in light of criticism of his 1980 book.

8 Boswell, "Concepts," p. 172, and J. J. Winkler, *Constraints of Desire: The Anthropology of Sex and Gender in Ancient Greece* (New York: Routledge, 1990), p. 4.

9. For a reconsideration of the implications of the word "patriarchy," see D. Kandiyoti, "Islam and Patriarchy: A Comparative Perspective," in *Women in Middle Eastern History: Shifting Boundaries in Sex and Gender,* N. Keddie and B. Baron, eds. (New Haven: Yale University Press, 1991), pp. 23–43, and Richlin, *Garden of Priapus,* pp. xvii–xviii; see also M. E. Combs-Schilling, *Sacred Performances: Islam, Sexuality, and Sacrifice* (New York: Columbia University Press, 1989), pp. 59ff.

Foucault scholarship on homoeroticism concentrates almost exclusively on male-male relations; see A. Richlin, "Zeus and Metis: Foucault, Feminism, Classics," *Helios* 18 (1991): 176; J. Brown, "Lesbian Sexuality in Medieval and Early Modern Europe," in *Hidden from History,* p. 500n53; and M. M. Henry, "The Edible Woman: Athenaeus's Concept of the Pornographic," in *Pornography and Representation in Greece and Rome,* A. Richlin, ed. (New York: Oxford University Press, 1992), pp. 251, 253. I am greatly indebted to Amy Richlin for the information in this paragraph.

10. Richlin, *Garden of Priapus,* p. xvii, and P. Sanders, "Gendering the Ungendered Body: Hermaphrodites in Medieval Islamic Law," in *Women in Middle Eastern History,* p. 79. Classic statements of feminist anthropology and sexuality are S. B. Orter and H. Whitehead, eds., *Sexual Meanings: The Cultural Construction of Gender and Sexuality* (Cambridge: Cambridge University Press, 1981), and P. Caplan, *The Cultural Construction of Sexuality* (London: Tavistock, 1987).

11. M. Skinner, "*Ego Mulier:* The Construction of Male Sexuality in Catullus," *Helios* 20 (1993): 107–9, 110–11, 120–21, and Richlin, *Garden of Priapus,* p. xviii–xx. For Richlin, Foucault and feminism are at cross-purposes, as feminism has as its goal social change while Foucault scholarship has lost its social agenda. See also N. Hartstock, "Foucault on Power: A Theory for Women?," in *Feminism/Postmodernism,* L. J. Nicholson, ed. (New York: Routledge, 1990), pp. 157–75.

12. A. Rousselle, *Porneia: On Desire and the Body in Antiquity,* F. Pheasant, trans. (New York: Basil Blackwell, 1988), p. 2, and R. Just, *Women in Athenian Life and Law* (New York: Routledge, 1989), chapter 1. See the discussion in J. C. Bürgel, "Love, Lust, and Longing: Eroticism in Early Islam as Reflected in Literary Sources," in *Society and the Sexes in Medieval Islam,* A. Lutfi al-Sayyid-Marsot, ed. (Malibu, Calif.: Undena, 1979), pp. 86–91, of the *Qābūsnāma* and how it caters only to males, even though much of it is dedicated to marriage and love. On whether male-authored texts can be used in feminist scholarship in the classics, see the debate in *Helios* 17(2)(1990); see also A. Richlin,

Introduction to *Pornography and Representation,* p. xiii, and "Reading Ovid's Rapes," in ibid., pp. 159–61. For studies of how such texts constructed female desire in ancient Greece, see L. Dean-Jones, "The Politics of Pleasure: Female Sexual Appetite in the Hippocratic Corpus," *Helios* 19 (1992): 72–91, and A. E. Hanson, "Conception, Gestation, and the Origin of Female Nature in the *Corpus Hippocraticum," Helios* 19 (1992): 31–71, with bibliography.

13. On these dreambooks, see G. Guidorizzi, *Pseudo-Niceforo: Libro dei sogni* (Napoli: Associazione di Studi Tardoantichi, 1980), and "L'interpretazione dei sogni nel mondo tardoantico: oralità e scrittura," in *I sogni nel medioevo, seminario internazionale, Roma, 2–4 ottobre 1983* (Roma: Edizioni dell'Ateneo, 1985), pp. 149–70; S. M. Oberhelman, *The Oneirocriticon of Achmet: A Medieval Greek and Arabic Treatise on the Interpretation of Dreams* (Lubbock, Tex.: Texas Tech University Press, 1991), and "Dreams in Graeco-Roman Medicine," in *Aufstieg und Niedergang der römischen Welt,* Teilband II, 37, 2 (Berlin: De Gruyter, 1993), pp. 121–56; G. Dagron, "Rêver de dieu et parler de soi: Le rêve et son interprétation d'après les sources byzantines," in *I sogni nel medioevo,* pp. 37–55; G. Gigli, "Gli onirocritici del cod. Paris. Suppl. Gr. 690," *Prometheus* 4 (1978): 65–86, 173–88. For the value of interpreters like Artemidorus as culture observers, see Winkler, *Constraints of Desire,* pp. 24–25; Oberhelman, *Oneirocriticon of Achmet,* chapter 2, II.A–B; and the introduction in Guidorizzi, *Pseudo-Niceforo.*

14. A. P. Kazhdan and A. W. Epstein, *Change in Byzantine Culture in the Eleventh and Twelfth Centuries* (Berkeley: University of California Press, 1985), pp. 14–15, 130, 133, 175, 182, 186n69; G. E. von Grunenbaum, *Medieval Islam* (Chicago: University of Chicago Press, 1946), pp. 54–55, and *Classical Islam: A History 600–1208,* K. Watson, trans. (London: George Allen and Unwin, 1970), pp. 87–88; F. Rosenthal, *Das Fortleben der Antike im Islam* (Zürich: Artemis, 1965), pp. 72–73.

15. See, for example, Halperin, *One Hundred Years,* chapter 1, and E. Keuls, *The Reign of the Phallus: Sexual Politics in Ancient Athens* (New York: Harper and Row, 1985).

16. This is the thesis of his book, *Christianity, Social Tolerance, and Homosexuality: Gay People in Western Europe from the Beginning of the Christian Era to the Fourteenth Century* (Chicago: University of Chicago Press, 1980); see his remarks on pp. 6–7.

17. M. Skinner, "*Ut decuit cindaediorem:* Power, Gender, and Urbanity in Catullus 10," *Helios* 16 (1989): 7–23, and "*Ego Mulier,*" pp. 107–30; Richlin, *Garden of Priapus;* Keuls, *Reign of the Phallus;* Winkler, *Constraints of Desire,* pp. 29–30, 36–39; Halperin, "Sex Before Sexuality," p. 48, and *One Hundred Years,* pp. 29–30. On the completely impersonal act of sexual intercourse among ancient Athenians, see R. F. Sutton, "Pornography and Persuasion on Attic Pottery," in *Pornography and Representation,* pp. 7–12, and B. Zweig, "The Mute Nude Female Characters in Aristophanes' Plays," in ibid., p. 83.

18. D. Greenberg, *The Construction of Homosexuality* (Chicago: University of Chicago Press, 1988), p. 147, and Halperin, *One Hundred Years,* pp. 34–35. Similar constructs of homosexual male relationships were common in Roman society; see A. Richlin, "Not Before Homosexuality: The Materiality of the *Cinaedus* and the Roman Law Against Love Between Men," *Journal of the History of Sexuality* 3 (1993): 523–73.

19. Halperin, "Sex Before Sexuality," p. 48, and *One Hundred Years,* p. 30; but see the cautionary remarks about Halperin's formulations in L. Barkan, *Transuming Passion:*

Ganymede and the Erotics of Humanism (Stanford: Stanford University Press, 1991), pp. 22–24. See also Greenberg, *The Construction of Homosexuality,* pp. 233–34; H. N. Parker, "Love's Body Anatomized: The Ancient Erotic Handbooks and the Rhetoric of Sexuality," in *Pornography and Representation,* pp. 98–99; Winkler, *Constraints of Desire,* pp. 11, 42–43; Halperin, "Sex Before Sexuality," p. 49, and *One Hundred Years,* pp. 23, 30.

20. Boswell, "Revolutions," p. 203, and "Concepts," pp. 154–55; Halperin, *One Hundred Years,* p. 30; Winkler, *Constraints of Desire,* pp. 11, 40; P. Mason, "Third Person/Second Sex: Patterns of Sexual Asymmetry in the *Theogony* of Hesiodos," in *Sexual Asymmetry: Studies in Ancient Society,* J. Blok and P. Mason, eds. (Amsterdam: J. C. Gieben, 1987), p. 158. Richlin, "Reading Ovid's Rapes," p. 169, formulates this as *pati* ("to suffer, to endure") and *vis* ("violence, force"); that is, suffering and submission characterize the woman, and forceful domination the man.

21. Greenberg, *The Construction of Homosexuality,* p. 158; Halperin, "Sex Before Sexuality," p. 49, and *One Hundred Years,* pp. 32–33; see also Winkler, *Constraints of Desire,* p. 40.

22. Keuls, *Reign of the Phallus,* pp. 275–76; Skinner, "*Ego Mulier,*" p. 111; Halperin, "Sex Before Sexuality," pp. 31–32, 49; A. Ide, *Gomorrah and the Rise of Homophobia* (Las Colinas, Tex.: Liberal Press, 1985); E. Rowson, "The Categorization of Gender and Sexual Irregularity in Medieval Arabic Vice Lists," in *Body Guards: The Cultural Politics of Gender Ambiguity,* J. Epstein and Kristina Straub, eds. (New York: Routledge, 1991), p. 72; P. Veyne, "Homosexuality in Ancient Rome," in *Western Sexuality: Practice and Precept in Past and Present Times,* Ph. Ariès and A. Béjin, eds. (Oxford: Basil Blackwell, 1985), p. 29.

23. Keuls, *Reign of the Phallus,* pp. 98–100; Sutton, "Pornography and Persuasion on Attic Pottery," pp. 3–35; H. A. Shapiro, "Eros in Love: Pederasty and Pornography in Greece," in *Pornography and Representation,* p. 53–72; J. Bremmer, "An Enigmatic Indo-European Rite: Paederasty," *Arethusa* 13 (1980): 279–98; R. Scroggs, *New Testament and Homosexuality,* pp. 38–40; S. Lilja, *Homosexuality in Republican and Augustan Rome* (Helsinki: Societas Scientiarum Fennica, 1983), p. 102 with literature in *n*65; Richlin, *Garden of Priapus,* pp. 33, 221–22, 224–25; D. Cohen, *Law, Sexuality, and Society: The Enforcement of Morals in Classical Athens* (Cambridge: Cambridge University Press, 1991), chapters 6 and 7, for laws and regulations on pederasty as well as on homosexuality; Rousselle, *Porneia,* pp. 65–66, 82, 97; Halperin, *One Hundred Years,* p. 35, and "Why Is Diotima a Woman?" in *Before Sexuality,* pp. 265–67; Just, *Women in Athenian Life and Law,* chapter 2; Boswell, *Christianity,* pp. 74–75, "Concepts," p. 154, and *Same-Sex Unions,* p. 55; Scroggs, *New Testament and Homosexuality,* pp. 38–40; M. Golden, "Slavery and Homosexuality at Athens," *Phoenix* 38 (1984): 308–24. For cross-cultural comparisons, see Greenberg, *The Construction of Homosexuality,* pp. 152, 157, 260–61; the many essays in Duberman, Vicinus, and Chauncey, *Hidden from the Past;* and Herdt, "Ritualized Homosexual Behavior," pp. 62–63.

24. Greenberg, *The Construction of Homosexuality,* pp. 149–50, 158; P. Brown, *The Body and Society* (New York: Columbia University Press, 1988), p. 432; Richlin, *Garden of Priapus,* p. 171; Lilja, *Homosexuality in Rome,* pp. 86, 89–97, on Cicero's attacks on opponents for being passive partners in anal sex. For example, Cicero accused M. An-

tony of enjoying the passive role as a youth—a devastating charge, since there was a stigma attached to the Roman freeborn male who submitted to penetration except *per vim.* See also J. Wright's paper in this volume and Rowson, "Arabic Vice Lists."

25. Keuls, *Reign of the Phallus,* pp. 267–68, and Veyne, "Homosexuality in Ancient Rome," p. 30.

26. See Keuls, *Reign of the Phallus,* pp. 276–77; Veyne, "Homosexuality in Ancient Rome," p. 29; Lilja, *Homosexuality in Rome,* p. 135; J. J. Winkler, "Laying Down the Law: the Oversight of Men's Sexual Behavior in Classical Athens," in *Before Sexuality,* p. 177, on the pathic as a social deviant since he violated social definitions of masculinity; Richlin, *Garden of Priapus,* p. 220. This construct held until the Renaissance; see J. M. Saslow, "Homosexuality in the Renaissance: Behavior, Identity, and Artistic Expression," in *Hidden from History,* pp. 98–99.

27. Greenberg, *The Construction of Homosexuality,* pp. 149–50; Scroggs, *The New Testament and Homosexuality,* pp. 40–42; Halperin, "Sex Before Sexuality," p. 46; Richlin, *Garden of Priapus,* pp. 15, 225; Lilja, *Homosexuality in Rome,* p. 135; Skinner, "*Ego Mulier,*" p. 120.

28. Greenberg, *The Construction of Homosexuality,* pp. 149–50.

29. See S. R. F. Price, "The Future of Dreams: From Freud to Artemidorus," in *Before Sexuality,* pp. 365–87; P. C. Miller, *Dreams in Late Antiquity: Studies in the Imagination of a Culture* (Princeton: Princeton University Press, 1994), pp. 29–31, 77–91; Oberhelman, *Oneirocriticon of Achmet,* pp. 38–41, with bibliography in *n*123, and "Dreams in Graeco-Roman Medicine," p. 152*n*177. On the incompatibility of modern psychoanalysis and Artemidorus, see Price, "The Future of Dreams," pp. 368ff., and Oberhelman, *Oneirocriticon of Achmet,* pp. 74–76.

30. MacAlister, "Gender as Sign and Symbolism in Artemidorus' *Oneirokritika:* Social Aspirations and Anxieties," *Helios* 19 (1992): 140–60; Winkler, *Constraints of Desire,* chapter 1; Halperin, *One Hundred Years,* chapter 1. On the male-centeredness of Artemidorus, see MacAlister, p. 141; similar remarks may be found in Oberhelman, *Oneirocriticon of Achmet,* pp. 78–81, regarding the medieval dreambook of Achmet.

31. MacAlister, "Artemidorus' *Oneirokritika,*" pp. 143–45; Price, "The Future of Dreams," pp. 373–74; Winkler, *Constraints of Desire,* pp. 28ff., to which I am indebted for much of the following paragraphs.

32. Ibid., pp. 30–31, is overly laudatory of Artemidorus as a value-free, unbiased culture observer. MacAlister, "Artemidorus' *Oneirokritika,*" is an excellent corrective to Winkler. Criticism of Halperin and Winkler for their use of Artemidorus in recovering sexual codes of fifth-century B.C.E. Athens is at times harsh (e.g., B. Thornton, "Constructionism and Ancient Greek Sex," *Helios* 18 (1991): 181–93). But it must be noted that in Greece sexual and gender codes did not change much over the centuries. Rome is a different matter; for example, Lilja points out that in the Republic sexual contact between freeborn males was considered improper, but during the Augustan age active partners in relationships between freeborn males were tolerated and accepted (although passive partners remained objects of contempt); moreover, P. Brown and Boswell both point to an ever-conservative and restrictive set of sexual codes in the later empire.

33. MacAlister, "Artemidorus' *Oneirokritika*," p. 150: "Expression of gender difference [in Artemidorus's dreambook] . . . has less to do with a person's anatomical sex than with a person's social status and identity: Artemidorus is not talking about a male/female dichotomy, but a masculine/feminine one. The feminine must adhere to its ideal of weakness, passivity, and obedience in order to evoke a corresponding notion of subordination. This, by way of the masculine/feminine contrast, serves to affirm the superordinate, active, and authoritative face of masculine identity and, thereby, to maintain the higher social status which the masculine affords."

34. Winkler, *Constraints of Desire*, p. 36, and MacAlister, "Artemidorus' *Oneirokritika*," p. 151.

35. I am speaking here of Artemidorus's and the Greeks' relative indifference; the Romans' opinions are different, as Richlin and Skinner have shown. On male homosexual protocols in the Roman Empire, see Boswell, *Christianity*, pp. 67–87, 161ff; Richlin, *Garden of Priapus* and "Not Before Homosexuality"; B. Verstraete, "Slavery and the Social Dynamics of Male Homosexual Relations in Ancient Rome," *Journal of Homosexuality* 5 (1980): 227–36; Boswell, *Christianity*, p. 78; Lilja, *Homosexuality in Rome*, pp. 16–32; Veyne, "Homosexuality in Ancient Rome," pp. 31–32; R. MacMullen, "Roman Attitudes to Greek Love," *Historia* 31 (1982): 484–502. On female homoeroticism, see J. Hallett, "Female Homoeroticism and the Denial of Roman Reality in Latin Literature," *Yale Journal of Criticism* 3 (1989): 209–27.

36. Keuls, *Reign of the Phallus*, p. 6; Winkler, *Constraints of Desire*, pp. 36–37, 40; Halperin, "Sex Before Sexuality," p. 51; Shapiro, "Eros in Love," pp. 57–58; MacAlister, "Artemidorus' *Oneirokritika*," pp. 145, 149.

37. Keuls, *Reign of the Phallus*, pp. 1–2, 86. Keuls's statements (p. 54) about the Athenian preoccupation with heterosexual and homosexual rape may be extended to Roman and even medieval Islamic literature. On rape and related imagery in early Islamic society, see S. P. Stetkevych, *Abū Tammām and the Poetics of the ʿAbbāsid Age* (Leiden: E. J. Brill, 1991). I owe this reference to J. Wright.

38. The association of cunnilingus and fellatio with strongly sanctioned rules on incest proves how strong an aversion there must have been to oral sex; Richlin, *Garden of Priapus*, esp. pp. 26–29 and 69, remains the best discussion here.

39. Winkler, *Constraints of Desire*, pp. 37–38, 43; Boswell, *Christianity*, pp. 56, 145, 162; P. Brown, *Body and Society*, p. 432; Keuls, *Reign of the Phallus*, p. 180; Rousselle, *Porneia*, p. 124; Richlin, *Garden of Priapus*, pp. 145–51 on oral rape of men and pp. 26–28 on reasons for revulsion to oral sex (see pp. 69, 99–100). Veyne, "Homosexuality in Ancient Rome," pp. 31–33, points out that Romans considered fellators so base and depraved that some would pass themselves off as penetrated partners in anal sex simply to avoid the label. As will be pointed out below, oral sex appears to have been so taboo to the Arabs and Persians that it was not even mentioned.

40. Winkler, *Constraints of Desire*, pp. 17–20, 42–43, and "Laying Down the Law," p. 203. Scroggs, *The New Testament and Homosexuality*, pp. 140–44, and Keuls, *Reign of the Phallus*, pp. 82–85, both stress that the use of dildos by women is probably a fantasy of male painters and authors—as if women could be satisfied only by a penis or its substi-

tute. See Dean-Jones, "Politics of Pleasure," p. 90n45: "[A] woman has no need of [dildos] to excite herself, though many men would like to think that she has. The descriptions of women lusting after dildos in *Lysistrata* and in Herodas' *Mime* 6 reflect how men would like to think women masturbated rather than actual women's practices, and the vase paintings represent entertainments which were staged for men by courtesans rather than wives."

41. Winkler, *Constraints of Desire,* p. 39, and Veyne, "Homosexuality in Ancient Rome," p. 33. Scroggs, *The New Testament and Homosexuality,* p. 144, asserts that lesbianism was rarely mentioned in ancient texts because men did not consider it important enough or interesting enough to record; see Richlin, *Garden of Priapus,* pp. 132–34, on lesbianism in Greek epigrams and Martial's epigrams. J. Brown, "Lesbian Sexuality," pp. 69ff., shows that men in medieval and early modern Europe were willing to *disbelieve* that female homoeroticism occurred: there is little mention of it until the mid-seventeenth century. Brown lists reasons for this willingness to disbelieve or ignore: lesbianism was not a serious threat, women were merely trying to emulate men (hence, lesbianism actually reaffirmed social hierarchy), and imperfect knowledge of male and female biology.

42. G. Chauncey, "From Sexual Inversion to Homosexuality: Medicine and the Changing Conceptualization of Female Deviance," *Salmagundi* 58/59 (1982/83): 114–46; see also Boswell, "Revolutions," p. 32: "At the outset sexual deviance is perceived only in women who violate the sex role expected of them by playing an active part in a female–female romantic relationship. The "passive" female, who does not violate expectations of her sex role by receiving, as females are thought naturally to do, the attentions of her "husband," is not considered abnormal."

43. J. Brown, "Lesbian Sexuality," pp. 72ff., and Saslow, "Homosexuality in the Renaissance," p. 96.

44. Oberhelman, "Prolegomena," "Interpretation of Dream Symbols," *Oneirocriticon of Achmet,* pp. 52–55; Guidorizzi, *Pseudo-Niceforo;* H. G. Beck, *Geeshichte der byzantinische Volksliteratur* (München: Beck, 1971), pp. 203–4; Gigli, "Onirocritici."

45. V. Bullough, "Formation of Medieval Ideals: Christian Theory and Christian Practice," in *Sexual Practices and the Medieval Church,* V. Bullough and J. Brundage, eds. (Buffalo, N.Y.: Prometheus Books, 1982), pp. 18–20; see Boswell, *Christianity,* p. 230, on the factors that led to increased hostility toward homosexuals in the third through sixth centuries C.E.

46. V. Bullough, *Sexual Variance in Society and History* (New York: Wiley Interscience, 1976), p. 325, and "Medieval Ideals," pp. 14–16, 20; Boswell, *Christianity,* pp. 22, 333–34.

47. For the various approaches to homosexuality within the Christian church from its beginnings to the present fundamentalist debate, see the excellent summary in Scroggs, *The New Testament and Homosexuality,* pp. 7–16.

48. Ide, *Rise of Homophobia,* pp. 4–20; Boswell, *Christianity,* pp. 114–15; Greenberg, *The Construction of Homosexuality,* pp. 135–41, 211–18, objects to Boswell's theories; P. Coleman, *Christian Attitudes to Homosexuality* (London: SPCK, 1980), pp. 29–50 (He-

brew Bible), pp. 86–111 (New Testament); Scroggs, *The New Testament and Homosexuality,* pp. 70–84 (Palestinian Judaism), pp. 85–97 (Hellenistic Judaism), pp. 99–122 (New Testament); T. Horner, *Jonathan Loved David: Homosexuality in Biblical Times* (Philadelphia: Westminster Press, 1978), pp. 24, 102–3.

49. Scroggs, *The New Testament and Homosexuality,* pp. 16, 127; Boswell, *Christianity,* p. 113, and "Concepts," p. 137. For the hundreds of reviews of Boswell's books on this subject, see the exhaustive bibliography on the World Wide Web, at http://www.bway.net/halsall/lgbh/lgbh-boswell-reviews.html.

50. Many scholars assert that the injunctions in the Hebrew Bible deal with idolatry, not homosexuality per se; see Horner, *Jonathan Loved David,* chapter 6, and Boswell, "Concepts," p. 153. For the influence of Zoroastrianism, see Greenberg, *The Construction of Homosexuality,* pp. 190–92.

51. See Horner, *Jonathan Loved David,* pp. 48–57, and Boswell, Christianity, pp. 113–14.

52. Horner, *Jonathan Loved David,* p. 97; P. Brown, *Body and Society,* pp. 51–55; Coleman, *Christian Attitudes,* pp. 92, 95ff.; Ide, *Rise of Homophobia,* pp. 46–49; Scroggs, *The New Testament and Homosexuality,* p. 121; Boswell, *Christianity,* p. 115, with Appendix I, and *Same-Sex Unions,* pp. 219–20n4 with extensive discussion there.

53. See P. Brown, *Body and Society,* pp. 95, 230, 335, on nonorthodox Christian groups that accepted any sort of sexual intercourse, including pederasty and bestiality.

54. Bullough, *Sexual Variance,* p. 331, and "Medieval Ideals," p. 18; P. Brown, *Body and Society,* pp. 132–33, 175, 308; Greenberg, *The Construction of Homosexuality,* pp. 223–25, 227–28, 276–77; Boswell, *Christianity,* pp. 157–58. See Brown, *Body and Society,* pp. 205–7, on the tightening of sex codes in the late empire, concurrent with a glorification (pp. 207–9) of the renunciation of all sex (virginity).

55. Bullough, *Sexual Variance,* p. 317; Greenberg, *The Construction of Homosexuality,* pp. 225–26; M. Goodich, *The Unmentionable Vice: Homosexuality in the Later Medieval Period* (Santa Barbara, Calif.: Chico Press, 1979), pp. 15–19; Boswell, *Christianity,* p. 128.

56. P. Brown, *Body and Society,* pp. 24, 319–20, 430, and W. Kaegi, *Army, Society and Religion in Byzantium* (London: Variorum Reprints, 1992), pp. 243–75. On prostitution in the early and middle Byzantine periods, see J. Beaucamp, *Le Statut de la femme à Byzance (4e–7e siècle): I. Le droit impérial* (Paris: De Boccard, 1990), pp. 122–32.

57. A. Laiou, "Observations on the Life and Ideology of Byzantine Women," *Byzantinische Forschungen* 9 (1985): 59–102; Beaucamp, *Le droit impérial,* pp. 195–201, 296–306, and *Le Statut de la femme à Byzance (4e–7e siècle): II. Les Pratiques sociales* (Paris: De Boccard, 1992), pp. 357–58.

58. Kazhdan and Epstein, *Change in Byzantine Culture,* p. 83.

59. Greenberg, *The Construction of Homosexuality,* pp. 266–67, 283; P. Brown, *Body and Society,* p. 431; Bullough, *Sexual Variance,* pp. 317, 322; Rousselle, *Porneia,* p. 141; Boswell, *Christianity,* chapter 6; Greenberg, *The Construction of Homosexuality,* pp. 266–67. On the repression, see Boswell, *Christianity,* chapter 10 (pp. 286, 334), and Greenberg, pp. 268–80, 295. Major forces behind the repression were the association of homosexuality with heresy (Goodich, *The Unmentionable Vice,* pp. 7–10; Greenberg,

pp. 268–80) and with Islam (Boswell, *Christianity,* pp. 278–82, and B. F. Musallam, *Sex and Society in Islam: Birth Control Before the Nineteenth Century* [Cambridge: Cambridge University Press, 1983], p. 11).

60. Bullough, *Sexual Variance,* pp. 332–38; Rousselle, *Porneia,* pp. 134–35, 141, 147–48, 151–52; P. Brown, *Body and Society,* pp. 232–33; see Saslow, "Homosexuality in the Renaissance," pp. 92–93, on homosexual poetry among clerics of the Renaissance.

61. Bullough, *Sexual Variance,* pp. 319, 331, 339–40; Rousselle, *Porneia,* pp. 148–49; Greenberg, *The Construction of Homosexuality,* pp. 282–85.

62. M. Goodich, "Homosexuality in Medieval Secular Law," *Journal of Homosexuality* 1 (1976): 295–302, and "Homosexuality in Ecclesiastical Law and Theory," ibid.: 427–34; Boswell, *Christianity,* pp. 176–77; Greenberg, *The Construction of Homosexuality,* pp. 261–68.

63. W. Treadgold, *The Byzantine Revival* (Stanford: Stanford University Press, 1988), p. 50. This explains why for women every extramarital sexual relation was considered criminal, but not so for men; see Beaucamp, *Le droit impérial,* p. 139. On the penalties for same-sex behavior, see Greenberg, *The Construction of Homosexuality,* p. 262, and Boswell, *Christianity,* pp. 182–83.

64. Bullough, *Sexual Variance,* pp. 326, 341, and Greenberg, *The Construction of Homosexuality,* pp. 228–30; for the laws, see Boswell, *Christianity,* pp. 70, 122–35.

65. Many medieval states allowed prostitution despite the church's position; see Boswell, *Same-Sex Unions,* pp. 173*n*53 and 174*n*57, with literature.

66. Bullough, *Sexual Variance,* pp. 325–29, and "Medieval Ideals," pp. 16–17; J. Herrin, "In Search of Byzantine Women: Three Avenues of Approach," in *Images of Women in Antiquity,* A. Cameron and A. Kuhrt, eds. (Detroit: Wayne State University Press, 1983), pp. 170–71; Kazhdan and Epstein, *Change in Byzantine Culture,* p. 67.

67. Bullough, *Sexual Variance,* pp. 332–33; P. Brown, *Body and Society,* p. 23; and Boswell, "Concepts," pp. 156–57, with full discussion in *n*30 on the continuation of same-sex marriages in the church despite legal sanctions; see his *Same-Sex Unions, passim,* esp. chapter 3 (same-sex unions in the Greek and Roman world) and chapters 5 and 7 (same-sex unions in early modern Europe). Boswell's thesis has come under strong attack from many church scholars; see P. Reynolds, "Same-Sex Unions: What Boswell Didn't Find," *Christian Century* (January 18, 1995): 49–54.

68. Boswell, *Christianity,* p. 170; P. Brown, *Body and Society,* p. 23; Bullough, *Sexual Variance,* pp. 332–33; Boswell, *Same-Sex Unions,* pp. 242–43.

69. Bullough, *Sexual Variance,* pp. 333–34, and Boswell, *Christianity,* p. 171. On later legal codes see Boswell, *Same-Sex Unions,* pp. 243ff., and S. Troianos, "Kirchliche und weltliche Rechtsquellen zur Homosexualität in Byzanz," *Jahrbuch der Österreichischen Byzantinistik* 39 (1989): 29–48.

70. Bullough, *Sexual Variance,* p. 335, and Boswell, *Christianity,* pp. 172–73.

71. See Bullough, *Sexual Variance,* pp. 336–38, on Nicephorus I, Michael III, Basil II, and Constantine VIII; but see also J. Norwich, *Byzantium: The Apogee* (New York: Alfred A. Knopf, 1992), pp. 80–81. From my reading of the primary sources all these

emperors were active partners, which may explain the lack of censure of emperors by imperial Roman historians.

72. Bullough, *Sexual Variance,* pp. 329–30, 341, and Greenberg, *The Construction of Homosexuality,* p. 292.

73. Bullough, *Sexual Variance,* pp. 325–26, 331–32; P. Brown, *Body and Society,* p. 250; Greenberg, *The Construction of Homosexuality,* p. 228.

74. See Oberhelman, *Oneirocriticon of Achmet,* chapter 1, for full discussion. The Greek edition of F. Drexl, *Onirocriticon Achmetis* (Leipzig: Teubner, 1925) is over 300 pages long. The dreambook was translated into many languages during the Middle Ages and the Renaissance; it was particularly popular in Italy.

75. Abū Bakr Muḥammad b. Sīrīn (late seventh and early eight century C.E.) was considered the greatest dream interpreter in medieval Islam. By claiming to be his son, Achmet (the author's pseudonym) attempted to lend prestige to his work. Achmet's Christianity is evident in passages where he quotes the New Testament (but never the Qur'ān) and in his discussions of such matters as the Christian clergy, Mariology, and the Trinity.

On al-Ma'mūn and his interest in Byzantine learning, see von Grunebaum, *Classical Islam,* pp. 87–88; Rosenthal, *Fortleben der Antike,* pp. 72–73; I. Shahid, "Byzantium and the Islamic World," in *Byzantium: A World Civilization,* A. Laiou and H. Maguire, eds. (Washington, D.C.: Dumbarton Oaks, 1992), pp. 51–52.

76. T. Fahd, *La divination arabe: Études religieuses, sociologiques et folkloriques sur le milieu natif de l'Islam* (Leiden: E. J. Brill, 1966), pp. 250–55.

77. Fahd, *La divination arabe,* pp. 252–53, 269–73; and the following essays in *The Dream and Human Society,* G. E. von Grunebaum and R. Callois, eds. (Berkeley: University of California Press, 1966): J. Lecerf, "The Dream in Popular Culture: Arabic and Islamic," pp. 365–79; F. Meier, "Some Aspects of Inspiration by Dreams in Islam," pp. 421–29; H. Corbin, "The Visionary Dream in Islamic Spirituality," pp. 381–419.

78. T. Fahd, "Les songes et leur interprétation selon l'Islam," in *Sources Orientales, II: Les Songes et leur interprétation,* A-M. Esnoud et al., eds. (Paris: Éditions du Seuil, 1959), pp. 127ff.; idem, *La divination arabe,* pp. 256–68; idem, "The Dream in Medieval Islamic Society," in *The Dream and Human Society,* p. 356; and Bausani, "Sogni," p. 31.

79. For these, see ibid., pp. 26–31.

80. Some of the theoretical discussions in both works, pertaining to the effect of the seasons on dreams and the methodology of deciphering symbolic images, and many symbolic interpretations are the same. See Oberhelman, *Oneirocriticon of Achmet,* p. 17, and N. Bland, "On the Muhammedan Science of Tabîr, or Interpretation of Dreams," *Journal of the Royal Asiatic Society* 16 (1856): 118–30.

81. Fahd, *La divination arabe,* pp. 330–63, lists 181 extant dreambooks from classical Islam.

82. Oberhelman, *Oneirocriticon of Achmet,* pp. 17–18.

83. R. Pack, "On Artemidorus and his Arabic Translator," *Transactions of the American Philological Association* 98 (1967): 313–26, and "Artemidoriana Graeca-Arabica," *Transac-*

tions of the American Philological Association 106 (1976): 307–12; F. Rosenthal, "From Arabic Books and Manuscripts, XII: The Arabic Translator of Artemidorus," *Journal of the American Oriental Society* 85 (1965): 139–44. Oberhelman, *Oneirocriticon of Achmet,* Appendix III, points out numerous places where Achmet and Artemidorus agree on the interpretation of symbols; the agreement in wording and phrasing is often too exact to indicate a common tradition. On the Christian materials, see Oberhelman, *Oneirocriticon of Achmet,* pp. 15–20.

84. See Dagron, "Rêver de dieu," p. 49. The interpretations from Artemidorus are scattered throughout all the chapters and were used apparently as a supplement to the Byzantine and Arabic texts.

85. A. Bouhdiba, *Sexuality in Islam* (London: Routledge and Kegan Paul, 1985), pp. 30–31. Compare Combs-Schilling, *Sacred Performances,* p. 58: "Islam did not invent patriarchy and patrilineality, but it did make them sacred. . . . From the beginning, patriarchy and patrilineality were central to Islam. Patriarchy went unquestioned, while patrilineality was both utilized and transcended. . . . A transcendent God was, and is, the center of Islam, but patrilineality and patriarchy were from the beginning worldly means of connection to him. Islam's patrilineal and patriarchal foundations . . . are crucial to the political templates that were built." Combs-Schilling's remarks certainly pertain to medieval Islam. Whether they are relevant to the Qur'ān and pure Islam is debatable; see below on this point.

86. B. F. Stowasser, "The Status of Women in Early Islam," in *Muslim Women,* F. Hussain, ed. (London: Croom Helm, 1984), p. 23; F. Hussain and K. Radwan, "The Islamic Revolution and Women: Quest for the Quranic Model," in *Muslim Women,* p. 60; Bouhdiba, *Sexuality in Islam,* pp. 7–8, 12.

87. Combs-Schilling, *Sacred Performances,* p. 60; N. Saadawi, *The Hidden Face of Eve: Women in the Arab World,* S. Hetata, trans. and ed. (Boston: Beacon Press, 1982), p. 79; Bouhdiba, *Sexuality in Islam,* p. 11; see Bürgel, "Love, Lust and Longing," pp. 109–11, for antifemale literature.

88. Bouhdiba, *Sexuality in Islam,* pp. 72–87; S. P. Stetkevych, "Intoxication and Immortality: Wine and Associated Imagery in al-Maʿarrī's Garden" (this volume); F. Sabbah, *Woman in the Muslim Unconscious,* M. J. Lakeland, trans. (New York: Pergamon Press, 1984), pp. 93–94; Bouhdiba, *Sexuality in Islam,* p. 80 (see also p. 85).

89. Ibid., pp. 75–76; Sabbah, *Woman in the Muslim Unconscious,* pp. 90–97; J. Smith and Y. Haddad, *The Islamic Understanding of Death and Resurrection* (Albany, N.Y.: State University of New York Press, 1981), pp. 164–65, point out that all references to the houris are early Meccan and may be related to social factors; see also A. Wadud-Muhsin, *Qur'an and Woman* (Kuala Lumpur: Penerbit Fajar Bakti Sdn. Bhd., 1992), pp. 54–55, who relates this to purposes of conversion of desert Arabs.

90. Combs-Schilling, *Sacred Performances,* pp. 61, 95ff., on whom I depend here.

91. Saadawi, *Hidden Face of Eve,* pp. 2–5.

92. F. Mernissi, *The Veil and the Male Elite: A Feminist Interpretation of Women's Rights in Islam,* M. J. Lakeland, trans. (Reading, Mass.: Addison-Wesley, 1991), pp. 146–47, and Bouhdiba, *Sexuality in Islam,* p. 89. There were some limits; a man could not practice *coitus interruptus* with a wife without her permission, although he might freely prac-

tice it with a concubine or slave. See Musallam, *Sex and Society in Islam,* pp. 28, 31–32; S. Spectorsky, *Chapters on Marriage and Divorce: Responses of Ibn Ḥanbal and Ibn Rāhwayh* (Austin: University of Texas Press, 1993), pp. 69, 236; M. Farah, *Marriage and Sexuality in Islam: A Translation of al-Ghazālī's Book on the Etiquette of Marriage from the* Iḥyā' (Salt Lake City: University of Utah Press, 1984), pp. 35–36. I owe this point to an anonymous referee of this volume.

93. See Saadawi, *Hidden Face of Eve,* p. 121; Sabbah, *Woman in the Muslim Unconscious,* pp. 107–8; Bouhdiba, *Sexuality in Islam,* pp. 90–91, 105; Farah, *Marriage and Sexuality in Islam,* pp. 10–16; B. F. Stowasser, *Women in the Qur'ān, Traditions, and Interpretation* (New York: Oxford University Press, 1994), pp. 121–23; and Musallam, *Sex and Society in Islam,* p. 11.

94. See N. R. Keddie, "Introduction: Deciphering Middle Eastern Women's History," in *Women in Middle Eastern History,* pp. 2–3, on the purpose of segregation and veiling. For the provenance of these phenomena in medieval Islam, see Stowasser, *Qur'ān, Traditions, and Interpretation,* pp. 90–94, 97–99, who concludes: "Women's secluded space, concealing clothing, and unfitness for public activity emerged as three powerful determinants in medieval Islamic paradigms on women's societal order."

95. R. Brunschvig, "'Abd," in *The Encyclopaedia of Islam,* 2nd ed., 7 vols. (Leiden: E. J. Brill, 1960), 1:25–28; S. Marmon, "Concubinage, Islamic," in *Dictionary of the Middle Ages,* 12 vols. (Cambridge: Cambridge University Press, 1982), 3:527; Bouhdiba, *Sexuality in Islam,* pp. 106, 108–9, 187. The children of a female slave or concubine were free and legitimate; thus, female slaves and concubines could function as childbearers for both their masters and their masters' kinship groups, without the social and economic encumbrances of marriage. See S. Marmon, "Slavery, Islamic World," in *Dictionary of the Middle Ages,* 12 vols. (Cambridge: Cambridge University Press, 1982), 11:333, and "Concubinage, Islamic," 3:527–28; Spectorsky, *Chapters on Marriage and Divorce,* pp. 68, 106, 110, 121–22, 134–35, 158–62, 177–79, 209, 211–12, 236–37, gives some of the legal rulings on sex between a master and his slave. I owe this point to an anonymous referee of this volume.

96. Combs-Schilling, *Sacred Performances,* pp. 92–93; Bouhdiba, *Sexuality in Islam,* pp. 117ff.; and Sanders, "Gendering the Ungendered Body," pp. 74–75.

97. See Saadawi, *Hidden Face of Eve,* chapter 6 ("Man the God, Woman the Sinful"). This polarity explains, perhaps, the emphasis on pederasty among the mystical Ṣūfīs, on which see A. Schimmel, "Eros—Heavenly and Not So Heavenly—in Sufi Literature and Life," in *Society and the Sexes in Medieval Islam,* pp. 119–41, esp. pp. 119, 131–32.

98. Ibid., p. 130; see also Combs-Schilling, *Sacred Performances,* pp. 62, 88.

99. Ibid., pp. 190, 264. See also Schimmel, "Eros in Sufi Literature and Life," pp. 124–30, and Farah, *Marriage and Sexuality in Islam,* pp. 26–30, on the Ṣūfīs and their dislike of women, particularly how they constructed a whole literature of women as stupid, dangerous, impure, and imbued with powers that hinder men's ascent to higher spheres.

100. Combs-Schilling, *Sacred Performances,* pp. 170ff., and H. Bloch, *Medieval Misogyny and the Invention of Western Romantic Love* (Chicago: University of Chicago Press, 1991), p. 27. Bloch, p. 213n64, quotes Origen: "Our actions are feminine or mascu-

line. Feminine, they are corporeal or carnal. If we plant a seed in flesh, the child of our soul is female, not male: but without nerves, soft and material. If we look toward the eternal, raising our intelligence toward the best, and if we fructify with the fruits of the spirit, all our children are male. All those who are brought before God, presented to the view of the Creator, are male, not female. For God does not deign to look at what is feminine and corporeal."

101. Ibid., p. 9. Combs-Schilling, *Sacred Performances,* p. 269, cites the medieval tradition that Augustine stated that females at the point of death became male, since only men could enter heaven; see also J. Drijvers, "Virginity and Asceticism in Late Roman Western Elites," in *Sexual Asymmetry: Studies in Ancient Society,* J. Blok and P. Mason, eds. (Amsterdam: J. C. Gieben, 1987), pp. 266–68. Woman as decoration and cosmetic is a constant feature of dreams in Achmet's dreambook, discussed below; while men's dreams dictate a change in their public status, women's dreams usually involve a change in their physical appearance or childbearing and household functions—the public and private spheres are thus reinforced in the dream world.

102. Cited in Bloch, *Medieval Misogyny,* p. 30; further references on pp. 29–31. See also the medieval Islamic opinions cited in D. Spellberg, *Politics, Gender, and the Islamic Past* (New York: Columbia University Press, 1994), chapter 5, and Sabbah, *Woman in the Muslim Unconscious,* p. 113.

103. Cited in Bloch, *Medieval Misogyny,* p. 30; see also M. Miles, *Carnal Knowing* (Boston: Beacon Press, 1989), p. 17: "The order of creation—man first, woman second—was understood to reflect cosmic order and to stipulate social order." See Bouhdiba, *Sexuality in Islam,* pp. 31–33.

104. Proudhon, cited in Bloch, *Medieval Misogyny,* p. 28. A good parallel in medieval Islam is the way in which the *ḥadīth* operated to remove woman from the spiritual realm; see Mernissi, *The Veil and the Male Elite,* pp. 64–70.

105. C. Bynum, "' . . . And Woman His Humanity': Female Imagery in the Religious Writing of the Later Middle Ages," in *Gender and Religion: On the Complexity of Symbols,* C. Bynum et al., eds. (Boston: Beacon Press, 1986), p. 257. On the medieval Islamic formulation in the *ḥadīth,* see Stowasser, *Qur'ān, Traditions, and Interpretation,* p. 113; F. Malti-Douglas, *Woman's Body, Woman's Word: Gender and Discourse in Arabo-Islamic Writing* (Princeton: Princeton University Press, 1991), pp. 1–16; and Sabbah, *Woman in the Muslim Unconscious,* p. 114: "The male principle represents: reason, order, God, control. The female principle represents: desire, disorder, devil, the uncontrollable."

106. Combs-Schilling, *Sacred Performances,* pp. 88–98, calls this dichotomy the kingdom of mothers and the kingdom of sirens; see also Malti-Douglas, *Woman's Body, Woman's Word,* p. 59, on the "consistent underlying binary opposition operating between woman and the deity."

107. Bloch, *Medieval Misogyny,* chapters 1 and 3. On medieval Islamic women, see Stowasser, "Status of Women in Early Islam," pp. 29–32; Malti-Douglas, *Woman's Body, Woman's Word,* pp. 60, 105–10, with literature; Schimmel, "Eros in Sufi Literature and Life." D. Spellberg, "Political Action and Public Example: 'Ā'isha and the Battle of the Camel," in *Women in Middle Eastern History,* pp. 45–57, discusses the wordplay on *fitna,* which can mean either an evil woman who is dangerous sexually, or civil war; woman,

therefore, unless controlled in the public and private realms, becomes a metaphor for civil disorder and chaos; this thesis is developed much more fully in Spellberg's 1994 study of ʿĀʾisha bint Abī Bakr (*Politics, Gender, and the Islamic Past*). Moreover, while ʿĀʾisha came to symbolize *fitna,* Zulaykhā (the Egyptian woman who tried to seduce Joseph) came to symbolize in medieval Islam *kayd,* trickery and deceit. These two concepts, *fitna* and *kayd,* were used as justification for the suppression of medieval Muslim women, according to Spellberg (p. 149). This line of inquiry is also developed in great detail in Malti-Douglas, *Woman's Body, Woman's Word.* On Byzantine women, see E. Fisher, "Theodora and Antonia in the *Historia Arcana:* History and/or Fiction?" in *Women in the Ancient World: The Arethusa Papers,* J. Peradotto and J. P. Sullivan, eds. (Albany, N.Y.: State University of New York Press, 1984), pp. 294ff.; J. Beaucamp, "La situation juridique de la femme à Byzance," *Cahiers de civilisation médiévale* 20 (1977): 145–76; J. Grosdidier de Matons, "La femme dans l'Empire byzantin," in *Histoire mondiale de la femme,* P. Grimal, ed., 3 vols. (Paris: Nouvelle Librairie de France, 1966), 3:11–43; K. Thraede, "Frau," in *Reallexicon für Antike und Christentum* (Stuttgart, 1972), with bibliography on cols. 266–69; E. Patlagean, "Byzance X^e^–XIe siècle," in *Histoire de la vie privée,* Ph. Ariès and G. Duby, eds., 2 vols. (Paris, 1985), 1:531–614.

108. Hussain and Radwan, "The Islamic Revolution," p. 57; J. A. Bellamy, "Sex and Society in Islamic Popular Literature," in *Society and the Sexes in Medieval Islam,* pp. 30, 35–38; Ch. Pellat, "Liwāṭ," in *Sexuality and Eroticism Among Males in Moslem Societies,* A. Schmitt and J. Sofer, eds. (New York: Haworth Press, 1992), pp. 151–53; N. J. Coulson, "Regulation of Sexual Behavior Under Traditional Islamic Law," in *Society and the Sexes in Medieval Islam,* pp. 63–68; Bouhdiba, *Sexuality in Islam,* p. 40; Rowson, "Arabic Vice Lists," pp. 59–62; L. Abu-Lughod, "Zones of Theory in the Anthropology of the Arab World," *Annual Review of Anthropology* 18 (1989): 287–94; Farah, *Marriage and Sexuality in Islam,* pp. 30ff.

109. The following discussion is rather broad-based (see also Rosenthal's criticism of Bouhdiba in "Fiction and Reality: Sources for the Role of Sex in Medieval Muslim Society," in *Society and the Sexes in Medieval Islam,* p. 5), but one cannot question the prevalence of the sexual and gender codes described here in much of medieval Islam.

110. The edited volume of Keddie and Baron (*Women in Middle Eastern History: Shifting Boundaries in Sex and Gender*) is highly recommended, particularly the essays by Kandiyoti, Spellberg, Ahmed, Sanders, Lutfi, and Petry.

111. See A. al-Hibri, "A Story of Islamic Herstory: Or How Did We Ever Get into This Mess?" *Women and Islam: Women's Studies International Forum Magazine* 5 (1982): 193–206, and Malti-Douglas, *Woman's Body, Woman's Word,* pp. 3–6.

112. Kandiyoti, "Islam and Patriarchy," p. 23, with bibliography in *nn*2–3; Mernissi, *The Veil and the Male Elite,* pp. 111, 118–19; Saadawi, *Hidden Face of Eve,* p. 5. See Stowasser, *Qur'ān, Traditions, and Interpretation,* pp. 5–7, for different approaches (modernist, conservative, fundamentalist) to the study of women in the Qur'ān and in history and society.

113. Sabbah, *Woman in the Muslim Unconscious,* pp. 69, 74; N. R. Keddie, "Introduction: Deciphering Middle Eastern Women's History," in *Women in Middle Eastern History,* pp. 1–21; Mernissi, *The Veil and the Male Elite,* pp. 23, 64ff., 126, 129ff., 154ff.; F.

Hussain, "Introduction: The Ideal and Contextual Realities of Muslim Women," in *Muslim Women,* pp. 1–9; Stowasser, "Status of Women in Early Islam," pp. 11–43, esp. 34–35 with notes, and *Qur'ān, Traditions, and Interpretation,* pp. 7–8, 21; H. Strange, "A Traditional Ceremony in an Islamic Milieu in Malaysia," in *Muslim Women,* p. 128; B. Callaway and L. Creevey, *The Heritage of Islam: Women, Religion, and Politics in West Africa* (Boulder: Lynne Rienner, 1994); V. Moghadam, *Modernizing Women: Gender and Social Change in the Middle East* (Boulder: Lynne Rienner, 1993); Spellberg, *Politics, Gender, and the Islamic Past;* L. Ahmed, "Early Islam and the Position of Women: The Problem of Interpretation," in *Women in Middle Eastern History,* pp. 58–73, esp. pp. 70–71; Saadawi, *Hidden Face of Eve,* chapter 15.

114. See the discussion with literature in Keddie, "Introduction," esp. pp. 1–2, 5–6, 19, 23; see also Kandiyoti, "Islam and Patriarchy"; Saadawi, *Hidden Face of Eve,* p. 6; Hussain and Radwan, "The Islamic Revolution," pp. 60–61. Also important are the essays in *Muslim Women* by Stowasser, Gerner, Ahmed, Salem, and Hussain.

115. M. Hodgson, *The Venture of Islam, Vol. II: The Expansion of Islam in the Middle Periods* (Chicago: University of Chicago Press, 1974), p. 146. Bellamy, "Sex and Society," p. 28, records cases where young men expressed their wish to sodomize their social superiors as a sign of dominance.

116. Saadawi, *Hidden Face of Eve,* p. 51; Bürgel, "Love, Lust, and Longing," p. 88; Greenberg, *The Construction of Homosexuality,* pp. 175ff.; C. Bosworth, "Ghulām," in *The Encyclopaedia of Islam,* 2nd ed., 3:1082; Brunschvig, "ʿAbd," pp. 25–33. Some scholars make reference (perhaps a little too much, in search of a "cause" for the occurrence of medieval Arabic homoeroticism) to Arab warriors' imposition of homosexual relations on conquered peoples; see Pellat, "Liwāṭ," p. 154; Hodgson, *The Venture of Islam,* pp. 140–46; Goitein, "Sexual Mores of the Common People," in *Society and the Sexes in Medieval Islam,* p. 47.

117. Bouhdiba, *Sexuality in Islam,* pp. 107, 141–42, 201–2; Boswell, *Christianity,* p. 195. An anonymous referee of this volume points out an in-depth study of this in H. Zayyat, "al-Mar'a al-ghulāmīya fī l-Islam," *al-Mashriq* 50 (1956): 153–92, which I have not seen.

118. Pellat, "Liwāṭ," pp. 155, 159; Goitein, "Sexual Mores," p. 58, and *A Mediterranean Society: The Jewish Communities of the Arab World as Portrayed in the Documents of the Cairo Geniza. Vol. V: The Individual* (Berkeley: University of California Press, 1988), pp. 318–21; Bouhdiba, *Sexuality in Islam,* pp. 130–31, 160–68; Boswell, *Christianity,* p. 190n100 (male prostitutes in medieval Spain).

119. Bouhdiba, *Sexuality in Islam,* pp. 203–5; the absolute loathing of female genitalia described here is similar to that in Greek and Roman sources. Professor Rowson points out to me that men were also expected to depilate their pubic hairs, and still quite regularly do so.

120. Bürgel, "Love, Lust, and Longing," p. 85; Bouhdiba, *Sexuality in Islam,* pp. 127–28; Greenberg, *The Construction of Homosexuality,* p. 175; Rowson, "Arabic Vice Lists," p. 57; Sabbah, *Woman in the Muslim Unconscious,* p. 9; Malti-Douglas, *Woman's Body, Woman's Word,* p. 47; see Bellamy, "Sex and Society," pp. 25–27, for a survey of primary source materials on sex in medieval Muslim society; and on the *topos* of the beardless

youth in medieval Islam as homoerotic, see Malti-Douglas, *Woman's Body, Woman's Word,* p. 44*n*121. See Bürgel, "Love, Lust, and Longing," pp. 85, 111 (although he points out that boys were preferred because of the impurity of women); Rowson, "Arabic Vice Lists," pp. 57 and 58–59 (on the debate on the relative merits of sex with boys versus sex with women); Bouhdiba, *Sexuality in Islam,* pp. 202–3; Musallam, *Sex and Society in Islam,* p. 108 with *n*154, on sodomy as a form of birth control. The medieval schools of Islamic law condemned heterosexual anal intercourse; see Rowson, p. 57, and note 129 below. For comparative purposes, see Richlin, *Garden of Priapus,* pp. 37–49, on the ancient Romans' obsession with the buttocks.

122. Pellat, "Liwāṭ," pp. 155, 157; Bouhdiba, *Sexuality in Islam,* p. 119; Boswell, *Christianity,* pp. 27, 194–95, 197, 233–34 (with *nn*87–90); Goitein, "Sexual Mores," p. 48, and *Mediterranean Society,* pp. 211–12, 318–21.

123. Schimmel, "Eros in Sufi Literature and Life," pp. 130–32; Bouhdiba, *Sexuality in Islam,* pp. 118–19, 142–48; Ch. Pellat, "Djins," in *The Encyclopaedia of Islam,* 2nd ed. 2:550; Hodgson, *The Venture of Islam,* pp. 145–46; Goitein, *Mediterranean Society,* pp. 21, 202, 320 (with literature on p. 593), and "Sexual Mores," pp. 48, 59 (with notes); Boswell, *Christianity,* pp. 196–97, and "Revolutions," p. 27; Greenberg, *The Construction of Homosexuality,* pp. 172, 174. See also Stetkevych, "Intoxication and Immortality" (this volume) on the eroticization of the young male *sāqī* (cupbearer).

124. Bellamy, "Sex and Society," p. 37, notes that the *ḥadīth* are less concerned with two adult males than with a man and a boy, since boys are greater temptations. But see Bürgel, "Love, Lust, and Longing," p. 112, and Boswell, *Christianity,* p. 27, on the isolated occurrences of homosexual love between mature adults.

125. Goitein, *Mediterranean Society,* pp. 318–21; Saadawi, *Hidden Face of Eve,* pp. 74–75; Rowson, "Arabic Vice Lists," pp. 54–55.

126. Richlin, *Garden of Priapus,* p. 15; see also Lilja, *Homosexuality in Rome,* pp. 54–57, on oral and anal rape.

127. Bellamy, "Sex and Society," p. 34, notes that not a single reference to oral sex can be found in Islamic medieval popular literature; see also Rowson, "Arabic Vice Lists," p. 75*n*8. I can find no mention of it in any Byzantine or Arabic dreambook, even though there are numerous sections on adultery, bestiality, sodomy, and transvestism, all of which were proscribed by Christianity and Islam (Bellamy, p. 30).

128. Not to mention anxieties about gender violations and gender expectations. The medieval physician al-Rāzī stated that men who desire to be penetrated by other men should have their penises subjected to oral and manual stimulation by female slaves and should also practice penetration of women as much as possible, in order to counteract this "disease." See F. Rosenthal, "Ar-Râzî on the Hidden Illness," *Bulletin of the History of Medicine* 52 (1978): 58–59.

129. Greenberg, *The Construction of Homosexuality,* p. 176; Boswell, "Revolutions," p. 479*n*25, with literature and discussion; Rosenthal, "Hidden Illness," pp. 45–51; Rowson, "Arabic Vice Lists," p. 64. It bears repeating that the legal scholars, the Qur'ān, and the Prophet were against sodomy, whether heterosexual or homosexual; see Spectorsky, *Chapters on Marriage and Divorce,* p. 236; Farah, *Marriage and Sexuality in Islam,* pp. 37–39; Sabbah, *Woman in the Muslim Unconscious,* p. 116. But see Malti-Douglas, *Woman's Body,*

Woman's Word, p. 15, on the attitudes of classical Arabic scholars, and the literature cited on p. 40*n*48 and p. 47 on the hyperactivity of homosexuals.

130. Boswell, *Christianity,* p. 158; J. Brown, "Lesbian Sexuality," pp. 70–71; Musallam, *Sex and Society in Islam,* p. 154*n*8; Rowson, "Arabic Vice Lists," pp. 63–64.

131. Sanders, "Gendering the Ungendered Body," pp. 75–76, 79, 85, 88–89.

132. For an argument for basic continuity in sexual practices and attitudes between the ancient world and medieval Islam, see Rowson, "Arabic Vice Lists," pp. 72–73.

133. As in society: E. Cantarella, *Pandora's Daughters: The Role and Status of Women in Greek and Roman Antiquity,* M. B. Fant, trans. (Baltimore: Johns Hopkins University Press, 1978), pp. 171–73. A prime example is the recurrent theme in all societies under discussion here, namely, the talkative woman. Achmet has much to say about the language of a woman and how it provokes men: "If a woman dreams that her tongue is cut off or grows smaller, she will receive joy and love from her husband: for it is through her tongue that every woman irritates her husband"; and "If a woman dreams that she has a quicker and more adroit tongue for speaking, her husband will experience her hatred and shamelessness" (section 62; see also section 115). Achmet's remarks echo Arabic views (Schimmel, "Eros in Sufi Literature and Life," p. 127; Sabbah, *Woman in the Muslim Unconscious,* p. 118; Malti-Douglas, *Woman's Body, Woman's Word,* p. 29), Greek (Keuls, *Reign of the Phallus,* p. 88), and Byzantine (Cantarella, *Pandora's Daughters,* p. 174). Compare Bloch, *Medieval Misogyny,* pp. 15ff., with primary and secondary literature given there.

134. Examples in Oberhelman, *Oneirocriticon of Achmet,* p. 80, to which may be added: "If the king dreams that gems and pearls are brought to him, he will be happy in proportion to their number; if anyone else dreams that he procures gems and pearls, he will receive proportionate wealth, glory, and fame. If a woman has this dream, she will find glory and joy in her husband" (section 246). And "if the king dreams that he has an eye in his heart with which he can see, he will beget a son who will advise him on financial matters; if a commoner dreams this, he will suddenly get wealth and honor; if a married woman, she will move on to a wealthier husband; if an unmarried woman, she will marry a rich man" (section 52).

135. Oberhelman, *Oneirocriticon of Achmet,* pp. 79–81. On woman as cosmetic and as signified by sexual status, see Achmet, section 127: "The interpretation of happiness in the case of women is greater if the woman in one's dream is a virgin; an unknown woman has a better interpretation than one known; a woman beautified with cosmetics better than an unadorned woman; and an unknown courtesan better than a familiar one. . . . One must know that the dream appearances of all women, young and old, are interpreted as joy analogous to their beauty." On woman as signified by the penis, see the dreams in the Appendix. Even sexual conduct is reinforced by the dreams: women who dream of committing "fornication" are told that they will fall into grave illness, while men who dream of having intercourse with either men or women will see changes, usually for the better, in their social status. Women's conduct is regulated and guarded everywhere with dangerous warnings of their fate; "If a woman dreams that she goes into a graveyard or that she speaks with a dead man, this signifies deceit toward her husband; if she is not married, she will spend her whole life in fornication" (section

132). Given the constant penalties and punishments that could befall women simply because of their dreams, the anxiety level among Byzantine and Arab women must have been extremely high.

136. MacAlister's comments on Artemidorus ("Artemidorus' *Oneirokritika*," p. 154) are worth replicating in full here:

> [Artemidorus' gender signs and symbolism] reflect a fundamental concern in Artemidorus' social and cultural environment to do with prestige and disgrace, dominance and subordination, strength and weakness, activity and passivity which, in turn, stand to be publicly manifested, on the one hand, by an individual's authority, power, and acquisition (whether of status or possessions) and, on the other, by loss, scandal, or exposure . . . The concept of masculinity is identified by signs of superior social status, dominance, strength, and activity. But although Artemidorus states univocally that such attributes belong to the male sex in terms of a biologically-given truth signified by the male penis, as signs of masculinity they depend for their sense and meaning on contrast with their polar opposites—inferior social status, subordination, weakness, and passivity—or, in other words, masculinity takes on meaning only through contrast and comparison with an "other."

137. It is very significant that all references to male homosexuality are to be found in the chapters dealing with women; the sole exception is section 14 where the passive partner is specifically labeled as acting as a woman. Obviously Achmet has collapsed male same-sex activity into the same rubric as heterosexual intercourse; even bestiality has its own chapters (sections 133 and 134).

138. Rowson, "Arabic Vice Lists," pp. 65–66.

139. I wish to thank the editors and the anonymous referees of this volume for excellent advice and constructive criticism; their suggestions have improved this paper considerably.

CHAPTER FOUR

The Striptease That Was Blamed on Abū Bakr's Naughty Son: Was Father Being Shamed, or Was the Poet Having Fun? (Ibn Quzmān's Zajal No. 133*)*

James T. Monroe

The Andalusī poet Ibn Quzmān's (d. 556/1160) *Zajal No. 133* is, strictly speaking, a *zajal*-like *muwashshaḥa.*[1] It contrafacts (*yuʿāriḍu*) an earlier *muwashshaḥa,* possibly composed by the distinguished Andalusī philosopher, poet, and musician Ibn Bājja ("Avempace" [d. 533/1138]). The melody of the latter must have been extremely popular, since S. M. Stern cites at least six other important imitations of it, both in Arabic and in Hebrew.[2] Ibn Quzmān's imitation is openly acknowledged by the quotation of Ibn Bājja's *kharja* at the end of his own poem. Although the *zajal* has been edited and translated into Spanish by both Emilio García Gómez[3] and Federico Corriente,[4] it still contains a few obscurities that when clarified allow for a new and somewhat different reading from those proposed by my distinguished predecessors. I would like to base my discussion of this new reading on my edition of the Arabic text,[5] followed by its prose translation into English.

Edition

0. *man daʿāni nafnī anā ʿumrī*
fī malīḥan yarā ṣawāb hajrī

1. anā naʿshaq li-man yaʿādīnī?
daʿnī min dhā! muhāwid aʿṭīnī;
idhā nashrab yamlā wa-yasqīnī.
w-ashshu maʿshūqan lā [yalāqīnī][6]
wa-naḍummu b-al-layl ilā ṣadrī
wa-naṣīr kadhā māʿu ṭūl dahrī?

2. lā taṣaddaq, fa-hadhā kullu muḥāl!
inna lam qaṭ yaṣil aḥad dhā l-wiṣāl!
innamā hu kalām an-nās an yuqāl!
yaʿtarī dhā ghayr fī [manām ar-rijāl]?[7]
tara dhā kullu f-al-manām yaʿtarī;
innamā f-al-yaqẓah fa-las nadrī.

3. habni naʿshaq ḥulū bi-ḥāl sukkar;
tadri man? walad qillīd [bū][8] bakar,
bi-fumaymah aʿṭar min al-ʿanbar,
wa-ḍuraysāt manẓūma min jawhar,
fa-bi-ḥaqq an yuqāl li-dhā ʿanbarī,
wa-matā mā nuẓim yuqāl jawharī.

4. law raʾaytum khurūj hadhā l-madhkūr,
wa-hu qad ḥalla ʿamda dhāk al-mazrūr,[9]
ʿalā sūsīyah bayḍa ka-l-kāfūr,
wa-rakab lak farasu ʾal-mashhūr,
wa-s-surayyaj matāʿ. . . . [10]
[ḥasra]tī,[11] law lā khawf abū bakri!

5. tadri ʾas-sā b-al-ḥaqq ash fazzaʿnī?
bayāḍ as-sāq ʿalā l-khiḍāb—da ʿnī!
inna sāʿat mā raytu ʾabhatnī;
taḥlaf annu min manbūtan maʿdanī,
fa-tarā s-sāq la-fawqu ʾabyaḍ ṭarī,
thumma dhuhhib an-niṣfi b-al-jaʿfarī.

6. raytu waḥd an-nahār kharaj b-al-kumayt,
wa-fī qalbī min ajlu mimmā darayt.
qultu fīh dhā z-zajal kamā qad raʾayt;
ʿāraḍ at-tawshīḥ alladhī sammayt:
"ʿaqada l-lāhu rāyata n-naṣri
li-ʾamīri l-ʿulā ʾabī bakri!"[12]

Translation

0. *Who invites me to waste my life*
On a beauty who deems it just to avoid me?

1. Should I love one who is hostile to me?
Deliver me from such! Give me one who is compliant;
[Who], when I drink, will fill and pour for me.
What sort of beloved is one who won't [meet me],
So that I can press him, all night long, to my breast,
And remain with him thus, all my life?

2. Don't believe it! The above is all far-fetched!
No one ever achieved such a love-union!
It is merely rumors mentioned by people!
Does this ever happen outside [men's dreams]?
You'll find that all this only happens in dreams;
As for waking, I don't know of it.

3. Let me love one who is sweet as sugar;
Do you know whom? The son of the *agellīd*[13] Abū Bakr,
Who has a little mouth more fragrant than ambergris,
And little teeth like pearls on a string,
Hence it is only fair [the mouth] be called "ambergris-like,"
And "pearly," insofar as its [teeth] are strung.

4. If only you could see the above mentioned's departure,
When he unbuttons, on purpose, the buttons
On his camphor-white *sūsīya,*[14]
And rides his thoroughbred horse for you,
While the little saddle of. . . .
[Alas], were it not that I fear Abū Bakr!

5. To be serious, do you know what now disturbs me?
Why, the white of his shank, above its stained part! Spare me!
The very moment I saw it, it overwhelmed me;
You'd swear it was the underground product of a mine,
For you could see his shank white and tender, up above,
While its [lower] half was gilded with *jaʿfarī* [gold].[15]

6. One day, I saw him ride forth on his bay horse,
While because of him, my heart suffered what you know.
As you see, I've composed this *zajal* about him,

Contrafacting the *muwashshaḥa* that I quote:
"May God raise the banner of victory
For the prince of glory, Abū Bakr!"

Surface Structure

In the *maṭlaʿ* ("refrain"), indicated by (0) in our text, the poet introduces a theme frequently encountered in classical Arabic poetry, that of unrequited love, the tyranny of which he expresses his desire to escape. However, it is a convention in the Arabic poetic tradition of chaste love for the poet to endure his beloved's cruel avoidance with total submission. Therefore the treatment of the theme offered here ("Why should I waste my life on one who avoids me?") clearly represents a rebellion against that literary convention. This idea is developed in strophe 1, where the poet decides to abandon a beloved who treats him with hostility in favor of one who will be compliant, who will pour his wine for him when he is drinking, and with whom he will be able to enjoy the delights of the love-union without interruption for the rest of his days. The ideal beloved the poet has in mind here is a cupbearer, and therefore a young male.

In strophe 2, with a sudden about-face that dismantles the previous construction, the poet reminds himself that such an ideal situation is both untenable and unattainable.[16] It only occurs in people's dreams; as far as their waking hours are concerned, he has never witnessed such a blissfully uneventful form of love. Having rebelled against reality in 1, then admitted that his rebellion is impossible in 2, the poet finally chooses a specific beloved in 3. This beloved is the son of the Berber *agellīd* or prince, Abū Bakr, who is described as being sweet as sugar, having a mouth more fragrant than ambergris and teeth like a pearl necklace.[17]

The above three strophes, in which the poet examines the general nature of both real and imagined love, constitute the first part of the poem. In its second part, he concentrates more specifically on the seductive qualities of Abū Bakr's son. In strophe 4, the boy is depicted as appearing with his camphor-white shirt unbuttoned "on purpose" (*ʿamda*) as he rides forth on his thoroughbred steed, in order, it is implied, to seduce his admirers with the charms of his bared flesh. The end of the first line of that strophe's *markaz,* along with part of the first word of the second line, has been cut off at the margin in the process of binding the manuscript. Nonetheless, we are left with enough of a context to perceive the malicious drift of ideas. After a reference, the end of which is also lopped off in the manuscript, to the horse's saddle, the poet implies that "were it not for fear of Abū Bakr" he would make amorous overtures to the latter's son (or sentiments to that effect).

The alluring portrait of the boy is developed in strophe 5, which concentrates on the beauty of his shank, the upper part of which is described as being white and tender while its lower half is stained. In turn, the staining of the lower shank is compared to gilding with *jaʿfarī* gold. A variant on this unusual image occurs in *Zajal No. 5,* strophe 3,[18] where a vizier named Ibn ʿUbāda is described as "having his shank stained halfway up" (*bi-khiḍāb ilā nisfi ṣaqu.*) Here, no gold is specified. These two passages have led García Gómez to the rather literal conclusion, for which he provides no documentation, that it was a fashion among Almoravid dandies to gild the lower halves of their shanks. Note, however, that only in *Zajal No. 133* is the image of gold mentioned, metaphorically, in conjunction with the stained shank. Could this image be a poetic reference to the well-known Berber custom of staining the hands, feet, limbs, and other parts of the body with henna? The latter is a custom still practiced in Morocco among women, children, boys, and men as a means of protection against harmful influences, particularly the evil eye and the *jinn.*[19] Note the extraordinary correspondence between the half-stained white leg described by Ibn Quzmān and the description of a half-stained white arm in a Judeo-Spanish version of the ballad of "Búcar at Valencia" collected in Morocco. Here, a Moor is introduced in the following grotesque terms, as he rides forth from the besieged city of Santafé (Granada):

> A las doze oras del día un moro se ha señalado,
> sobre un caballo afletado, de muchas marcas marcado.
> El moro que sobre él viene parece de grande estado;
> un oído trae sordo, y el otro trae tapado;
> un ojo trae de vidro y el otro alcoholado,
> la barba trae crecida y el cabello crespo y cano,
> *el braço blanco* y velludo, *la meatad del alheñado.*
>
> At twelve o'clock, noon, a Moor came into view,
> On a rented horse, branded with many brands.
> The Moor who rides him seems to be of high rank;
> One of his ears is deaf, the other is covered up,
> One eye is made of glass, the other, painted with collyrium,
> His beard is long and full, his hair, curly and gray,
> *His arm is white* and hairy, *its half is stained with henna.*[20]

Should the difference between an arm and a leg prove insurmountable to the skeptic, could Ibn Quzmān's description of the boy's leg be a poetic portrayal of a tan line? If so, the boy's lower shanks would have been exposed to the sun, thus acquiring a "golden" tan, while their upper areas, normally hidden beneath his robes but visible when viewed from below as he rides on horseback, would have remained white. Either way, the boy is being portrayed as a wanton and a tease, for he is *deliberately* exposing those parts of his body (chest and upper shanks) for which Islamic norms of decency recommend covering.[21] Furthermore, it makes little difference whether the leg of Abū Bakr's son is sunburned, dyed with henna, or actually painted with gold. The main point of this passage is that the lovesick poet, with unabashed prurience, is peering up the hem of the equestrian boy's robes from below in order to catch a glimpse of his legs.

In strophe 6 the boy is again portrayed riding on his horse; this time on the day he first smote the poet's heart. As a result, the poet declares that he has composed the present *zajal* about him, to the tune of a *muwashshaḥa,* the *kharja* of which he incorporates by adopting it as his own. The *kharja* involved is that of the famous *muwashshaḥa* beginning *jarriri dh-dhayla ayyamā jarrī / wa-ṣili s-sukra minka bi-s-sukrī* ("Trail proudly your cloak wherever it listeth / and add to your drunkenness intoxication"). The poem is a five-strophe composition of which the first two are anacreontic and the last three constitute a panegyric in praise of the Almoravid governor of Zaragoza, Abū Bakr b. Ibrāhīm al-Masūfī, known as Ibn Tīfalwīt, who was a brother-in-law of ʿAlī b. Yūsuf b. Tāshufīn, the Almoravid ruler (r. 500–537/1106–1142). The latter appointed Abū Bakr b. Tīfalwīt governor over Zaragoza in 508/1114. Abū Bakr died in battle in 510/1116. Authorship of the poem is attributed to Ibn Bājja (d. 534/1139) in a passage by Ibn Saʿīd (d. 673/1274)[22] and in Ibn Bushrā's *ʿUddat al-jalīs,*[23] but to Ibn al-Ṣayrafī (467–558/1074–1162) in the *Jaysh al-tawshīḥ* by Ibn al-Khaṭīb (713–776/1313–1374).[24] Aside from the name Abū Bakr, which appears in the *kharja* quoted by Ibn Quzmān, the *muwashshaḥa* has nothing in common thematically with *Zajal No. 133*. This lack of thematic correspondence between the model and its imitation lends support to the arguments I have developed elsewhere, to the effect that the phenomenon of *muʿāraḍa,* usually translated as "imitation" in a literary-thematic sense, may also be understood as musical contrafaction. In other words, by quoting the *kharja* of his model, Ibn Quzmān is not suggesting a thematic dependence of his own poem on that of Ibn Bājja/Ibn al-Ṣayrafī; he may instead be indicating that it is intended to be sung to the tune of the latter.[25] This is not to deny, of course, that in all likelihood Ibn Quzmān chose the earlier poem as a model precisely because its *kharja* contained a name that conveniently coincided with that of the unknown Abū Bakr to whose son he was dedicating his own love song.

The second part of the poem thus moves specifically from a picture of the boy riding on horseback with his shirt unbuttoned, so that his bared flesh arouses in the poet a strong desire to engage with him in certain acts the full description of which we are spared and which he would gladly do but for fear of the boy's father, to a minute description of the boy's shanks, of which the white upper areas are seductively visible. The final strophe returns to the initial image of the boy on horseback, who is portrayed as causing such havoc in the poet's heart that he is inspired to compose a *zajal* ending with a *kharja* containing the father's name.

Like most of Ibn Quzmān's *zajal*s, this one is based on the principles of ring composition.[26] On the one hand, each tripartite half of the six-strophe poem exhibits its own circular pattern, which may be outlined as follows:

(A) 1. The poet rejects the conventions of chaste love poetry (passivity of lover).
(B) 2. The poet rejects his previous rejection (activity of lover).
(A′) 3. The poet accepts the conventions of chaste love poetry (passivity of lover).
(C) 4. The beloved, on horseback (active), charms the poet, who cannot (and does not) take action sexually (passive).
(D) 5. The beloved's shank (static) charms the poet, who is reduced to stasis.
(C′) 6. The beloved, on horseback (active), charms the poet, who can (and does) take action poetically (active).

On the other hand, the entire poem also exhibits its own set of rings: if 1 is a rejection of the normal conventions of Arabic sentimental love poetry (the poet will not submit to an unattainable beloved), 6 embodies the acceptance of those conventions (the poet has submitted, in this *zajal,* to an unattainable beloved). Similarly, if 2 is a return to the normal themes of classical Arabic poetry (attainable beloveds are only encountered in dreams), 5 is a departure from the normal images of classical Arabic poetry (the beloved's shank is like a mineral; the stain on its lower area is like gold). Finally, if 3 embodies the acceptance of a beloved who is (A) *unattainable* (because of Abū Bakr's princely status), and (B) *charming* (his mouth is like ambergris; his teeth are like pearls—both normal images in classical poetry), 4 inverts the order of terms by depicting a beloved who is (B′) *charming* (his shirt is unbuttoned—an abnormal image in classical Arabic poetry), and (A′) *unattainable* (because of Abū Bakr's watchful fatherly eye). Furthermore, the father's name appears in its colloquial form in 3, and in its classical form in 4. From the above analysis it becomes clear that, on one level at least, Ibn Quzmān's poetic launching pad is the tradition of idealized classical Arabic love poetry, which, as a prince of disorder, he then proceeds to deconstruct by every possible means available to him, ranging from colloquial diction through nonstandard imagery to idiosyncratic themes.

The Poem Itself

What are we to make of this strange poem? To begin, let us note that although the father's name is mentioned, the son's is not. Let us also note that, according to one mode of Arabic love poetry, introduced to ʿAbbāsid Baghdad by al-ʿAbbās b. al-Aḥnaf (d. ca. 192/807) and predominant in the classical Andalusī *ghazal,* it was a strict taboo to mention the name of the beloved. Therefore, given the general tenor of the poem, we would not go far astray in viewing it, on one level at least, as a love lyric composed in honor of Abū Bakr's son. Furthermore, in Andalusī panegyrical poetry of the *muwashshaḥa* type, it was common practice to invoke the patron's name in a metrically prominent position, be it the *maṭlaʿ*, the central strophe or strophes, the *kharja* (i.e., at the beginning, middle, or end of the poem), and/or in rhyme position. In this *muwashshaḥa*-like *zajal,* the name of Abū Bakr appears precisely in the two central strophes, and then, once again, at the end of the poem, in its *kharja.* Not only are all three invocations of the name in rhyme position, but its inclusion in the *kharja,* which provides the rhyme for all the previous *markaz*es plus the *maṭlaʿ*, means that all the strophes end with *markaz*es rhyming upon Abū Bakr's name. This singular *tour de force* on the part of the poet hammers home the point that this love poem is simultaneously intended as a panegyric to the father, who is indeed praised in the *kharja.* But how can a father be praised convincingly when the poet is simultaneously making amorous overtures to his son?

To understand this seeming paradox, let us turn to the Arabic genre of *hijāʾ* or "invective poetry" and consider some of its manifestations in the literary tradition. In his treatise on poetics entitled *Kitāb al-ʿUmda,* Ibn Rashīq (d. 457/1064 or 464/1071) cites an epigram by Ibn al-Rūmī (d. 283/896), which he describes as "the most malicious thing I have ever heard in this genre of poetry":

la-hū sāʾisun māhirun / yajūlu ʿalā matnihī
wa-yaṭʿunu fī dubrihī / afānīna min ṭaʿnihī
bi-aṭwala min qarnihī / wa-aghlaẓa min dhihnihī[27]

He has a skillful groom / who rides upon his back,
And pokes him in the ass, / with thrust on piercing thrust
Of what is longer than his horns / and thicker than his wits.

Here Ibn al-Rūmī's unfortunate male victim is abused on several counts, for he is not only accused of being habitually on the receiving end of anal intercourse, but also charged with cuckoldry and stupidity. According to G. J. Van Gelder, who has recently published a book on *hijāʾ*, in which he studies the above poem, it appears that in early Arabic poetry *hijāʾ* was aimed primarily at men, and when women were reviled the indirect aim of the poet was to put their menfolk to shame.[28] This was certainly true in the case of the Umayyad poet Jarīr (d. 110/728), who, in many poems, insulted the women of Mujāshiʿ, the clan of his arch-rival al-Farazdaq (d. 110/728). In particular, he made disparaging sexual remarks about Jiʿthin, the sister of the latter, accusing her (without foundation, according to the commentators) of having been the victim of a gang rape.[29] The following is one example of Jarīr's treatment of this subject:

Your betrayal of Zubayr at Minā summed you up entirely, along with the rape of Jiʿthin at Dhāt Ḥarmala.
Farazdaq spent the night looking out for himself, while Jiʿthin's ass was being used like a highway.
Where were those you imagined would not arrive to rape Jiʿthin, O son of an abscessed mother?
You surrendered Jiʿthin, when she was dragged off by the foot, and the Minqarī pierced her with his skewer.
Her ass sank to the ground as she cried out: "Help Mujāshiʿ!"[30] while the crack of her hole squinted like an eye.[31]

There existed, then, in early Arabic poetry, a tradition of reviling women in order to shame their menfolk. A more subtle form of *hijāʾ* in the Umayyad period praised women in order to shame their menfolk. The anthologist Ibn Sallām al-Jumaḥī (d. ca. 231/845), in his *Ṭabaqāt al-shuʿarāʾ*, ignores the Jiʿthin episode and writes about Jarīr that, "in spite of his excessive *hijāʾ*, [he] abstained from mentioning women, and never made love poetry on women other than his own."[32] Van Gelder comments that "*hijāʾ* and love poetry are not always as clearly opposite as they seem: the description of female charms (*tashbīb*) was not rarely interpreted as a form of invective by the indignant husbands, brothers, and other relatives; an interpretation that was often intended by the poet himself."[33] As a result, love poetry was often condemned by the guardians of religion, to such an extent that the caliph ʿUmar (r. 13–24/634–644) "actually threatened to flog poets composing erotic poetry."[34] Two Medinese poets, Ḥassān b. Thābit al-Khazrajī (d. ca. 39/649) and his contemporary, Qays b. al-Khaṭīm al-Awsī,[35] had already resorted to the genre of satirical love-poetry in the pre-Islamic period.[36] This form of invective was further cultivated by the Umayyad poets. Ḥassān's son, ʿAbd al-Raḥmān,[37] wrote love poems about Ramla, the daughter of the caliph Muʿāwiya (r. 41–61/661–680), "to annoy her father and family."[38] Al-Aḥwaṣ al-Anṣārī (d. 105/723) and ʿAbdallāh b. ʿUmar al-ʿArjī (d. 121/738) also composed satirical love songs.[39] In the case of the latter, Ṭāhā Ḥusayn explains:

> Al-ʿArjī was . . . a righteous man who disliked those in authority, and both his bluntness and his dislike destroyed him. It is claimed that when Hishām b. ʿAbd al-Malik was made caliph (r. 106–126/724–743), he appointed his maternal uncle Muḥammad b. Hishām al-Makhzūmī to be the governor of Mecca. Soon al-ʿArjī began to exceed all bounds in satirizing Muḥammad b. Hishām. Next, he ceased restricting himself to excessive satire and began to compose love poetry about the mother and wife of the governor, and to hand over his love poems to singers, and very swiftly did men's tongues burst forth in singing them! . . . Thus Muḥammad b. Hishām became intensely angry with him, and began to look for excuses to pounce upon him, and he soon found a way of doing so![40]

The following is a love poem composed by al-ʿArjī to Jabra al-Makhzūmīya, wife of Muḥammad b. Hishām:

> "Turn toward me, and greet me, Jabra; why this avoidance just as you're departing?
> Of itself, the latter is separation enough for you and me. Why this too? Know what separation is.
> We will not meet again until the third day of Minā, when the stampede will soon tear us apart,
> One month after this year is over; fate is but a year plus one month!

If you'd but stay, I would excuse you for preventing me from reaching you, and I'd be patient,
For love of you, and I would hold your avoidance sacred at times, yet does an impassioned lover enjoy a sacred pledge?"
She glanced with the pupil of a fawn-bearing gazelle; one fond of tender shoots whose growth is fresh,
Whose cares are redoubled by a tender fawn whose languor slows its pace,
In a place where slanderers raised glances just like burning embers.
I recognized an abode, and said to it, beside its castle: "An age has passed since my acquaintance with it."
The castle was emptied of dear Jabra's people, along with its surroundings and dust-covered hillsides.
Then the well was abandoned, along with its place at Sidra and its reddish eastern hills,
By every tender, slender-waisted maiden, empty of waistband, like the full moon,
Bright-eyed, who is prevented from rising, when she sits down, by the fullness of her shape and by the weight that leaves her breathless,
She is like a palm tree, laden down with dates, rising high on the top of a sand dune, bending down its heavily laden branch.
She walks with the gait of one deeply intoxicated, who trails his garment, when wine has snatched away almost all his senses.
It is a castle in which dwelt a girl of tender youth, before whose ancestry Glory falls short.
She is radiantly beautiful, while her forefathers and their radiant, noble wives raise her to a lofty rank.
From her female elders she inherited virtue, along with the memorable good deeds they performed of old,
Yet when ice and snow together lashed the thorny trees, while the region remained rainless,
And the north wind overpowered the area's garments, and the dates faded to yellow,
The sharp edge of winter did not trouble her, nor was a curtain raised for her to go out and earn her living.[41]

To the mother of the exasperated governor of Mecca, al-ʿArjī dedicated these lines:

> Turn toward me, mistress of the howdah; if you do not do so, you will commit a crime.
> The easiest gift a lover can offer upon the departure of the beloved is to say: "Turn aside,"
> That his need be granted; or to say: "Can I escape my suffering?"
> You have departed from your quarter [or: lover], but the passion in the heart of one deeply in love, by love exhausted, will not depart.[42]

One objection to the love poetry of the Meccan aristocrat ʿUmar b. Abī Rabīʿa (d. ca. 102/720) was that in singing the praises of the forty-odd ladies mentioned in his *dīwān* he was dishonoring their menfolk. One of his loves was Fāṭima, daughter of the Umayyad caliph ʿAbd al-Malik (r. 66–86/685–705), to whom he dedicated several songs before he was compelled to desist by the indignant caliph's threats.[43] The ʿUdhrī poet Jamīl (d. 82/701) became the subject of a complaint made against him by the father, husband, and clan of Buthayna, his beloved, to the governor of Medina (or possibly the latter's representative in Wādī l-Qurā), for composing love poems to her that compromised their honor. After a virulent exchange of *hijāʾ* between the poet and a defender of Buthayna's clan, the governor ruled that Jamīl could lawfully be killed by her male relatives, should he be apprehended by them in her vicinity. To save his life, he fled to Syria and later to Egypt, where he died.[44] Jamīl's tender love lyrics, all dedicated to Buthayna, were hardly intended as satires, but it is significant that they were perceived as such by the lady's outraged male relatives. Possibly the most famous example of a satirical love poem of this type was composed by ʿUbaydallāh b. Qays al-Ruqayyāt (d. ca. 85/704). This poet was at first a supporter of the Zubayrids, under whom the Hijaz had revolted against the Umayyads, and he transferred his loyalty to the Umayyad cause only after the death, in 72/691, of his Zubayrid patron Muṣʿab b. al-Zubayr. Ibn Qays al-Ruqayyāt's poem contains a passage in which the poet claims to have made love to Umm al-Banīn, the wife of the future al-Walīd I (r. 86–97/705–715), in order to irritate her father-in-law, ʿAbd al-Malik (r. 66–86/685–705), who was the reigning caliph at the time the poem was composed.[45] However, the poet adds the disclaimer that the night of love he enjoyed with Umm al-Banīn only took place in his dreams! Here is a translation of the entire poem:

A certain damsel of Quraysh, whose retinue were rocking on their camels' backs, once ridiculed me,
When she deduced, all from the hoar-frost on my head, a state that drove her far away,
And so she asked: "Is that Ben Qays?" for something else, besides my hoariness, had caused her to exult:
She saw my youth had gone for good, while in her company were fresh young maids.

Yet I remember many women just like her, with whom I dallied formerly, whose greatest fault was sheer perfection in their loveliness:
One had a jealous husband parked before her door, whose only aim was to conceal her from my gaze.
He saw me passing by in vain; and then he threatened her and thrashed her cruelly.
And yet I often tarried on her cushions, the while I offered up my relatives in ransom for her, all the more to charm.
I thus cajoled her so she would believe me, being both sincere and insincere to her.

But now I'll leave this subject. Let me speak, instead, of pressing needs I sought to satisfy
With Umm al-Banīn, whose longing for me caused her to draw near.
She came to visit me in sleep; this poem I said, the time I was given her in dreams.
When I enjoyed her and her mouth, the sweetest part of her, inclined toward me,
I sipped the liquor of her lips until I'd taken an initial draught, and then I whiled away the night by giving her the liquor of my lips to drink.
I spent the night in highest spirits, bedded down with her, while she delighted me and I delighted her;
I caused her to both laugh and cry; I covered and uncovered her;
I felt her flesh until she made me swoon; I caused her satisfaction and I angered her.
Oh, what a night was that, if only in my sleep, when I conversed and played with her!

Announcing soon the prayer of dawn, a muezzin, its arrival waiting long, finally awoke me,
And then the image of my dreams, just like some female *jinn,* made off for sites unknown;
She kept me wide awake the while I slept, but now the place to which she sped is far removed from me.

When serious words are spoken, Muṣʿab[46] has far more than they, and far more sweet.
He puts them into execution using flags, whose cohorts block the mountain breach.
When enemy detachments and their troops emerge upon a hill,
With God's support he overcomes, exhausts, and conquers them,
And makes them burst in flame with but two hands, when all the stars, that are their spear-tips, shine for you to see.[47]

The poem is divided into four sections: (1) a traditional amatory prelude in which the poet complains that he has been ridiculed, because of his lost youth, by an unnamed damsel of the tribe of Quraysh; (2) a passage in which he recalls a past adventure with a married lady, the tone of which is a triumphantly malicious response to the Qurayshī damsel's ridicule; (3) the dream-seduction of Umm al-Banīn, which is a satire directed against the Umayyad caliph ʿAbd al-Malik; (4) a panegyric of Muṣʿab, the Zubayrid governor of Iraq, who was at the time challenging the authority of the Umayyads. The underlying implications of the poem are therefore straightforwardly political.

It appears that love lyrics dedicated by poets to other men's women, in which the women are praised while the men are not always, or necessarily, satirized, came to be perceived as a potential form of satire, albeit indirect. It is in this context that the following incident, reported about the Andalusī poet Abū ʿĀmir b. Shuhayd (382–427/992–1035), may be understood:

> The poet used to sit with his friends at the portal of the Great Mosque of Córdoba next to the minaret. Behold, there was a daughter of one of the notables of Córdoba, accompanied by slave girls who veiled and concealed her. And she sought a place for private converse with her Lord, desiring a spot where she might beseech pardon for her sins. She was veiled to prevent her being observed, and was alert against that possibility, while before her went a child of hers. So when her eye fell upon Abū ʿĀmir, she turned

> away hurriedly and went off in distress, fearing lest he be inspired by her and divulge her name. So when he saw her, he improvised these lines of poetry, wherein he dishonored her and made her notorious:
>
> I remember a woman looking out from under the fold of her veil,
> whom a caller summoned to God and to good.
> She advanced with her child, seeking a place in which to be joined
> to piety and devotion.
> Thus she walked proudly like a gazelle fondling its young, expressing concern for a gazelle in the height of youth.
> She came to us walking with a stately gait, yet she alighted in a valley full of lions.
> She grew frightened from concern for her little one, so I called
> out: "You there, do not be afraid!"
> Immediately she turned away, and the musk from her hem left
> upon the ground a trail like the back of a serpent.[48]

In Ibn Shuhayd's *Risālat al-Tawābiʿ wal-zawābiʿ*, the above poem is introduced as a "scandalous" or "obscene" (*mujūn*) piece of poetry. Since there is nothing inherently obscene in the poem itself, the obscenity must be taken to reside in the poet's intention to provoke scandal by dishonoring the lady, thereby shaming her menfolk.[49] This custom must have been common in Andalus, where we are told that the poet Ibn Ṣāra al-Shantarīnī (d. 517/1123)

> was madly in love with well-guarded females, made them notorious, and used them as barbs which he hurled, in the form of insults concocted against the grandees of his time with which he stigmatized the pride of their reputations, leaving them as a warning example to their descendants. . . . I have seen many pieces by him on *hijāʾ*, so numerous that they exceed the number of pebbles on the desert plain for, in [that genre], his arrow is accurate and his judgment effective. But I have [generally] kept them to myself and ignored them—even if I have very infrequently alluded to them—so that you may observe and be informed, for had I deemed it permissible for part of what he wrote in this genre to be recorded in this book, you would have realized that such of his compositions are an entirely covert, indirect insult and a defamatory thunderbolt. I have included a vast amount of [such poems], composed both by him and

by a large group [of other poets], in my book entitled *Dhakhīrat al-dhakhīra.*[50]

The technique of compromising a man's honor by composing love poems to his womenfolk is very ancient in the shame-oriented cultures of the Mediterranean, as may be concluded from the story (whether true or not, it was universally known in antiquity) of the Greek poet Archilochus, who was born in the first half of the seventh century B.C., and Neobulé, daughter of Lycambes and Amphimedo. Archilochus was engaged to be married to Neobulé, but when her father broke off the engagement, the disgrace produced by the satirical iambs Archilochus composed drove either Lycambes or, according to another version, his daughters, to suicide.[51] The surviving poetry of Archilochus is frustratingly fragmentary, but in 1974 a relatively long poem, discovered on a papyrus mummy-wrapping some ten years earlier, was first published. In this poem, the poet introduces the figure of Neobulé's younger sister, who declares her love for him. Taking advantage of the situation, the poet suggests to her that they engage in an act of sex and, after making several disparaging remarks about Neobulé, provides the reader with a detailed account of how he seduced her all-too-willing younger sibling:

[. . . . .]
Back away from that, [she said]
and steady on [.]
Wayward and wildly pounding heart,
There is a girl who lives among us
Who watches you with foolish eyes.

A slender, lovely, graceful girl,
Just budding into supple line,
And you scare her and make her shy.

O daughter of the highborn Amphimedo,
I replied, of the widely remembered
Amphimedo now in the rich earth dead,

There are, do you know, so many pleasures
For young men to choose from
Among the skills of the delicious goddess,

It's green to think the holy one's the only
When the shadows go black and quiet,
Let us, you and I alone, and the gods,

Sort these matters out. Fear nothing:
I shall be tame, I shall behave
And reach, if I reach, with a civil hand.

I shall climb the wall and come to the gate.
You'll not say no, Sweetheart, to this?
I shall come no farther than the garden grass.

Neobulé I have forgotten, believe me, do.
Any man who wants her may have her.
Aiai! She's past her day, ripening rotten.

The petals of her flower are all brown.
The grace that first she had is shot.
Don't you agree that she looks like a boy?

A woman like that would drive a man crazy.
She should get herself a job as a scarecrow.
I'd as soon hump her as [kiss a goat's butt].

A source of joy I'd be to the neighbors
With such a woman as her for a wife!
How could I ever prefer her to you?

You, O innocent, true heart and bold.
Each of her faces is as sharp as the other,
Which way she's turning you never can guess.

She'd whelp like the proverb's luckless bitch
Were I to foster get upon her, throwing
Them blind, and all on the wrongest day.

I said no more, but took her hand
Laid her down in a thousand flowers,
And put my soft wool cloak around her.

I slid my arm under her neck
To still the fear in her eyes,
For she was trembling like a fawn,

Touched her hot breasts with light fingers,
Spraddled her neatly and pressed
Against her fine, hard, bared crotch.

I caressed the beauty of her body
And came in a sudden white spurt
While I was stroking her hair.[52]

Let us add that according to the traditions of Provençal love poetry of an idealized nature it was conventional for the lady addressed by the poet to be married to another man. Such an arrangement, within a religious context that, being Christian, did not permit divorce, guaranteed that the poet's erotic aspirations would be suitably hopeless and therefore pure. But when the Provençal tradition was introduced to Christian Spain, the requirement that the beloved be previously married was the first to be eliminated. Either because of an as yet unstudied Arab influence, or because of a shared, pan-Mediterranean ethos, Christian Spaniards sided with their traditional Muslim Arab antagonists in being outraged at the thought of another man praising their wives.[53]

A further dimension, necessary to our understanding of Ibn Quzmān's *Zajal No. 133,* is that Arabic love poetry includes a sizable corpus of poems written by male poets in celebration of the charms of boys. This tradition was evidently introduced to Arabic literature during the ʿAbbāsid period by poets such as al-Ḥasan b. Hāniʾ, better known by the nickname of Abū Nuwās ("The Kiss-Curled One" [d. ca. 195/810]). Here is one of his poems on the subject:

Hey, pour me some wine, and let me know it is wine; don't pour in secret when it can be done openly!
A pleasant life consists in getting drunk time after time; if this goes on for a long time, then time will become too short.
It is a disadvantage to find me sober; the advantage lies in drunkenness that staggers me.
Reveal the name of the one you love; spare me the use of pseudonyms, for there is no good in veiled pleasures,

Nor is there any good in disorderly conduct without debauchery, nor in depravity without blasphemy,
That is enjoyed in the company of every roisterer, whose brow is bright as a crescent moon surrounded by shining stars.
I remember a tavern maid whom I awakened as she was snoozing, when Gemini had set and Aquila had risen.
She asked: "Who's knocking at this time of night?" We answered: "A gang lightened of their wineskins; in need of wine,
Who want to screw a woman!" She added: "Or to be satisfied by a boy bright as a gold coin, with languor in his glance?"
Then we said to her: "Hand him over; the likes of us cannot restrain ourselves from such as he—may we ransom you with our relatives!"
So she produced him, like the full moon in its final phase, such that you would think him to be enchantment itself, although he was for real.
We got on him, one after another, and with him we broke the fast of our abstinence.
We spent the night, while God watched us: a most evil crowd, trailing the robes of depravity, and that is no boast![54]

In turn, Abū Nuwās was greatly admired by Ibn Quzmān, who alludes to and imitates him in several of his *zajals*. In *Zajal No. 123,* for example, the poet specifically declares his preference for the licentious poetry of al-Ḥasan b. Hāni', that is to say, Abū Nuwās, over the chaste love of the seventh-century ʿUdhrī poets ʿUrwa b. Hizām (d. 30/650) and Jamīl. He then proceeds to illustrate a typically Nuwāsian technique of seduction, which involves getting the beloved so drunk that he is unable to resist the lover's advances:

0. *I'm my time's lover and heedless of anger:*
Censor, you bore me;
Listen I'll not, any longer!

1. Passion's transformed me: I'm thin and I'm yellow;
Look, my complexion is altered and sallow;
Yet I'm still crying "Alas," my dark fellow!
See how my robe holds no body's remainder?
You can't behold me:
Hear then a constant bewailer!

2. Truly, in love I am deeply impassioned!
Proof of this fact is my state, now you're rationed;
Also this song that's so skillfully fashioned.
Clever by nature, I'm poetry's unsheather:
Tongue's sword before me,
Armor won't be its defeater!

3. ʿUrwa's pure love, with Jamīl's I've forgotten;
Better's the license of Ḥasan besotten;
Ask one believing true love's misbegotten:
"Say, you who honor, than Ḥātim,[55] one grander,
What kind's your whoring,
Mocked in all lands as you wander?"

4. Lose all restraint chasing boys who are beardless!
If your love's waistband is fastened, be tearless:
Pour him a drink; pour another; be fearless.
Offer the largest of cups. If still sober,
Seconds then pour him:
Watch him, a lion, keel over!

5. After my lover much wine had been drinking,
During a party he drank himself stinking;
Raising his head, I poured more without blinking;
Eager, he drank it, and then he rolled over:
Fair game he's for me,
Now that he's soused and a dozer![56]

In light of the tradition we have considered, Ibn Quzmān's *Zajal No. 133* begins to make sense in more ways than one. By naming the father, Abū Bakr, yet refraining from making any disparaging comments about him while describing the erotic charms of his son, who is simultaneously being portrayed as a flirt, Ibn Quzmān has joined in unholy matrimony the Umayyad genre of love poetry, composed about women in order to satirize their men, with the genre of Abū Nuwās, composed to extol the delights of boys. By telling Abū Bakr that his son is a charmer who aims to seduce men, he is in effect both provoking and attempting to shame the father. Therefore, on one level at least, this *zajal* represents a special form of the genre *hijāʾ*, insofar as its immediate aim is invective.

Van Gelder notes that "one of the differences between ʿAbbāsid and earlier poetry is the far greater amount, in ʿAbbāsid times, of light-hearted *hijā*ʾ, humorous epigrams, coarse jokes instead of angry invective,"[57] adding that "mock panegyric, mock love-poetry or mock elegies turn into satire or invective."[58] He also claims that "great masters of invective that bear comparison with Jarīr or Ibn al-Rūmī are not to be found in al-Andalus."[59] Certainly, if we consider that Ibn Quzmān was satirizing an Almoravid prince, that is to say a member of the ruling Berber ethnicity, we are entitled to assume that he could not have gotten away with this strategy if his invective had been perceived as anything other than playful. His approach appears to be what the Arab rhetoricians dubbed *taʾkīd al-dhamm bimā yushbih al-madḥ* ("emphasizing blame through what resembles praise").[60] Yet were the underlying blame perceived as virulent, the poet might have found himself deep in hot water.

At this point in our analysis, a face-saving deconstruction of the satire contained in the poem, of the sort that can only be performed by a ritual clown, is called for, and this is precisely what Ibn Quzmān sets out to provide. By portraying himself as one hopelessly smitten with the boy's charms and madly in love with him, he is saying that he is no better (but, as we shall see below, possibly worse) than Abū Bakr's son, morally speaking, and therefore the implied invective, coming as it does from the mouth of a fool, becomes harmless and ineffective; it becomes the sort of invective that a man of princely status can well afford to ignore. In this way, the invective directed against Abū Bakr at the expense of his son's reputation becomes the poet's self-satire, insofar as he portrays himself as one who is caught on his own hook. As a result, it becomes apparent that all the multileveled about-faces in the poem are integral parts of its structure. The poet begins by asking why he should waste his life on a beloved who avoids him. Instead, he will choose one who will be compliant. On second thought, he reconsiders, such an approach is hardly possible because in real life no beloved is ever compliant. Therefore, he will choose an unattainable beloved, namely Abū Bakr's son; that is to say, he will, after all, waste his life on a beloved who avoids him. Given the Arabic tradition of *hijā*ʾ examined above, the poet's expression of his love is, on a secondary level, a form of invective against Abū Bakr and therefore the poem is a satire. But insofar as it is a satire composed by a fool, that is to say by one who ends up doing precisely what he had expressly set out not to do, on a third level, it is presented as entirely ineffective.[61] The fool may not be taken to task for the product of his foolishness only if he is really a fool. In its endless deconstructive complexities, therefore, this *zajal* has its own enduring literary beauty. It has survived long after the precise identity of Abū Bakr and his son have been forgotten.

Through his many contradictions, the poet thus points to his art as a monument to the beauty, endurance, and power of words, which have made the charms of Abū Bakr's son, as well as his father's shame, notoriously immortal.

The Poet as Pederast

In medieval Christian terminology, the word *sodomy* was applied to all those forms of sexual intercourse that precluded the production of offspring, often but not exclusively between two men or between a human being and an animal. Sodomy was further characterized by the Church as a *vitium* or *peccatum contra naturam* (a "vice" or "sin against nature"). Let us note that the Latin word *vitium* means a "fault" or "defect," be it physical or moral, and that it therefore implies a failure to live up to a socially admired norm. *Natura* ("the qualities with which one is born," "nature") is, in turn, a future participle of the Latin verb *nascor,* "to be born," and designates that particular combination of qualities belonging to a person by birth. In contemporary jargon, we might therefore venture to translate the phrase *vitium contra naturam* as a "defect that runs contrary to the genetically programmed instincts with which one is born." Such a definition implies that the sodomite is an *abnormal, pathological* individual. His disease needs curing; failing that, steps (often radical) must be taken to neutralize his effect (which is considered negative) on *normal, healthy* society. The term *sodomy* includes, but is by no means restricted to, homosexual behavior.

In contrast, the term *homosexuality* is a Græco-Latin linguistic bastard of nineteenth-century creation, used to designate a condition, also deemed pathological by the modern medical profession that coined the term, in which sexual desire or behavior is directed toward a person of one's own sex.[62] Thus sodomy may, but need not necessarily be, homosexual, whereas homosexuality must always be sodomitic. Put differently, homosexuality is a subcategory of sodomy, not its equivalent.

Within the limited context and scope of this study, which is not about homoeroticism per se but about a poem, the categories described above are far too deeply entrenched in Western culture, and far too familiar to Western scholars, to need further explanation. What may possibly be less well known is that traditional Islamic teachings and beliefs concerning sexuality are based on an entirely different set of assumptions about the individual.[63]

In Modern Standard Arabic, the term for a homosexual is *shādhdh jinsī* ("sexual deviant"), of which the component *shādhdh* means, among other things, "isolated, separated, irregular, abnormal, queer, peculiar, exceptional." This term is a learned one; it was artificially coined to express a concept borrowed from Western medicine and is not generally understood by the uneducated majority. In contrast to Modern Standard Arabic, the Classical Arabic language, which reigned supreme as the vehicle of culture until very recent times, has no precise word for *homosexual.* When a word does not exist in a given language, we may safely assume that the concept it denotes does not exist in the culture that speaks and writes that language. Keeping in mind that our discussion deals with culturally specific perceptions, categorizations, and value systems applied to otherwise universal acts, and not with those acts themselves, we can state categorically that there were no homosexuals in premodern Arabic civilization and that as a consequence there were no heterosexuals or bisexuals in it either, simply because the concepts did not exist. In approaching Ibn Quzmān's poem, we must therefore cleanse our minds of our own culturally conditioned preconceptions.

There does exist, however, a Classical Arabic term equivalent to the word *sodomy,* namely *liwāṭ*. This word seems to be a back-formation based on the name of the prophet Lūṭ ("Lot"), whose dealings with the inhabitants of Sodom are repeatedly mentioned in the Qur'ān. In the legal sources, *liwāṭ* is defined as *ʿamal qawm Lūṭ* ("the act of the people of Lot"). Conventional jurisprudence distinguishes between two types of *liwāṭ*. *Al-liwāṭ al-akbar* ("grand sodomy") is described as that which takes place between two adult males (*rijāl*). As we shall see below, this term is ambiguously applicable to pubescent boys. Theoretically, grand sodomy is punishable by the death of both participants, in accordance with a *ḥadīth,* dubiously attributable to the Prophet, that declares: "Whomsoever you find committing the act of the people of Lot, kill both the active and the passive partner."[64] *Al-liwāṭ al-asghar* ("petty sodomy") is usually understood as anal intercourse between a man and a woman. This practice is allowed by the Shīʿites but forbidden by all the Sunnī schools of jurisprudence, with the notable exception of the Mālikīs, who permit it, conditional upon the woman's consent.[65] From the above clarifications, it is apparent that the term *liwāṭ* may cover some but not all homosexual or heterosexual activities, and that it cannot therefore be equated exclusively with homosexuality, for which there is no precise term in the Classical Arabic language.

In sharp contrast to Christianity, which considers homosexuality to be a pathological character defect and homosexuals to be abnormal, perverted individuals, Islamic jurisprudence adopts a more restrained attitude, according to which attraction toward members of one's own sex[66] is viewed as entirely normal and natural. Thus, the Ḥanbalite jurist Ibn al-Jawzī (d. 597/1200) is quoted as having expressed the opinion that "He who claims that he experiences no desire when looking at beautiful boys or youth[s], is a liar, and if we could believe him, he would be an animal, not a human being."[67] In this respect, it should be indicated that the mystics of Islam included among their meditative practices the contemplation of beautiful pubescent boys, who were considered witnesses "to the beauty of God and the glory of His creation."[68] For the Ṣūfīs, we may thus conclude, boyishness was next to godliness. In his *Epistle of Singing Girls,* al-Jāḥiẓ (d. 256/869), who otherwise shows little sympathy for grand sodomy, discusses passion between male and female, which he declares to be an instinct natural to the animal world. He then adds: "If this passion (*ʿishq*) is felt by a male for a male, it is only derivative from this fundamental carnal instinct. [Yet passion between two males produces the same symptoms as true *ʿishq*.] Otherwise it could not be called passion when the carnal instinct is absent."[69]

But just because Islamic law views mutual attraction between males to be *natural* does not mean that it considers homosexual acts between them to be *appropriate.* On the contrary, such acts are punishable by the death of both partners if either (1) the transgressors confess to having committed the deed (in which case they are given three chances to retract their confession), or (2) four reputable witnesses can be found, all of whom have personally seen the act of penetration take place. But since neither of these two requirements is easy to satisfy, the penalty prescribed in theory often remains inapplicable in practice.

Thus, as is the case with crimes such as *zinā*ʾ (fornication), wine drinking, and theft, erotic attraction between males is viewed as a natural temptation to which the religious law forbids the believer to yield and for which it prescribes the specific and severe penalty of death. Grand sodomy, like fornication, wine drinking, and theft, is in Islamic law a crime against religion, as opposed to a crime between individuals, such as homicide.[70] Within these parameters, the person committing an act of grand sodomy may personally feel the guilt incurred by a sinner or a criminal, but unlike his Christian counterpart he need not necessarily feel that he is an abnormal or perverted individual. Indeed, he may even be inclined to boast about his homoerotic exploits, just as the fornicator or adulterer may boast about his heterosexual conquests before an approving audience of confidants.

In this area, Islamic jurisprudence was concerned exclusively with acts rather than preferences, proclivities, tendencies, or personalities. Individuals may commit acts of sodomy, but not necessarily because of an inherently sodomitic nature. Since same-sex attraction is viewed as natural, surrendering to a natural temptation cannot make the individual abnormal—merely sinful. Hence, within the restricted limits of discussion set by Islamic law, there was no room for the emergence or delineation of a homosexual personality per se. As a result, in the vast corpus of licentious poetry produced by medieval Arabic writers that triad of sins constituted by fornication, pederasty, and wine drinking tends to be interconnected, in the sense that the same poet will frequently boast, occasionally within the very same poem, of having committed all three activities.[71] In *Zajal No. 133,* Ibn Quzmān extols wine drinking and pederasty, leaving fornication to other poems, where it is often combined with the former two sins to make no sense in realistic terms: a roaring drunk, too intoxicated to walk a straight line, portrays himself as alternately seducing women and boys. If he were heterosexual in modern, Western terms, he would not be attracted to boys; if he were homosexual, he would not be attracted to girls. In either case, his ability to perform sexually would, no doubt, be severely limited by the claimed frequency and intensity of his libations. Therefore, we should not take this particular genre of poetry more literally than any other. Authors such as Abū Nuwās and Ibn Quzmān, had we accused them of composing homosexual poetry, would simply not have understood the nature of our accusation and would have responded by pointing to their poems dealing with equally illicit, if heterosexual, escapades and even anacreontic themes; for to them, it was the *illicit* nature of the escapades they extolled that mattered, not their gender-specific orientation. Moreover, since homoerotic attraction was viewed as perfectly natural by medieval Islamic society (as adulterous attraction is viewed as natural by ours), the forms of repression, internalized guilt, and bids for freedom that characterize homosexuality in modern European and American societies could not and did not develop.

Human sexuality is a complex phenomenon, the full nature and true underlying causes of which are so poorly understood that one may easily imagine future, more enlightened generations looking back upon our crude attempts to understand and legislate it with the same incomprehension we feel when looking back upon the claims of humoral pathology and Aristotelian psychology. With many gross oversimplifications, what has been described above are the main features of a system constructed by medieval Islamic jurists to deal with one aspect of human sexuality, namely the homoerotic. As with all systems, it is a production of the feeble human mind; a theory erected to control a more-often-than-not stubbornly recalcitrant reality. In this specific instance, the reality represented by the homoerotic experience of Islamic societies was somewhat different from the theory, and it shared with classical antiquity[72] many ideas that, despite Islam and Christianity and possibly because of human nature, have survived to the present day in several Mediterranean societies.

Pan-Mediterranean beliefs about sexuality are based upon the premise that the male is sexually empowered, by nature, if not by divine rights, to dominate the female absolutely. This concept is currently expressed by the pseudo-Spanish term *machismo*[73] and requires the male's constant and unquestioned penetration of the submissive female. The adult male is therefore idealized par excellence in the popular imagination of Mediterranean peoples as a Penetrator. Mediterranean societies also draw a sharp demarcation between private and public life that may not be crossed without serious consequences. In terms of sexuality, this means that there are two categories of women: those inhabiting his private domain (his mother, sisters, cousins, wives, daughters, etc.) whom the Penetrator is expected to protect against other males, all of whom are potentially predatory, failure to do so earning him undivided scorn; and the mothers, sisters, cousins, wives, daughters, etc. of other males, all of whom are potential fair game for the Penetrator's own predatory instincts. Underlying this antagonistic and jungle-like system is a certain logic, inspired by the spirit of competition for honor among males: he who gets the most women is the dominant Penetrator and therefore the highest on the phallic totem pole. Within such a system, it is inevitable that women who have no one to protect them will end up in the public domain, as prostitutes available to all potential penetrators. The Penetrator will perceive no double standard in jealously guarding his own women while at the same time subjecting all others' women to his own penetration, to the full extent of his abilities.

Once the male role is perceived as that of one competing for sexual dominance, as an aspirant to the title of Supreme Penetrator, the nature or gender of the object of penetration soon becomes secondary. Since real *machos* are respected by their peers for being systematic penetrators and lose all respectability if they ever manifest the slightest inclination to being penetrated, a second double standard is established: in male-to-male sexual encounters, it is honorable to penetrate and an unmentionable disgrace to be penetrated. Thus a new dichotomy arises: that of the honorable Penetrator, who may and often does boast of his exploits to admiring inner circles, and the dishonorable penetrated one, who is required to conceal his unmentionable role on pain of public infamy. Sometimes the Penetrator will rape a defenseless enemy or subordinate in order to humiliate him, whereupon the victim will plot his revenge, sometimes with devastating consequences.[74]

In Arabic, the active partner is called *lūṭī* and the passive, *ma'būn*. While both are, from a legal point of view, sinners against the religious law, the *ma'būn* is considered the more shameful partner from the angle of public opinion. Since a man is admired for being a Penetrator, the act of being penetrated robs him, ipso facto, of his virility. Within this system of values, pubescent boys occupy an ambiguous position: not being adult males, they are not yet virile; therefore, penetration cannot rob them of manliness. This is the rationalization underlying sexual relationships between adult males and boys, descriptions of which abound in Arabic as in Greek literature. Sexual acts are universal in nature, only limited by the anatomical, gymnastic, and imaginative abilities of the species; however, the position they hold within the value system of any given society is culture-specific. What was viewed by both ancient Greeks and medieval Arabs as a perfectly normal kind of relationship was for Edwardians "the unspeakable vice of the Greeks"[75] and is for us, at the close of the twentieth century, a particularly reprehensible form of child molestation.[76]

A further complication, of dramatic relevance to the poem under analysis, is that if a boy is sodomized by an older male the ensuing disgrace reflects upon his family and particularly upon his father or its other male members. This point is eloquently made in a tragic story by the late Egyptian writer, Yahya Taher Abdullah, entitled "The Free-for-All Dance":[77]

> Isma'il Ab Ali is the caretaker of Hajj Abdul Kareem Mohammed Abdullah's orchard. One day, he catches two boys committing sodomy in it. The larger boy manages to climb over the wall that encloses the orchard. The smaller one is unable to do so and conceals himself within it. Isma'il, who is a drug addict and a hypocrite, is outraged by the monstrosity of the sin he has witnessed and swears to catch the smaller boy, in order to teach him a lesson by sodomizing the boy himself. At that very moment, the worshipers are coming out of the mosque, having completed their evening prayer. Isma'il persuades the boy to come out of hiding by promising that he will not be hurt, and opens the orchard gate that leads to the street through which the congregation is passing as it leaves the mosque. When the all-too-trusting boy comes out of hiding, Isma'il announces the boy's sin publicly to the passersby. The boy is immediately identified as the son of Shahhat who, being in the crowd, first

> rends his garments and shrieks in extreme pain. His second reaction is to ask his son whether he has played the active or the passive role. When the son replies that he was the active partner, he is disbelieved by his father (the precise nature of the sexual role adopted by either boy is never explicitly established within the story). After having extracted the information that the other boy involved was Mustafa, son of Fikri al-Kour, Shahhat drowns his son by throwing him into a well, in order to restore his paternal honor. In light of Shahhat's supreme sacrifice, Fikri al-Kour feels exposed to public infamy. The Hajj Abdul Kareem Mohammed Abdullah, owner of the orchard, is asked to judge between the two fathers and decrees that Fikri's son Mustafa is to be forever banished from the village. Although Fikri knows that without village ties, his son will die honorless "like a gypsy," he realizes that he cannot battle against an entire village and accepts the Hajj's judgment, thereby swallowing his pride. That night, Isma'il has dark thoughts. They instruct him to search out Mustafa and kill him in order to restore Fikri's honor. However, he abandons such thoughts and falls asleep.

The above story is far more complex than this summary could possibly hope to convey; nevertheless, it makes clear that, in Arab society, sodomizing a boy is perceived as an immediate and direct affront to his father, whose honor can only be restored by the death of the offending son.

In Arabic literature the homoerotic relationship almost invariably takes place between an adult male and a pubescent boy and is therefore pederastic. To emphasize this fact, it is even a poetic *topos* to declare that the first appearance of the boy's beard (which, in all those cultures featuring at least two sexes, represents the attainment of sexual virility) is a harbinger of forthcoming separation between the two partners in the relationship. Even when this convention is violated, as in the following example, the violation itself implies a norm:

> With his pure golden complexion, he almost make the clouds weep;
> But he felt ill at ease with his first beard, like a colt which has never known the bridle.
> And when he saw me he hung down his head, disconsolate, and was wrapped in shame.
> For he was thinking that his new beard would make my love for him disappear,

> But I see his bearded cheeks as sword belts from which hangs the saber of his glance.[78]

As we consider *Zajal No. 133* further in light of the above remarks, it will be helpful to note that in many literary traditions, including that of the Arabs, the image of riding or mounting on horseback is a metaphor for sexual intercourse.[79] In the poem we are considering, it is Abū Bakr's son who is specifically portrayed as mounting a horse, whereas the poet, who is peering up the boy's legs, must be on foot. Perhaps it is not too far-fetched to assume that in the sexual union with the boy to which the poet aspires, it is the boy who will perform the socially honorable function of being the rider (i.e., the *lūṭī*), whereas the poet will adopt the shameful role of the ridden *maʾbūn*. If this is what the poet is hinting at, then he has inverted traditional sexual roles: the poet, an adult male, is expressing his desire to be penetrated by a boy. In so doing, the poet is presenting himself as an object of derision; as one who surrenders all pretension to respectability in society. He is a sexual laughingstock, a buffoon, and an effeminate (*mukhannath*). In medieval Islamic society, the effeminate publicly avowed his role as a passive sexual partner, in return for which he was granted tolerance as a distinct inferior and was allowed to conduct his affairs outside the pale of social respectability. He was, furthermore, often a member of the entertainment industry. The same was not the case for the *maʾbūn,* who was usually married and who attempted (unsuccessfully) to pass himself off as a Penetrator, and thus posed a perceived threat to the integrity of the adult male insofar as the latter was idealized by society as a Penetrator par excellence.[80]

In Mediterranean societies, the Penetrator is viewed as a normal individual, regardless of the gender of the person he penetrates. Such is not the case with the penetrated, who is considered pathological but can in some instances be successfully cured, as follows:

> One possible treatment consists in strengthening the penis and testicles by gently descending them. The most suitable person to perform this operation for the patient would be a pretty, young, hot-blooded servant-girl. Her infectious eagerness will render the massage she gives all the more efficacious. Between such massages, the patient should thoroughly and completely rub down his whole lower abdomen and genitals with Egyptian willow oil in which horehounḍ and musk-mallow leaves, or a little Persian asafetida, have been previously steeped. He should take especial care to oil his penis well with this mixture and should not hesitate to insert a

> little of it into the urinary canal. The preparation should be allowed to sink into the tissues for a moment, and then he should take a good bath, seated in a tub of really hot water, in the course of which he should once more vigorously massage his penis and testicles. Once a week he should soak his genitals in pine-resin gum diluted with hot water. That's one of the surest-acting medicines I know of for this kind of treatment. If, during the course of treatment, the patient begins to feel the slightest sexual excitation, if his testicles begin to descend, or if he starts to get an erection at the same time as his sexual appetite awakens, that's a sure sign that the method being used is the right one. But the patient must be very careful to follow all the above instructions without exception, and for the prescribed period of time, without the slightest interruption—that is, to repeat, he must be conscientiously massaged by good-looking young servant girls; then, he must rub himself down with the ointments mentioned, and then with the resin.
>
> Besides doing this, he should at the same time attempt to alleviate the burning sensation in his intestines, his buttocks and his anus—this is just as important. This can be achieved by sitting as often as possible on a floor that has been sprinkled with cold water, or by spreading a cloth previously dipped in ice water over the affected area, while at the same time keeping the genitals warm, by wrapping them up, for example in the folds of a long, loose shirt. A possible supplement to this course of treatment is enemas with rosewater inspissated by heating and laced with vinegar, warmed up to the point of complete dissolution, or, in lieu of that, simply a solution of rosewater and vinegar. If the patient wishes to keep his intestines good and cool and at the same time retain the heat that is advisable for his genitals, he should follow this regimen faithfully, for it's one of the most effective.
>
> One last important point. Experience demonstrates that nothing is more harmful to the patient than prolonged abstinence from sexual intercourse with women. He should therefore do his best to have sexual relations as often as possible. These are, in short, the most direct ways we possess of treating the disease of sexual inversion, by means of legitimate medical procedures.[81]

It seems a mysterious paradox that those three specific activities—wine drinking, fornication, and pederasty—the practicing of which, on this earth, is hardly recommended in the Qur'ān,[82] are assigned a legitimate place in the Islamic paradise. Nor should we forget that these three activities constitute the three major themes of Arabic licentious poetry. The semantics of wine, along with its connections to fornication and pederasty, have been carefully studied in a recent article by Suzanne Pinckney Stetkevych, which is reprinted in this collection.[83] The author points out that, given the river of wine that flows through Paradise, the Qur'ānic prohibition of wine drinking in this world requires some explanation. She then argues that in those scriptural passages where wine is forbidden, it is normally associated with pagan rituals alluded to in pre-Islamic Arabic poetry. Since the Prophet was at some pains to disassociate his new religion from such pagan practices, wine drinking was inevitably proscribed. Furthermore, just like the waters of the river Kawthar that flows through the eternal Garden, the river of wine in Paradise bestowed immortality on those who drank of it. The cupbearer, who is ever-present at drinking parties in Arabic poetry and is also to be found in Paradise, is a symbol of immortality that Stetkevych relates to certain prominent symbols of the Dionysiac cult. She also indicates that the youthful cupbearer, be he the Greek Ganymede,[84] who is the aging Zeus's wine pourer as well as his catamite, or the equally ambivalent *sāqī* of Arabic poetry, who is both cupbearer and sex object, is not only an eternal youth but also a bestower of immortality.[85] His Qur'ānic counterparts, the *wildān mukhalladūn* ("immortal youths") who minister to the inhabitants of the Garden of Paradise,[86] are not merely immortal themselves; they also confer immortality upon the blessed. Stetkevych concludes:

> In this world, man is obligated to perpetuate himself by sexual reproduction; this is precisely what is meant by the Islamic prohibition of monkery. Licit sex is that which is sanctioned by marriage for the express purpose of propagation of the species. Illicit sex is that which for social and biological reasons is nonproductive. In the afterlife, however, immortality renders reproduction redundant. This too is the logic behind the Islamic absolute denial of offspring to Allah: paternity and immortality are incompatible. However, that which is illicit on earth because it distracts the mortal from his obligation is unobjectionable in the Garden. The delights of the Garden are thus the immature and carefree—or even as Freud put it, "perverse, polymorphous"—ones of youth.[87]

In claiming to represent absolute truth, the Qur'ān views most poets as being the spokesmen for relative untruth: "As for poets, the erring follow them. Do you not see that they wander in every valley *and say what they do not do?*"[88] The holy text does, however, provide one exception to its general condemnation of poets: "those who believe, work righteousness, engage much in the remembrance of God, and defend themselves only after they are unjustly attacked."[89] Thus the themes of wine drinking, fornication, and pederasty that pervade the poetry of licentious authors such as Abū Nuwās and Ibn Quzmān represent an act of rebellion against established authority. At the same time, such a rebellion, insofar as it is portrayed as ultimately unsuccessful, recognizes by implication the legitimacy of the very authority it seeks to challenge. Whereas in pre-Islamic times, as the mouthpiece and champion of its value system, the poet enjoyed a central position in society, he has now become a marginalized "half-outsider."[90] Displaced by the authority of the revealed text, he can neither subscribe wholeheartedly to its teachings nor survive entirely without them. By couching his rebellion in the form of a pseudo-panegyric that is, in reality, a satire against a member of the ruling class, the voice speaking in Ibn Quzmān's poem carries its rebellion one step closer to total anarchy, attempting through subversion of the genre to disrupt the entire social order. However, the speaker's program is presented from the very outset as unsuccessful. He is doomed to failure in his attempt to win the boy's favors because of his prudent, pusillanimous, and decidedly unheroic fear of Abū Bakr, if for no other reason. Thus it may be concluded that the speaker's anarchic program is being presented ironically, as one of which the implied author heartily disapproves. In this sense, Ibn Quzmān's *Zajal No. 133* seems to validate the eternal truth contained in the Qur'ān, to be far less licentious than a preliminary reading might suggest. Paradoxically, licentiousness, insofar as it is presented as being unsuccessful, may in certain cases have the ritual function of reaffirming the very values it seems to flout.

A further step in the arguments I have suggested could be formulated as follows. A mock panegyric, such as *Zajal No. 133,* has the potential to become a satire (as pointed out by Wright elsewhere in this volume). But if, as in this case, the satire is also undercut, what does it become?—a mock satire with the potential to become a true panegyric? Since that panegyric is also undercut, the poem becomes a satire that is a panegyric that is a satire that is a panegyric that is a satire that is a panegyric, with no amen. Thus the poet has found a unique way to circumscribe his patron with a vicious circle from which he cannot escape and within which he is rendered utterly neutral and helpless. The poem is therefore an instrument for patronly entrapment: having been roundly insulted, the patron must now graciously pay the poet for his efforts while secretly remaining thankful that matters have gone no further. In this sense, the poem illustrates the poet's superiority over the patron, based upon the poet's unique mastery of words. But when a superior poet praises an inferior patron, the genre of panegyric has been totally subverted.

Verse Adaptation

0. *Who invites me to waste all my days*
On the fair who deem just their delays?

1. Should I love one who's always defiant?
Just forget it! I'll take one compliant;
One who pours when I drink, and is pliant,
What beloved would be [uncompliant]?
I'll embrace him all night in our frays,
And remain with him thus all my days.

2. Don't believe the above—it's absurd!
Of a union like that, no one's heard;
It is merely what men have averred,
For alone in [their dreams] it's occurred.
Only happens when one's in a daze;
When awake, I have known no such ways.

3. Let me love a young lad sugar-sweet.
Who? The son of [Bū] Bakar 'gellīd!
His mouth's scent can no ambergris beat,
While his teeth with strung seed pearls compete.
Hence, as "ambrous" his mouth I will praise,
And as "pearly" his teeth I'll appraise.

4. Oh, if only you'd seen him appearing!
All unbuttoned *on purpose,* endearing,
Was the camphor-white shirt he was wearing,
While the thoroughbred steed he was steering,
And the saddle of. . . . .
But I feared Abū Bakar's stern gaze!

5. Do you know what has caused me most pain?
Why, the white of his shank, next its stain,
Which as soon as I saw, I was slain.

You would swear in a mine it had lain:
See his shank, white and tender, amaze,
While below, it's with gold all ablaze!

6. Lo, one day he rode forth on his bay,
And my heart fell right under his sway.
I then sang about *him* my love-lay,
To the tune of this song I will say:
"God, the banner of victory raise,
For Bū Bakar, the prince of great praise!"

NOTES

1. The strophic form of poetry known as *zajal,* which is couched in colloquial Arabic and originated in Andalus as an oral form, probably derived from its Romance cognate genre variously known as *cantiga, villancico, dansa, ballata,* and *virelai.* It has the basic rhyme scheme AA bbba (AA), ccca (AA), ddda (AA), etc., where AA is the refrain. The more learned *muwashshaḥa,* which was invented in Andalus around the year 287/900, has the rhyme scheme [AA] bbbaa (AA), cccaa (AA), dddaa (AA), etc.; it is probably a derivative of the *zajal* and is couched in Classical Arabic, save for its final aa element, called *kharja,* which is normally in colloquial Arabic, Romance, or a combination of the two. In sum, mother and daughter genres differ both in poetic form and in language. A third development, the granddaughter, is the *zajal*-like *muwashshaḥa,* written, like the *zajal,* in colloquial Arabic but exhibiting the rhyme scheme of the *muwashshaḥa.* For a more detailed description, see James T. Monroe, "Zajal and Muwashshaḥa: Hispano-Arabic Poetry and the Romance Tradition" in Salma Khadra Jayyusi, ed., *The Legacy of Muslim Spain,* Handbuch der Orientalistik, 12 (Leiden: E. J. Brill, 1992), pp. 399–419.

Two preliminary versions of this study were presented as papers at the Colloquium on Medieval Spain held at Cornell University, in November, 1991, and at the Annual Meeting of the American Oriental Society held at Harvard University, in April, 1992.

2. "Studies on Ibn Quzmān," *Andalus* 16 (1951): 398.

3. *Todo Ben Quzmān,* 3 vols. (Madrid: Gredos, 1972), 2:660–63.

4. Arabic text in *Gramática, métrica y texto del Cancionero hispanoárabe de Aban Quzmán* (Madrid: Instituto Hispano-Árabe de Cultura, 1980), pp. 843–47. Corrected in "Istidrākāt wa-qtirāḥāt jadīda ʿalā hāmish *Dīwān Ibn Quzmān,*" *Awrāq* 5–6 (1982–1983): 18; Spanish translation in *Ibn Quzmān: Cancionero andalusí* (Madrid: Hiperión, 1989), pp. 238–39, 317. See also Corriente's second edition: *El cancionero hispano-árabe de Aban Quzmán de Córdoba (m. 555/1160) "Iṣābat al-Aġrāḍ fī ḏikr al-aʿrāḍ"* (Cairo: al-Hay'a al-Miṣrīya al-ʿĀmma li-l-Kitāb, 1995), pp. 385–87.

5. With a few minor modifications, I have adopted elements from both of Corriente's excellent editions of this poem, which I have checked against the manuscript published in photocopy by David de Gunzburg, *Le Divan d'Ibn Guzman* (Berlin: Calvary, 1896).

6. *Gramática, métrica, y texto,* restoration of text cut off at the margin of the manuscript.

7. Ibid., restoration of text cut off at the margin of the manuscript.

8. Ibid., emendation of text on metrical grounds.

9. Corriente, *El cancionero hispano-árabe: zurūr.*

10. Here, there is a lacuna in the text, but ibid. p. 387, n. 3, invites comparison with *Zajal No. 70:* 8, 3 (p. 219). The latter is another love poem to an Almoravid youth, also described as riding a horse, *wa-l-sarji maḥlūl lam yarbaṭuh* ("with the saddle loose; not tied").

11. *Gramática, méttica, y texto,* restoration of text cut off at the margin of the manuscript.

12. Corriente, *El cancionero hispano-árabe* follows the manuscript, reading Abī Zikrī. Since the numerous other *muwashshaḥas* that quote this famous *kharja* consistently read Abī Bakri, which was, incidentally, the name of the patron to whom the original poem attributed to Ibn Bājja was dedicated, I prefer in this case to accept Stern's emendation.

13. A Berber prince.

14. A type of shirt made from the fine linen cloth fabricated in Sūs (Sousse), a town in Tunisia.

15. Relying on Ibn al-ʿAwwām, a Sevillian botanist who flourished toward the end of the twelfth century or the first half of the thirteenth and who wrote a major work on agriculture entitled *Kitāb al-Filāḥā,* R. Dozy explains that this is the name of a type of gold (*al-dhahab al-khāliṣ al-ja ʿfarī* ["pure, *jaʿfarī* gold"]). See *Supplément aux dictionnaires arabes,* 3d ed., 2 vols. (Leiden, Paris: Brill, Maisonneuve, 1967), 1:198, col. A.

16. If for no other reason, because the youthful cupbearer/catamite will inevitably grow up and stop providing his services to the poet, according to a convention we shall discuss below.

17. The identity of Abū Bakr is unclear. S. M. Stern states that his "full name seems to be Abū Bakr b. Bukar (see strophe 3, 1.2: *walad qalīd Bukar:* the son of the nobleman Bukar)," ("Studies on Ibn Quzmān," pp. 396–97, n. 5). García Gómez's suggestion that he may be the "rey Búcar" of the *Cantar de Mío Cid* is based exclusively on the fact that the manuscript reads *bukar,* which *Gramática, métrica, y texto* views as an unmetrical scribal error for *bū bakar,* a colloquial form required by the meter. Either *bukar* or *bakar* is required if the name is to rhyme with *sukkar, ʿanbar,* and *jawhar.* In contrast, Abū Bakri, the classical form of the same name, appears in the final line of strophe 4 and, with Stern's emendation, in the final line of 6, where this form is required in order to rhyme with *hajrī, dahrī, nadrī,* etc. There is no substantial reason to conclude, on the basis of this questionable evidence alone, that Ibn Quzmān's Berber prince was the same "rey Búcar" of an admittedly semihistorical Spanish epic, at least not without more convincing proof than a single passage that is possibly a scribal error.

Corriente describes this poem as a "panegīrico y requiebro de un muchacho almorávide, hijo de un *agellid,* de nombre Bū Bakr, o llamado así él mismo, si en 3/2 traducimos "un chico, el *agellid* Bū Bakr" (*Cancionero andalusí,* p. 317, *No. 133,* n. 1). However, this alternate translation proposed by Corriente is syntactically less likely. *Walad qillīd bū bukar* means "the son of the agellid Abū Bakr." To derive Corriente's translation from it, one would have to correct the manuscript to *walad: al-qillīd bū bakar,* which would be unmetrical since it would add one syllable to the line. *El cancionero hispano-árabe,* p. 386, n. 1, adds the information that *bukar* is a colloquial contraction for Abū Bakr, and goes on to subscribe to the "rey Búcar" theory. The "rey Búcar" of the *Cantar* is introduced as a "rey de marruecos" who attacks the Cid in Valencia (besieged by the Cid in 486/1093), and is killed by him. Ramón Menéndez Pidal at one point adopted the view that he was the Almoravid general Sīr b. Abī Bakr, who was appointed governor of Seville from 484/1091 and governed until his death in 507/1113. He outlived the Cid, who was born abound 435/1043 and died in 486/1099. Menéndez Pidal furthers admits that there is no record of Sīr b. Abī Bakr ever having attacked the Cid in Valencia, since that was done by the Almoravid *qā'id* Muḥammad b. ʿAysha (see R. Menéndez Pidal, *Cantar de Mío Cid: texto, gramática y vocabulario,* 3 vols. [Madrid: Bailly-Baillière, 1911], 2:515–16). It is hardly likely, therefore, that the Abū Bakr with whom the Cid crossed swords was the same man praised by Ibn Quzmān, who could not have been born before the battle of Sagrajas (480/1087), at the very earliest (see É. Lévi-Provençal, "Du nouveau sur Ibn Quzmān," *Al-Andalus* 9 [1944]: 347–69, at p. 356), and who died in 556/1060. In an early article, García Gómez (who appears to have changed his mind on the subject by the time he got around to *Todo Ben Quzmān*) was of the less unsound of two preposterous opinions, according to which *Zajal No. 133* was addressed not to the "rey Búcar" of the *Cantar,* but to that character's son (see "El 'rey Búcar' del *Cantar de Mío Cid,*" *Studi Orientalistici in Onore de Giorgio Levi Della Vida,* 2 vols. [Rome: Istituto Per L'Oriente, 1956] 1: 371–77).

As I shall attempt to show, Ibn Quzmān's poem was written to annoy an as yet unidentified Abū Bakr. It is *his* name, not that of his son, that is mentioned throughout the poem, while the whole malicious point would have been lost entirely were Abū Bakr no longer to be counted among the living. Therefore, we must seek out and identify those Abū Bakrs who were contemporaries of Ibn Quzmān, who were Almoravids, who were princes of the royal family, and who held high office either in our author's native Córdoba or in other Andalusī cities he is known to have visited. Since there are several likely candidates, the matter is a complex one, to which I hope to devote a separate article. For the moment, let me unmask a few of my leading suspects: (1) Abū Bakr Yaḥyā b. Rawwād, who governed Córdoba from 514/1120 to 515/1121; (2) Abū Bakr b. ʿAlī b. Yūsuf, governor of Seville from 518/1124–522/1128 who, incidentally, had a son named Yaḥyā al-Ṣaḥrawī, (3) Abū Bakr b. Mazdalī, governor of Seville from 539/1144 until the collapse of Almoravid rule; (4) ʿAlī b. Abī Bakr Fannū, last governor of Granada, appointed in 539/1144, although there is a *dīnār* from Granada dated 540/1145 and issued in the name of the Almoravid *amīr* Isḥāq b. ʿAlī b. Yūsuf, along with the name Bakr, presumably the governor (see Hanna E. Kassis, *A Numismatic History of the Almoravids* [forthcoming], No. 742); (5) Abū Bakr Yaḥyā b.ʿAlī, appointed governor of Valencia and Murcia in 529/1134 and destined to be the last representative of Almoravid power in Andalus (see Ambrosio Huici Miranda, "ʿAlī b. Yūsuf y sus empresas en el Andalus," *Tamuda* 7[1959]: 110). Let me also express my deep-felt gratitude to two friends and colleagues: Samuel G. Armistead, who has provided me with exhaustive bibliographical materials clearly showing that the "rey Búcar" of the *Cantar* cannot possibly be Ibn Quzmān's Abū Bakr, and Hanna E.Kassis, who has generously offered me materials from his important forthcoming book, *A Numismatic History of the Almoravids.*

18. Not 7, as misprinted by García Gómez, *Todo Ben Quzmān,* vol. 2, p. 663, n. 3.

19. See Edward Westermarck, *Ritual and Belief in Morocco,* 2 vols. (London: Macmillan, 1926; reprint, New York: University Books, 1968), 1:310, 443, 516, 540, 582, 2: 92; Samuel G. Armistead and Joseph H. Silverman, *Folk Literature of the Sephardic Jews, 1: The Judeo-Spanish Ballad Chapbooks of Yacob Abraham Yoná* (Berkeley: University of California Press, 1971), pp. 344–45, n. 1; G. S. Colin, "Ḥinnā'," *Encyclopaedia of Islam,* 2nd ed., 3:461.

20. Samuel G. Armistead, Joseph H. Silverman, and Israel J. Katz, *Folk Literature of the Sephardic Jews, II: Judeo-Spanish Ballads from Oral Tradition: I, Epic Ballads* (Berkeley: University of California Press, 1986), p. 249. My translation; emphasis mine. The authors note that the grotesque figure of the Moor is not found in the Peninsular version of the ballad contained in a manuscript dated 1598, but is based on a line found in the latter: *el braço blanco y velloso / asta el medio rremangado* ("His arm is white and hairy/ its sleeve rolled up halfway." [Armistead, Silverman, and Katz, p. 248, n. 31]). This means that the detail relevant to *Zajal No. 133* was added in Morocco, by Sephardic singers who must have been describing a fashion familiar to them. See also the comment of Diego Catalán: 'Esta fantasmagórica figura es invención de la tradición sefardí,' in *Siete siglos de romancero (historia y poesía),* (Madrid: Gredos, 1969), p. 128.

21. See, for example, the following *ḥadīths*: "The Prophet of Allah, peace and blessings of Allah on him, said: 'Eat and drink and wear clothes and be charitable, not being extravagant or self-conceited'" (transmitted by Bukhārī); "Miswar said: 'I took up a heavy stone, and whilst I was going along (with it), my garment fell down. So the Messenger of Allah, peace and blessing of Allah on him, said to me: 'Don thy garment, and you should not walk naked'" (transmitted by Abū Dāwūd). In Maulana Muhammad Ali, *A Manual of Hadith* (London: Curzon Press, 1944; reprint, 1977), pp. 359–60.

22. See Sayyid Ḥanafī Ḥasanayn, ed., *al-Muqtaṭaf min azāhir al-ṭuraf,* (Cairo: Markaz Taḥqīq al-Turāth, 1983), p. 207. This passage was reproduced by Ibn Khaldūn (733–809/1332–1406). See *The Muqaddima: An Introduction to History,* Franz Rosenthal, trans., 3 vols. (New York: Pantheon, Bollingen Series XLIII, 1958), 3:443–44.

23. Nothing is known about the compiler ʿAlī b. Bushrā al-Ighranāṭī ("the Granadan"). The manuscript appears to have belonged to the prince al-Mustaḍī', son of Muley Ismāʿīl of Morocco (d. 1173/1759). See E. García Gómez, 'Veinticuatro *jarŷas* romances en *muwaššaḥas* árabes (ms. G. S. Colin), *Andalus* 17 (1952): 63–64. See also Alan Jones, ed. *The ʿUddat al-jalīs of ʿAlī b. Bishrī: An Anthology of Andalusian Arabic Muwashshaḥāt,* (Cambridge, England: E. J. W. Gibb Memorial, New Series, 31, 1992).

24. See S. M. Stern, "Four Famous *Muwaššaḥs* from Ibn Bušrà's Anthology," *Andalus* 23 (1958): 357–62, where the Arabic text and an English translation are provided. Stern is inclined to think that the poem should be attributed to Ibn Bājja; this is a valid and even likely opinion, but one that can be neither contested nor defended with any

degree of certainty. See also Jones, *The ʿUddat al-jalīs of ʿAlī b. Bishrī,* pp. 161–62, who follows Stern. If the poem was composed by Ibn al-Ṣayrafī, who was a contemporary of Ibn Quzmān, it could not have been addressed to Abū Bakr b. Tīfalwīt.

25. For a summary of this view, see Benjamin M. Liu and James T. Monroe, *Ten Hispano-Arabic Strophic Songs in the Modern Oral Tradition: Music and Texts* (Berkeley: University of California Publications in Modern Philology, University of California Press, 1989), vol. 125.

26. For further examples of ring composition previously analyzed by me, see (1) "Prolegomena to the Study of Ibn Quzmān: The Poet As Jongleur," in Samuel G. Armistead, Diego Catalán, and Antonio Sánchez Romeralo, eds., *El Romancero hoy: historia, comparatismo, bibliografía crítica,* (Madrid: Gredos, 1979), 78–128 (On *Zajal No. 12*); (2) "Prolegómenos al estudio de Ibn Quzmān: el poeta como bufón," *Neuva Revista de Filología Hispánica* 34 (1985–1986): 769–99 (On *Zajal No. 137*); (3) "Wanton Poets and Would-be Paleographers (Prolegomena to Ibn Quzmān's *Zajal No. 10*)," *La Corónica* 16 (1987): 1–42; (4) "Salmà, el toro abigarrado, la doncella medrosa, Kaʿb al-Aḥbār y el concimiento del árabe de don Juan Manuel: prolegómenos al *Zéjél Núm. 148* de Ibn Quzmān," *Nueva Revista de Filología Hispánica* 36 (1988): 853–78; (5) "The Underside of Arabic Panegyric: Ibn Quzmān's (Unfinished?) *Zajal No. 84*," *Al-Qanṭara* (forthcoming); (6) "The *Zajal* within the *Zajal*: Ibn Quzmān's *Zajal No. 20*" (forthcoming).

27. Abū ʿAlī al-Ḥasan b. Rashīq al-Qayrawānī, *Kitāb al-ʿUmda,* 3d ed., 2 vols. (Cairo: M. al-Saʿāda, 1963), 2:44. My translation. Arabic poems of this type bear some resemblance to those in Latin edited and translated in W. H. Parker, *Priapea: Poems for a Phallic God* (London: Croom Helm, 1988). See, for example, No. 13, pp. 116–17:

> Donec proterva nil mei manu carpes,
> licebit ipsa sis pudicior Vesta.
> sin, haec mei te ventra arma laxabunt,
> exire it ipsa de tuo queas culo
>
> If you don't steal from me with wanton hand,
> You may as chaste as goddess Vesta stand:
> My member else had carved a hole so vast
> That through your own backside you could have passed.

28. *The Bad and the Ugly: Attitudes Towards Invective Poety* (Hijāʾ) *in Classical Arabic Literature* (Leiden: Brill, 1988), p. 55.

29. Ibid., pp. 48, 114. On this subject, Salma K. Jayyusi comments: "Jiʿthin, al-Farazdaq's sister, known for good character, was a victim of another incident. Al-Farazdaq had accosted a girl from another tribe, which retaliated by sending one of its men, who surprised Jiʿthin and touched her shoulder insultingly. Jarīr spent his life describing, in one poem after another, Jiʿthin's sexual orgies." "Umayyad Poetry" in *The Cambridge History of Arabic Literature: Arabic Literature to the End of the Umayyad Period* (Cambridge: Cambridge University Press, 1983), p. 411.

30. The name of al-Farazdaq's clan. Nor did al-Farazdaq neglect this approach to

satire. In one poem, he speaks about seducing a lady while he ridicules her husband and portrays him as a fool. See Régis Blachère, *Histoire de la littérature arabe des origines à la fin du XIe siècle de J.-C.,* 3 vols. (Paris: Maisonneuve, 1966), 3:565. In general, as Blachère points out, "la génération en cause s'attaque avec fureur à la mère, aux soeurs, aux femmes de ses rivaux" (p. 575). See also the remarks of Jayyusi, pp. 404, 412.

31. Arabic text in Anthony Ashley Bevan, ed., *The Naḳāʾid of Jarīr and al-Farazdaḳ,* 3 vols. (Leiden: E. J. Brill, 1905), 1: *Poem No. 40,* pp. 211–31, pp. 222–23, ll. 25–29. Translation mine.

32. Van Gelder, *The Bad and the Ugly,* p.47.

33. Ibid., p. 105.

34. See S. A. Bonebakker, "Religious Prejudice against Poetry in Early Islam," *Medievalia et Humanistica: Studies in Medieval and Renaissance Culture,* new series, 7 (1976): p. 84. See also pp. 85, 87–88.

35. He seems to have died at some unspecified date before the Hijra.

36. Jayyusi, "Umayyad Poetry," p. 419.

37. Dates not known.

38. Jayyusi, "Umayyad Poetry," p. 397.

39. Ibid., p. 419.

40. Ṭāhā Ḥusayn, *Ḥadīth al-Arbiʿāʾ* (Cairo: Dār al-Maʿārif, 1954), p. 232.

41. *Dīwān al-ʿArjī,* Khiḍr al-Ṭāʾī and Rashīd al-ʿUbaydī, eds. (Baghdad: al-Shirka al-Islāmīya li-l-Ṭibāʿa wa-l-Nashr, 1956), pp. 42–45. Translation mine.

42. Ibid., p. 17.

43. See Abū l-Faraj al-Iṣbahānī, *Kitāb al-Aghānī,* Ibrāhīm al-Abyārī, ed., 31 vols. (Cairo: Dār al-Shaʿb, 1969), 1:192–95.

44. Ibid., 8: pp. 2841, 2845, 2854–2855, 2867–2870, 2875, 2878–2881, 2890–2891, 2893–2895; Francesco Gabrieli, "D̲jamīl," *Encyclopaedia of Islam,* 2nd ed., 2:427–28. The biography of Jamīl is, of course, legendary in part, but here we are not necessarily dealing with what is historically true but with what is perceived as such.

45. Jayyusi, "Umayyad Poetry," p. 424.

46. Brother of the famous ʿAbdallāh b. al-Zubayr (d. 74/693). The latter was an enemy of the Umayyads, who declared himself anticaliph in the Hijaz, Iraq, South Arabia, Egypt, and parts of Syria. Ibn al-Zubayr appointed Muṣʿab to be his governor in Iraq.

47. ʿUbaydallāh b. Qays al-Ruqayyāt, *Dīwān,* Muḥammad Yūsuf Najm, ed. (Beirut: Dār Ṣādir, 1958), *No. 48,* pp. 121–23. My translation.

48. Ibn Khāqān, *Maṭmaḥ al-anfus* (Constantine: no publ., 1884), pp. 18–19. See also *Risālat at-Tawābiʿ wa z-zawābiʿ: The Treatise of Familiar Spirits and Demons by Abū ʿĀmir b. Shuhaid al-Ashjaʿī, al-Andalusī* James T. Monroe, trans. (Berkeley: University of California Press, University of California Publications in Near Eastern Studies, vol. 15, 1971), p. 67.

49. Ibn Shuhayd's poem pales in comparison, however, with the sentiments expressed in the following *cantiga* by the medieval Galician-Portuguese poet Martín Soárez (fl. 1220–1270):

Pero Rodríguiz, da vossa molher
non creades mal que vos ome dia,
ca entend' eu dela que ben vos quer
e quen end' al disser, dirá nemiga;
e direi-vos en que lho entendi:
en outro día, quando a fodi,
mostrou-xi-mi multo por voss' amiga

Pero Rodríguiz, about your wife.
Believe not the evil that anyone tells you,
For she has led me to believe that she loves you well,
And anyone saying the contrary, is saying slander.
I'll tell you how I've reached that conclusion:
The other day, when I was screwing her,
She showed me how much she loved you.

Cantigas d'escarnho e de mal dizer dos cancioneiros medievais galego-portugueses, M. Rodrigues Lapa, ed. (Coimbra: Editorial Galaxia, 1965), p. 442. My translation. For more on Martín Soárez, see Valeria Bertolucci Pizzorusso, *Le poesie di Martin Soares* (Bologna: Palmaverde, 1963). On the theme of cuckoldry, see also the humorous Castilian *villancico:*

Cornudo sois, marido.
—Mujer ¿y quién te lo dijo?

"You're a cuckold, husband."
"Who told you so, wife?"

Julio Cejador y Frauca, *La verdadera poesía castellana: floresta de la antiqua lírica popular,* 4 vols. (Madrid: Revista de Archivos Bibliotecas y Museos, 1921), 1:147, *No. 431.*

50. Ibn Bassām, *Kitāb al-Dhakhīra fī maḥāsin ahl al-jazīra,* Iḥsān ʿAbbās, ed., (Beirut: Dār al-Thaqāfa, 1978), part 2, vol. 2, pp. 834–35.

51. Albin Lesky, *A History of Greek Literature,* James Willis and Cornelis Heer, English trans. (New York: Crowell, 1966), pp. 111–12.

52. *Archilochus, Sappho, Alkman: Three Lyric Poets of the Late Greek Bronze Age,* Guy Davenport, trans. (Berkeley: University of California Press, 1980), pp. 22–24. For an edition of the Greek text and a literal translation, see H. D. Rankin, *Archilochus of Paros* (Park Ridge, N.J.: Noyes Press, 1977), pp. 69–71. See, especially, the editions, interpretations, and translation of Gregory Nagy in "*Iambos:* Typologies of Invective and Praise," *Arethusa* 9:2 (Fall 1976): 191–205, and Elvira Gangutia in *Cantos de mujeres en Grecia* (Madrid: Ediciones Clásicas, 1994), pp. 8–12, 136–39.

53. See Pierre Le Gentil, *La poésie lyrique espagnole et portugaise à la fin du moyen âge,* 2 vols. (Rennes: Plihon, 1949), 1:102, 103, 110, n. 77; Álvaro Alonso, ed., *Poesía de cancionero* (Madrid: Letras Hispánicas, 1986), p. 21: "Es raro que la dama aparezca explícitamente como mujer casada . . . la poesía cancioneril se aparta de los trovadores

provenzales, cuyo amor era esencialmente adúltero." This one feature of Arabic and Spanish love poetry in which both coincide in differing from Provençal poetry is not, to the best of my knowledge, either discussed or accounted for by proponents of the hypothesis according to which Arabic poetry influenced that of Provence.

54. Arabic text in *Dīwān Abī Nuwās* (Beirut: Dār Ṣādir, 1962), p. 242. Translation mine. The often-expurgated licentious poems of Abū Nuwās have been recently and conveniently collected and edited in *Abu Nuas: The Forbid[d]en Poems,* Jamal Jumaʿa, ed. (London: Riad El-Rayyes Books Ltd., 1994). This type of poetry became thoroughly acclimatized in classical Andalusī verse, as may be seen in the examples contained in *Ibn Saʿīd al-Maghribī, The Banners of the Champions: An Anthology of Medieval Arabic Poetry from Andalusia and Beyond,* James A. Bellamy and Patricia Owen Steiner, trans. (Madison: Hispanic Seminary of Medieval Studies, 1989), pp. 177–204.

55. In Arabic literature, Ḥātim al-Ṭāʾī (fl. second half of the sixth century) became a figure proverbial for his chivalry and generosity. Therefore, in this context the reference is to be understood ironically.

56. My versification. For another reference to Abū Nuwās, see *Zajal No. 63:* 4:4. On the *topos* of getting the beloved drunk, all the better to seduce him, as it was adopted into the classical poetry of Andalus, see specifically the following poem by Ibn Shuhayd:

> When he was fully drunk, and so, fell asleep, and the eyes of the night-watch slept,
> I approached him, despite his distance, as does a friend who knows what he is after,
> Crawling toward him as does slumber; rising upon him as does a sigh,
> And I spent the night with him in bliss, until the mouth of Dawn smiled,
> While I kissed the whiteness of his neck and sipped the darkness of his red lips.

Risālat at-Tawābiʿ wa z-zawābiʿ, James T. Monroe, trans., pp. 41–42. See also "On Sodomy and the Tricks of Sodomites, Their Love for Boys and Their Preference for Boys over Good-looking Girls," in *The Glory of the Perfumed Garden: The Missing Flowers (An English Translation from the Arabic of the Second and Hitherto Unpublished Part of Shaykh Nafzawi's* Perfumed Garden), H. E. J. (sic), trans. (London: Neville Spearman, 1975), pp. 32–58, especially pp. 42–58 ("The Vicious Practice of *Crawling*"). For more on crawling in particular, and other illicit Islamic sexual practices in general, both homo- and heterosexual, see Shihāb al-Dīn Aḥmad al-Tīfāshī (580–651/1184–1253), *Nuzhat al-albāb fīmā lā yūjad fī kitāb,* Jamal Jumaʿa, ed., (London: Riad El-Rayyes Books Ltd., 1992). There exists a French translation of this work, by René R. Khawam: *Les délices des coeurs, ou, ce que l'on ne trouve en aucun livre* (Paris: Éditions Phébus, 1981), which appeared before Jumaʿa's edition of the Arabic text and was based directly on manuscripts. In turn, a derivative English translation of chapters 5, 6, 8, 9, and 12 of the French translation was made by Edward A. Lacey: *The Delight of Hearts, Or What You Will Not Find in Any Book* (San Francisco: Gay Sunshine Press, Inc., 1988). The chapters selected for translation into English by Lacey were the homoerotic ones exclusively; the heterosexual ones appear to have been deemed too indecent for translation.

57. Van Gelder, *The Bad and the Ugly*, p. 50.

58. Ibid., p. 51.

59. Ibid., p. 92. This statement is, however, patently untrue. It would be more accurate to say that much of Andalusī satire was censored, or has subsequently been lost. In discussing the literary figure of Ibn Ṣāra al-Shantarīnī (d. 517/1123), Ibn Bassām (also named al-Shantarīnī; d. 542/1147) specifically indicates that Ibn Ṣāra was known for satirizing notables by alluding to their womenfolk, adding that he has omitted such poetry from his anthology, *Kitāb al-Dhakhīra fī maḥāsin ahl al-Jazīra* (which has survived), while collecting a large body of it, both by Ibn Ṣāra and others, in his other work, *Dhakhīrat al-Dhakhīra* (which has not). See n. 50 above.

60. Van Gelder, *The Bad and the Ugly*, p. 113.

61. See also the lengthy *ḥadīth* concerning "The Punishment of One who Commands Others to Do Good but Does Not Do It Himself and He Forbids Others to Do Evil but Does Not Himself Refrain from It," in *Ṣaḥīḥ Muslim*, ʿAbdul Ḥamīd Ṣiddīqī, trans., 4 vols. (Lahore: Sh. Muhammad Ashraf, 1981), 45:1539.

62. The first English usage of the term occurs in C. E. Chaddock's 1892 translation of Richard von Krafft-Ebing, *Psychopathia Sexualis* (Stuttgart: F. Enke, 1892; reprint, New York: Rebman, 1904), p. 255 (see the *Oxford English Dictionary*). For Christian attitudes toward homosexuality in the period that concerns us, see John Boswell, *Christianity, Social Tolerance, and Homosexuality: Gay People in Western Europe from the Beginning of the Christian Era to the Fourteenth Century* (Chicago: University of Chicago Press, 1980).

63. For a general treatment of the subject, see Abedelwahab Bouhdiba, *Sexuality in Islam* (London: Routledge and Kegan Paul, 1985); Abdelkebir Khatibi, "La sexualité selon le Coran" in *Maghreb pluriel* (Paris: Denoël, 1983), pp. 149–76.

64. Jamāl Jumʿa, "al-Īrūtīkīya al-ʿarabīya: al-saṭḥ wal-qāʿ," *al-Nāqid* 52 (October 1992): 12.

65. Ibid. The Mālikī school of jurisprudence predominated in Andalus, and its rulings would therefore have been relevant to Ibn Quzmān's environment.

66. The discussions deal largely with *male* homosexuality. Female homosexuality (*saḥq, siḥāq, musāḥaqa*) seems to have stimulated little discussion within the male-dominated profession of jurisprudence, and is sometimes classified along with "harmless" practices such as masturbation, an activity that was nevertheless forbidden by the Mālikī school.

67. The passage is discussed in Arno Schmitt, "Different Approaches to Male-Male Sexuality/Eroticism from Morocco to U[z]bekistān" in Arno Schmitt and Jehoeda Sofer, eds., *Sexuality and Eroticism Among Males in Moslem Societies* (New York: Harrington Park Press, 1992), p. 5. For his quotation, the author refers to James A. Bellamy, "Sex and Society in Islamic Popular Literature" in A. Lufti al-Sayyid-Marsot, ed., *Society and the Sexes in Medieval Islam* (Malibu: Undena, 1976), p. 37, where that particular passage is not found, although others equivalent in kind are: "Don't sit with the sons of the rich, for they have features like women, and they are a worse temptation than virgins"; "I have less fear for a pious young man from a ravening beast than from a beardless boy who sits with him"; "A man should never spend the night in a house with beardless youths" (p. 37). The idea that beautiful boys are sexually attractive to normal adult men

has led, in Islamic jurisprudence, to prolonged discussions concerning what to do about the presence of young boys in mosques during prayer time. The problem perceived by the jurists is that in the course of the boys' genuflections the movements of their buttocks might sexually arouse the men praying in the rows immediately behind them. As a result, the adult males might experience emissions, which would leave them in a state of pollution that would invalidate their prayers. In this case, the ultimate concern of the jurists is to safeguard the validity of prayer, but to do so they begin by assuming that beautiful boys are sexually attractive to normal men.

68. Everett K. Rowson, "The Categorization of Gender and Sexual Irregularity in Medieval Arabic Vice Lists" in Julia Epstein and Kristina Straub, eds., *Body Guards: The Cultural Politics of Gender Ambiguity* (New York: Routledge, 1991), p. 62. See also Joseph Norment Bell, *Love Theory in Later Ḥanbalite Islam* (Albany: State University of New York Press, 1979), pp. 20–24.

69. A. F. L. Beeston, ed. and trans., *The Epistle of Singing Girls of Jāḥiẓ* (Warminster, Wilts, England: Aris and Phillips Ltd., 1980), p. 29. Bracketed insertion provided by Beeston on p. 57. Al-Jāḥiẓ also wrote two essays dealing with pederasty: "Boasting Match over Maids and Youths" and "The Superiority of the Belly over the Back," available in English translation. See William M. Hutchins, *Nine Essays of al-Jahiz* (New York: Peter Lang, 1989), pp. 139–66 and 167–73, respectively. In the former, a spokesman in favor of maids as sexual partners wins a debate against a spokesman for youths, whereas in the latter an attempt is made to persuade a pederast to give up his predilection for youths and pursue maids instead. Although the author, who also wrote a lost *Attack on Liwāṭ* (see Rowson, "Medieval Arabic Vice Lists," p. 76, n. 19) was clearly not sympathetic to pederasty, he still treats it as a natural instinct rather than a perversion.

70. Rowson, "Medieval Arabic Vice Lists," p. 75, n. 9.

71. See the example by Abū Nuwās, n. 54 above.

72. For a general study of Greek homoeroticism, see K. J. Dover, *Greek Homosexuality* (New York: Vintage, 1978).

73. The word is, paradoxically, of English coinage, based upon the Spanish elements *macho* + *ismo,* neither of which were originally combined by native Spanish speakers to form that specific word, although it has been subsequently incorporated into the Spanish language. Presumably, Hispanic peoples were so overwhelmingly *machistas* that they could conceive of no pattern of behavior other than *machismo;* hence they graciously accepted a term describing what they had happily been all along as soon as it was coined by Anglo-American anthropologists eager to describe them. In turn, those anthropologists appear to have been unaware that the Spanish word *macho* can, unfortunately, designate the mule, i.e., the *sterile,* though male, offspring of hybridization between the horse and the donkey.

74. See Isabel Allende, *El plan infinito* (New York: Harper Libros, 1995), where an instance of homosexual rape within a Hispanic social environment is vividly portrayed on pp. 79–83 along with a subsequent, horrible act of revenge by the victim on pp. 95–98. (*The Infinite Plan,* Margaret Sayers Peden, English trans. [New York: HarperCollins, 1993], pp. 82–86, 101–4).

75. E. M. Forster, *Maurice* (reprint, New York: W. W. Norton, 1971), p. 51. In a religion such as that of the Greeks, exhibiting a Trinity consisting of Father, Mother, and Holy Catamite, it would of course have been difficult to disapprove of pederasty.

76. Our current approach rests upon the idea that childhood is, or should be, an age of innocence. Such a belief has also given rise to modern child-labor laws, the first of which were only passed in 1830. The innocence of childhood is a relatively recent concept in human history. In England, it was preceded by the Calvinist belief that children were innately evil and therefore deserving of punishment. Education of the young, prior to Rousseau's *Émile,* was accompanied by copious beatings. In Spanish, the pithy saying *la letra, con sangre entra* (loosely paraphrased, "letters should be instilled to the accompaniment of bloodshed") exemplifies such an attitude. Earlier ages were far more brutal in their treatment of children, as any reader of Dickens will be aware. See Roy Porter, *English Society in the Eighteenth Century* (London: Penguin, 1990), pp. 266–68.

77. In *The Mountain of Green Tea,* Denys Johnson-Davies, trans. (Cairo: American University in Cairo Press, 1983), pp. 10–18.

78. Ibn Rashīq al-Qayrawānī (391–457/1000–1064). Arabic text in Ibn Saʿīd al-Andalusī, *Rāyāt al-mubarrizīn wa-ghāyāt al-mumayyizīn,* al-Nuʿmān ʿAbd al-Mutaʿāl al-Qāḍī, ed. (Cairo: al-Majlis al-A ʿlā li-l-Shuʾūn al-Islāmīya, 1973), p. 138. English translation, Bellamy and Steiner, *Ibn Saʿīd al-Maghribī, The Banners of the Champions,* p. 67, no. 65.

79. See n. 27, above. Rowson, "Medieval Arabic Vice Lists," cites further examples, pp. 56–57, 71–72.

80. On the social marginalization and tolerance of the *mukhannath* (the term is sometimes translated as "transvestite," although "transsexual" is not impossible, and "hermaphrodite" is often meant) who was always a passive sexual partner and often a member of the entertainment industry, see Rowson, "Medieval Arabic Vice Lists," pp. 69–72; Bellamy, "Sex and Society," p. 36. Rowson stresses "the general acceptance of a public role for the male effeminate" insofar as he entirely renounced all pretensions to respectability (p. 74). This was not the case for the *maʾbūn*. Bellamy points out that, although thoroughly despised, the *mukhannath* "was not classified with the sodomites." He seems to have held the position of a harmless (and therefore tolerated) marginal character, wielding no power, enjoying no honor, and existing merely for the amusement and gratification of others. See especially Rowson, "The Effeminates of Early Medina," *Journal of the American Oriental Society* 111 (1991): 671–93.

81. The above treatment is attributed to the famous physician Muḥammad b. Zakarīyā al-Rāzī (251–313/865–925). The Arabic text is found in Aḥmad al-Tīfāshī, *Nuzhat al-albāb,* pp. 305–6; English translation, Edward A. Lacey, *The Delight of Hearts,* pp. 231–32. The recommendation that the penis be massaged with Pinesol, while the offending anus is simultaneously submerged in ice water, betrays an underlying hot-cold approach based upon the time-honored principles of humoral pathology.

82. As far as sexual relations between males are concerned, see Qurʾān 7:81: "You desire men *(rijāl)* instead of women; indeed, you are a group of men *(qawm)* who transgress"; 26:165–66: "Of all the creatures of the world, do you desire males *(dhukrān)*,

and ignore those whom your Lord has created for you, to be your wives? Indeed you are a group of men (*qawm*) who transgress"; 27:55: "Do you really desire men (*rijāl*) instead of women? Indeed you are a group of men (*qawm*) lacking self-restraint"; 29:29: "Do you indeed approach men (*rijāl*) and commit highway robbery?"; 54:37: "And they even sought to snatch away [Lūṭ's] guests." Note that the word *rijāl* denotes adult males, not boys, while the term *qawm,* in Old Arabic, meant properly "those men of the tribe who stand up and fight," i.e., its virile men (compare Algerian *goum*). The term excludes women and children. The Qur'ān, therefore, does not seem to be concerned, in its overall disapproval of grand sodomy, with the special case of pederasty. Once again boys seem to have been assigned an ambiguous sexual role.

83. Suzanne Pinckney Stetkevych, "Intoxication and Immortality: Wine and Associated Imagery in Al-Maʿarrī's Garden" (this volume).

84. The latter's name, in its Latin form Catamitus ("catamite"), entered the Arabic language as *qaṭīm* ("minion"). See Dozy, *Supplément,* 2, p. 337, col. A.

85. The word *sāqī,* cognates of which are found in all the major Semitic languages, appears as *shaqu* in Assyrian. Among the Assyrians, the office of royal *rab shaqe* ("chief cupbearer") was so important that its holders doubled as governors of provinces and commanders-in-chief of the army. See A. T. Olmstead, *History of Assyria* (reprint, Chicago: University of Chicago Press, 1975), p. 605. For references to the Assyrian *shaqu* and to the institution of *rab shaqe,* see John A. Brinkman et al., eds., *The Assyrian Dictionary of the Oriental Institute of the University of Chicago* (Chicago: Oriental Institute, 1992), 17: 24–32. In 2 Kings 18:17–36 and Isaiah 36–37, a *rabshakeh* appears before the walls of Jerusalem (in 701 B.C.) to demand the surrender of the Jewish king Hezekiah in the name of Sennacherib, king of Assyria (the siege is discussed in H. W. F. Saggs, *The Might That Was Assyria* [London: Sidgewick and Jackson, 1984], pp. 91, 256–57, 306). The relationship between an ancient Middle Eastern cupbearer and his king was so close that on occasion a cupbearer was able to usurp his master's throne by violent means. Thus the legendary Sargon of Akkad, a man of unknown parentage, became cupbearer to Ur-Zababa, King of Kish, whom he overthrew in 2334 B.C. (Georges Roux, *Ancient Iraq,* 2nd ed. [New York: Penguin, 1980], pp. 145–46). For the portrayal of Ashurnasirpal II being ministered to by his cupbearer, who is conventionally represented as beardless, see J. E. Curtis and J. E. Reader, *Art and Empire: Treasures from Assyria in the British Museum* (New York: Harry N. Abrams Inc., 1995), pp. 121, 219; Michael Roaf, *Cultural Atlas of Mesopotamia and the Ancient Near East* (Oxford: Equinox, 1990), p. 163. In the story of Joseph (Genesis 40; Qur'ān 12), when that prophet is imprisoned by Potiphar, he finds himself in the company of Pharaoh's cupbearer and baker, whose dreams he successfully interprets: "As for one of you, he will pour out the wine for his lord to drink; as for the other, he will hang from the cross, and the birds will eat from off his head" (Qur'ān 12:41).

Any sexual relationship that may have existed between cupbearer and monarch is not spelled out in the above examples, but in Hittite mythology Alalu, the first king of the gods, after reigning uneventfully for nine years, was overthrown by his cupbearer Anu and sought refuge beneath the earth. After nine more years, Anu was himself overthrown by his own cupbearer Kumarbi (who was a son of Alalu). In the second uprising, the conflict is characterized as being far more excruciating: Kumarbi bites off Anu's testicles but in the process ingests his seed, which he attempts to spit out. Failing to do so, he is impregnated and flees to Nippur, where he spends the months of his pregnancy and eventually gives birth to three gods. See Franca Pecchioli Daddi and Anna Maria Polvani, *La mitologia ittita* (Brescia: Paideia Editrice, 1990), p. 117; *Hittite Myths,* Harry A. Hoffner, Jr., trans. (Atlanta, Ga.: Scholars Press, 1990), pp. 38–42. The Hittite myth is not only an astonishing analog to the Greek story of Zeus's revolt against Kronos, but also adds the detail that Kumarbi, Anu's cupbearer, unmanned him orally, thereby strongly suggesting a sexual dimension to the relationship. Taking into account the case of Zeus and Ganymede, we have reasons to suspect that in the ancient Middle East, royal cupbearers at times functioned simultaneously as minions by appointment to his majesty the King.

As far as the connection between wine and immortality is concerned, aside from the all-too-familiar New Testament doctrines according to which wine is the blood of Christ while Christ is in turn the resurrection, let us note that in the Old Testament, after the Lord has realized the mistake He has committed by creating sinful humankind and has sent down the flood, saving from it only Noah, his immediate family, and the paired beasts, one of the very first things Noah does upon disembarking from the ark is plant a vineyard: "And Noah began to be an husbandman, and he planted a vineyard: And he drank of the wine, and was drunken; and he was uncovered within his tent" with all the attendant injustices that followed (Genesis 9:20–21). Noah is a symbol of the survival of the species; his close connection with wine suggests that the latter is also a symbol of eternity. In Greek mythology, *ambrosia* is the food (but sometimes also the beverage) of the gods. The word is derived from *ámbrotos* ("immortal"), of which the *a* is privative, whereas the element *brotós* <*mbrotós ("mortal") is a cognate of the Latin root *morior* ("to die"). See Émile Boisacq, *Dictionnaire étymologique de la langue grecque, étudiée dans ses rapports avec les autres langues indo-européennes,* 2nd ed. (Paris: C. Klincksieck, 1923), p. 134.

86. See Qur'ān 56:17–18: "Immortal youths shall circulate around them, with goblets and beakers, and cups filled from clear-flowing fountains"; 76:19: "Immortal youths shall circulate around them. If you saw them, you would think they were scattered pearls"; 52:24: "Boys destined for them shall circulate around them like well-guarded pearls."

87. Stetkevych, "Intoxication and Immortality" (this volume).

88. Qur'ān 26:224–26. Emphasis mine.

89. Qur'ān 26:227.

90. For the concept of the "half-outsider" in picaresque literature, see Claudio Guillén, *Literature as System: Essays Toward the Theory of Literary History* (Princeton: Princeton University Press, 1971), p. 80.

CHAPTER FIVE

Al-Sharīf al-Ṭalīq, Jacques Lacan, and the Poetics of Abbreviation

Richard Serrano

Despite attempts to bring contemporary critical concerns to the study of classical Arabic poetry, there lingers among scholars a belief that literary theory is still somewhat antithetical to this field. Admittedly, the complexity of the medieval Arabic language and the distance of its historical context, not only from contemporary Western thought but from the modern Arab world as well, reinforce the necessity of basing every act of exegesis in rigorous philological practice. Nonetheless, critical moves such as James Monroe's application of Lord and Parry's theories of oral-formulaic composition[1] and Suzanne Pinckney Stetkevych's use of anthropologist Victor Turner's theories in her studies of pre-Islamic poetry[2] suggest that judicious consideration of contemporary literary theory is not necessarily inimical to the study of classical Arabic poetry.

Still, traditional scholars would be understandably skeptical of the relevance of French psychoanalyst Jacques Lacan's theories to a literary tradition of which he was barely, if at all, aware.[3] In its infancy, and even today on talk shows and in books of pop psychology, psychoanalytic theory was and is often used to unintentionally comic effect. We do not want to turn Arabic poetry of the previous millennium into case studies like Marie Bonaparte's study of Edgar Allen Poe in the 1940s, which reduced all his texts to his "sadonecrophiliac . . . desire for his dead mother."[4] Nor do we want to use Arabic poetry as yet another example to "prove" that Freud or Lacan was right. The point of this study of the tenth-century Andalusian poet al-Sharīf al-Ṭalīq (350–400/961–1009) is not to demonstrate that he wanted to kill his father and sleep with his mother, although he *did* kill his father. Instead, the intent is first, to provide a reading of al-Sharīf al-Ṭalīq's *qaṣīda* rhymed in *qāf,* "A branch wavers on a rounded sand dune of a desert plain," with reference to a few pertinent remarks by Jacques Lacan, and second, to comment on the reading of Arabic poetry based on this Lacanian-informed exegesis. I want to suggest that what Lacan and other psychoanalysts have to say about language and the unconscious can point us toward a strategy for resolving the difficulties peculiar to the reading of Arabic poetry.

Jacques Lacan is perhaps most famous—and is often criticized—for his allusive and elusive writing and teaching styles. More important for our purposes, however, are two theoretical innovations he developed from his self-declared return to Freud. Lacan insists that the unconscious is structured like a language, and that the purpose of psychoanalysis is to listen for that language struggling to break through the surface noise of the analysand's discourse. His second, perhaps more controversial, innovation was the psychoanalytic session of variable length. Traditionally, the psychoanalytic session has a fixed length of an hour, or fifty minutes. Lacan instead terminated his sessions at will, sometimes after a mere ten minutes. He assumed that in ending a session on a crucial word or at a critical moment the analyst is better able to guide the analysis, yet also, somewhat paradoxically, leaves greater responsibility to the analysand in the work to be done during the silence between sessions. At first glance, these innovations might seem to have little relevance to the study of any literature, let alone Arabic, but it is Lacan's insistence on the centrality of language that makes his theories useful to the study of literature, particularly poetry.

This article purports to uncover the motivation of the poem. By this I do not mean a reconstruction of the poet's purpose in writing it which, unfortunately, is forever lost to us. Instead, I return to the motive force of the poem: the image, the lyric moment, even the mystery from which the poem develops and to which it constantly returns. I want to consider this moment the original trauma of the poem. In Lacanian terms, the trauma is an event in the realm of the Real, a moment that cannot be translated into the accessible Symbolic Order. In other words, this event is somehow always beyond (or before) language. Attempts to account for this moment—and, simultaneously, to hide it—result in language that constantly obscures the original trauma yet relentlessly points back to it. The trauma sets this language in motion; the something unspeakable of al-Sharīf al-Ṭalīq's poem is the *raison d'être* of the poem itself.

We know very little of al-Sharīf al-Ṭalīq's life; what biographical information there is in contemporary and near-contemporary sources borders on the legendary. The poet's life seems to have fallen neatly into three sections: the sixteen years prior to his imprisonment, the sixteen years of his incarceration, and the sixteen years following his release.[5] Such a perfectly tripartite division warns us that the stories surrounding al-Sharīf al-Ṭalīq should not necessarily be taken at face value. That does not, however, mean that we should disregard them. In some sense, the stories attached to a poet and poem are the first attempts at interpreting the poem. Apparently, al-Sharīf al-Ṭalīq was jailed for murdering his father, who had taken for his own the slave girl who had grown up with (and been promised to) the future poet.[6] I will avoid the temptation to evoke Freud's Oedipal complex, except to note that the poet's good fortune in avoiding neurosis by *knowingly* killing his father for taking the son's sexual property is all the more reason to turn to Lacan.

More important than a reconstructed psychohistory of the poet are two other details that blur our conception of the boundaries of his erotic attractions and attractiveness. At the time of his imprisonment, the poet was only sixteen and described as a *ghulām wasīm,* or an adolescent with an exceedingly beautiful face. The only story we have about al-Sharīf al-Ṭalīq from his prison days centers on his acquaintance with another famous, and older, poet, Ibn Masʿūd, also incarcerated, who later became his enemy and wrote nasty things about him. While still an admirer, however, Ibn Masʿūd compared the younger poet to Joseph, the son of Jacob, who was the medieval Arabic model of masculine beauty and, coincidentally, also served some time in prison.[7] In the twelfth sura of the Qur'ān, as in Genesis, Potiphar's wife falls madly in love with Joseph and attempts to seduce him. The Qur'ān relates an interesting additional moment. After she hears that the women of the city are gossiping about her immorality, the wife sends a servant to the women to prepare a banquet and distribute knives. As the women peel their dessert fruit, Potiphar's wife sends Joseph in. "They so admired him that they cut their hands and said, 'God protect us! This is not a man. Truly this is a noble angel'" (Sura 12:31).[8]

There is some debate among Western translators as to how the Arabic word *muttaka'an,* which appears in this passage, should be rendered in a Western language. It may be a pillow to recline against during a meal, although this is not an acceptable custom among Arabs. It may by extension be a room where such a meal is taken or even the meal itself. These meanings of *muttaka'an* all stem from the triconsonantal root *w-k-'*.[9] The French orientalist Régis Blachère prefers to translate *muttaka'an* "oranges," which suggests that he reads the word as based on a different triconsonantal root, *m-t-k, matk* or *mitk.*[10] Even if we do not accept Blachère's translation, the meaning seems to involve the presence of fruit, otherwise there would be little reason for the knives with which the gossiping women cut their hands.[11] A peculiarity of the words *matk* and *mitk* is that an Arabic word for clitoris, *mutuk,* has the same triconsonantal root. It would seem that the Qur'ān's reluctance to represent the fruit masks an even greater reluctance to refer to female sexual organs.

Regardless of whether it is behind oranges, pillows, banquets, or banquet halls that clits lurk in the story of Joseph, the reference to this tale is hardly innocent. Joseph—and by extension al-Sharīf al-Ṭalīq, since Ibn Masʿūd's allusion is hardly innocent either—is beautiful in a way that inspires uncontrollable sexual desire. When Joseph enters, the Egyptian women cannot concentrate and accidentally cut themselves as their thoughts turn from citrus (?) fruit to sexual pleasure. The selection of this anecdote for the biography of al-Sharīf al-Ṭalīq is obviously intentional.[12] Since we have so little knowledge of the poet's life, his apparent sexual appeal to an older man, indeed an older poet—despite his attraction to the beautiful slave girl who inspired the murder of his father—is intended not only as a commentary on his life, but also as a clue to a possible reading of his work.

The biography, even if there is not a shred of truth in it, is relevant to our project. The "facts" surrounding the life of the poet are in themselves the first exegesis of the poetry: the legends attach themselves to the poet's name because some Arab scholar, in this case al-Ḍabbī, believed them relevant to his poetic fragments as well. The legends provide a contest for his poetry, set the exegetical parameters. Just as we do not have full biographical information for al-Sharīf al-Ṭalīq, neither do we have a complete text of the poem in question. The *qaṣīda* in *qāf* as we know it is composed of four fragments of ten lines, seven lines, sixteen lines, and eight lines scattered among six sources.[13] We cannot be certain that we have all the lines in their proper order, or even that we know the sequence of the four fragments. However, we can label them with some confidence. The first is a *ghazal,* therefore concerned with eros; the second a *khamrīya* about wine drinking; the third a *nawrīya* or floral section of the poem; and the fourth a *fakhr* or offer of praise, in this case from the poet to himself.[14]

The poem exists in scattered fragments and lines because traditional Arab poets and scholars appreciated and conserved their poetry by quoting favorite lines or groups of lines and compiling long collections of these fragments. The ʿAbbāsid poet Abū Tammām's *Ḥamāsa,* for example, "is composed of 882 selections of poetry comprising some 3,760 verses."[15] Since Abū Tammām arranges these fragments by topic and not by poet, "one can scarcely remember whether a particular poet has spoken before, or if so, which of the hundreds of voices was his," and hundreds of years of Arabic poetry are rendered univocal. Similarly, the absence of so much of al-Sharīf al-Ṭalīq's *qaṣīda* does not completely efface the distinctions among the four sections; rather, it seems to lend them a greater unity, if not in content, then in approach to poetic expression. In part, our attempts to understand the poem demand that we find meaning in the empty spaces among the fragments. Reading a fragmented poem, then, mimics to some degree the traditional process of reading by breaking poems into smaller, more easily digested bits. The reconstruction of these poems is a mania peculiar to Western scholars.

In keeping with that mania, I present a full translation (which does not acknowledge the fragmentary nature of the various recensions) of the poem as currently reconstructed:[17]

> A branch wavers on a rounded sand dune in the desert, my heart gathering from it a flame;
> From his face Beauty presents to us a moon never seen waning.
> He enchants with a white gazelle's eyes, the contrast of black and white startling, his glance a notched arrow in my heart;
> He smiles with a string of pearls that I believed he snatched from our necks for his gums.
> The *lām* of his curls flows over his cheek, the flow of gold over silver;
> In him Beauty reaches its zenith; for a branch achieves beauty only with leaves.
> So slender is his waist that I believe it, from the thinness of its thinness, enamored;
> It is as if the hips had enslaved it in love, so that it became distressed and disquieted.
> Emaciated, it came attacking them, supple like my beloved when he remains in my embrace;
> Wondrous that they resemble us and have not begun to split or separate.
> I passed the night offering many a cup—which clothed the wing of Darkness with a garment of light that from its flash shone—
> To a gazelle fawn in whose eyes was a languor that the gaze of my eye kept awake.
> It hid itself from the eyes so that I believed it feared from the glance what is feared;
> It glowed in his immaculate palm, like the sun's rays meeting daybreak.

It is as if the cup in his fingers were the yellow of narcissus rising from silver leaves;
It made day like the sun, his mouth the West, the hand of the blushing cupbearer the East;
So whenever it sets in his mouth, it leaves a red afterglow on his cheek.
Many a cloud sending down rain, its showers drinking companion to the garden, sings and pours drink.
It is as if the earth were its prison, as if the plants were criminals imprisoned;
The lightning clothes its sides in embroidered robes when it flashes.
It is as if the dense cloud in it is black with a black-and-white horse blanket upon it;
It is as if the wind blowing it along sends into flight magpies in the sky.
On nights whose stars stray, lost, unable to distinguish the paths;
The lightning lights its lamp for them so that the face of their night-darkness turns to the East,
The thunder humming sobs so that cups of the rain cloud run over, watering it,
The sun rising, weaning it; having wrapped it in its brilliance, drowning it.
So it is as if the sun reviving itself were the first light of the beloved reviving one burning with lust;
It is as if the rose, dew upon it, were the beloved's cheek bedewed with perspiration.
It blooms beside a pure yellow narcissus that I believe hid love for the rose;
Like two lovers joined, one come blushing, the other timid.
Oh they of the stars in the garden from their hills to the horizon have risen;
They stared in delight at the morning sun, pupils of flowers captivating pupils.
It is as if the rain drop by drop when it flowed generously left quicksilver on their leaves.
What noble youth is like me in audacity and generosity, in word, deed, and piety?
My nobility is my soul, my ornament my knowledge, and my

sword my eloquence in an encounter.
My tongue, for one who tries it, is a viper that spells turn not away;
My right hand is the good fortune of an indigent seeker, having joined a praise that was scattered.
My grandfather is al-Nāṣir li-l-Dīn, whose palms dispersed the dispersal,
The noblest of the noble in himself and his fathers when they rival him, the highest, in superiority.
I am the glory of those of ʿAbd Shams, through me their worn glory is renewed;
I clothe what has been effaced of their illustrious example with the ornament of my splendid poetry.

Although this is our best guess at the original arrangement, the fragmentation of the poem permits some license in the order of analysis. So let us begin with the final fragment. It probably was intended to be the final section of the poem, or at least part of it, since traditionally the poet reserves praise for himself or his patron for the end of the poem. All that which precedes the *fakhr* is a demonstration of the poet's mastery of traditional language and tropes. The *fakhr* itself can follow only after the poet has proven himself worthy to give or receive praise; it is a reward for having proven himself a poet.

What noble youth is like me in audacity and generosity, in word, deed, and piety?
My nobility is my soul, my ornament my knowledge, and my sword my eloquence in an encounter.
My tongue, for one who tries it, is a viper that spells turn not away;
My right hand is the good fortune of an indigent seeker, having joined a praise that was scattered.
My grandfather is al-Nāṣir li-l-Dīn, whose palms dispersed the dispersal,
The nobles of the noble in himself and his fathers when they rival him, the highest, in superiority.
I am the glory of those of ʿAbd Shams, through me their worn glory is renewed;
I clothe what has been effaced of their illustrious example with the ornament of my splendid poetry.

Lines 37–38 and lines 40–41 hint at al-Sharīf al-Ṭalīq's poetic purpose. Like his grandfather, the first Caliph of Córdoba, who established centralized political power in the tenth century[18] and reversed the political fragmentation of al-Andalus, al-Sharīf al-Ṭalīq wants to reverse the poetic decline of the Arabs. This poem gathers together the dispersed force and power of Arabic poetry. Like his grandfather, and like the twentieth-century critic culling errant lines from various recensions, the poet wants to transform fragmentation into unity.

The final two lines of the *fakhr* begin with *'Ana* "I." Al-Sharīf al-Ṭalīq is emphatic that it is he who can accomplish the poetic equivalent of his grandfather's political successes. But he reaches yet farther back into history: he is not only the grandson of the first Caliph of Córdoba,[19] he is also the *fakhr,* the glory of those descended from the ancestor of the Umayyads, ʿAbd Shams.[20] He insists that he is the inheritor of imperial Arabic culture, which unfortunately has settled into a decline. The image of this poetic inheritance is not entirely positive. The poet likens it to a worn-out cloak in need of a bit of patching; the ornaments or jewelry of his poetry are necessary to cover up the bald spots. In a sense, the last line works against the penultimate line. Line 40 evokes the renewal of the tradition, but the last line suggests that the worn spots are not so much renewed as covered up.

The poet seems to be papering over the tradition's exhaustion with his own work. We need to ask just what is being covered up by or in the poem. As we know, the point of the psychoanalytic session is, in part, to discover what is hidden. "The unconscious," Lacan tells us, "is that chapter of my history which is marked by a blank or occupied by a falsehood: it is the censored chapter. But the Truth can be found again; it is most often already written down elsewhere."[21] Al-Sharīf al-Ṭalīq is not necessarily a liar, but the key to reading this poem is finding out what is being covered up, what is being censored, and how this affects the construction of the poem. In the final two lines al-Sharīf al-Ṭalīq ostensibly describes the relationship of his poetry to the tradition from which it springs, but he also describes the relationship of the poem to its content.

Working backward, the third and longest fragment of the poem, the *nawrīya* or floral part of the *qaṣīda,* is also concerned with cloaking.

> Many a cloud sending down rain, its showers drinking companion
> to the garden, sings and pours drink.
> It is as if the earth were its prison, as if the plants were criminals
> imprisoned;

> The lightning clothes its sides in embroidered robes when it flashes.
> It is as if the dense cloud in it is black with a black-and-white horse blanket upon it;
> It is as if the wind blowing it along sends into flight magpies in the sky.
> On nights whose stars stray, lost, unable to distinguish the paths;
> The lightning lights its lamp for them so that the face of their night-darkness turns to the East,
> The thunder humming sobs so that cups of the rain cloud run over, watering it,
> The sun rising, weaning it; having wrapped it in its brilliance, drowning it.
> So it is as if the sun reviving itself were the first light of the beloved reviving one burning with lust;
> It is as if the rose, dew upon it, were the beloved's cheek bedewed with perspiration.
> It blooms beside a pure yellow narcissus that I believe hid love for the rose;
> Like two lovers joined, one come blushing, the other timid.
> Oh they of the stars in the garden from their hills to the horizon have risen;
> They stared in delight at the morning sun, pupils of flowers captivating pupils.
> It is as if the rain drop by drop when it flowed generously left quicksilver on their leaves.

Rather than seeing the lightning of line 20 as illuminating the cloud and allowing us to see into or through sections less dense than others, suggested by the motley pattern of the horse blanket in line 21, the poet insists with his choice of image that the lightning *covers* the cloud: blackness with whiteness, monotone with embroidered pattern. According to the logic of the image, the lightning is not powerful enough to clothe the black with robes entirely, purely white; it falls short in its attempt to again clothe the cloud in robes of honor, the complete meaning of the verb *kh-l-ʿ*, which I have translated "to clothe." Line 21 attempts to remedy this defect by insisting that even the black parts of the cloud are part of the robes—now become horse blanket—covering them. The images depict how the lightning is unable to penetrate the cloud even as they attempt to explain this inability away. Having already interpreted the final lines of the poem, one can see an analogy between the poet trying to cover up with poems the defective robe of his inherited tradition and the lightning trying to render white the dark cloud. As a result, both images end up more troubling than they might otherwise seem.

As already noted, Lacan's most controversial innovation in the practice of psychoanalysis was the abbreviated session of variable length. Lacan felt that to assign the psychoanalytic session a specific length, and then to silence the analysant when the clock ran out, was arbitrary; instead, he cut off the analysand at what he perceived to be a crucial moment. This action had two important and perhaps contradictory effects. The first was to take away a certain amount of the analysand's power to control the session; if he has no idea when the session will end and, indeed, has good reason to believe that the session could end at any moment, he is more likely to speak without attempting to control his discourse, permitting the repressed unconscious-as-language to surface. Since most of the psychoanalytic work must go on between sessions, the second effect of ending the session on a crucial phrase or image was to return responsibility for his progress to the analysand.

The accidents of literary history, the selections of al-Sharīf al-Ṭalīq's contemporaries and successors, and the informed opinions of contemporary scholars leave us with a poem in four fragments or sessions (*séances* in French). There is no such thing as an objective interpretation of a poem, dream, or psychoanalytic session. Just as al-Sharīf al-Ṭalīq inherited a tradition with worn sections that he must cover, we have inherited a poem with missing—lost, suppressed, elided—pieces. Our task is not to imagine what filled those gaps, but to take the poem in its current abbreviated, punctuated form and make sense of it both as a whole and as fragmentary, as Abū Tammām rearranged the fragments of several hundred poets in order to make sense of them.

In the floral fragment we can see how carefully al-Sharīf al-Ṭalīq articulates his images. This careful articulation is lost when sections of the poem are lost, but we can use these dislocations to better understand the force of the images. First, let us look at how carefully he interweaves the images of lines 18 to 33. The frequent occurrence of "it" in the translation is misleading, replacing in each instance (except in the construction "it is as if," *kaʾanna*) a subject understood in the conjugation of the accompanying verb. As a result, the language of the original Arabic is, in most instances, less ambiguous than the English translation.

Nonetheless, the images are particularly unstable in this section of the poem. The *kaʾanna* construction is used six times and most of the rest of the lines are devoted to noting the transformation from one metaphor to the next. The rain cloud seems to be the sole constant, appearing at both the beginning and the end of this fragment. Its showers are a drinking companion to the garden that exists as a direct result of the standing water sent down by the cloud. The earth is called a prison and the plants springing from it prisoners. The sites of the cloud are embroidered robes. The further articulation of this image turns the robes into a horse blanket, making the cloud a horse. We are suddenly back to a more naturalistic rendering of the sky, with magpies in flight, stars, lightning, darkness, and thunder, but the poet lends increasingly human characteristics to these images. The stars stray, the lightning is a lampbearer attempting to lead them back to their paths, and the darkness of night has a face that turns eastward in anticipation of sunrise. The rain cloud gives way to the sun, which replaces the drenching water with drowning sunlight, weaning the garden from the cloud.

The first light of the sun, permitting a view of the garden at last, reveals a mass of images intertwined and dizzying in the shifting of their referents. The sun and the garden are lover and beloved. The narcissus and rose are lovers. The stars of the night are now the stars of the garden risen from their flower beds to the horizon, again made stars of the sky. The centers of the star-flowers are pupils capturing the gaze of human eyes, the lovers' eyes. Then in the final line of this fragment we are suddenly reminded of the rain again: the drops on the leaves resemble quicksilver, the word for leaves itself here referring to silver as well.

To begin to make some sense out of this welter of images, we will examine which parts of the fragment seem extraneous to the central conceit of rain, sunlight, and gardens. In line 18 is a drinking companion who in pouring out drink for the garden is something of a *sāqī*. The suggestion of crime and punishment in line 19 seems even more out of place. Who has done wrong? Although we can see how the dewy rose would bring to mind the cheek of the beloved, the sudden appearance of the beloved's cheek and the lovers' eyes in lines 28 and 32 is somewhat disorienting. Do the lovers' eyes spring to mind from the sight of the flowers? What lovers are these? Finally, the quicksilver on the leaves is also somewhat jarring; the intrusion of the merely metallic into natural images seems to require explanation.

We turn to the preceding fragment for answers. The second fragment, lines 11–17, is a haunting evocation of a *sāqi,* a young, not unattractive boy serving as cupbearer, pouring forth wine for the poet. On rereading, the fragment just discussed, lines 18–33, now seems like a florid reworking of the images evoking the boy and his function.

I passed the night offering many a cup—which clothed the wing of Darkness with a garment of light that from its flash shone—
To a gazelle fawn in whose eyes was a languor that the gaze of my eye kept awake.
It hid itself from the eyes so that I believed it feared from the glance what is feared;
It glowed in his immaculate palm, like the sun's rays meeting daybreak.
It is as if the cup in his fingers were the yellow of narcissus rising from silver leaves;
It made day like the sun, his mouth the West, the hand of the blushing cupbearer the East;
So whenever it sets in his mouth, it leaves a red afterglow on his cheek.

The poet offering cup after cup of wine to the cupbearer—something of a reversal, since that is the boy's task, and certainly not without intentions—becomes the showers of the cloud pouring out rain. The threatening image of an older man trying to inebriate a little boy becomes that of a boon companion pouring forth mere rain; the image is robbed of its danger. The staring man keeping the drunken boy awake with his gaze—so threatening that even the cup holding the wine hides itself, fearing that the man's intention is what "is feared" in general when you put a poet, a boy, and wine together—becomes people looking at flowers, or perhaps just flowers looking at flowers. The image is naturalized and recontextualized, the threat of sexual malfeasance transformed into mere flower-gazing. In the image of the boy about to bring the cup to his lips, the yellow of the wine is narcissus; the white of his hands is silver, like a flower in its vase or surrounded by its leaves (*waraqu* refers to both leaves and silver), and becomes nothing but dew. The prohibited behavior upon which the poet is about to embark with his cupbearer is effaced, censored—clothed.

There are other parallels between the two fragments. In the *khamrīya* the poet tells us how he passed the night; in the *nawrīya* he describes the passing of night into day. Similarly, the motion of the *ṣāqī* lifting the cup of wine to his mouth is described in terms of the passing of the sun over the sky, moving from morning to evening, reversing the movement of the *nawrīya*. The cup full of luminous wine in the *sāqī*'s hand takes on the functions of both the lightning and the sun in the third fragment. In line 11 it clothes the darkness with a garment of light—in fact, the cup outperforms the lightning, since there is no suggestion that the robe here is anything less than pure white. Indeed, the cup of wine so illuminates the cloud that the poet compares it to the light of the sun at dawn. The *khamrīya* fragment ends not with sunshine or sunrise, of course, but with dusk. A gulp of the wine leaves the cupbearer with a red glow on his cheek, an image echoed in the third fragment when the dewy rose is compared to the beloved's cheek, suggesting in retrospect that the *sāqi*'s blush is due as much to *pudeur* as to the effects of wine.

The sight of the wine entering the boy's mouth and the afterglow that spreads across his cheek seems all but unbearable for the poet. The entire fragment is an attempt to avoid just such a carnal image of the boy. In line 11 the cup at first mention becomes clothing over darkness, the poet insisting that it is covering when instead it is illuminating. In line 12 the first reference to the cupbearer is actually to a gazelle fawn; so transfixed is the poet by the fawn/boy's eyes that he no longer sees the cup. He breaks his gaze to see the cup in the boy's hand, but even this is too corporeal—the cup and palm become rays of sun and daybreak. Then in line 15 the cup and fingers become narcissus and vase, but this still does not distract the poet from the boy's body, so he sees the cup as the sun, the mouth as an abstraction (the West), and the boy's hand as another abstraction (the East). The contact of hand, cup, wine, and mouth reveals—undresses—the poet's desire to make physical contact with the cupbearer. The rush of blood to the boy's face, perhaps the corresponding rush of blood through the poet's body, are unbearable. The poet's attempts to make the boy increasingly abstract fail one after the other until he can see nothing but the boy's mouth and cheek. He flees from this fragment into the third and, apparently, much less erotic fragment of the poem. This is perhaps the original trauma, the central, indescribable, unwatchable, unavoidable, unbearable physical moment around which the poem constructs itself, moving ever farther from the boy yet leaving clue after clue traceable to his body.

So is this the key to the poem? Is the boy's body the trauma from which the poem and the poet flee? Consider the first fragment, the *ghazal* that traditionally concerns itself with the erotic:

> A branch wavers on a rounded sand dune in the desert, my heart
> gathering from it a flame;
> From his face Beauty presents to us a moon never seen waning.
> He enchants with a white gazelle's eyes, the contrast of black and
> white startling, his glance a notched arrow in my heart;

He smiles with a string of pearls that I believed he snatched from our necks for his gums.
The *lām* of his curls flows over his cheek, the flow of gold over silver;
In him Beauty reaches its zenith; for a branch achieves beauty only with leaves.
So slender is his waist that I believe it, from the thinness of its thinness, enamored;
It is as if the hips had enslaved it in love, so that it became distressed and disquieted.
Emaciated, it came attacking them, supple like my beloved when he remains in my embrace;
Wondrous that they resemble us and have not begun to split or separate.

The use of the masculine pronoun in referring to the beloved (the word for which itself takes a masculine form in line 9, *ḥabīb* rather than the feminine *ḥabība*) does not necessarily mean that he is male. Love poems of this period sometimes addressed women with masculine pronouns and masculine forms of nouns. The gender of the addressee here is ambiguous and probably irrelevant. Unless the poet is addressing his wife—and it is hard to imagine a good Muslim doing so, since dedicating a love poem to a woman was generally considered an insult to her family—the desire evoked is illicit. We have no reason to believe the poet has any particular person in mind, male or female; the beloved is a poetic fiction. In keeping with the language of the poem, however, we will refer to the beloved as male.

These first lines of the poem take us through a series of transformations in which the beloved seems to be everything but a person. The first line by itself seems to be nothing more than a desert scene. Only in line 6 are the branches explicitly connected to the beloved. But even in line 1 it is difficult to read the landscape as "real," since the poet's heart gathers from the branch not fruit but a flame. By the end of the first fragment we realize that the branch evokes the slenderness of the beloved's waist, the sand dune the curves of his hips. In the second line we see the beloved's face as a full moon. In the rest of the poem there are clouds and lightning, the sun and stars, even a flock of magpies in the sky, but no other reference to the moon, although this is a moon never seen waning; it seems more like a moon never seen again. Perhaps the most intriguing aspect of the opening lines is that the beloved is never there, is always something else. The solitary branch on a sand dune in a desert plain is an evocation of great loneliness. The beloved is the branch, his face is a moon, his eyes belong to a white gazelle whose glance is a notched arrow, his smile is a stolen string of pearls. Even the golden *lām* of his curls is just a thin sheet of gold over silver; both are precious metals, but pure gold would be more valuable.

Despite the omnipresent moon of the boy's beautiful face, the heart-rending arrow of his glance, the blinding smile of pearls, the precious curls, the poet cannot keep from returning obsessively to the beloved's waist, or more specifically the juncture of waist and hips. A branch on the sand dune is the beloved's waist in line 1. Five lines later the poet returns to the waist, reminded of it by his own conceit of silver *waraq* under gold, which shares a tri-consonantal root with *awraqa* (to put forth leaves), which of course leads back to the branch in line 6. Line 7 leaps immediately from branch to waist. We are no longer in the realm of metaphorical mediation; the waist is thin because the beloved is pining away. But before we can relax, in line 8 the waist and hips are in love, the waist taking the part of the poet, enslaved in love. The poet identifies with the waist in the following line, likening the supple hips to his beloved when in the poet's embrace. Wondrous, the poet tells us, that like us they have not begun either to either split or to separate.

Wondrous indeed that the poet spends the first six lines of the poem running from the body of the beloved as quickly as he can, transforming every attractive body part into something else, only to end up picturing himself as the waist snuggling between his beloved's hips. The metaphoric representation of the poet's longing is lodged in the very body of the beloved, indeed in a crucial part of that body. But it is not simply the intersection of hips and waist that the poet must flee. The very important final line of this fragment contrasts the union of the beloved's hips and waist with the separation of the beloved and the poet. The separation of the lovers makes about as much sense as rending the beloved's hips from his waist.

The point, however, is not merely to explicate the poet's complex conceit, but to determine what he has covered up, which according to the final line of his poem is his task. The trauma from which the poem springs and around which it circles is not only the separation from the beloved, but the inextricable intertwining of that separation with the unity of the beloved's body and union *with* the beloved's body. It is not the eyes of a white gazelle, face like a moon, or smile like a string of pearls that both attracts and drives away the poet, but the covered-up space of the beloved's body where the waist joins the hips. There the poet hangs his ornaments, sheaths his eloquence (his sword)—this place that requires the clothing of his poem. Ironically, the ambiguity of the gender of the beloved does not permit us to speculate on what is adorned by the poem, what is hidden at the juncture of waist and hips; the organ of the beloved is effaced in the poem. All that matters is that the poem covers it—and in doing so, glorifies the poet.

I hope I have demonstrated that the poem is remarkably coherent, the obsessions of the poet remarkably consistent. Despite the fragmentation of the poem, the missing lines and the uncertainties of organization, the poet repeatedly returns to the same images and tropes. The precipitous endings of the fragments, cut off from their own extensions or from the longer beginnings of succeeding sections, emphasize rather than work against the coherence of the poem, for even in their foreshortened state they point ahead or back to other moments in the poem. Perhaps most crucial are the last two lines of the final fragment of the poem, in which the poet reveals his artistic intentions, and the last two lines of the first fragment, in which he provides a startlingly corporeal vision of these intentions. Perhaps the somewhat abstract goals of self-glorification and renewal of his poetic inheritance are born in the obsession with covering the private parts of the beloved, although again, this is not to suggest that there is any counterpart to the beloved in the "real" world outside the poem. Poetic language itself is corporeal enough to provoke obsession and compulsion; the poetic image is traumatic enough to motivate a poem—and like any trauma must remain ambiguous and unreachable.

NOTES

1. James T. Monroe, "Oral Composition in Pre-Islamic Poetry," *Journal of Arabic Literature* 3 (1972): 1–53.

2. Suzanne Pinckney Stetkevych, *The Mute Immortals Speak: Pre-Islamic Poetry and the Poetics of Ritual* (Ithaca: Cornell University Press, 1993).

3. As opposed to another oriental tradition, the Chinese, which he knew somewhat.

4. Shoshana Feldman, "On Reading Poetry: Reflections on the Limits and Possibilities of Psychoanalytical Approaches" in *The Purloined Poe: Lacan, Derrida, and Psychoanalytic Reading,* John P. Muller & William J. Richardson, eds. (Baltimore: Johns Hopkins University Press, 1988), p. 148.

5. Emilio García Gómez, *Cinco Poetas Musulmanes: Biografías y Estudios* (Madrid: Espasa-Calpe, 1944) p. 71. García Gómez takes most of his biographical material from al-Ḍabbī's *Bughya* (Bibliotheca Arabico-Hispana, F. Codera and J. Ribera, eds., vol. III [Madrid, 1885]), dating from 1343, although other information can be found attached to the various recensions or partial recensions of the poem. See note 15.

6. This seems to be where the poet's mania for blonds began as well. Even the wine in the poem we will read is "dorado," or golden, rather than red. See A. R. Nylel,

Hispano-Arabic Poetry and Its Relations with the Old Provençal Troubadours (Baltimore: J. H. Furst, 1946), pp. 61–62; García Gómez, *Cinco Poetas Musulmanes,* p. 77.

7. Ibid., p. 73.

8. The way in which Potiphar's wife stage-manages the whole scene is striking: she has the props distributed and times Joseph's entrance for maximum effect.

9. These versions can be found in Hashim Amir-Ali, *The Message of the Qur'an Presented in Perspective* (Rutland, Vt.: C. E. Tuttle Co., 1974), p. 263; A. J. Arberry, *The Koran Interpreted* (New York: Macmillan, 1965), p. 257; Ahmed Ali, *al-Quran: A Contemporary Translation* (Princeton: Princeton University Press, 1988), p. 202; Mohammed Marmaduke Pickthall, *Meaning of the Glorious Koran* (New York: New American Library, 1976), p. 176; N. J. Dawood, *The Koran Translated with Notes* (Harmondsworth, N.Y.: Penguin, 1974), p. 40.

10. Régis Blachère, *Le Coran* (1923; reprint, Paris: G.-P. Maisonneuve & Larose, 1980).

11. Abdullah Yusuf 'Ali's footnote to his translation amplifies the verse so that the fruit appears from the obscurity of *muttaka'an*: "When her reputation began to be pulled to pieces by Mrs. Grundy, with sundry exaggerations and distortions and malicious innuendoes, the wife of 'Aziz invited all the ladies in society to a grand banquet. We can imagine them reclining at ease after the manner of fashionable banquets. When dessert was reached and the talk flowed freely about the gossip and scandal which made their hostess interesting, they were just about to cut the fruit with their knives, when, behold! Joseph was brought into their midst. 'If fruit is good enough for Mrs. Grundy . . .'" 'Abdullah Yusuf 'Ali, *The Holy Qur'an: Text, Translation and Commentary* (Brentwood, Md.: Aman Corporation, 1989).

12. Not even the name by which we know the poet is innocent. García Gómez translates all al-Sharīf al-Ṭalīq as "el Príncipe Amnistiado" (the pardoned prince), which reminds us of his crime as well as his pardon and which he also uses as the title of his chapter on the poet. His real name was Abū 'Abd al-Malik Marwān b. 'Abd al-Raḥmān b. Marwān b. 'Abd al-Raḥmān al-Nāṣir (A. R. Nykl, *Hispano-Arabic Poetry,* p. 61).

13. James T. Monroe, *Hispano-Arabic Poetry: A Student Anthology* (Berkeley: University of California Press, 1974), p. 154.

14. Ibid., p. 11.

15. Stetkevych, *The Mute Immortals Speak,* p. 257.

16. Ibid.

17. Although the translation is my own, I follow the Arabic text presented by James Monroe in *Hispano-Arabic Poetry: A Student Anthology.* Monroe notes the following sources: "Main text in Ibn al-Abbār, *apud* R. Dozy, *Notices sur quelques manuscrits arabes* (Leiden: E. J. Brill 1847–1851), pp. 116–19; scattered lines in al-Maqqarī, *Analectes sur l'histoire et la littérature des arabes d'Espagne,* R. Dozy, G. Dugat, L. Krehl, and W. Wright, eds. (Leiden: E. J. Brill, 1855–1861), 2:398; Ḥimyarī, *Kitāb al-Badī' fī wasf al-rabī',* Henri Pérès, ed. (Rabat: Publications de l'Institut des Hautes Études Marocaines, 1940), 8:33–34; Ḍabbī, *Bughyat al-multamis,* F. Codera and J. Ribera, eds. (Madrid: Bibliotheca Arabico-Hispana, 1885), 3:447; Ibn Sa'īd al-Maghribī, *'Unwān al-murqiṣāt wa-l-muṭribāt,* 'Abd al-Qādir Maḥdād, ed. (Algiers: Bibliotheque arabe-francaise, 1949),

4:16; Ibn Saʿīd al-Maghribī, *Kitāb Rāyāt al-mubarrizīn: Libro de las banderas de los campeones,* E. García Gómez, ed. and trans. (Madrid: Seix Barral, 1942), p. 38."

18. Monroe, *Hispano-Arabic Poetry,* p. 8.

19. It should be noted that Córdoba of this period saw itself as surpassing even Baghdad, which in its eighth-century heyday was the greatest city of the world, rivaled only by Chang An, capital of Tang China.

20. Monroe, *Hispano-Arabic Poetry,* p. 159.

21. Lacan, Jacques, *Écrits* (Paris: Éditions du Seuil, 1966), p. 259. All translations from Lacan are my own, as are all the translations from the Arabic.

CHAPTER SIX

Two Homoerotic Narratives from Mamlūk Literature: al-Ṣafadī's Lawʿat al-shākī *and Ibn Dāniyāl's* al-Mutayyam

Everett K. Rowson

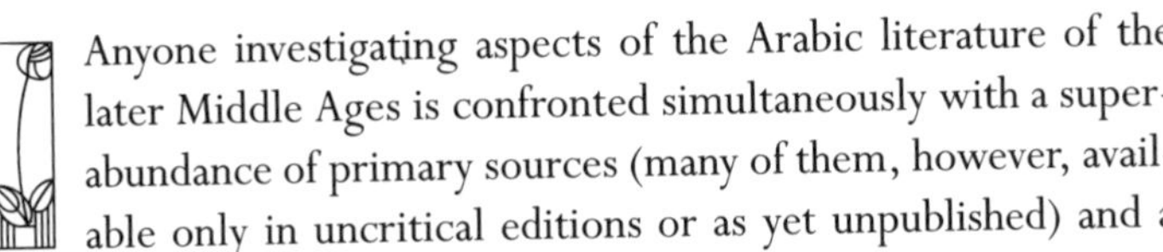

Anyone investigating aspects of the Arabic literature of the later Middle Ages is confronted simultaneously with a superabundance of primary sources (many of them, however, available only in uncritical editions or as yet unpublished) and a paucity of secondary studies. With the exception of Andalusian literature, whose formal innovations in stanzaic and popular poetry have generated considerable heat as well as light in modern scholarship, the modern Western "canon" of classical Arabic literature may be said to close with al-Maʿarrī (d. 449/1058) in poetry and al-Ḥarīrī (d. 516/1122) in artistic prose. Only a few later figures have attracted much attention, and these for somewhat peripheral reasons: Ibn al-Fāriḍ (d. 632/1235), who is seen as an Arabic equivalent to the major Persian Ṣūfī poets; Ibn Dāniyāl (d. 710/1310), whose shadow plays provide relief for those who would consider the lack of a dramatic tradition in Arabic an embarrassing literary lacuna; and al-Būṣīrī (d. 694/1294), whose Mantle Ode in praise of the Prophet is simply too famous to ignore completely. Beyond the work of these writers, Arabic literature of the Ayyūbid, Mamlūk, and Ottoman periods has been given sporadic scholarly attention at best.

The principal reason for this neglect is undoubtedly the perceived lack of accord of this literature with modern taste. Rhetorical embellishment occupied an increasingly important place in both poetry and prose from the eleventh century on, and al-Ḥarīrī's *Maqāmāt,* seen as a *ne plus ultra,* is as far as most scholars have been willing to go; it is easy to dismiss all the subsequent *ultra,* of which there is indeed a very large quantity, as collectively too clever by half. Equally discouraging has been the apparent lack of innovation and initiative, as evinced most obviously by the fondness for such forms as the commentary and the *takhmīs* (the expansion of an older poem by supplementing each original line with four new ones). Even the rich development of stanzaic and colloquial poetry in fourteenth- and fifteenth-century Egypt and Syria has been neglected in favor of their earlier efflorescence in Arabic Andalusia.

Given the quantity of unstudied material from this period, it would be rash to attempt any comprehensive statements about the role of homoerotic sentiment in later Arabic literature, or to what extent it differs from what we find in earlier periods. Yet some general observations may be ventured, and two works in particular, each innovative in its way and concerned centrally with homoerotic sentiment, offer a basis for some more specific analysis.

First, the general observations. By the time the Mamlūks took power in Egypt and Syria in the mid-thirteenth century, Arabic poems by male poets about the love of boys and their beauty had long been as common, and canonical, as those about the love and beauty of women. From its beginnings, which may be dated roughly to the appearance of the ʿAbbāsid poet Abū Nuwās (d. ca. 200/815), this homoerotic poetry can be divided into two broad categories. In the poetry of licentiousness (*mujūn*) the poet celebrates his antinomian defiance of societal values. Coarse descriptions of homosexual seductions, anatomical preoccupations, and later a significant admixture of scatology characterize this kind of poetry; since homosexual acts (specifically, anal intercourse) were proscribed in the strongest terms in Islamic law, antinomianism would seem to be a natural prerequisite for treatment of such themes. On the other hand, a much more chaste, discrete, and romantic tradition of homoeroticism is also represented, modeled on the already well-developed tradition of heterosexual love poetry in all its subgenres, ranging from the playful (but not profligate) to the tragic.[1] In this "higher" tradition, the basic illicitness of homosexual relations is essentially elided; where explicit references to sexual acts—which are what the law specifically proscribed—are inappropriate, the poetical treatment of the emotions of love need not be affected by the sex of the beloved, given, as was clearly the case from the ninth century on, that men's attraction to boys was considered as natural as their attraction to women.

The situation in prose is more complex, badly under-studied, and correspondingly difficult to summarize succinctly. In early literary encyclopedism, the prose equivalent to the poem was the anecdote, which concerned itself with content much more than form.[2] Anecdotes about homosexual passion are not rare, and *mujūn* anecdotes are common; both have their heterosexual equivalents. Monographic treatments of love, a genre that begins with the *Book of the Flower* of Muḥammad b. Dāwūd in the late ninth century, incorporated many love anecdotes as well as poems but varied in their treatment of homoeroticism; the best-known of these, Ibn Ḥazm's *Ring of the Dove,* offers homoerotic and heteroerotic anecdotes (including personal ones about the author) in an indifferent mix, and concludes with praise of chastity and condemnation of licentiousness, the latter explicitly including both homosexual relations and any heterosexual relations outside of marriage or concubinage.[3] A folk tradition of prose romances, virtually entirely lost to us except for bibliographic citations, seems to have been exclusively heterosexual.[4] Artistic prose, originally much more restricted in its subject matter than poetry, expanded its scope in the course of the tenth century to become the latter's serious rival, but nothing like a "prose poem" of love seems to have developed.

A basic continuity of earlier forms in the Mamlūk period is easy to document. Homoerotic love poetry remained as popular as ever, perhaps even gaining in popularity at the expense of heteroerotic verse, although verifying this impression would require careful documentation as well as, and prior to, analysis of its possible causes. One obvious index of the continued parallelism between the two forms of love poetry is the appearance of a series of paired anthologies of poems describing the beauty of boys and of girls, the earliest of which, to my knowledge, are the *Thousand and One Boys* and *Thousand and One Girls* of al-ʿĀdilī (fl. mid-seventh/thirteenth century).[5] Both biographical dictionaries and literary anthologies of the Mamlūk period include large numbers of poems of both sorts, as well as *mujūn* poems, by all the major poets of the era.[6] Further evidence comes from the ongoing production of monographs on love.[7] All these sources, as well as chronicles, contain abundant anecdotal evidence for the prevalence of homoerotic sentiment in life as well as in art, particularly among the Mamlūks themselves (who are in any case overrepresented in our documentation).

But it is in artistic prose that we find the most striking innovations in the treatment of homoerotic themes. The early Mamlūk period produced two works of extended narrative, each focused on a homosexual love affair. To my knowledge, these works are unprecedented. *Ghazal* poetry could be narrative in its fashion but was necessarily limited in scope, rarely extending beyond a sketch of a single incident (normally, a seduction). Factual, or ostensibly factual, anecdotes about homosexuals and homosexual affairs could be quite long and are of the greatest importance for social history, but do not present the literary interest and the kind of idealized or generalized picture offered by these texts. Furthermore, these works appeared at approximately the same time—they are separated by only about thirty or forty years—but treat their subject in radically contrasting ways, one embodying the chaste, romantic tradition and the other presenting homoerotic *mujūn* at perhaps its most extreme. The preliminary analysis of both texts presented here, then, may offer some insight into the general concept of homoeroticism and its place in literature in the Mamlūk period, as well as into the specifics of its actual role in that society.

The earlier of these two texts, a shadow play by the Cairene littérateur Ibn Dāniyāl (d. 710/1310), is the licentious one. Since, however, a proper appreciation of Ibn Dāniyāl's approach requires some understanding of the chaste ideal that his play is intended to undermine, it will be more convenient to look first at a slightly later text that expresses this ideal directly, an "epistle" by the well-known littérateur al-Ṣafadī (d. 764/1363) entitled *The Plaint of the Lovelorn and Tears of the Disconsolate.*[8]

Khalīl b. Aybak al-Ṣafadī, the son of a Mamlūk, occupied various government posts throughout his life, in his native Ṣafad, al-Raḥba, Aleppo, Cairo, and especially Damascus, where he died of the plague.[9] He was a leading writer of his day and is best known now for his massive biographical dictionary of everyone who was anyone, from Muḥammad to his own time.[10] But he wrote dozens of other works, mostly in belles lettres, including a lengthy (and highly digressive) commentary on the famous poem by al-Ṭughrāʾī (d. 515/1121), the *Lāmīyat al-ʿajam*;[11] studies of specific rhetorical figures and tropes, as well as a general work on literary theory;[12] various anthologies of prose and verse, both general and specific; and a massive commonplace book running to at least forty-four volumes, many of which are extant but none of which have been published.[13] Besides the *Plaint of the Lovelorn,* his unpublished poetic anthology entitled *The Pure Beauty of One Hundred Handsome Boys*[14] also takes homoeroticism as its subject.

The Plaint of the Lovelorn is referred to by some later writers as a *maqāma,* but this seems to be due to the progressive widening of the term's application until it could refer to any piece of fine writing in prose. Al-Ṣafadī himself would probably have called it an epistle (*risāla*), although we have no contemporary evidence for any generic label at all for the work and it lacks the real or putative address to a "friend" that most often characterizes epistles.[15] In the edition I have used, it runs to eighty pages and is composed throughout in elaborate rhymed prose (*sajʿ*) although interrupted frequently by poetic citations, usually of only two or three lines; these are never attributed, but in fact most if not all of them are by earlier poets, not the author himself.[16] After a five-page introduction explaining the purpose or "moral" of the work, al-Ṣafadī begins his first-person narrative, which extends to the end.

The "plot," such as it is, proceeds extremely slowly, being constantly interrupted not only by poetry but also by extensive passages of pure description; it is clear that the writing itself, in all its exuberant rhetoric, is the real point, the subject matter serving largely as a vehicle.[17]

This does not mean, however, that the latter lacks significance. The story, in barest terms, is this: One day the narrator goes out for a walk with a trusted friend and reaches a beautiful garden. At this time he is not in love, and mocks those who are. But then a troop of seven beautiful young men appears, all of them Turks mounted on horseback and carrying bows, and the narrator is entranced. Heedless of the danger of gazing on such beauty, he feasts his eyes, particularly on one of them, and immediately loses his heart. He advances alone to the group and greets them, and the one who has captivated him returns the greeting and then leads him apart to another part of the garden for a private conversation. This youth asks how, for all his good sense, he could have let himself fall prey to this disaster, and the narrator replies that it was simply God's decree. When pressed to prove his love, the narrator appeals to his tears and his misery as witnesses and swears, repeatedly, his eternal devotion. Convinced, the beloved declares himself at his service and obedient to his wishes. The lover has difficulty controlling his tears and articulating his desires, but when prompted by the beloved he embraces and kisses him, although fearful of spies. Anxious to rejoin his waiting companions, the beloved promises to return to the same place the following Saturday, when they can enjoy uninterrupted intimacy, and rides off.

The narrator, now desolate, is joined by his friend, who is appalled to discover that he has fallen victim to love and counsels him to conceal his passion as befits his social status. The following days and sleepless nights are sheer torture for the lover, who must also endure his friend's reproaches, but at last the appointed day arrives and he and his friend return to the garden, where they sit and wait. When the beloved fails to appear, the friend offers to go seek him out and after a time returns, alone but smiling. He has found the beloved riding with his companions, and brings a message that he will join the narrator as soon as he can, then accompany him home where they can enjoy wine and spend the night together. The lover is beside himself with joy, which only increases when the beloved arrives, declares his own love, and asks for a kiss. After indulging in some teasing, the beloved suggests that they have had enough of pretty speeches and should retire to the lover's home. The friend is sent ahead to make preparations, and when the lovers arrive they find food, candles, sweet-smelling herbs, and wine awaiting them. The beloved acts as cupbearer, urging the lover not to fear the sin of wine drinking but to trust in God's forgiveness.

At midnight, the narrator asks his friend to take away the wine and prepare a bed; the friend is to sleep in the house himself, but outside the room. Invited to the lover's bed, the beloved protests that embracing is a sin, but the lover makes light of his objections. The beloved strips to his shirt and skullcap and the two fall into each other's arms. Neither sleeps at all throughout this night of love, over whose brevity the lover weeps when morning breaks. The beloved insists he must go, grants a final kiss, promises to visit again if he finds the opportunity, and departs. The friend appears to congratulate the lover on his night of passion, but the latter is already weeping in his agony over its end. Hoping and waiting for a repeat of that night, he must content himself in the meantime with the phantom of the beloved. The epistle ends with his expression of faith in the beloved's promise and his prayer that God grant that they be reunited.

Clearly, there is nothing remotely realistic about this story. An example from the narrator's first encounter with the group of young men will suffice to illustrate the artificiality of both the language and the situations depicted. His first words, addressed to the group as a whole, are, "May God preserve these beautiful features, these bodies envied by swaying branches, these faces gleaming with the water of loveliness, these eyes that are the snare of souls and fetters of minds! Will you not have pity on one infatuated and lovesick, bound in the chains of ardor and passion. . . ? The just-encountered beloved then replies, "May God preserve you and exalt you, and keep you safe from the call of passion and protect you! May he not make your eyelid sleepless from the cruelty of the beloved . . . may He rather cause the sides of his body to incline to you, grant you the fruit of his intimacy near for plucking,[18] bestow on you a share of healthful rest, give you to drink from his lips their wonderfully cool and refreshing water, lay you beside the beloved in a single bed, make his wrist and arm a collar for your neck, permit you to kiss those cheeks and drink from that mouth, give you the pleasure of undoing the knot of the drawstring from that waist and buttocks, and bring you together with the one you love and have chosen. . . ." His next words, after drawing apart with the lover from his companions, are, "I have known you to be stout of heart and proud of soul, keen of mind and incisive of judgment; what then is it that has caused you to embark on this extraordinary course and delivered you over to weeping and sobbing? How have you fallen prey to something from which you have warned others off, and for which you have showered contempt on every unrequited lover?"[19] Yet the two have clearly never met before.

The succession of events is, in fact, to be understood less as a fully coherent story than as a reasonably logical sequencing of occasions for the literary expression of standard topoi, originally poetic, here in elaborate prose. The uniting principle of these topoi is indicated by the work's title: lovesickness and tears. The narrator weeps on every page, occasionally with joy but usually with longing. Even when the beloved declares himself the lover's slave the latter weeps to the point that the beloved must ask, "Why do you weep when I am here before you?" to which he replies, "Only because of my certainty of our imminent parting."[20] Secondary topoi are also occasions for long pauses; the descriptions of the beauty of the garden and the beauty of the beloved take up many pages. Equally verbose are the passages that precede inserted verses, which often seem to bend the narrative to make the insertions fit and amount to anticipatory prose paraphrases of the poetry. Rather than being perceived as awkward duplication, however, this procedure would probably have been understood as a deliberate demonstration of the author's power to render verse into fine prose.[21]

But the contradictions in the love situation itself go beyond the sacrifice of full narrative coherence to the exigencies of literary thematics. The unresolved tensions between the pleasures and the pains of unfulfilled love, between the poetic richness of longing and the comparative poetic poverty of fulfillment, and between the religiously tinged avoidance of passion and the heady immersion in it are basic to the thematics of love throughout the Arabic literary tradition. And while the *Plaint* builds its plot and bases its general tone on the first two of these tensions, the third raises urgent questions about the very coherence of the narrator's message, particularly in light of his introduction, which offers a rationale for presenting his narrative that is difficult to reconcile with the tale as actually told.

This introduction begins conventionally, with an elaboration of the requisite praise of God and blessing on His prophet, shaped in accordance with the subject to be treated in the epistle:

> In the name of God, the Merciful, the Compassionate
>
> Complaint must be directed to him who possesses manly virtue (*murūwa*)
> Who will commiserate with you, console you, or share your pain.[22]
>
> After praising God, who decreed love and passion, ordained the burning of hearts for every lover and impassioned one and humilia-

tion for all those in love's throes . . . and invoking blessing and peace on our master Muḥammad . . . who said—and his words in their surpassing wisdom bring near all that is remote—"He who loves, hides his love, and is chaste, and then dies, is a martyr"—may God bless him, and his family and companions, who poured out their souls in love for him, pursued only his path, and sought only to follow his exemplary speech and behavior (*sunna*), so long as the east wind blows and brings consolation to the distracted lover, and comes from the abodes of those he loves and evokes his tears over them—

I know better than any of my brethren and companions, friends and colleagues—may God deliver them from the attacks and ravages of passion, the terrors and sorrows of love . . .[23]—that the most harmful thing that can befall a man at any time is that his eye wander unrestrained, roam through the plazas of loveliness and beauty, and graze amidst the branches of charm and allure, so that he sees what he has no patience to withstand once he has gazed on it, and is unable to flee once he has drawn near it, and finds himself, after enjoying comfort and respect, reduced to a state of ignominy and wretchedness.[24]

After describing at some length the resulting catastrophe, al-Ṣafadī appeals to the Qur'ānic injunction that the believers "lower their eyes" in modesty,[25] then cites verses to the effect that one who sends out his eyes as scouts for his heart brings trouble on himself, since he can neither obtain all of what he sees nor be satisfied with a part. He concludes his introduction with verses describing how the hapless lover takes revenge on his eyes by making them shed tears of blood, then makes the transition to his narrative by saying, "The occasion for this admonitory introduction and these words expressing warning is that I went out one day . . ."[26]

In this introduction, al-Ṣafadī invokes two major themes from the love tradition whose complex history can only be touched on here: the problem of gazing on the beautiful and the martyr status granted to those who die of love. That love and desire are awakened by gazing was more than a commonplace; it was an occasion for religious and legal discussion. Besides the Qur'ānic reference cited by al-Ṣafadī, there were a number of traditions from the Prophet (*ḥadīth*) that dealt with this question and on which legal scholars relied in debating the permissibility of a second, deliberate glance as opposed to the first, inadvertent one. The legal discussions took on more urgency when the Ṣūfīs initiated the practice of deliberate *naẓar,* that is, gazing at a beautiful boy (called a *shāhid* or "witness"—to God's glory and beauty) as a spiritual exercise. By al-Ṣafadī's time, the conservative Ḥanbalite legists, in particular, had had much to say against such deliberate *naẓar.*[27] Al-Ṣafadī's own Shāfiʿī school was rather less concerned with the question, but there too the standard view was that gazing on a beardless boy with lust was forbidden, and some jurisprudents prohibited gazing without lust as well.[28]

The *Plaint* is not, however, a work of jurisprudence, and despite his invocation of the Qur'ān al-Ṣafadī stresses not the sinfulness of *naẓar* but its peril. Gazing leads to love, which leads inevitably to unhappiness, specifically tears. Yet love, whether or not induced by a deliberate gaze, is not in itself a sin; indeed, a celebrated prophetic tradition on passion (*ḥadīth al-ʿishq*) promises those who die of love, so long as they keep the secret and remain chaste, immediate admission to paradise as martyrs. Unlike the Ḥanbalites, who were uncomfortable with this tradition and attacked both its authenticity and its apparent sense, al-Ṣafadī acknowledges its validity.[29] And if its invocation in this introduction were to precede an account of tragic, unfulfilled heterosexual passion, with a full complement of tears, no problem would arise. The difficulty lies in the fact that al-Ṣafadī proceeds to describe an apparently consummated homosexual affair, something unequivocally condemned by Islamic law and hardly to be justified by this *ḥadīth.*

The question of consummation aside, the homoerotic nature of the narrator's passion is not in itself in contradiction with the *ḥadīth al-ʿishq.* Islamic law condemned homosexual activity, not homoerotic sentiment; and even a pietistic moralist like the Ḥanbalite Ibn al-Jawzī (d. 597/1200) insists that anyone who claims that a man can gaze on a beautiful youth without desire is either lying or not fully human.[30] Both the discussions of *naẓar* and the *ḥadīth al-ʿishq* are equally applicable to both heterosexual and homosexual passion, at least in theory. In practice, however, there were reasons why both were particularly associated with the homoerotic. Given the seclusion of women from the onset of puberty in respectable society, the problem of *naẓar* was much more likely to arise with boys, and in its institutionalized form among the Ṣūfīs it was exclusively so directed. The *ḥadīth al-ʿishq* has obvious roots in the resolutely heterosexual passion of the ʿUdhrī lovers of the Umayyad period, who died or went mad when denied union with their beloveds. Yet it first acquired celebrity through association with Muḥammad b. Dāwūd and citation in his *Book of the Flower,* and while this anthology includes both heteroerotic and homoerotic poetry, the anecdotal tradition insists not only that Muḥammad b. Dāwūd wrote the book for his beloved Ibn

Jāmiʿ, but also that he later died of love for this man.[31] Ibn Dāwūd was the son of the founder of the Ẓāhirī, or literalist, school of Islamic jurisprudence (which did not survive to al-Ṣafadī's time), and it was his reported advocacy of the "permitted gaze" (*al-naẓar al-mubāḥ*) and the *ḥadīth al-ʿishq,* associated with this school, that became the particular target of the Ḥanbalites.[32]

It is difficult to imagine a piece of high literature of al-Ṣafadī's time, such as the *Plaint of the Lovelorn,* concerning itself with a heterosexual affair rather than a homosexual one. Whether this is in part a function of social class—one might posit that heterosexual romances existed on the folk level but were not reflected in respectable writing—is an important question, but beyond the scope of this essay. The nature of the male beloved over whom al-Ṣafadī's narrator waxes so passionate, however, is worth pausing to consider. First of all, he is a Turk. This represents a shift from the situation in classical Arabic poetry, but conforms entirely to the canons of beauty in the Mamlūk age (as well as to its social hierarchy). Many erotic verses by al-Ṣafadī and his contemporaries celebrated the beauty of Turkish boys, sometimes explicitly to the disadvantage of Arabs, and the beauty of both the boys and women of the Mongol Oirats, a group settled in the quarter of al-Ḥusaynīya in Cairo at the end of the thirteenth century, was particularly renowned.[33]

The further, interrelated questions of the beloved's age and his presumed sexual role are more problematic. The conventions of literature, and presumably of society, had always dictated that the lover, who assumed the active role in homosexual (anal) intercourse, be a mature man, and more insistently that the beloved, assuming the passive role, be an adolescent. In the classical tradition, the sharp distinction between the two roles was generally more important than the age differentiation. While convention ruled that a boy lost his beauty once his beard began to grow, there were protests against this dictum from an early period. By al-Ṣafadī's day, poems for and against the continued desirability of a bearded young man were a standard subgenre of erotic verse.[34] Nevertheless, even a bearded beloved was assumed to be relatively young, and younger than the lover. Whether this was the case with Ibn Dāwūd, to whom are attributed two pro-beard poems, said to have been composed about Ibn Jāmiʿ, is unclear, because our sources are too meager and contradictory to draw any firm conclusions about the later image of their relationship, let alone about its historicity.[35] In the *Plaint* also, specific indications of age (including any reference to the beloved's beard or lack of one) are missing, except for the conventional description of him as a gazelle fawn (*rashaʾ*, *ẓaby*), and there is no explicit reference to sexual role.

Strictly speaking, where there is no question of consummation, that of sexual role need not arise. Even in Ibn Dāwūd's case, however, the transmitted reports leave no room for doubt about who was the lover and who the beloved; a basic asymmetry in love relationships, clearly grounded in the assumed inequality in power and status between men and women, would be as unquestioned in homosexual as in heterosexual relationships.[36] Similarly, in the *Plaint,* despite the beloved's enthusiasm he remains unambiguously the beloved; but there are also abundant indications throughout the work, even apart from the description of the final night of union, that the relationship is a fundamentally sexual one. And while the citations of Qur'ān and *ḥadīth* in the introduction may seem to suggest both the possibility and desirability of combining love passion with chastity, later religious references in the work point in a quite different direction. A notable example, which also underlines the asymmetry between lover and beloved, is the latter's appeal to God, at his first meeting with the lover, that He "give you the pleasure of undoing the knot of the drawstring from that waist and buttocks." Given the consensus among all the legal schools that anal intercourse between men was a major sin, and among most of them (including the Shāfiʿīs) that the punishment for both participants was death, such a prayer would appear both risible and impious.[37]

Yet neither laughter nor outrage seems to be the appropriate, or intended, response to al-Ṣafadī's rather frequent commingling of erotic and religious topoi in this work. For example, when the beloved first wonders how the lover has permitted himself to fall into the trap of love, he asks, "Do you know that when someone is killed by passion no talio is applied to his killer, no crime counted against the deliberate perpetrator, no blood-revenge demanded, and no proceedings against the one who did it initiated? Has not your *imām* al-Shāfiʿī (may God be pleased with him!) said, by way of stressing the terrors of such a situation and warning against it—

> Hold that gazelle responsible for the loss of my life,
> For he shot me with the arrows of his eyes, and with intent.
> But do not kill him, for I am his slave,
> And according to my school a free man is not put to death for (killing) a slave![38]

When the lover is then asked to swear to the sincerity of his love, he appeals to his tears and misery as witnesses, insisting that they are "known for their probity, acceptable to you in their statements, and duly registered with the

Judge of Love."[39] And the beloved, insisting that the lover be true *until death* (thus dying in, if not of, love), cites the following verse:

> Die on the straight path and you will have a good reward for your passion,
> For in the Law (*shar*ʿ) of Passion death is the best thing for you.[40]

Some interpreters, seeing a blatant contradiction between being "on the straight path" (*rāshid*) and indulging in homosexual passion and being under the spell of the "didacticism" of medieval literature in general, might be tempted at this point to read al-Ṣafadī's epistle as an admonitory tract in the most direct sense, taking such passages as these as illustrations of the protagonists' depravity, assuming the author's condemnation of their love, and finding in the lover's unremitting tears the just recompense for an immoral indulgence in sin. To my mind, such an interpretation would make nonsense of the aesthetics of the epistle as a whole. It may be rhetorically effective to depict the Devil as beautiful, but a compelling sermon will not dwell unduly on the delectability of sin and will certainly not conclude with the sinner's fervent hope—and prayer—for further occasions to pursue it. Despite all his tears, the protagonist's experience of love is simply portrayed too positively here to be meant as nothing but a negative example.

How, then, can al-Ṣafadī depict someone as being "on the straight path" (*rāshid*) while engaged in a homosexual love affair? There seem to be three possibilities. The lover could love from afar and keep his love secret, perhaps even from the beloved; such a course finds frequent literary expression, but is ultimately poetically interesting only if the secret is betrayed (conventionally, by the lover's tears). The lover could permit himself some dalliance with the beloved, falling short of the specific acts proscribed by the law, but the degree of freedom permitted is legally fraught.[41] Or one could simply say that piety and homosexual love *are* incompatible in real life, but literature is not real life. Such, for instance, is the interpretation offered by Ibn Saʿīd al-Maghribī (d. 685/1286) of the scandalous verses by the thirteenth-century Egyptian poet al-Jazzār (d. 679/1280):

> He was unlike the (generality of) poets in avoiding addiction to wine and any confirmation (in his life) of the various sorts of prohibited activities of which he speaks in his poetry. Indeed, he followed the path of chastity and virtuous behavior, despite all his playful (verses) to newly bearded young men, which are to be taken

> (simply) as displays of elegance and exercises in composing love poetry.[42]

But Ibn Saʿīd clearly considers al-Jazzār an exception, and one must count a fourth possibility—not a reconciliation of piety and profligacy at all, but a simple damn-the-consequences attitude that, at best, counts on God's boundless mercy and forgiveness in the end.

This last possibility is by definition the way of *mujūn,* and certainly inapplicable to the register at which the *Plaint* is composed. Nor does the first possibility, the keeping of the secret demanded by the *ḥadīth al-ʿishq,* seem relevant to the protagonist's behavior, despite the author's appeal to it in his introduction. After all, it is not only the beloved but also the audience of the epistle to whom this secret is betrayed. But between the remaining possibilities—an ultimately unconsummated relationship and a sort of default position dissociating literature from real life—there is room for some degree of constructive ambiguity, as can be seen from al-Ṣafadī's handling of the crucial scene when the lovers are finally united for a night of passion.

At the end of their evening of carousal, just before preparations are made for bed and the lover's friend retires, he asks the lover, "By God, do you incline more toward this one, or toward singing slave girls?[43] Explain to me what it is that you really want, and lay bare for me what you hide inside." The lover replies, "If love of Salmā is better (*aslam*) for one's life, and passion for Nuʿmā is more delightful (*anʿam*) for one's eye, I have nevertheless contented myself—with a beloved in a turban![44]

> I love him in his turban, but the one who upbraids me
> Will never leave off wronging me with his fanatical
> partisanship.[45]

For the passion I have for him takes away not only my breath but my very soul . . ." To this rather evasive reply the lover then adds a long poem on the beauty of his "Turkish gazelle."[46] He then says to the beloved, "Come, let us go to bed, and give me the pleasure of kissing that mouth and embracing that body." The beloved replies, "I will come with you, but embracing is forbidden." The lover says, "On my neck be any burden of sin!" and cites a verse to the same effect. The beloved protests, "I take refuge in God from immortality and vicious gossip (*laghaṭ*), and from your falling, my dear sir, into error (*ghalaṭ*)." But the lover responds, "Do not think that love of you is sinful and wicked (*sayyiʾāt*), and do not imagine that your lover's page (of good and bad deeds) is black like your moles and beauty marks (*ḥasanāt*)!

Know rather that passion for you is one of the greatest virtues and best of pious acts!

> I ask God for forgiveness for anything but my love for you,
> For it will be counted as my good deed on the day I meet Him.
> But if you claim that love is a sin,
> Love is surely the most trivial of ways that one can sin against God.

Come then—may I be your ransom—and let us make doubt into certainty (*yaqīnā*), and call an embrace to our aid, for perhaps an embrace will protect us (*yaqīnā*)!" Without further protest the beloved is then led to bed and stripped to his shirt and skullcap. The description of the lovers' night of passion occupies five pages of the text but is couched throughout in the most discreet of phraseology: "we abandoned restraint, and cast aside sobriety . . . and what we sought and intended happened"; "he moved (*sāq*) my heart to bliss by the intertwining of leg (*sāq*) with leg"[47]; "we ran through the plaza of passion and profligacy"; and, in verse,

> Generous Time gave us a wonderful night,
> But do not ask what happened between us.[48]

"Do not ask" would seem in fact to be the appropriate reply to all the above questions. A work that wishes to include descriptions of the ultimate joy of love must at least imply that this love was sexually consummated, but the sublimated register of the work, marked by the introductory appeal to the *ḥadīth al-ʿishq,* equally requires that the description of love not turn into one of sex and that the possibility be left open that this affair did remain, in the narrowest of senses, chaste. The lover seems far from dying of love at the end, but his passion endures, so perhaps ultimately this will be his fate. The beloved's surprisingly casual remark that he will visit again if he finds a chance may seem to leave the story without a conclusion, but in fact it leaves the lover in exactly the most "poetic" of circumstances: distracted by his passion and unable even to take comfort in despair.

In other words, the *Plaint* presents all the idealized aspects of love, without any awkward or sordid intrusion of reality. As an idealized portrait, it is fiction: not only are the events not "true," but physical, moral, and even logical constraints are all suspended. What matters is the elegant description of the emotional heights and depths of passion—longing, frustration, consummation—for the ideal beloved, a beautiful Turkish boy in late adolescence. In an ideal—that is, ultimately gratifying—world, such a passion would indeed be a virtue, or at the very least an eminently forgivable peccadillo.

Not that al-Ṣafadī was any stranger to sordid reality—or at least to the sordid. In other works, he shows no hesitation in quoting, or composing, scabrous verses and anecdotes; his *al-Ghayth al-musajjam,* in particular, is replete with the coarsest *mujūn.*[49] Since *mujūn* was an established genre, as much so as refined *ghazal* and its prose equivalents, we must beware of mistaking it for the real as opposed to the ideal, but an investigation of some homosexual *mujūn* will at least balance out the picture of Mamlūk literary treatments of the homoerotic.

Rather than al-Ṣafadī himself, however, it is a poet of the previous generation who provides the most apposite *mujūn* correlate to the *Plaint.* Ibn Dāniyāl was an ophthalmologist from Mosul who settled in Cairo in the days of the Mamlūk amir Baybars (658–76/1260–77) and set up shop just inside the Bāb al-Futūḥ.[50] He composed poetry in all genres, including panegyrics of the Mamlūk amirs, who offered him at least sporadic patronage, but his forte was licentious verse. Al-Ṣafadī, who admired him greatly, described him in an oft-quoted passage as "the Ibn Ḥajjāj of his age (*ʿaṣr*), and the Ibn Sukkara of his city (*miṣr*)," thus comparing him to the two most notorious exponents of obscene (*mujūn*) and scatological (*sukhf*) poetry during its first peak of popularity, in late tenth-century Baghdad.[51] And it is to al-Ṣafadī that we owe the preservation of extensive selections from Ibn Dāniyāl's *Dīwān,* itself apparently lost.[52]

What set Ibn Dāniyāl apart from other poets of his time, however, was not his indulgence in *mujūn,* which was common to virtually all of them, but his innovation in composing shadow plays, a genre not previously attempted by representatives of serious literature. Before his time we have only scattered references to this genre of entertainment, which probably found its way west from southeast Asia in the tenth century or earlier and was clearly a purely folk phenomenon. Marionette-like flat figures of colored translucent leather were held against a sheetlike screen onto which a strong light was projected from behind so that the figures' outlines, color, and articulations could be seen from the front; performances were held at night. Only from Ibn Dāniyāl's own work and from much later "scripts" do we have an idea of the nature of the "plays" presented with these figures, although allusions in a poem by Ibn al-Fāriḍ suggest a wide range of subject matter.[53]

Ibn Dāniyāl published his three shadow plays in a book he entitled *Ṭayf al-khayāl* (approximately, "The Imaginary Phantom"), punning on a cliché of love poetry that refers to the phantom visit of the beloved in the lover's dreams, and on the term for the shadow play itself (*khayāl al-ẓill*). Al-Ṣafadī stresses the novelty of this work, following his characterization of the poet, quoted above, with the statement that "he composed the book *Ṭayf al-khayāl,* in which he forged a new and unheard-of path, and in which it was in fact he who produced both the singing and the dancing."[54] The exact implications of this last comment are unclear, but it may serve as a caution against the usual assumption that Ibn Dāniyāl's plays were in some way typical and intended as real scripts for performance. Although they do read as scripts, with dialogue interrupted by stage directions, the latter are, like the former, couched in rhymed prose and cannot be taken as purely functional. Furthermore, the adaptation of a folk genre by a literary figure, no matter how broadly conceived his potential audience, presumably involved some shift—upward—in form if not content, and indeed the roguish charm of these plays must have consisted in part in the incongruity between the two.[55] This is implied by Ibn Dāniyāl himself in the introduction to his book, which reads as a parody of the conventional opening of a literary epistle (*risāla*), in this case a reply to a request from ʿAlī b. Mawlāhum the shadow-play artist (*khayālī*):

> You wrote to me, O artful master and debauched degenerate—may your screen remain high and your privacy inviolate—to say that people have turned a deaf ear to the shadow play and ceased to respond to it because of its hackneyed repetition, and to ask me to compose for you in this genre something that will be an innovation (*badīʿ*) for the characters in the puppet box. I was at first constrained by modesty from providing you with what you desired to transmit from me; but I feared that if I refrained from fulfilling your request you might imagine that I did so out of lack of ambition, insufficient intelligence, and an inability to respond creatively to the copious wellsprings and natural quickness of my imagination. So I let my thoughts range through the wide fields of my profligacy, and was able to fulfill your request without the slightest delay. I have composed for you some licentious plays (*bābāt al-mujūn*), pieces of high, not low, literature (*al-adab al-ʿālī lā l-dūn*), which, once you have made the puppets, divided the script into scenes, assembled your audience, and waxed the screen, you will find to be entirely novel (*badīʿ al-mithāl*) and truly superior to the usual shadow play.[56]

Whether intended for actual performance or not, these plays do represent high, but licentious, literature. They are composed in an approximately equal mix of prose and poetry; the prose is uniformly parallelistic and rhymed, the poetry ranges from formal odes to such stanzaic forms as the *muwashshaḥ, dōbayt, zajal, ballīq,* and *mawāliyā.* The last three of these are, by definition, composed in the vernacular, and there is strong admixture in the prose as well of colloquial vocabulary, and even on occasion of the argot of the underworld.[57] In their content, each of the three plays deals, in its own way, with popular life and the demimonde of entertainers and other marginal types. The first play, which shares the title of the entire book, *Ṭayf al-khayāl,* is presented as a reaction to the amir Baybars' well-known campaign to repress vice in Cairo; the hero, the amir Wiṣāl, decides to clean up his life and get married, with farcical consequences. The second play, *ʿAjīb wa-Gharīb,* offers simply a parade of entertainers and other itinerants, including quack physicians, monkey trainers, sword swallowers, and the like. But it is the third play, *al-Mutayyam wa-l-Ḍāʾiʿ al-Yutayyim* (The Man Distracted by Passion and the Little Vagabond Orphan), that is of particular interest here.

In his introduction to this play, Ibn Dāniyāl gives a preview of what is to come, saying, "I have included in it something about the states of lovers, some love poetry that is patent magic, some games, and some blameless *mujūn.*" This is a reasonably accurate description of the four-part, rather episodic plot, although surely some would have quibbled with the word "blameless." The play as a whole is about homosexuality, and can be seen as a progressive undermining of the ideal which was soon to be expressed so eloquently in al-Ṣafadī's *Plaint.* In the first part, al-Mutayyam laments his frustrated passion for al-Yutayyim, explains how they met, and describes a subsequent encounter in which he managed to steal a kiss but was left literally prostrate by the coy beloved. The second part presents an encounter, and a love duet of a sort, between the two parties after the beloved's heart has been somewhat softened through the good offices of a go-between. In the third part al-Mutayyam plays to his beloved's passion for sport, and the two initiate a series of animal fights between their cocks, rams, and bulls. When al-Mutayyam's bull is killed in the third of these contests and his beloved departs, he decides to throw a banquet for all and sundry, hoping to attract al-Yutayyim (and presumably to get him drunk and thus make him more pliant). Al-Yutayyim does not reappear, however, and in his stead we are entertained by a procession of unsavory characters, each representing a sexual alternative to such a hopeless romantic love. The play concludes with a token gesture to morality as the Angel of Death appears, al-Mutayyam repents and dies, and the guests disperse.

The lovesick al-Mutayyam who introduces himself to the audience at the beginning of the play sounds very much like the narrator of al-Ṣafadī's *Plaint,* and the beloved by whom he is distracted also conforms to the ideal, as is clear from a poem he recites which begins:

Is every brother of passion in such a state,
  Or I am alone in this madness?
I am tormented by a dusky (*aḥwā*), black-eyed (*aḥwar*) Turk
  Whose gaze is languid (*futūr*) and seductive (*futūn*).

This is followed by a further description of the beloved and al-Mutayyam's version of love at first sight:

> Your servant is al-Mutayyam, distracted over al-Ḍāʾiʿ al-Yutayyim, who has enchanted people's hearts, and closed the door on other beauties, with his willowy build, tiny waist, large eyes and thick eyebrows, copious buttocks, bright forehead, and well-separated teeth, whose cheeks are roses and whose downy beard is violets; he is perfect in features (*awṣāf*) but lacking in justice (*inṣāf*). The way I first fell for him, and began to stumble in pursuit of him, is this: I happened to pass by the palaestrum, where there were huge crowds of people massed at the door. They were all staring at a youth who had stripped off his *qabā* and was being closely watched by his guardians; he had boxed his way to a perfect 150 (?),[58] and the lovers were invoking God's protection on him by chanting the Qurʾānic chapters *Ṭāhā* and *Yāsīn*; *dirhams* and *dīnārs* had been scattered all about him, and he was coming toward me with a face like the full moon. When I saw him, my heart skipped a beat and my thoughts were scattered, and I extemporized a *muwashshaḥa* on him . . .

Wrestling is an even more virile activity than hunting with bow and arrow on horseback, and as in the *Plaint* the beloved is clearly identified as an ephebe, not a pudgy adolescent. Characteristically, however, Ibn Dāniyāl is not content merely to imply this fact, but proceeds to spell it out in the most explicit way. Al-Mutayyam's former boy (*ghulāmukum al-qadīm*) joins him on stage, gives a Bronx cheer and a snort, and proceeds to criticize his new choice:

> Mutayyam, your religion has betrayed you, and you've exchanged jasmine for thorny tragacanth; you've exposed your honor to attack, and treated your illness with what will only make you sicker; you've fought the spearthruster with your own spearthrust, and met his spearpoint with your own spearpoint. Suppose you attain

your desire—are not two penises under a single blanket a danger? Do not argue against me (*bi-khilāfī*), or be dazzled by the crack of a backside (*shiqq al-khilāfī*)[59], for you will not be safe with him from the evil of a serpent that can harm you, or peck you like a rooster. Why not try a young gazelle fawn, easy to obtain, sincere in his coquetry, fair when it comes to the in-and-out, who can be pleased with a bite to eat, and abashed with a box on the ears, small in years but perfect in beauty? How can one compare the meat of a lamb to that of a woolly ram? Is there anything more restorative to life than chicken soup? One eats almonds with their husks only because they're so soft and small, and only small fish, not big ones, can be consumed whole—

They said: You're in love with a little one! I said: What of it:?
  A little one is light on the scales!
A little one is like a flower in a garden that you sniff
  When it's fresh, from time to time.
He's smooth as silk to the touch,
  And the scent of his armpits is as pleasant as basil.
His lips are sweet, his airs delectable, his breath fresh,
  His limbs supple, soft, and lovely.

When you see a little one peeved and embarrassed, pluck the delicious apples from his cheeks. When you see him coming from school, he has ink smudges for a beard and there is lapis on his golden cheek. Only the lucky man attains him, and the day one puts it in him is a festival day.

To this al-Mutayyam replies:

May God break your teeth, and give you neither security nor sustenance! Chant the Qur'ān (*mathānī*) to cure yourself of your madness, and acknowledge that a downy beard is a second (*thānī*) beauty! How can the crescent be compared to the full moon, or a ripe pomegranate fruit to the pomegranate blossom? Alas for you! Would you prefer an unripe date to a ripe one, or verjuice to wine? A young fig can be eaten only with the blemish of its acidity, and is too narrow to accommodate more than a goosing with a finger.[60]

Here we see Ibn Dāniyāl drawing from the pro- and anti-beard tradition, as well as displaying his rhetorical skills on a *mujūn* topic. The general tone, which was not unequivocally parodic at the beginning of the play, has taken a definite turn downward and from this point continues to do so. Al-Muttayyam complains about the torture "this toothsome (?) gazelle, this wretched pretty-boy"[61] has caused him, and says he has daydreamed about running him through with his sword—but when he saw him again and their eyes met, his heart melted.

One of these occasions was at the baths, as al-Mutayyam proceeds to recount in one of Ibn Dāniyāl's most famous poems (here slightly abridged):[62]

I have become notorious for my slip in the baths,
  And you have all heard it talked about everywhere.
What happened happened, and it's over; but
  That slip of mine was one of the marvels of the age.[63]
I crossed over from my house to the Bath of Bāb al-Kharq,[64]
  Just as dawn was putting a blaze on the forehead of the night;
And there I encountered my beloved strutting about provocatively,
  With his willowy build, like a branch on a sand dune.
I said, "What! Here, too, my dear sir?" And he said,
  "Here, too," with a beautiful smile.
He had stripped, like a sword when the blacksmith
  Takes it from its scabbard.
He was wearing two wrappers, one of hair,
  The other his own hair, and looking like a full moon.
Pearls of sweat covered him,
  Like the pearls of a necklace, scattered, unstrung.
When his inky mole indiscreetly disclosed
  The tale of his musky (new) beard,
The rose swore that his cheeks were more dazzling than it was
  Itself when bedewed with the showers from the clouds.
Then the fingers of the bathman made manifest
  The strands[65] of musk on the camphor of his flanks,
And he appeared like the silk brocade of a lote-tree
  In a garden of beauty, where the roses of his cheeks grew.
And the water streamed, overflowing, like me with love,
  Or like my tears, which streamed in torrents.
He was so delicate as to melt under that water,
  And flow over that marble.
Then the hand of the groomer fell with its comb

On the morning of his part, to divide it.
I said, "Comb[66] the beloved's hair well,
And free me from my ties to this boy;
Then manicure him and give him victory[67] over hearts,
As wished by my passion and infatuation in his love."[68]

I stumbled just behind him on my way out,
Desires causing feet to slip,
And he found me thrown down prostrate before him
And recited healing charms over me with the charms of his body.
I pretended to have swooned from my passion,
And stole a kiss from what he had covered with his face-scarf.
What a slip! With it I healed my heart,
Even if I also broke all my bones!
So hear (these verses) from me, O noble one,
Like necklaces of bubbles on the surface of wine,
With both serious and lighthearted *mujūn*
And permitted and forbidden magic.

The end of this story is given in prose: "Then I put my hand on that gentle hill of his buttock, seeking a draught from that reservoir. But he said to me, 'Not so fast, Mutayyam! Not everything smooth is a pancake!'[69] Then he made his way through the crowd, and left me prostrate on the floor of the bath." Rescued by his friend Nuṣayr, who rolls him up a in a mat, takes him out, and then revives him with wine, al-Mutayyam expresses his gratitude with a panegyric.[70]

At this point al-Yutayyim's servant Bayram enters and informs al-Mutayyam that he has been interceding on his behalf with his master. When al-Yutayyim asked him whether al-Mutayyam really loves him, he reports, he had responded that he does, with a love as great as the grains of the sands and even greater than his love for his own parents: "if he sits with you he keeps you company, if you stretch your legs he massages you, if you stand up he dresses you, and if you lie down at night under him he covers you." Emphasizing to al-Yutayyim al-Mutayyam's attractiveness as a beautiful and cultured young man, not to mention his being a champion wrestler, he had gone on to laud his prowess in other games and also to praise the superiority of the animals he raised for fighting contests. He had then pointed out that al-Mutayyam was also an aficionado of animal fights, and in this way persuaded his master to relent and pay the distraught lover a visit. Al-Mutayyam is overjoyed at this news, and when al-Yutayyim himself appears he bursts into a *muwashshaḥa* on his love. But al-Yutayyim complains that "you have tarnished my reputation, and treated me badly; you have abashed me before my family, and shamed me among the youth of al-Ḥusaynīya."[71] This is followed by an exchange of seven quatrains (*dō-bayt*) between lover and beloved, al-Mutayyam complaining of his lovesickness and emaciation and al-Yutayyim replying with coyness and aloofness, until in the final quatrain al-Mutayyam turns to praise of his fighting cock.

The implied challenge in these verses provides the transition to the third episode of the play, the fights between the protagonists' animals. Such animal contests were clearly popular among the rowdy youth of Cairo, and it seems likely that they would have been standard in shadow plays because of the ease and vividness with which they could be represented on the screen.[72] For Ibn Dāniyāl they offer an opportunity to display his talents at parody. All three contests, between cocks, rams, and bulls, follow a similar pattern: each contestant first recites a mock panegyric on his animal,[73] and then the referee and holder of the wagers (*ḥakam*) enters and pronounces a mock invocation (*khuṭba*) before initiating the fight. Al-Mutayyam's cock wins the first contest. Before the second begins, al-Yutayyim's mother (the only woman in the play) puts in an appearance to describe how she has applied spells and charms to her son's ram to protect it from defeat;[74] these are to no avail, however, and al-Mutayyam's animal wins again.

In an interlude before the third contest, a bit of business between al-Mutayyam and his beloved serves further to destroy any illusions about the former's high-minded intentions. As al-Yutayyim eavesdrops, his lover, clearly aware of his presence, soliloquizes about offering him his ram, along with two calves, in exchange for a kiss or at least a kind word. When al-Yutayyim withdraws for a moment, however, he says, "Where is that well-screwed pretty-boy with the well-punched pot?[75] I swear I will"—and here al-Yutayyim reappears—"kiss his feet, lay before him a bolt of silk, and swear to him with every oath that he must accept from me an ornamental belt and a scimitar." When al-Mutayyam then breaks into further plaintive verses, al-Yutayyim replies,

> Woe to you, Mutayyam! Leave off this babble (?)[76] or I'll slap you,
> And subject you to my destructive enmity and hatred;
> Vice simply lowers you in my eyes, while virtue raises you,
> So leave off this absurdity and treat me the way that will profit you.

Ignoring a further poetical protest by al-Mutayyam, al-Yutayyim then proposes the third match, between bulls. Al-Mutayyam's luck has clearly run out, for this time his animal is not only defeated but killed, and he recites a mock elegy over its body.

At this point al-Yutayyim makes what is to be his final exit from the play, leaving al-Mutayyam to attempt one final stratagem. He proposes to the puppeteer that a feast be mounted with the flesh of the bull and plenty of wine, and the doors thrown open for any passerby, on the chance that al-Yutayyim will be attracted by the revelry. This is done, and al-Mutayyam opens the banquet with a wine song (*khamrīya*). Instead of al-Yutayyim, however, he attracts a parade of characters representing, in the main, different sorts of male-male sexual practices and underscoring the implied message that love is only sex misspelled. For us, this procession serves as a convenient review of the way Ibn Dāniyāl's society categorized such activities.

First on the scene are a pair of effeminates (*mukhannath, mu'annath*) named Narjisa and Bashnīna.[77] The latter sings a song replete with puns on Arabic terms for "penis" (*zubr* or *zubb*), which begins:

> If I should desire anyone other than al-Zubayrī,[78]
> May my anus never enjoy a penis.
> Give me a cup of raisin-wine (*zabīb*) to drink,
> Tasting better than grape-wine,[79]
> Amongst a company of blacks from Zabīd
> Who come to us bringing everything nice . . .

Narjisa follows this with an elaborate prose description of his parturition of a turd, which was attended by a group of effeminate friends with "their men," all having comic names;[80] he then apologizes for not letting al-Mutayyam "beat me with that pestle of yours" because of his recent experience, recommends to him the company of effeminates in general, and asks for wine. Al-Mutayyam offers to give Narjisa anything he wants, and the latter dances and drinks until he passes out.

Next to appear is Abū l-Sahl,[81] a plump young catamite who recites verses on the "wide" welcome he offers everyone and commiserates with al-Mutayyam on the "narrow" morals of his absent beloved. Then he too drinks until he collapses (as do all the subsequent arrivals).

Then comes al-Bukhaysh b. al-Khannāqa,[82] an apprentice of al-Zallāqa,[83] who is "narrow" in what he offers, insisting on intercrural intercourse (*tafkhīdh*) rather than penetration. As he puts it, "I do not like to associate with bad people, will lie down only outside the house, and drink only in moderation; when a small person has a headache, he does not have the capacity for large cups"—

> My breastplate cannot withstand your arrows,
> And I do not have the strength to engage in love combat with you.
> Fear God when you deal with me, for I am small;
> Do not make me bear more than I can.
> Do not trick me into bringing lowliness on myself,
> But enjoy embracing without any hoisting.[84]

He also commiserates with al-Mutayyam, and after drinking but before passing out becomes more explicit in his poetry, reciting a *zajal* that begins:

> How big your thing is, Uncle! Slowly, slowly! Ouch! Mother!
> Be content with it outside! Not inside!
> Let it rub against the hair,
> Or put it in the gap,
> But don't tear up my anus with it!

The next arrival, who introduces himself as "Baddāl, famous for *bidāl*," that is, for taking turns with a partner in the active and passive roles in anal intercourse, has no sympathy for al-Mutayyam's plight and urges him to give up pursuit of his standoffish beloved and find someone like himself. In both prose and verse he lauds the equity—and economy—of such an arrangement, and before passing out he insists that were al-Yutayyim present he would debate this point with him (*jādaltuhu*), and perhaps have a go with him himself (*bādaltuhu*).

The identity of the next person to show up, Dāwūd al-Qabbāḍ,[85] is unclear to me. His brief self-description suggests that he may be a "groper" or *frotteur*, but offers too many lexicographical puzzles to permit more definite conclusions.

He is followed by ʿUmayra al-Jallād, the masturbator,[86] who extols the advantages of his specialty: he can have intercourse with any boy he finds attractive (although only in his imagination), avoids the messiness of actual anal intercourse as well as its legal penalty (*ḥadd*), and can pursue his pleasure in the baths or almost anywhere else. He advises al-Mutayyam to "summon your beloved [in your imagination], despite his aloofness, and whip ʿUmayra and say 'this is in him!'"

Next comes Nabhān al-Dabbāb,[87] whose specialty is *dabīb*, that is, sneaking up on sleeping boys and raping them. He describes his technique in prose and verse, leading al-Mutayyam to remark "No sleep for me tonight!" and to ply him hurriedly with drink.

As with al-Qabbāḍ, I have been unable to identify the specialty of the next arrival, Ziyād al-Shashshī. He urges al-Mutayyam to take advantage of one of the sleeping forms at his feet, but recites verses praising his own chastity before succumbing to the wine offered him.

The penultimate "guest" is the only one who clearly has nothing to do with sex. This is Salhab[88] al-Ṭufaylī, the proverbial gluttonous gate-crasher, who vaunts his insatiable appetite and total lack of shame. Al-Mutayyam apologizes for having run out of food before his arrival and offers him wine, which he gladly accepts.

With all the attendees except al-Mutayyam in a heap on the floor, the action of the play is brought to an abrupt close by the arrival of the Angel of Death. Terrified, al-Mutayyam asks if there is still time to repent; when told there is, he utters a quick prayer for forgiveness, turns to the *qibla,* and dies. The revived guests then disperse, and al-Mutayyam is shrouded and buried.

Leaving aside the problematical al-Qabbāḍ and al-Shashshī as well as the nonsexual figure al-Ṭufaylī, the remainder of the guests at al-Mutayyam's banquet are all well-known, nameable types, and a clear progression can be discerned in the order of their appearance, namely, a decreasing remoteness from standards of virility. Effeminacy (*takhnīth*) combines sexual role inversion (penetrated rather than penetrator) with nonsexual gender inversion; the former but not the latter characterizes passive prostitution (*bighāʾ* or *muʾājara*); a boy who submits only to intercrural intercourse (*tafkhīdh*) is still passive, but not penetrated;[89] masturbation (*jald ʿUmayra*) occupies a neutral position between passive and active roles; homosexual rape (*dabīb*) is active. The order is thus from greater to lesser depravity, gradually approaching the position of al-Mutayyam himself on this scale.[90] The *ṭufaylī* who appears at the end may seem somewhat out of place in this crowd but is a stock character in the *mujūn* tradition, and does serve to mark, so to speak, the emergence to the surface from this swamp of sexual irregularities; in any case, a *ṭufaylī* who arrives when the food has run out is an appropriate way to conclude such a banquet.

The restoration of the moral order with the appearance of the Angel of Death parallels the conclusions of Ibn Dāniyāl's other two plays. *Ṭayf al-khayāl* ends with the repentance of the title character and his partner's resolution to make pilgrimage, and the character Gharīb concludes *ʿAjīb wa-Gharīb* with a more perfunctory poem of repentance. Just as the admonitory introduction to al-Ṣafadī's *Plaint* should not be overread, any temptation to read back from the conclusions of these plays so as to make them into morality tales or warnings by negative example should be strongly resisted. The kind of literary indulgence represented by *mujūn* is fun precisely because one can temporarily suspend moral constraints, and this "harmless" *mujūn*—after all, this is literature, not life—loses its point if weighed down with preachy subtexts. Even Ṭayf al-Khayāl's palliative statement at the end of the first play that "Repentance is better, and we say things that we do not do"[91] should not be taken too seriously; while this standard topos, reflected also in Ibn Saʿīd's statement about al-Jazzār quoted above, does serve to get the poet off the hook, what the poet does or does not do is ultimately irrelevant to his art. And a more licentiously inclined reader is perfectly welcome to rely on the other aspect of the Angel of Death's appearance at the end of *al-Mutayyam*: "The door of repentance is ever open, so feel free to repent so long as you still have life in you, before you are snatched and your senses obliterated."

Like al-Ṣafadī in his *Plaint,* Ibn Dāniyāl in his *al-Mutayyam* presents a series of set pieces, ordered by means of a simple plot, about a homosexual love affair, except that instead of exalted passion his protagonist suffers from straightforward lust. If tears unite al-Ṣafadī's various themes, deflation and parody unite Ibn Dāniyāl's. Instead of a tender exchange on the dangers and desirability of falling in love, we have a debate on the comparative merits of pubescent and post-pubescent boys, and instead of a romantic first encounter, a pratfall in the baths. Courtship is reduced to a series of animal contests that allow Ibn Dāniyāl to parody formal prose invocations, panegyrics, and elegies.[92] And the final parade of "alternatives" offers a series of poems in which self-revelation through choice of vocabulary ("wide," "narrow," "penis," etc.) undercuts an ostensibly innocuous conventional theme.[93] The final irony is that it is the high-minded protagonist of the *Plaint* who (probably) consummates his love affair, while the hapless al-Mutayyam never really gets to first base; on the other hand, it is the latter who dies—although certainly not of love—and through his last-minute repentance is assured of his heavenly reward, while we can only wonder about the ultimate fate of al-Ṣafadī's lovelorn protagonist.

Neither al-Ṣafadī's *Plaint* nor Ibn Dāniyāl's *al-Mutayyam* attempts to deal directly with reality. Al-Ṣafadī builds a work of stylistic and rhetorical beauty upon all that is sublime in homoerotic sentiment; where that sublimity lies, despite whatever intrusions reality may make upon it, is assumed to be obvious to his readership. Ibn Dāniyāl exploits the gap between sublimity and reality, not so much to depict the latter as to mock the former, presenting a

Rabelaisian world in which all kinds of male-male lusts find their gratification in open defiance of conventional restraints. Here rhetorical finesse combines with deflating humor to offer a joyride through the *boue* just as accessible, and just as unreal, as al-Ṣafadī's soaring through the clouds.

As for the reality that lies behind these excursions, both texts presuppose a society in which male erotic attraction to males, in some form, is assumed to be natural and, if not universal, sufficiently widespread to be treated on its own terms rather than as a "marked" minority version of an "unmarked" heterosexual eroticism. At the same time, this society puts constraints on homosexual eroticism (again, not presented as differing in either intensity or nature from those on heterosexual eroticism) that encourage its treatment in terms of either sublimated frustration or antinomian indulgence. Much more remains to be said about the precise nature of homoeroticism in this milieu, but while such literary depictions as these have much to contribute, further research must be at least equally grounded in other varieties of texts offering different perspectives on both behavior and *mentalités*.

NOTES

1. The distinction between these two genres can be seen most clearly in the thematic subdivisions imposed on Abū Nuwās's oeuvre by the editors of his *Dīwān*, who separated his love poems into *ghazal* on males (*mudhakkarāt*), *ghazal* on females (*muʾannathāt*), and licentious poems (*mujūnīyāt*). See Ewald Wagner, *Die Überlieferung des Abū Nuwās—Dīwān und seine Handschriften* (Mainz: Akademie der Wissenschaften und der Literatur, 1957), pp. 316–26; idem, *Abū Nuwās: Eine Studie zur arabischen Literatur der frühen ʿAbbāsidenzeit* (Wiesbaden: Franz Steiner, 1965), pp. 308–29.

2. This is not to deny the value of recent studies by Fedwa Malti-Douglas, Stefan Leder, and others of the formal properties of the Arabic anecdote, but to contrast the situation with that of later formal artistic prose, discussed below.

3. The monographic love tradition is surveyed in Lois Anita Giffen, *Theory of Profane Love Among the Arabs: The Development of the Genre* (New York: New York University Press, 1971).

4. The titles of many of these are recorded by al-Nadīm in section 8.1 of his *Fihrist*, Riḍā Tajaddud, ed. (Beirut: Dār al-Masīra, 1988), pp. 363–67.

5. See Carl Brockelmann, *Geschichte der arabischen Litteratur*, 2nd ed., 2 vols. (Leiden: E. J. Brill, 1943–49), 1:352; Jürgen W. Weil, *Mädchennamen-verrätselt: Hundert Rätsel-Epigramme aus dem Adab-Werk Alf Ǧāriya wa-Ǧariya (7./13. Jh.)* (Berlin: Klaus Schwarz, 1984). Similar anthologies were compiled by Ibn al-Wardī (d. 749/1349) (*al-Kalām ʿalā miʾat ghulām* and *al-Kawākib al-sāriya fī miʾat jāriya*, extant in an Azhar manuscript); al-Nawājī (d. 859/1455), *Marātiʿ al-ghizlān fī [wasf] al-ḥisān min al-jawārī wa-l-ghilmān*, partial translation by René R. Khawam, *La Prairie des gazelles* (Paris: Phébus, 1989); and others. For al-Ṣafadī's contribution, see below, note 14. For those by al-Ḥijāzī (d. 875/

1471) and al-Badrī (d. 894/1489), see the essay by Franz Rosenthal in this volume, above, p. 33.

6. See Muḥammad Zaghlūl Sallām, *al-Adab fī l-ʿaṣr al-Mamlūkī,* 2 vols. (Cairo: Dār al-Maʿārif, 1971), 2:105–245.

7. Giffen, *Theory of Profane Love,* pp. 31–42.

8. *Lawʿat al-shākī wa-damʿat al-bākī* (more literally, "The love-sickness of the complainer and tear of the weeper"); frequently printed but never critically edited. My citations are to the edition of Muḥammad Abū l-Fadl Muḥammad Hārūn (Cairo: Muḥammad Afandī Fahmī Ḥusayn al-Kutubī, 1922).

9. See Donald P. Little, "Al-Ṣafadī as Biographer of His Contemporaries," *Essays on Islamic Civilization Presented to Niyazi Berkes,* Donald P. Little, ed. (Leiden: E. J. Brill, 1976), pp. 190–210; and Josef van Ess, "Ṣafadī-Splitter," *Der Islam* 53 (1976): 242–66, and 54 (1977): 77–108.

10. *Al-Wāfī bi-l-wafayāt,* various editors (Istanbul and Wiesbaden: Deutsche Morgenländische Gesellschaft, 1931–). A smaller work of the same nature but limited to his own contemporaries, the *Aʿyān al-ʿaṣr wa-aʿwān al-naṣr,* has recently begun to appear in a facsimile edition (Frankfurt am Main: Institute for the History of Arabic-Islamic Science, 1990–). On his dictionary of blind scholars, the *Nakt al-himyān fī nukat al-ʿumyān,* see Fedwa Malti-Douglas, "Dreams, the Blind, and the Semiotics of the Biographical Notice," *Studia Islamica* 51 (1980): 137–62.

11. *Al-Ghayth al-musajjam fī sharḥ lāmīyat al-ʿajam,* 2 vols. (Beirut: Dār al-Kutub al-ʿIlmīya, 1990).

12. *Nuṣrat al-thāʾir ʿalā l-mathal al-sāʾir,* Muḥammad ʿAlī Sulṭānī, ed. (Damascus: Majmaʿ al-Lugha al-ʿArabīya bi-Dimashq, 1972).

13. *Al-Tadhkira al-Ṣalāḥīya*; for some of the manuscripts see Brockelmann, *Geschichte,* 2:32, and *Geschichte der arabischen Litteratur, Supplementbände* 1–3 (Leiden: E. J. Brill, 1937–42), 2:28. See also note 52 below.

14. *Al-Ḥusn al-ṣarīḥ fī miʾat malīḥ*; see Brockelmann, *Geschichte,* 2:32, and *Supplementbände,* 2:28. Unlike al-ʿĀdilī and his own contemporary Ibn al-Wardī, al-Ṣafadī seems not to have composed a companion anthology on girls.

15. The attribution of the work to al-Ṣafadī is not beyond question. Among the twenty-five manuscripts listed by Brockelmann (*Geschichte,* 2:32, 335 and *Supplementbände,* 2:28, 463), seven attribute it rather to Zayn al-Dīn Manṣūr b. ʿAbd al-Raḥmān al-Ḥarīrī Khaṭīb al-Saqīfa (d. 967/1559), as does Ḥājjī Khalīfa (*Kashf al-ẓunūn,* 7 vols. [Leipzig-London: Oriental Translation Fund of Great Britain and Ireland, 1835–58], 5:344, 1336); two others attribute it to Jamāl (or Jalāl) al-Dīn Yūsuf al-Khaṭīb al-Manadī al-Ṣāliḥī, with a date of 988/1580; one to ʿAlā al-Dīn b. Sharīf [read al-Musharraf: see Brockelmann, *Geschichte,* 2:161 and *Supplementbände,* 2:200] al-Māridīnī (fl. 845/1441); and one to Ṣafī al-Dīn al-Ḥillī (d. 749/1349). Al-Ṣafadī himself informs us that he read under his older contemporary Ibn Faḍlallāh al-ʿUmarī (d. 749/1349) the latter's work entitled *Damʿat al-bākī wa-yaqẓat al-sāhir* (*Wāfī,* 8:255). None of the biographies of al-Ṣafadī I have consulted, including those by al-Subkī, Ibn Shākir, Ibn Kathīr, and Ibn Taghrī Birdī mention this work, but none of them offer complete bibli-

ographies (for references see Ibn Taghrī Birdī's *al-Manhal al-ṣāfī,* Muḥammad Muḥammad Amīn, ed., 7 vols. [Cairo: al-Hay'a al-Miṣrīya al-ʿĀmma li-l-Kitāb, 1984], 5:241–57). Stylistically, there is nothing to militate against al-Ṣafadī's authorship, and the bulk of the manuscripts support it.

16. Some of these are identified in the edition of the text I have used; I have found a few others, and further investigation would undoubtedly result in additional identifications. The verses cited come from all periods of Arabic literary history. Al-Ṣafadī was accused of stealing verses from his contemporaries, notably from his mentor Ibn Nubāta, who wrote a book pointing out his thefts; see Sallām, *Adab,* 2:94–95.

17. In the edition I have used, the editor has obligingly marked with parentheses the first word of each sentence that actually advances the story; these appear rather less frequently than once a page.

18. This is an allusion to Qur'ān 69:23 and 76:14, where the fruits of Paradise are so described.

19. Al-Ṣafadī, *Lawʿat al-Shākī,* pp. 17–20. The author's prolixity necessitates my resorting to abridgment, here and in subsequent quotations from his work. Of course much of the rhetorical brilliance of the original, which is replete with paronomasia and other "figures of sound," is unavoidably lost in translation.

20. Ibid., p. 25.

21. The rendition of poetry in prose (*ḥall al-naẓm*) and vice versa was by al-Ṣafadī's time not only a school exercise but an established genre of *adab.* To my knowledge, works of this sort have not yet been investigated seriously by scholars. Two published examples are al-Thaʿālibī's (d. 429/1038) *Nathr al-naẓm wal-ḥall al-ʿiqd* (Cairo: al-Maṭbaʿa al-Adabīya, 1317 [1899–1900]) and al-Nayramānī's (d. 413/1022) *Manthūr al-manẓūm li-l-Bahā'ī* (Frankfurt am Main: Institute for the History of Arabic-Islamic Science, 1984), the latter a prose rendition of Abū Tammām's *Ḥamāsa.*

22. A line from an unidentified poet.

23. This parenthesis extends for half a page and includes two lines of verse.

24. Al-Ṣafadī, *Lawʿat al-Shākī,* pp. 4–5.

25. Qur'ān 24:30–31.

26. Al-Ṣafadī, *Lawʿat al-Shākī,* pp. 6–8.

27. See Joseph Norment Bell, *Love Theory in Later Ḥanbalite Islam* (Albany: State University of New York Press, 1979), pp. 19–28, 125–44, and Giffen, *Theory of Profane Love,* pp. 117–32.

28. See al-Ramlī, *Nihāyat al-muḥtāj ilā sharḥ al-Minhāj,* 8 vols. (Cairo: Muṣṭafā al-Bābī al-Ḥalabī wa-Awlāduhu, 1967), 6:192. In his *al-Ghayth al-Musajjam,* 1:165–66, al-Ṣafadī expresses his surprise that the Shāfiʿī al-Nawawī (d. 676/1278) listed those who die of love among the martyrs without adding the usual proviso that they keep their love secret and remain chaste, despite this scholar's insistence that gazing on a beardless boy was forbidden whether or not accompanied by lust. Al-Ṣafadī does not venture a personal opinion on this latter point.

29. On the *ḥadīth al-ʿishq,* see Bell, *Love Theory,* pp. 38, 133–39, and Giffen, *Theory of Profane Love,* pp. 99–115. In his discussion in the *al-Ghayth al-musajjam* (see previous

note), al-Ṣafadī notes criticisms of this *ḥadīth*'s claim to authenticity but seems himself to support it.

30. Ibn-al-Jawzī, *Dhamm al-hawā,* Aḥmad ʿAbd al-Salām ʿAṭā, ed. (Beirut: Dār al-Kutub al-ʿIlmīya, 1987), p. 101; cited in Bell, *Love Theory,* p. 27.

31. See W. Raven, *Ibn Dāwūd al-Iṣbahānī and His* Kitāb al-Zahra (Amsterdam, 1989), pp. 32–57. According to one celebrated anecdote, Ibn Dāwūd confessed on his deathbed that it was love for his friend (unnamed: keeping the secret!) that brought him to his wretched state; when asked why he had not permitted himself to enjoy his love, he distinguished between permitted enjoyment—the gaze that had occasioned his love—and forbidden enjoyment, and then quoted the *ḥadīth al-ʿishq*. Al-Ṣafadī gives an abbreviated version of this account in his *Wāfī,* 3, 59f. Raven surveys all the anecdotes about Ibn Jāmiʿ, and expresses considerable skepticism about their historicity.

32. See notes 29 and 41.

33. Sallām, *Adab,* 1:58–59, 71–72, and 2:114, quoting from the sequence of verses in al-Ṣafadī's *al-Ghayth al-musajjam,* 2:19–21. Al-Ḥusaynīya was also famous for the rowdiness of its inhabitants, a reputation it retains today.

34. Some early examples can be found in al-Thaʿālibī, *Taḥsīn al-qabīḥ wa-taqbīḥ al-ḥasan,* Shākir al-ʿĀshūr, ed. (Baghdad: Wizārat al-Awqāf wa-l-Shuʾūn al-Dīnīya, 1981), pp. 63–64. The first monograph on the subject of which I am aware is that of al-Nawājī (d. 859/1455), *Khalʿ al-ʿidhār fī waṣf al-ʿidhār* (unpublished); Brockelmann (*Geschichte,* 2:56 and *Supplementbände,* 2:56) notes that one manuscript of this work attributes it to al-Ṣafadī. Three other treatises on the same topic, not yet investigated, are preserved in a Birmingham manuscript; see the *Catalogue of the Mingana Collection . . . , 4: Islamic Arabic manuscripts* (Birmingham: Selly Oak Colleges Library, 1963), p. 1732.

35. See Raven, *Ibn Dāwūd,* pp. 34–35, 47–48.

36. One report (Raven, *Ibn Dāwūd,* pp. 35, 47), remarking that Ibn Jāmiʿ was the only beloved known to have spent money on (*anfaqa ʿalā*) his lover (rather than vice versa), offers a rare hint of a breakdown in this asymmetry, but its very remarkability and the terms in which it is put confirm the point being made here.

37. On the legal status of homosexual anal intercourse (*liwāṭ*) see, provisionally, *The Encyclopaedia of Islam,* 2nd ed., 7 vols. (Leiden: E. J. Brill, 1960–), s. v. Liwāṭ. This topic is sorely in need of detailed study. The Shāfiʿīs either analogized the offense to heterosexual fornication, stipulating the death penalty only for married offenders, or relied on *ḥadīth* to impose the death penalty regardless of marital status; see Abū Isḥāq al-Shīrāzī, *Kitāb al-Muhadhdhab fī fiqh al-Imām al-Shāfiʿī,* 2 vols. (Cairo: Musṭafā al-Bābī al-Ḥalabī wa-Awlāduhu, 1976), 2:244. The Ẓāhirī Ibn Ḥazm permits only a discretionary punishment (*taʿzīr*), short of execution, in all cases; see his *Muḥallā,* 11 vols. (Cairo: Idārat al-Ṭibāʿa al-Munīrīya, 1347–52 [1928–33]), 10:380–94.

38. See Abū Isḥāq al-Shīrāzī, *Muhadhdhab,* 2:222; this contrasts with the view of the Ḥanafīs.

39. For professional witnesses in Mamlūk Cairo, see Carl F. Petry, *The Civilian Elite of Cairo in the Later Middle Ages* (Princeton: Princeton University Press, 1981), pp. 225–27.

40. Al-Ṣafadī, *Lawʿat al-Shākī,* pp. 20–23. The verses are unattributed. The parallels

to European courtly love in this passage are arresting, but do not to my knowledge represent more than an isolated rhetorical trope in their own tradition. This seems to be the only instance in the *Plaint* after its introduction where any allusion to the *ḥadīth al-ʿishq* can be detected.

41. For various opinions on this question, see Giffen, *Theory of Profane Love,* pp. 121–32, and especially Bell, *Love Theory,* pp. 127–39; the more liberal views were based on the distinction drawn between major (*kabīra*) and venial (*lamam*) sins at Qurʾān 53:32, as well as (spurious) verses attributed to pre-eminent jurisprudents (especially al-Shāfiʿī) permitting kisses, embraces, etc.

42. Quoted in Sallām, *Adab,* 2:138.

43. In comparing love for boys with love for slave girls (rather than for potentially marriageable women), al-Ṣafadī conforms to the conventions of the Arabic debates on this topic (which, however, are usually more a part of the *mujūn* tradition). On these debates, see Everett K. Rowson, "The Categorization of Gender and Sexual Irregularity in Medieval Arabic Vice Lists," in *Body Guards: The Cultural Politics of Gender Ambiguity,* Julia Epstein and Kristina Straub, eds. (New York: Routledge, 1991), pp. 58–59, and the article by Franz Rosenthal in this volume.

44. "Contentment" (*qanāʿa*) might be better translated "being satisfied with less," as is clear from the extensive treatment al-Ṣafadī gives this theme in his *al-Ghayth al-musajjam* (2:395–407). With regard to sexual activity, he notes that the term *qanāʿa* is applicable to tribadism between women (*saḥq*), taking turns at the active role in homosexual intercourse between boys (*bidāl*), and masturbation (*jald*), and appends a series of *mujūn* verses to this effect. The monograph by Stefan Weninger, *Qanāʿa (Genügsamkeit) in der arabischen Literatur: anhand des Kitāb al-Qanāʿa wa-t-taʿaffuf von Ibn Abī d-Dunyā* (Berlin: Klaus Schwarz Verlag, 1992), does not discuss such *mujūn* uses of the term.

45. The verses cited here and below are all unattributed.

46. Here unattributed, but assigned by al-Khafājī (*Shifāʾ al-ghalīl fīmā fī kalām al-ʿarab min al-dakhīl,* Muḥammad ʿAbd al-Munʿim Khafājī, ed. [Cairo: Maktabat al-Ḥaram al-Ḥusaynī al-Tijārīya al-Kubrā, 1952], p. 127) to al-Ṣafadī's older contemporary Abū Ḥayyān (d. 745/1344).

47. Echoing the description at Qurʾān 5:29 of the Last Day, when "leg will be intertwined with leg."

48. Al-Ṣafadī, *Lawʿat al-Shākī,* pp. 66–72. These unattributed verses echo the celebrated line from Ibn al-Muʿtazz's poem "Dayr ʿAbdūn": "What happened happened, but I'm not telling / Think well, and do not ask for specifics." This line (originally referring to a boy Ibn al-Muʿtazz picked up at a monastery) was used prominently by al-Ghazālī in his *al-Munqidh min al-ḍalāl* (ʿAbd al-Ḥalīm Maḥmūd, ed. [Cairo: Dār al-Kutub al-Ḥadītha, 1968], p. 133) to describe the mystic experience. Al-Ṣafadī quotes a different line from this poem earlier in the *Plaint* (p. 53).

49. See, e.g., *al-Ghayth al-musajjam,* 2:234–43, where a discussion of regret over past joys leads to a digression on loose vaginas and anuses, impotence, and related topics.

50. On him see *The Encyclopaedia of Islam,* 2nd ed., s. v. Ibn Dāniyāl (J. Landau) and references there; Ibrāhīm Ḥamāda, *Khayāl al-ẓill wa-tamthīlīyāt Ibn Dāniyāl* (Cairo: al-

Mu'assasa al-Miṣrīya al-ʿĀmma li-l-Ta'līf wa-l-Tarjama wa-l-Ṭibāʿa wa-l-Nashr, 1963), pp. 82–100; Aḥmad Ṣādiq al-Jammāl, *al-Adab al-ʿāmmī fī Miṣr fī l-ʿasr al-Mamlūkī* (Cairo: al-Dār al-Qawmīya li-l-Ṭibāʿa wa-l-Nashr, 1966), pp. 200–9; Sallām, *Adab,* 2:166–73; Muḥammad Nāyif al-Dulaymī, ed., *al-Mukhtār min shiʿr Ibn Dāniyāl . . . ikhtiyār Ṣalāḥ al-Dīn Khalīl b. Aybak al-Ṣafadī* (Mosul: Maktabat Bassām, 1979), pp. 5–25; M. M. Badawi, "Medieval Arabic Drama: Ibn Dāniyāl," *Journal of Arabic Literature* 13 (1982): 83–107; ʿAlī Ibrāhīm Abū Zayd, *Tamthīlīyāt khayāl al-ẓill* (Cairo: Dār al-Maʿārif, 1983), pp. 83–112.

51. Al-Ṣafadī, *Wāfī,* 3:51. On Ibn al-Ḥajjāj (d. 391/1001) see *The Encyclopaedia of Islam,* 2nd ed., s. v. Ibn al-Ḥadjdjādj; C. E. Bosworth, *The Mediaeval Islamic Underworld,* 2 vols. (Leiden: E. J. Brill, 1976), 1:64–67; Fuat Sezgin, *Geschichte des arabischen Schrifttums,* 9 vols. (Leiden: E. J. Brill, 1967–), 2:592–94. On Ibn Sukkara, see ibid., 2:571–72.

52. Some 217 poems and parts of poems are reproduced by al-Ṣafadī in volume five of his *Tadhkira,* preserved in a Cairo manuscript. They have been edited by Muḥammad Nāyif al-Dulaymī (see note 50), who has supplemented this selection with verses found in other sources (not including other unpublished volumes of the *Tadhkira*). Unfortunately, al-Dulaymī has heavily bowdlerized his edition.

53. See Badawi, "Medieval Arabic Drama," pp. 84–87. On Arabic shadow plays generally, see the works cited in note 50 and the older literature to which they refer. Among Paul Kahle's many publications in this field, a particularly useful summary is "The Arabic Shadow Play in Medieval Egypt (Old Texts and Old Figures)," *Journal of the Pakistan Historical Society* 2 (1954): 85–97.

54. *Fa-kāna huwa l-muṭrib wa-l-murqiṣ ʿalā l-ḥaqīqa* (*Wāfī,* 3:51).

55. Compare the discussion of classical and medieval European parody and travesty in M. M. Bakhtin's essay, "From the Prehistory of Novelistic Discourse," in *The Dialogic Imagination* (Austin: University of Texas Press, 1981), pp. 51–82.

56. I translate from my personal collation of the four known manuscripts of *Ṭayf al-khayāl.* The recent edition of the plays prepared by Derek Hopwood from Paul Kahle's Nachlass (*Three Shadow Plays by Muḥammad Ibn Dāniyāl* [Cambridge: E. J. W. Gibb Memorial, 1992]) is marred by numerous misprints and other errors; see my review in *Journal of the American Oriental Society* 114 (1994): 462–66. Even with four manuscripts (two with extensive lacunae), severe textual problems as well as lexical difficulties remain; my translations are all tentative.

57. See Bosworth, *The Mediaeval Islamic Underworld,* 1:119–31.

58. *Wa-qad lakaza muqāyadat/muqāmarat/muqāyarat al-miʾa wa-khamsīn*; the reading and sense are uncertain.

59. Translation uncertain.

60. The use of "fig" to mean "anus" is fairly common in the literature.

61. *Hādhā l-ẓaby al-mulaʿwas/malʿūs wa-l-ʿilq al-mukhassas/manḥūs. ʿIlq,* which in classical Arabic means "precious object," had by this time long acquired the significance "catamite."

62. In the *Mukhtār* edited from al-Ṣafadī's *Tadhkira* by al-Dulaymī, this poem appears (pp. 88–92) with numerous variants, as well as six added verses at the end that turn it

into a poem of apology (*iʿtidhār*) for Ibn Dāniyāl's absence from an unnamed patron's *majlis.* It is unclear whether the poet has incorporated parts of a previously composed poem into his shadow play or (less probably) expanded lines from the shadow play for a new purpose. There are instances of similar doublets elsewhere in the *Mukhtār.* I see no justification, however, for positing interpolation by later copyists into Ibn Dāniyāl's text; this suggestion has been repeatedly made by modern scholars, mostly to absolve the author of responsibility for some of the more extreme obscenity found in the texts.

63. Yet another echo of Ibn al-Muʿtazz's famous line (compare note 48 above). But Ibn Dāniyāl, of course, goes on to tell exactly what happened.

64. Modern Bāb al-Khalq.

65. *Fatāʾil,* black rolls of dirt rubbed from the skin.

66. *Sarriḥ,* also meaning "to let go free."

67. *Ẓaffir* has both these meanings.

68. The following verses, which bristle with lexicographical difficulties, pun on the various accoutrements of the bath (towels, boiler, pipes, etc.) in describing the lover's passion but recount no further events.

69. *Mā kullu zalaqa zalābiya. Zalaqa* and *zalaq* mean a slippery rock or place; *zalaq* is also the hindquarters of an animal. The sense seems to be "all that glitters is not gold" with an added sexual innuendo.

70. Almost certainly a previously composed poem; see note 62 above. In the *Mukhtār* (p. 99), al-Ṣafadī gives only the first line of the poem, referring the reader to the (lost) ninth volume of his *Tadhkira* for the full text.

71. See note 33 above.

72. This is implied by Ibn Dāniyāl's stage directions for the fights, which he says are to be carried out in the way "customary in the shadow play" (*ʿādat al-khayāl*).

73. For the cocks these are in verse; for the other two, in rhymed prose.

74. Unfortunately, the text is severely disturbed here, partly because of overlapping lacunae in two of the four manuscripts; how it should be restored is by no means clear.

75. *Al-ʿilq al-marhūz al-makhsūf al-kūz*; I have found no attestations for *kūz* with the meaning "anus," but it seems certain from context.

76. *Tasṭīʿ,* unattested in the lexica available to me. It does appear in Yūsuf al-Maghribī, *Dafʿ al-iṣr ʿan kalām ahl Miṣr,* facsimile edition by ʿA. A. ʿAwwād (Moscow: Nauka, 1968), of which I have only a list of entries.

77. "Narcissus" and "Lotus," both in the feminine form.

78. A common name, famous in Islamic history; *zubayr* is the diminutive form of *zubr.*

79. *Khumayr,* diminutive of *khamr.* The constant use of diminutives is a cliché in the speech of effeminates. Perhaps *zabīb* in this line should also be read in the diminutive form, *zubayb.*

80. The effeminates' names are mostly diminutives, e.g., Muwayza ("little banana"), while their men bear such names as Abū l-Kamar ("father of glans penes") and Zallūm ("elephant's trunk").

81. "Father of the Easy One."

82. "Little Hole, son of the Choker."

83. "Pipe of a Privy."

84. This last line—*lā tasumnī bi-l-naṣbi jarran li-khafḍin // wa-tamatta' bi-l-ḍammi min kulli raf'ī*—puns on five grammatical terms, following a common trope in rhetorical poetry.

85. "The Grabber."

86. The most common expression for masturbation is *jald 'Umayra,* "whipping 'Umayra."

87. "Wide-awake the Creeper."

88. The lexica define this word as meaning "long-bodied (of horses)," but R. Dozy, *Supplément aux dictionnaires arabes,* 2 vols. (Leiden: E. J. Brill, 1881), 1:679, notes a passage in the *Thousand and One Nights* describing someone as "more rapacious than Salhab," which suggests a proverbial proper name.

89. If the order postulated here is accurate, al-Qabbāḍ, who appears in this position, should represent a "mildly" passive but nonpenetrative act, and he does recite the following verses:

> Where is the one whose penis
> Was erect, filling the sky,
> Who would never turn away a beggar?
> God have mercy on those who have passed away!

90. This does not correspond, of course, to an order by the severity of sin according to Islamic law, which would consider masturbation the mildest of these activities and condemn the passive and active roles in anal intercourse equally. The coercive nature of *dabīb* is less central to its evaluation, both in religious law and in social morality, than we might expect; this is a topic deserving further, and careful, consideration. Al-Shashshī, coming after al-Dabbāb, should be a more acceptable sort of sexual penetrator; perhaps his invitation to "read my inscription" (*iqra' naqshī*) can be interpreted to mean "look at the color of my money," suggesting that, unlike al-Dabbāb, he pays for his pleasures.

91. Echoing the famous Qur'ānic statement about the poets (26:226) that "they say what they do not do"; one manuscript makes the allusion more direct by reading "and we are poets, who say things that we do not do."

92. Parodic elegies over the death of animals are a much-exploited genre; see, for example, al-Ṣafadī, *al-Ghayth al-musajjam,* 2:234–35.

93. These poems constitute a variation on the theme of "professional illiteracy," in which various artisans use metaphors derived from their crafts to describe a common subject (e.g., a battle or love); this theme has been traced through the literature by Joseph Sadan in "Kings and Craftsmen—A Pattern of Contrasts: On the History of a Medieval Arabic Humoristic Form," *Studia Islamica* 56 (1982): 6–49 and 62 (1985): 89–120.

CHAPTER SEVEN

Le beau garçon sans merci: *The Homoerotic Tale in Arabic and Persian*

Paul Sprachman

The Arabic Foundation

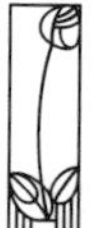

In Arabic, the tale in which a man, typically Muslim, becomes infatuated with a boy, typically Christian, appears in two genres, one literary and the other biographical. This obscene tale in its barest formulation comes in the *Maqāmāt* of Badīʿ al-Zamān al-Hamadhānī (d. 398/1008). The *Maqāmāt,* a highly allusive mélange of poetry and rhymed prose that influenced the literary essay in Persian, contains a homoerotic poem attributed to Abū Nūwās. Yāqūt al-Ḥamawī's *Dictionary of Learned Men* offers a fuller version, attributing it to the poet Muḥammad b. Aḥmad Al-Ṣanawbarī (d. 334/945). When this tale, which begins in Arabic bawdy (*sukhf* and *mujūn*), enters Persian literary expression, it undergoes various transformations but remains faithful to the obscenity of its Arabic precursors. This article explores the ways in which the basic homoerotic tale found in Arabic belles lettres of the tenth century was adapted to meet the literary needs of Persian authors who lived centuries later. The narrative begins as the Arabic story of an interfaith infatuation and evolves into such forms as the homiletics of Sanāʾī of Ghaznī (d. ca. 525/1130–31), the bawdy of Saʿdī of Shiraz (d. 691/1292), and the irony of ʿUbayd-e Zākānī (d. ca. 772/1371).

Readers of the published editions of the *Maqāmāt* are lucky to have the brief outline of the tale that Hamadhānī attributes to Abū Nuwās. The poem does not appear in any of the poet's published works I examined,[1] and Hamadhānī's most influential editor, Muḥammad ʿAbduh, tried to purge the *Maqāmāt* of all its obscenities.[2] The poem is found in the so-called "Satanic Maqāma" (*al-Maqāma al-Iblīsīya*), in which Hamadhānī's narrator, ʿĪsā b. Hishām, relates what happened when he went out looking for an errant camel.

He wanders into a idyllic grove of lofty trees where the presence of a Shaykh takes him by surprise. When the Shaykh asks ʿĪsā what he knows of Arabic poetry, he responds with the standard pre-Islamic canon of Imru' al-Qays, ʿAbīd b. al-Abraṣ, Labīd b. Rabīʿa, and Ṭarafa b. al-ʿAbd, all of whose poems in the *Muʿallaqāt* bemoan the loss of desert abodes or past loves. Hamadhānī does not have his narrator recite any of these poems; presumably they were too well known to need even partial quotation. Unmoved by the standard canon, however, the Shaykh asks ʿĪsā about his own poetry, whereupon the narrator, reciting only the opening line, tries to pass off as his own another *ubi sunt* poem by the invectivist Jarīr b. ʿAṭīya. ʿĪsā readily admits the fraud, but also notes that practically every schoolboy, woman, and literary gathering would know that the poem belongs to Jarīr.

At this point the tenor of the recitation changes dramatically. The *maqāma* lives up to its name when the Shaykh asks ʿĪsā to recite what he knows of the poetry of Abū Nuwās, and ironically, it is only this poem that ʿĪsā quotes in full. Invoking "Abū Nuwās" is pure artifice here; the Shaykh is not testing ʿĪsā's knowledge of the canon anymore. Instead, the Shaykh is changing the rhetorical register of the *Maqāmāt* by slipping into the bawdy world of *sukhf* and *mujūn,* the obscene genre that marked a revolution of sorts in the literature of the time.[3] The poem begins pointedly:

> I will not lament the deserted above
> Nor will I yearn after the drivers of the white camels.[4]

This is to eschew the "days forgotten, when Salma was near" of Imru' al-Qays; the absent "head-ropes or dung, the Chandlers, Bakers and Whitbys all gone" of ʿAbīd b. al-Abraṣ; the desolate "abodes . . . halting place and encampment at Mina" of Labīd b. Rabīʿa; and the "traces yet of Khaula in the stony tract of Thahmad" of Ṭarafa b. al-ʿAbd.[5] What is devilish about this *maqāma* is that "Abū Nuwās" serves as a conduit for the homoerotic lines that follow.

ʿĪsā's Abū Nuwās poem takes place in the aftermath of a debauch during which all but the narrator have become stone drunk. Safe from the prying eyes of "those who would condemn him" (*shūs*), the narrator, styled "Shaykh Satan," goes after his Christian prey, "a gazelle in the full bloom of youth" (*shādin*):

> What a splendid night is that which is past. How delightful it was!
> When the cups took effect upon our scornful brethren;

And a young gazelle whose eye spoke enchantment,
Wearing a Christian's waistband, an ally of the rosary and
Consecration.
I struggled with him for a kiss and the wine was pure and ruddy,
In the garb of a Qāḍī [judge] with the piety of Shaykh Iblīs.[6]

The narrator feigns sleep, and as the boy rests in irresistible disorder, he couches the seduction in Christian terms:

Then he stretched himself on a couch that was finer to me,
In spite of its disordered condition, than the throne of Balqis.
So I made a pilgrimage to his sleeping place before dawn, and
When the sounds of church bells told the matins,
He asked, "Who's that?" I answered, "The priest has come to visit;
And your monastery needs a sacristan's care."
He said, "How vile a man you are, I never in all my life!"
I said, "On the contrary! In no way am I at fault."[7]

This short poem contains the basic literary elements of the tale of homoerotic infatuation. A boy in the full flush of adolescence, seductive yet combative, becomes the pitiless beloved, *le beau garçon sans merci*. He resists a Shaykh's advances and, despite his pious rejection and other factors that distance him from his lover, remains an indelible symbol of forbidden love. The lover, enslaved by his love, is not to blamed but pitied for his pathology. The transformation of vocabulary associated with the boy's faith or occupation into the language of seduction is an important part of the rhetoric of the tale. The pseudo-Abū Nuwās eroticizes emblems of the beloved's Christianity: "Consecration" (*taqdīs*), "wearing a waistband" (*muzannar*), "pilgrimage" (*ziyāra*), "performing the act of a sacristan" (*tashmīs*), etc. The beloved is typically situated in a "monastery" (*dayr*), where his pining lover cannot reach him. Here the lover poses as a priest; in Persian versions of the tale, he actually converts to Christianity, showing the depth and daring (apostasy being severely punished in Islam) of his infatuation.

All of these elements are also present in a more elaborate, prose version of the tale of homoerotic love, found in Yāqūt's *Dictionary of Learned Men* as a coda to the biography of Aḥmad b. Kulayb (d. 426/1035), the Spanish grammarian who was famous for his love of a handsome youth. Adam Mez's mining of the entry on Aḥmad b. Kulayb for evidence of pederasty in Islam ignores the literary aspects of the tale;[8] using it as a window on society is especially risky, considering its provenance. Like the homoerotic tale in the

Maqāmāt, Yāqūt's version comes indirectly, recorded in another work, transmitted by an intermediary poet, and ultimately attributed to another poet, Abū Bakr al-Ṣanawbarī, who died in 334/945.[9] An analysis of the tale shows that it recapitulates and elaborates the structure of Hamadhānī's spare Abū Nuwās poem.

According to al-Ṣanawbarī, there was once a stationer (*warrāq*) named Saʿd, who held a literary salon in his shop in Edessa. Al-Ṣanawbarī attends the salon along with other accomplished Syrian poets who recite poems of "sentimental" value. Also in Edessa at this time is a Christian merchant who has a son named ʿĪsā, "the most attractive of people facially, the most agreeable in stature, and the most delicate in nature and speech."[10] Saʿd the stationer falls in love with the boy and writes love poems to him. His poetry borrows from the tools of his own trade to express the self-sacrifice of his infatuation:

Make my heart an inkwell and my blood the ink;
Here take and notch my bones in place of a pen.[11]

After Saʿd's love for the boy becomes common knowledge, ʿĪsā expresses his desire to join the ministry. His rich father then buys him the position of sacristan in a monastery near the town of Raqqa along the Euphrates. His lover gone, Saʿd abandons his business, and the love poetry he writes to his Christian beloved takes inevitable advantage of the pun contained in the Arabic words "sacristan" (*shammās*) and "sun" (*shams*):

Having compared the sun to the sacristan, they had to admit:
That the *shams* and the *shammās* are one and the same.[12]

The head monk will not let Saʿd communicate with his beloved, and despite repeated, abject pleas remains steadfast in his decision, for he fears the local ruler. In despair, Saʿd closes his shop, burns all his belongings, and lapses into madness. At this point al-Ṣanawbarī encounters him "sitting in the shadow of the monastery, naked, his hair having grown long."[13] After censuring and reproving Saʿd for his obsession, al-Ṣanawbarī agrees to take down his last poem to his beloved. The end of the poem is Saʿd's epitaph, which can be interpreted as a reference to his beloved's Christianity:

And if I die, inscribe on my grave:
A lover who died for the absence of his beloved.
If a single watchman proved the ruin of a life;
What about one with a hundred of them?[14]

The head monk's fear of the local Amīr proves prescient, because when Saʿd dies the Christians are blamed for his death, and only the payment of 100,000 *dirhams* saves ʿĪsā from decapitation. Eventually the rabble of Edessa drive ʿĪsā from his home, and he is said to have found sanctuary in the Samʿān monastery in Aleppo.

In al-Ṣanawbarī's version of the homoerotic tale, the emphasis shifts from the beauty of the beloved to his abject lover. Saʿd is a miserable figure, disheveled, unnerved, and driven insane by his infatuation. He knows that his love is forbidden on two counts—it is both homosexual and heterodox—yet he persists. This impossible love causes him to fall from a position in society that allowed him to patronize eminent poets and run a salon in his shop, to sever his ties to the material world, and to assume the role of the crazed (*majnūn*) lover. Eventually he is a martyr to his infatuation, for he cannot compete with one hundred watchmen.

The Tale in Mystical Persian: Heterodox, Chaste, and Heterosexual

The most famous Persian version of the tale of heterodox infatuation is not homoerotic, but it contains some of the elements found in Arabic versions. It is the story of Shaykh Samʿān (also Sanʿān), told by the twelfth-century poet Farīd al-Dīn ʿAṭṭār in his great mystical epic *The Conference of the Birds.* In a sense, ʿAṭṭār's narrative is the continuation of al-Ṣanawbarī's tale, for if Saʿd had lived he would have followed his beloved sacristan to Samʿān and camped out near the monastery vainly trying to get a message to him. ʿAṭṭār tells the story of a fall from piety caused by hopeless infatuation. His Shaykh Samʿān is, in the beginning, a marvel of learning and erudition, pious and divorced from the world:

> Samʿān was once the first man of his time.
> Whatever praise can be expressed in rhyme
> Belonged to him: for fifty years this sheikh
> Kept Mecca's holy place, and for his sake
> Four hundred pupils entered learning's way.
> He mortified his body night and day,
> Knew theory, practice, mysteries of great age,
> And fifty times had made the Pilgrimage
> He fasted, prayed, observed all sacred laws—
> Astonished saints and clerics thronged his doors.[15]

This overpraise of the saint's piety is an important element in the Persian tale; ʿAṭṭār's paean to the Shaykh's goodness makes his fall even more spectacular.

Returning from one of his numerous pilgrimages, the Shaykh happens to see a Christian girl and is immediately smitten. ʿAṭṭār's description of the girl's beauty contains imagery found in conventional erotic poetry, but when he directs his attention to the Shaykh's infatuation the poem becomes quite polemical:

> Love sacked his heart; the girl's bewitching hair
> Twined round his faith impiety's smooth snare.
> The Shaykh exchanged religion's wealth for shame,
> A hopeless heart submitted to love's fame. . . .
> "I have no faith," he cried. "The heart I gave
> Is useless now; I am the Christian's slave."[16]

When his friends and disciples suggest Islamic pathways that the Shaykh might take toward salvation, he responds by playing on the heresy of his infatuation:

> Another asked: "Where is your rosary?"
> He said: "I fling the beads away from me;
> The Christian's belt is my sole sanctuary!" . . .
> One counselled prayer; he said: "Where is her face
> That I may pray toward that blessèd place?"[17]

Of course, the rosary mentioned here is the Islamic one and the Christian's belt is the *zunnār,* the same waistband worn by the boy in the Abū Nuwās poem. But ʿAṭṭār's tale, unlike Hamadhānī's Abū Nuwās, does not eroticize the habiliments of interfaith infatuation.

Ultimately the Shaykh's infatuation is so exigent that he replaces the Kaʿba with his Christian "idol." His love leads him literally and figuratively to idolatry; because of this, when the Shaykh admits his passion to the girl, she asks him to "bow down before idols, burn the Qur'ān, drink wine, and turn a blind eye on his faith."[18] The Shaykh's apostasy also exacts a heavy worldly cost. He must not only renounce his faith but also provide a bride price of silver and gold, and to make himself worthy of his Christian bride, he must undergo one more indignity aimed at his former faith: he becomes her swineherd.[19] In the end, however, the Shaykh is redeemed. His followers return to the Kaʿba and pray so hard that the Prophet Muḥammad appears to them. This prophetic agency not only cleanses the Shaykh of his impiety, it also causes the Christian girl to see the light and renounce her idolatry.

ʿAṭṭār's version of the tale strips the narrative of its prurient elements. The love between the Shaykh and the girl is heterodox but sterile. There is no eroticism in ʿAṭṭār's description of the infatuation, merely the poetically conventional beauty of a beloved and the abjectness of her heretic lover; the poem's obscenity is in the idolatry that attends apostasy. ʿAṭṭār's purpose was to write a parable (*ḥikāya, tamthīl*) of redemption, in which the *sukhf* and *mujūn* aspects of the Arabic homoerotic tale were replaced by elaborations on the Shaykh's steep fall from grace and the deus ex machina recovery of his faith.

Three Homoerotic Persian Variations: Anti-Ṣūfism, Bawdy, and Travesty

Although there are references to lesbianism in classical Persian, the most fully articulated form of literary homoeroticism in the works of the great Persian writers is unquestionably male. In those rare instances when a poet refers to erotic love between women, it is usually to picture them as freaks of nature wearing leather dildos called *machāchang.*[20] In an even rarer instance, the celebrated mystic poet Mawlānā Jalāl al-Dīn Rūmī uses homoeroticism to present the broad compass of God's creation, which can include sexually passive men and sexually active women. This representation comes in Book 6 of his *Mathnavī* (the "Persian Qur'ān," an epic explanation of the ineffable), in which he develops the theme of "congeniality" (*jinsīyat*). His general theory is that a being endowed by God with a certain disposition will naturally gravitate toward another with the same endowment. Rūmī adduces examples of this gravitation from prophet lore, anecdotes, and his observations of everyday life, e.g., "The reckless man gets a reckless man [as his comrade], because they are congenial in respect of their understanding."[21] His two homoerotic illustrations of congeniality are quintessentially Rumian, for even if such thoughts had occurred to any other mystic poet, he or she would not have used Mawlānā's explicit language to express them:

> Were God to give the man a woman's stripe,
>   He'd bare his hole like a catamite.
> Of woman if He fashions a male's like,
>   She'd fancy females like a rutting dyke.[22]

In both lines, Rūmī uses dysphemisms for homosexuals and their sexual activities. The male is a *mukhannath,* ("sissy," "pansy," or "catamite"), an Arabic term that stigmatizes boys and men who assume the passive role in intercourse,[23] and the female is a *saʿtarī* ("butch" or "dyke"), a term that maligns women who take the initiative in lovemaking. But not all authors are as even-handed as Rūmī in their dispraise of homoeroticism. Any survey of Persian literature on the subject will show that most classical authors burlesque the *saʿtarī,* painting lesbianism in uniformly dull and unflattering hues, and reserve some of their most imaginative eroticism for the love between men and boys.

The provenance of the pederasty found in Iran and the Fertile Crescent has always been a matter of dispute. Herodotus believed that the Persians learned "unnatural lust from the Greeks."[24] Richard Burton's research led him to conclude that pederasty was inevitable in these lands because they fell within what he called the "Sotadic Zone," a band comprising the regions along the northern and southern shores of the Mediterranean and extending eastward to Asia Minor, Mesopotamia, Chaldea, Afghanistan, Sind, and the Punjab and Kashmir.[25] Burton speculated that within these climes "there is a blending of the masculine and feminine temperaments, a crasis which elsewhere occurs only sporadically,"[26] and contradicted Herodotus: "I believe Iran borrowed her pathologic love from the peoples of the Tigris-Euphrates Valley."[27] Iranian writers also place the origins of Persian pedophilia elsewhere. The dean of Persian literary historians, Zabīh Allāh Ṣafā, calls pederasty "the shameful inheritance of a period of moral turpitude which began to contaminate Iran from the fourth and fifth centuries [A.H., tenth and eleventh centuries A.D.], especially from the reign of the [Turkic] slave [kings] and the yellowskin [Sinitic] tribes."[28]

In his tale of homoerotic love, the poet Sanāʾī of Ghaznī upholds the dysphemistic tradition in Persian. Sanāʾī's mystical and homiletic epic *Ḥadīqat al-ḥaqīqa wa-sharīʿat al-ṭarīqa* ("Garden of Truth and Path to Enlightenment") tells of the Khvāja of Herat who, out of necessity, makes love to a young boy. Like Shaykh Samʿān, the Khvāja is a paragon of learning and asceticism:

You've heard about the Khvāja of Herat,
  The Ṣūfī savant skilled in ev'ry art?
Fatigued by concerns of his times and age,
  His learning made him the world's foremost sage.
His wisdom propelled him ten million miles;
  But he was trampled by life's temptations and trials.
Alas, one test had always troubled him—
  The painful tug of his elastic limb.[29]

Sanāʾī's tale marks the emergence of Arabic *sukhf* and *mujūn* in Persian. He devotes some of his best derision to detailing the Khvāja's homosexual coupling:

Not finding shelter he became perturbed;
  The mosque, he reasoned, would be undisturbed.
The mosque was empty as was the mihrab,
  And now he wanted to begin the job.
When he unveiled that hill of silver ore,
  To drive his salmon upstream once more,
The mosque was filled with light as luminous,
  As sparks that fly from coal bituminous.[30]

Before the Khvāja is able to relieve his lust, a devout man (*zāhid*) barges in on him and the boy, and blames the calamitous weather of Herat on their pederasty:

"These sinful ways of yours"—this was his shout—
  "Have ruined all the crops and caused the drought!
In God's own house, how could you act this way?
  Your lamp of faith has lost its brilliant ray.
You so and so, you *hijo de putain,*
  In Islam such an act is judged a stain.
The time of our Apocalypse has come;
  Whose turn is it? The ignorant and dumb!
The people have no awe nor fear of Him;
  Their hearts are domicile to ev'ry whim.
Your wicked ways and wrongs the country stained;
  The land is barren and the sky is drained.
The surface of earth's bereft of greens;
  Our countryfolk have lost their ways and means.
Adultery and pederasty! Why,
  The source of April showers has gone dry!
When perverts use the mihrab for their lust,
  Our age has little choice but to go bust!"[31]

After this speech the Khvāja sidles out of the mosque, but when he takes one last look at his inamorato, he finds that the devout man has taken up his position over the boy and is completing the act. Ironically, it is this hypocrisy that restores Herat to prosperity.

Homoeroticism in Sanāʾī's version of the tale demeans the homosexuality of the Khvāja and then demonstrates the hypocrisy of those who protest it too much. The boy is not defined at all, unlike the *beaux garçons* of the Arabic tales. Sanāʾī's purpose is homiletic; his tale severely condemns homoeroticism but is even harsher when it comes to hypocrisy. Therefore, he exaggerates the *sukhf* and *mujūn* elements of the tale and downplays the humanity of the participants.

Not all Persian authors took Sanāʾī's severe tack. One of the most successful writers of bawdy in the classical period, Saʿdī of Shiraz, retained all the elements of Sanāʾī's homoerotic tale but reworked them into the kind of ribald entertainment found in the *Maqāmāt*. In Saʿdī's tale another super-ascetic falls in love with a wrestler. To introduce his story, the poet culls vocabulary from the inamorato's (*amrad*) profession and, like Hamadhānī's Abū Nuwās, eroticizes it:

> A learned Ṣūfī's heart was once enraptured,
> His reason by the face and ringlets captured.
> Of a well-muscled, power wrestler boy,
> A doe-eyed flirt whose arms could chains destroy.
> For days and days he thought with all his might
> About getting the lad alone one night;
> He groped the boy's apple in hot pursuit,
> To take his turn kissing that musky fruit.
> He wished to get inside the grappler's crotch
> And shoot his arrow to its very notch;
> But the *amrad* was quick-tempered and rough,
> He warned of cat-o'-nine and fisticuff.
> "Never will I permit this shame," he spat.
> "You'll never pin my face onto the mat;
> But if my hugs and kisses will suffice,
> I'm your young man—so come along, be nice."
> The Ṣūfī said, "This pact is fine with me,
> O budding youth, my stately cypress tree;
> I merely want to hold you in my arms,
> And fall down dead before your lofty charms."[32]

The Ṣūfī does not keep his end of the bargain and finds the wrestler's charms so delightful that he decides to share them with the other members of his order:

He brought the boy before his friends and mates,
And passed him on to his associates.
Everybody copped a kiss or two or three,
And probed his navel with proctoscopy;
This one declared his love and devotion,
That one proclaimed his deepest emotion.[33]

Like Sanā'ī's version of the homoerotic tale, Sa'dī's plays on the hypocrisy of Ṣūfīs who are more interested in self-satisfaction than self-denial. The love-starved novices compete so hard for the wrestler's favors that their order nearly disintegrates. They appeal to their superior, the Father Qalandar, and he opines in such a way that harmony is restored and the novitiates can continue to satisfy their cravings in peace:

Turmoil and scandal spread amongst the crowd;
The hubbub reached the sky, it was so loud.
This lasted till their necks were blue and bruised;
From slaps and stones the Order was contused.
They visited the master Qalandar
And told their chief what was going on "thar."
He bent his brow and went deep into thought,
His head now rose and this is what he taught:
"Our Order's poor, we share the food we eat;
One pair of boots is good for twenty feet."
The entire crew approved of what they heard;
To heal their wounds they had the master's word.
They fell prostrate and from all sides lauded;
They sang his praise in poems and applauded.[34]

Sa'dī refreshes the tale by amplifying the prurient elements found in Arabic versions and foregoing the heterodox or doctrinal aspects that 'Aṭṭār and Sanā'ī exploit. His primary purposes are to entertain and to poke gentle fun at outwardly ascetic but inwardly hedonistic Ṣūfīs. Thus the irony of his tale lies not in the fact that the Ṣūfīs can continue their homosexuality because of societal hypocrisy, as in Sanā'ī's version, but in the fact that they must stop: the wrestler boy finally goes through puberty and is disfigured by a beard. The Ṣūfīs forgo their sinful ways not because of some moral authority (Sanā'ī) or divine intervention ('Aṭṭār) but because of the inexorable course of nature:

The wrestler who was never nelsoned to the mat,
  Now had his forehead pinned—and that was that.
The boy took up hashish and bore disgrace,
  Until a beard blackened his rosy face;
He then repented, wishing to go straight,
  Thus the forlorn could do nothing but wait.[35]

In ʿUbayd-e Zākānī's *Rīshnāma* ("Book of the Beard"), the basic elements of the Arabic homoerotic tale—*sukhf* and *mujūn,* heterodoxy, and irony—come together. Zākānī's work is a highly allusive and playful *risāla* (literary essay) that owes a great deal rhetorically to Saʿdī's *Golestān* ("Rose Garden") and Arabic *maqāmāt*. It is a mock treatise on the passage from downy-cheeked boyhood to stubbly adolescence. In this sense, the *Rīshnāma* elaborates the ironic note sounded at the end of Saʿdī's homoerotic tale. Zākānī's admonitory satire is aimed at those *beaux garçons sans merci* who cruelly exult in their beauty as long as it lasts but are devastated when their beards sprout. In Zākānī's version, the main source of bathos is not the infatuated Muslim but the newly bearded Christian inamorato, who, betrayed by nature, must now beg for what he formerly took for granted.

In typical *risāla* fashion, the *Rīshnāma* begins with encomia of God and the Prophet Muḥammad. Like the *maqāmāt,* it has a narrator, a lover pining for his beloved who, thanks to the neutrality of the Persian pronoun, remains of undetermined gender throughout the essay. Suddenly a bearded figure emerges from the wall; he is Rīsh al-Dīn Abū l-Maḥāsin ("the Beard of Faith, Father of all Beauty.")[36] Like the narrator in Hamadhānī's *Maqāmāt,* ʿĪsā b. Hishām, Rīsh al-Dīn delights in mock or ironic appeals to the Qurʾān, *ḥadīth,* and Arabic poetry; he uses these citations to support his pro-whisker position.[37] For example, he appropriates Aaron's complaint "Seize me not by my beard nor by the hair of my head" (Qurʾān 20:94) to justify his own greatness—mere mention in scripture being reason enough to affect grandeur. He fails to give the context: Moses was expressing his anger at Aaron for not calling him when the Jews began to go astray. Rīsh al-Dīn and the lover engage in debate on the importance of the beard until the lover offers the following refutations of beard-hubris:

> When the beard talk had become too long and drawn out, I countered, "I can't agree; your premises are false. First, you say that you are the 'Beard of Faith, the Father of all Beauty.' What does that mean? As they say, '*Beard* is no surname, no honorific.'" He replied,

> "This much you don't know: 'A beard is a beard, to be specific.'" "Second, what you said about inscribing the cheeks of those moon-faced ones with the most delicate hand is also not beyond dispute, because any cheek that you brush up against finds its beauty lined out, as the back-stabbers say,
>
> Your beard has sprouted, and you've lost all your face,
> Better to lose your soul than bear that disgrace.
>
> Third, you said that the Almighty spoke of your greatness in the Glorious Qur'ān; but your greatness is cause for inadequacy. As they say, 'Long on beard, short on brains.' Fourth, you said that your origin is heaven; but this is also unfounded, for the Prophet (prayer and peace be upon him), opined, 'Verily the people of heaven are the hairless, beardless.'"[38]

This dense bilingual wordplay gives way to a series of anecdotes "from the annals of history," which the lover uses to illustrate his horror of the beard. One of these anecdotes is a retelling of the homoerotic tale that translates ʿAṭṭār's Shaykh Samʿān story into Arabic and Persian bawdy.

Zākānī's travesty of the Shaykh Samʿan tale begins appropriately with a pilgrimage *to* the holy places: i.e., in exactly the opposite direction ʿAṭṭār's pilgrim is traveling. The pilgrim stays at a retreat (*dayr*) where

> there was a Christian boy whose speech was like the Messiah Jesus' breath, it brought the dead back to life; and whose cheeks were like the bright hand of Moses, they worked its miracle on his lovers.[39]

Like Samʿān, the pilgrim replaces the rites of the *ḥajj* with his idolatry of the Christian boy and doubts the wisdom of God:

> It took just one unexpected look at the boy for the pilgrim to lose his heart to him, whereupon he recited,
>
> My Christian lover is the Kaʿba of my soul;
> Whence Kaʿba and retreat? Where's the truer goal?
>
> He thought to himself, There is no doubt that these folk are denizens of hell. I am truly perplexed by the wisdom of the Lord and His unbounded Grace, that He would consign one with such a comely face and excellent disposition to the torments of hell. When his caravan got under way, the pilgrim had no choice but to join it, lamenting,

I'm off but regretfully look around
For though I walk, my feet don't touch the ground.

When he stopped to pray, he would recite,

Five times each day this breast toward the Ka'ba prays,
While all its bearings are in church these days.[40]

While the pilgrim visited the holy places, the boy became a man, and the traveler did not recognize him on his way back, for

His moon that once had risen was now down,
His beard that once had molted was now grown.

> On his return trip, the pilgrim stopped at the same retreat where he saw the Christian boy. His beard bedraggled, a Christian's belt draped around his girth, a pressed-felt cap on his head, and a ropy rug on his chest, the boy was herding swine. After the boy respectfully acknowledged him, the pilgrim said, "I don't believe I've had the pleasure." The Christian said, "I am that boy who was in your company the time you first came." The chain of that circumstance jolted the pilgrim.[41]

Again Zākānī's version reverses the Shaykh Sam'ān story: instead of having the lover herding the abominable animal to prove his devotion, the beloved, as a former *beau garçon,* is punished with this demeaning chore.

At the end of Zākānī's homoerotic tale, a mysterious voice is heard. It could be the voice of a being from the unseen world (*'ālam-e ghayb*), a *hātif,* who says, "First we char their faces so that we condemn them to the flames; in the flower of youth they are birds of paradise, but at the end of the day denizens of hell."[42] This is the voice of Iblīs, who punishes the *beaux garçons sans merci* for their pride. His punishment is to blacken their faces with beard, the emblem of their sinful ways, and consign them to the hell of rejection and ridicule.

In Lieu of a Conclusion

In Arabic, homoeroticism has often been associated with the diabolical. As Richard Burton noted in his terminal essay on the Sotadic Zone, legend has it that "the angels, generally supposed to be three, Gabriel, Michael and Raphael, appeared to Lot as beautiful youths, a sore temptation to the sinners, and the godly man's arm was straitened concerning his visitors because he felt unable to protect them from the erotic vagaries of his fellow townsmen."[43] The Prophet Muḥammad is also said to have "damned the effeminate amongst young men and the masculine amongst women."[44] A diabolical obsession is one of the ties that bind the Arabic and Persian versions of the homoerotic tale. The lover in Hamadhānī's *al-Maqāma al-Iblīsīya* appears in the guise of a Qāḍī with the piety of Shaykh Iblīs. In al-Ṣanawbarī's tale, interfaith homoeroticism drives the lover to insanity and eventually to martyrdom. In Sanā'ī's tale, homoeroticism occasions natural calamities like drought and human ones like hypocrisy. Sa'dī's learned Ṣūfī is able to resist every temptation but the lure of an adolescent wrestler; their love proves to be the contagion that nearly causes the downfall of the Ṣūfī's order. In Zākānī's *Rīshnāma,* Iblīs himself appears to punish the sources of temptation with a hormonal vengeance.

There is an interesting symmetry in the demonization of temptation. The homoerotic tradition in Arabic and Persian led to a *beau garçon sans merci* in the same way that Western Romanticism created the analogous *belle dame.*[45] Other similarities invite scrutiny. Octavio Paz noted that in Mathew Gregory Lewis' *Matilda,* "the devil appears in the form of a very beautiful young man, his features overcast with melancholy—as is suitable for a fallen angel of the Miltonic school (with a touch, also, of *Eblis* in *Vathek*)."[46] He stopped with Milton and Beckford but could just as well have followed the idea of demonic love back to the homoeroticism in Arabic belles lettres.

NOTES

1. *Dīwān Abī Nuwās al-Ḥasan b. Hāni' al-Ḥakamī,* Ewald Wagner, ed. (Wiesbaden: F. Steiner, 1958–); *Dīwān Abī Nuwās* (Cairo: al-Maṭba'a al-Ḥamīdīya, 1904 or 05); *Dīwān Abī Nuwās al-Ḥasan b. Hāni',* Aḥmad 'Abd al-Majīd al-Ghazzālī, ed. (Cairo: Maṭba'at Miṣr, 1953); *Dīwān Abī Nuwās* (Beirut: Dār Ṣādir, 1962); and *Dīwān Abī Nuwās al-Ḥasan b. Hāni',* 'Alī Najīb 'Aṭawī, ed. (Beirut: al-Hilāl, 1986).

2. A. F. Kilito, "Le genre 'Séance': une introduction," *Studia Islamica* 43 (1976): p. 32, n. 7, calls 'Abduh's edition an "opération de castration," and James T. Monroe in *The Art of Badī' az-Zamān al-Hamadhānī as Picaresque Narrative* (Beirut: American University Press, 1983), p. 62, notes that censorship has caused some scholars to believe that the work contains one less *maqāma* than it actually does.

3. One of the most serious students of *sukhf* and *mujūn,* Adam Mez, noted this shift in style in his introduction to Muḥammad b. Aḥmad Abū l-Muṭahhar al-Azdī, *Abulḳâsim: ein baghdâder Sittenbild* (Heidelberg: Carl Winter, 1902), p. ix, and in *The Renaissance of Islam,* Salahuddin Khuda Bakhsh and D. S. Margoliouth, trans. (Delhi: Idarah-i Adabiyat, 1979), pp. 249–50.

4. Badī' al-Zamān al-Hamadhānī, *Sharḥ Maqāmāt Badī' al-Zamān al-Hamadhānī,* Muḥammad Muḥyī al-Dīn 'Abd al-Ḥamīd, ed. (Cairo: Maktabat Muḥammad 'Alī Ṣubayḥ,

1962), p. 268; *The Maqāmāt of Badīʿ al-Zamān al-Hamadhānī,* W. J. Prendergast, trans. (London: Luzac, 1915), p. 139.

5. The text of the *Muʿallaqāt* used here is *Sharḥ al-Muʿallaqāt li-l-Zawzanī* (Beirut: Dār Ṣādir, 1962). The translation of Imru' al-Qays's poem is from *Classical Arabic Poetry,* Charles Grenville Tuetey, trans. (London: KPI, 1985); that of ʿAbīd b. al-ʿAbraṣ' is from *Arabic and Persian Poems in English,* Omar S. Pound, trans. (Orono, Maine: University of Maine, 1986); and those of Labīd b. Rabīʿa's and Ṭarafa b. al-ʿAbd's are from *The Seven Odes,* A. J. Arberry, trans. (London: George Allen, 1957).

6. Al-Hamadhānī, *Maqāmāt,* p. 269; trans. p. 139 (modified). To compare a beautiful boy (*ghulām*) to a gazelle (*shādin*) is a common conceit, according to Abū Isḥāq Ibrāhīm b. ʿAlī al-Ḥuṣrī al-Qayrwānī, *Zahr al-ādāb wa-thamr al-albāb,* ʿAlī Muḥammad al-Bajāwī, ed. (Cairo: ʿĪsā al-Bābī al-Ḥalabī, 1970), 2:730.

7. Al-Hamadhānī, *Maqāmāt,* p. 270: trans. p. 139 (modified).

8. Mez, *The Renaissance of Islam,* pp. 359–61. Recently Robert Irwin in *The Arabian Nights: A Companion* ([London: Penguin, 1994], pp. 160–61) has criticized using such anecdotes as "data about Arab sexual practices"; on this point, see also *Suppressed Persian: An Anthology of Forbidden Literature,* translated with notes and an introduction by Paul Sprachman (Costa Mesa, Calif.: Mazda, 1995), pp. l-li.

9. Shihāb al-Dīn b. ʿAbdallāh al-Ḥamawī Yāqūt, *Yaqut's Dictionary of Learned Men,* D. S. Margoliouth, ed. (Leiden: E. J. Brill, 1907–27), 2:23. On the literary uses of "transmission" in the *Maqāmāt,* see Monroe, *The Art of Badīʿ al-Zamān al-Hamadhānī,* pp. 24–27.

10. Yāqūt, *Dictionary,* p. 24.

11. Ibid.

12. Ibid.

13. Ibid., p. 25.

14. Ibid.

15. Farīd al-Dīn Muḥammad ʿAṭṭār Nīshābūrī, *Manṭiq al-Ṭayr,* S. Ṣādiq Gowharīn, ed. (Tehran: Bongāh-e Tarjoma va Nashr-e Ketāb, 1969), p. 67, ll. 1185–1190; *The Conference of the Birds,* Afkham Darbandi and Dick Davis, trans. (New York: Penguin, 1984), p. 57.

16. ʿAṭṭār, *Manṭiq,* pp. 69–70, ll. 1230–1231, 1233, trans. p. 59.

17. Ibid., pp. 71–72, ll. 1271–1272, trans. p. 61.

18. Ibid., p. 75, l. 1343.

19. Shaykh Samʿān is often pictured as a swineherd in illustrated manuscripts of Ṣūfī works; for example, see Annemarie Schimmel, *Mystical Dimensions of Islam* (Chapel Hill, N.C.: University of North Carolina Press, 1975), p. 269.

20. *Machāchang* appears to have been first used this way in a poem attributed to Abū ʿĀsim (fl. 3rd/9th cent.), which is cited in Asadī Ṭūsī's early Persian lexicon *Lughat-e Fors,* Dabīr Sīāqī, ed. (Tehran: Ṭahūrī, 1957), p. 113. Later, Afẓal al-Dīn Badīl b. ʿAlī Khāqānī (b. 515/1121–22) caricatured *saʿtarīs* for their use of leather dildos in *Dīvān,* Sajjādī, ed. (Tehran: Zuvvār, 1338/1959), p. 809. Pūr Bahā of Jām (d. ca. 699/1300) ridiculed *saʿtarīs* for their "oxhide dildos" in Muḥammad b. Badr al-Jājarmī's *Muʾnis al-*

aḥrār fī daqā'iq al-ash'ār, Mīr Ṣāliḥ Ṭabībī, ed. (Tehran: Anjoman-e Āthār-e Millī, 1958–71), 2:910, and 'Ubayd-e Zākānī (*Kullīyāt,* 'Abbās Iqbāl, ed. [Tehran: Zuvvār, 1343/1964], p. 233) noticed a "little lady" (*zanakī*) who had donned a penis made of leather so that she "could fuck like a jackass" (*ke gādanī konad chūn khar-e nar*). *Machāchang* is analogous to the Greek *olisbos;* see Jeffrey Henderson, *The Maculate Muse: Obscene Language in Attic Comedy* (New Haven, Conn.: Yale University Press, 1975), pp. 221–22.

21. Jalāl al-Dīn Rūmī Balkhī, *Mathnawī,* R. A. Nicholson, ed. (Leiden: E. J. Brill; reprint, Tehran: Amīr Kabīr, 1350/1971), 6:1188, l. 2984; *The Mathnawī of Jalālu'ddīn Rūmī,* R. A. Nicholson, ed. and trans. (London: E. J. W. Gibb Memorial, 1977), 3:423.

22. Jalāl al-Dīn Rūmī, *Mathnawī,* 6:1188, ll. 2995–2996. Nicholson (*The Mathnawī,* 3:423) found the language in these verses so objectionable that he translated them into Latin. 'Abd al-Ḥusayn Zarrīnkūb, a contemporary critic and scholar, cites Rūmī's use of the word *sa'tarī* as an example of the profanities he used in his mystical poetry (*Sirr-e Nay* [Tehran: 'Ilmī, 1364/1985], 1:230).

23. *Al-Mukhannath,* the name of a "passionate lover," is translated as "The Impotent" in Abū l-Faraj Muḥammad b. Isḥāq b. Muḥammad al-Nadīm, *al-Fihrist,* Bayard Dodge, ed. and trans. (New York: Columbia University Press, 1970), 2:723. The Arabic term survives in the Omani word *khanīth,* a male transvestite prostitute, which Unni Wikan characterizes as a "third sex"; see *Behind the Veil in Arabia: Women in Oman* (Chicago: University of Chicago Press, 1991), pp. 168–88.

24. Herodotus, *The History of Herodotus,* George Rawlinson, trans. (Chicago: Britannica, 1952), p. 32; I, 135.

25. *The Book of the Thousand Nights and a Night,* Richard Burton, trans. (London: The Burton Club, 1886), 10:179.

26.Ibid., 10:180–81.

27. Ibid., 10:201.

28. Zabīh Allāh Ṣafā, *Tārīkh-e Adabīyāt dar Īrān* (Tehran, 1362/1983), 3:2:1272. Ṣafā's opinion is echoed in a study of Sa'dī's wisdom, *Ḥikmat-e Sa'dī* by Kaykhosrow Hakhāmaneshī (Tehran: Amīr Kabīr, 1977), p. 239: "It appears that Turkic tribesmen of the Oghuz and the Seljuk period popularized this unbalanced fixation, which is, in any event, an unnatural phenomenon and in reality a kind of mental disorder."

29. Abū l-Majd Majdūd b. Ādam Sanā'ī, *Ḥadīqat al-ḥaqīqa wa-sharī'at al-ṭarīqa* (Tehran: Dāneshgāh-e Tehrān, 1359/1980), p. 668.

30. Ibid., p. 668.

31. Ibid., pp. 668–69.

32. Abū 'Abdallāh Musharrif al-Dīn Sa'dī, *Kullīyāt-e Sa'dī,* Muḥammad 'Alī Furūghī and 'Abbās Iqbāl, eds. (Tehran: Iqbāl, 1340/1961), pp. 17–18.

33. Ibid., p. 18.

34. Ibid., pp. 18–19.

35. Ibid., p. 19. Sa'dī's *Golestān* (Book V, *ḥikāyat* 10; pp. 134–35) contains a similar tale, in which the narrator tells of his love for a fetching young boy (*shāhid*) who disappoints him in some way. The narrator warns him not to be so proud, but the boy does

not listen. In time the youth's "Yusof-like good looks suffer and a dusting of down settles on his dimpled chin causing the market of his beauty to become bearish."

36. Sprachman, *Suppressed Persian,* p. 72; trans. p. 65. On the title "Abū l-Maḥāsin" in Arabic, see Abū Manṣūr al-Thaʿālibī, *Kitāb al-Kināya wa-l-taʿrīḍ,* M. Badr al-Dīn al-Naʿsānī al-Ḥalabī, ed. (Cairo: Maṭbaʿat al-Saʿāda, 1908), p. 56.

37. On ironic citation of religious texts in the *maqāma,* see Kilito, "Le genre 'Séance'," pp. 32–33, 38; Monroe, *The Art of Badīʿ az-Zamān al-Hamadhānī,* pp. 20–21.

38. Sprachman, *Suppressed Persian,* p. 67.

39. Ibid., p. 69.

40. Ibid.

41. Ibid., pp. 69–70.

42. Ibid., p. 70.

43. Burton, *The Book of the Thousand Nights and a Night,* 10:193.

44. Quoted in Abū ʿUthmān ʿAmr b. Baḥr al-Jāḥiẓ, *Mufākharat al-jawārī wa-l-ghilmān* (Beirut: Dār al-Makshūf, 1957), p. 22.

45. On this strain of Romanticism, see Mario Paz, *The Romantic Agony,* Angus Davidson, trans. (London: Oxford University Press, 1970), pp. 203–300.

46. Ibid., p. 203.

CHAPTER EIGHT

Intoxication and Immortality: Wine and Associated Imagery in al-Maʿarrī's Garden

Suzanne Pinckney Stetkevych

Preface: Old Wine in a New Bottle

In accepting the editors' request to reprint "Intoxication and Immortality" in *Homoeroticism in Classical Arabic Literature,* I have chosen not to try to redirect, and thereby risk distorting, the original argument. I offer instead a few brief remarks on how the ideas in this article might contribute to the goals of this volume, in particular by helping to carry the study of the *sāqī* beyond gender studies, the poetics of homoeroticism, and Arabic studies into the broader realm of comparative myth and symbol. In the first place, "Intoxication and Immortality" demonstrates that there is an extensive and cohesive iconography of immortality that takes the form of a banquet scene. There the *sāqī,* the wine and its vessels, the singing girl or musician, the pearls, and so forth, contribute to the fuller image while functioning as symbols of immortality in themselves. The homoerotic aspect of the *sāqī* can be quite explicit, quite implicit, or even so deeply latent in some cases as not to function at all.

Having learned how to "read" the *sāqī* as symbol and archetype through his iconographical attendance at what we might term "the banquet of immortality," we may then identify him in related contexts or even when decontextualized. Knowing that the ephebe serving wine is an expression of immortality, of everlasting bliss, we can appreciate his role within the rhetorical strategy of the Qur'ānic message of salvation. At the same time, we can understand why within the broad Arabic cultural context the homoerotic interpretation of the Qur'ānic "immortalized ephebes" is virtually inevitable.

"Intoxication and Immortality: Wine and Associated Imagery in al-Maʿarrī's Garden" was first published in *Critical Pilgrimages: The Arabic Literary Tradition,* F. Malti-Douglas, ed., special issue of *Literature East & West* 25 (1989), pp. 29–48.

Similarly, the iconography of the *sāqī* allows us to identify the Qur'ānic Yūsuf/Joseph with his symbolic double, the youth of Yūsuf's dream who will "serve wine to his lord." This identification is essential to arriving at the true moral and spiritual intent of the Qur'ānic story of Yūsuf. In the Qur'ānic text the homoerotic element is not operative; rather, Yūsuf and the wine-serving youth function in a mythic-symbolic complex that reiterates the moral message of the Qur'ān: that righteousness, choosing the spiritual over the carnal, leads to salvation, i.e., immortality. However, when the figure of Yūsuf is seen outside of the Qur'ānic text, the homoerotic element inherent in the archetype emerges. The beauty of Yūsuf becomes a byword for the homoerotic allure of the graceful ephebe. This association should allow us to pursue this alluring fawn/ephebe/*sāqī* from his Arabic and Qur'ānic contexts to other Middle Eastern cultures in both the ancient and Islamic periods, most immediately to his role as the Joseph/Yūsuf figure in the Hebrew, Persian, and Turkish literary cultures.

The placement of this archetype in a broader comparative context allows us to identify the *sāqī* and Yūsuf with Ganymede and access a rich vein of myth, literature, and art rooted in classical Greek and Latin cultures and reemerging most strikingly in the Renaissance, as well as an extensive body of modern scholarly studies whose materials, methods, and ideas could enrich our understanding of our fawn. Two fairly recent studies are most pertinent to the subject of this present volume: James M. Saslow's *Ganymede in the Renaissance: Homosexuality in Art and Society* (New Haven: Yale University Press, 1986) and Leonard Barkin's *Transhuming Passion: Ganymede and the Erotics of Humanism* (Stanford, Calif.: Stanford University Press, 1991). Conversely, the study of the Middle Eastern *sāqī*-immortal ephebe-Yūsuf complex should add symbolic and mythic resonance to the name of Ganymede.

Intoxication and Immortality: Wine and Associated Imagery in al-Maʿarrī's Garden

Orientalist literary criticism has traditionally relied upon the rhetorical works of the medieval Arab literary critics to guide it in interpreting classical Arabic poetry. It is not surprising then that Orientalist discourse has, to a large degree, limited itself to the realm of rhetoric and has thereby failed to deal with ultimately more important semantic and formal issues. The reason for the rhetorical bent or bias of medieval Arabic literary criticism may well derive from the term *naqd al-shiʿr* itself. For although it is etymologically akin to our term—the Greek *kritikos,* able to discern, is from *krinein,* to separate, distinguish, but further to decide disputes, decide a contest for a prize, judge—the Arabic term seems to have clung more closely to its original sense, that of *naqada al-darāhima* (he examined the pieces of money to pick or separate the good from the bad), so that *naqada al-kalāma* or *al-shiʿra* means "he picked out the faults of the language or the poetry."[1] Thus whereas the Greek term came to encompass an overall judgment of aesthetic merit—the Judgment of Paris comes to mind, or Dionysus judging between Aeschylus and Euripides in Aristophanes' *Frogs*—the Arabic concept, preserving as it were an analogy between a *qaṣīda* and a bag of coins, never entirely went beyond the rhetorical analysis of, for the most part, single verses or images. Thus, for example, when al-Āmidī in his *Muwāzana* (Comparison) attempts to judge between Abū Tammām and al-Buḥturī, it is largely by listing the standard *topoi* of the Arabic *qaṣīda* and comparing examples of it from each of the poets in question.[2] Nor is al-Bāqillānī's sustained analysis of the *Muʿallaqa* (Suspended Ode) of Imru' al-Qays and of the *Lāmīya* (Ode rhymed in *lām*) of al-Buḥturī in his *Iʿjāz al-Qur'ān* (The Inimitability of the Qur'ān) any more than a line-by-line rhetorical fault-finding.[3] Van Gelder's recent attempt at analyzing this situation in his *Beyond the Line: Classical Arabic Literary Critics on the Coherence and Unity of the Poem,* although quite correct in its assessment of the failure of contemporary criticism to produce a convincing argument for poetic unity in the Coleridgean—or any other—sense, is methodologically flawed in that it concludes, as do most Orientalist studies of Arabic poetry based on the classical Arab critics, that since the classical Arab criticism is "atomistic," so too is the poetry.[4] Both the classical critics and those of the moderns who restrict themselves to a similar atomistic approach have failed to address what are perhaps the two most salient features of the classical Arabic poetic corpus and the ones that seem most to demand vindication: the domination, from pre-Islamic times until the beginning of our own century, of the tripartite (and later bipartite) form of the classical *qaṣīda* (ode) consisting of *nasīb* (amatory prelude), *raḥīl* (desert journey), and *madīḥ* (panegyric) or its alternatives[5] and, within that structure, the incessant and seemingly obligatory repetition of the same images, metaphors, and similes. In a series of studies, I have attempted to formulate an explanation of the *qaṣīda* form in terms of ritual or sacrificial paradigms.[6] In the present study, I would like to examine the archetypal aspect of one of the recurrent motifs of classical Arabic literature, that of wine and its associated imagery.

I should furthermore like to propose an experiment in literary-critical method: to approach the Arabic poetic text (*shiʿr*) and the Qur'ānic text, not through the classical Arabic literary critical text, but rather through the

Arabic belles lettres (*adab*) text. In doing so, I hope to elucidate the curious and often antagonistic interdependency between Arabic poetry, especially pre-Islamic, and the foremost Arabic prose work, the Qur'ān. In the first place, the Qur'ān condemns poets, "As for poets, the erring follow them. Do you not see that they wander in every valley and say what they do not do?. . ."[7] (Qur'ān 26:224–226). At the same time, the Qur'ān repeatedly refutes accusations that Muḥammad is a poet rather than a Messenger (21:5, 36:69, 37:36, 52:30, 64:41). When Muḥammad's enemies demand that he produce a sign, or miracle, to prove, as others of God's Messengers have, the divine provenance of his message (21:5), his only proof is their inability to respond to the challenge to produce anything like it (52:30–34). This failure on the part of both the poets and orators to produce a like discourse was then itself taken to be the proof of the miraculous nature of the Qur'ān, what later came to be formulated as the precept of *I'jāz al-Qur'ān* (the inimitability of the Qur'ān).[8] Thus the Qur'ān was ultimately dependent on poetry for the validation or confirmation of its divine provenance:[9] their relationship is the symbiotic one of text to antitext, scripture to antiscripture.[10]

But the relationship does not end there. The Qur'ān is described in sūrat al-Shu'arā' (sūra of the Poets) as being a revelation sent down "in a clear Arabic tongue" (*bi-lisānin 'arabīyin mubīnin*) (Qur'ān 26:195). This was taken to mean the same language that the poets used, with the result that when Qur'ānic passages were found to be obscure, recourse was had to poetic usage: "Abū 'Abbās used to say, 'If you read something in God's Book that you do not understand, then look for it in the poetry of the Arabs, for poetry is the register of the Arabs (*al-shi'r dīwān al-'Arab*).' And if he was asked about something in the Qur'ān, he would recite a verse [of poetry] concerning it."[11]

I intend to demonstrate that their relationship is not merely, as was traditionally claimed, lexical, syntactical, and rhetorical—i.e., that certain Qur'ānic lexical items, syntactical constructions, and rhetorical devices could be known only through pre-Islamic (poetic) usage—but is also, knowing what we know about the metalanguage of poetic images (especially within the limited image lexicon of pre-Islamic poetry), semantic. That is, the imagery of the Qur'ān can be understood (only) through the imagery of the *qaṣīda;* in other words, "in a clear Arabic tongue" refers to the metalanguage of poetic imagery, not just language in the abstract lexical, syntactical, and rhetorical sense.[12] Conversely, I would argue that Arabic poetic imagery, and the role of poetry in Arabo-Islamic culture, can be fully understood only with reference to the Qur'ān. This argument is strengthened by the fact that

Muḥammad was accused of being a poet (*shāʿir*) even though the Qur'ān is not, strictly speaking, poetic in form,[13] and further by the accusation, repeatedly refuted in the Qur'ān, that it was nothing but stories or myths of the ancients (*asāṭīr al-awwalīn*) (Qur'ān 6:25, 8:31, 16:24, etc.)—that is, that the Qur'ān did not strike some of Muḥammad's contemporaries as being entirely novel.

The work I have chosen is the *Risālat al-Ghufrān* (Epistle of Forgiveness) by Abū l-ʿAlā' al-Maʿarrī, the blind poet and littérateur of fifth/eleventh-century Syria.[14] The first part of the *Epistle* consists of an often ironic and satirical journey to an Arabo-Islamic Parnassus. In it the author places his protagonist, his fellow littérateur, the Aleppan Ibn al-Qāriḥ, in the heavenly Garden to discourse and carouse with those of the Arab poets and assorted literati that have been granted salvation.

In the opening fifty or so pages, al-Maʿarrī describes the delights of the Garden. The description focuses largely upon the rivers of wine and strained honey that meander through it, providing the souls of the blessed with a perpetual source of immortal and, it appears, immortalizing refreshment. Al-Maʿarrī's depiction of Paradise proceeds through a sustained series of wine descriptions and drinking (and, to a lesser extent, hunting) scenes from pre-Islamic poetry set in a bed of Qur'ānic paraphrase, allusion, and quotation. It is my contention that the intermingling of Qur'ānic and poetic images in al-Maʿarrī's Garden reveals much about that fifth/eleventh-century Muslim littérateur's perception and interpretation of poetic texts and how and why the Islamic age adopted the pagan pre-Islamic poetic corpus as a cultural and ideological foundation. The explanation of the pre-Islamic wine passages in the *Risālat al-Ghufrān* bears a synecdochic relation to the larger question of the place of pre-Islamic poetry in Arabo-Islamic culture. Conversely, it should provide a better understanding of the mythopoeic dimension of Qur'ānic imagery.

Given the Qur'ānic proscription of wine, the abundance of this drink in the Islamic paradise requires some explanation, and this is what our analysis of al-Maʿarrī's text hopes to provide. In the Qur'ānic passages proscribing wine, it is associated with what are, ultimately, pagan cultic practices: e.g., "O you who believe, verily wine, gambling, idols, and divining arrows are foul deeds of the work of Satan" (5:90; see also 5:91, 2:219). Otherwise, it is associated with the heavenly Garden: "rivers of wine (*khamr*)" flow through the Garden, (47:15) (quoted by al-Maʿarrī below, p. 216); the pious there will be given to drink a "sealed wine" (*raḥīq makhtūm*) (83:22); they will inhabit a "garden of palms and vines (*aʿnāb*)" (2:226); and, in the dream of

Yūsuf's fellow prisoner that he "was pressing grapes (*khamr*)" (12:36), which Yūsuf interprets as meaning "he shall serve wine (*khamr*) to his lord" (12:41), will achieve salvation.

Al-Maʿarrī's *Epistle* is ostensibly the reply to a much shorter epistle that he had received from Ibn al-Qāriḥ.[15] The dominant conceit (through which he proceeds to ridicule the addressee) is his placing Ibn al-Qāriḥ in the Garden of Paradise as a reward for the piety and skill displayed therein:

> In these lines are many words, all of them pleasing to the Creator—Blessed is He. Because of this praise there have been planted in the Garden of Paradise for my lord the great shaykh trees whose fruit is delightful to pluck. Each one of them encompasses all that is between the east and the west in an overspreading shadow. . . . In the shadows of these trees are the immortal youths, some standing, some sitting—for good fortune is gained through forgiveness!—saying . . . "We and these trees are a gift from God to ʿAlī ibn Manṣūr (Ibn al-Qāriḥ). We are concealed from him until the trumpet is sounded on the Day of Judgment."
>
> Through the roots of these trees run rivers that are quickened by the water of life, and al-Kawthar[16] supplies it to every vessel. Whoever drinks a draught of it will never die; he is safe there from passing away. There run there too wide rivulets of milk that are not curdled by the protraction of time and streamlets of the finest sealed wine—Mighty is He who decrees all that is decreed! This is the eternal liquor, not that which is blameworthy and disgraceful. Rather, it is like what ʿAlqama[17] described—and he was lying, for he never did seek pardon: It cures the headache;/Its fever does no harm;/No reeling from it mixes up the mind.
>
> The ladler betakes himself to it with cups of gold and pitchers crafted of crystal, through which the viewer looks at a clear wine. . . .
>
> Into this wine flow rivers of strained honey that was not obtained by bees going forth to blossoms in the early morning, nor secreted in wax, but rather the Almighty and Omnipotent said to it, "Be!" and it was (Qur'ān 2:117, 3:47, etc.), and by His munificence He bestowed potentiality. What a marvelous mead this is! It was never made sour and strong by the Fire.[18] If the feverish drinker made it his aliment for all eternity, he would never be stricken by the pox nor would he ever don the garment of fever. And there is proof of

> all this in what (God) the Exalted has said: "(This is) the likeness of the garden that is promised to the god-fearing: in it are rivers of water that is untainted, and rivers of milk whose taste never sours, rivers of wine delightful to its drinkers and rivers of strained honey, and in it they will partake of every fruit" (Qur'ān 47:15).[19]

Central to our argument is that al-Maʿarrī's rivers of *māʾ al-ḥayawān* (*aqua vitae*), the water of life, and its branches of wine, honey, milk, and fresh water, are described not merely as a delightful reward or refreshment for those whom God has granted life everlasting, but as the *source* of that eternal life, immortalizing as well as immortal. The wine with which the paradisiac rivers flow is the "eternal liquor" (*al-rāḥ al-dāʾima*)—a term that suggests the immortal soul (*al-rūḥ al-dāʾima*)—as distinct from the blameworthy terrestrial beverage. Al-Maʿarrī is careful to distinguish between the earthly, mortal wine that is fatal and condemns its drinker to hell and the heavenly wine that immortalizes the blessed. Furthermore, just as imbibing the heavenly wine is an expression of salvation, so conversely is having one's wine jug broken a metaphor of damnation:

> If ʿAlqama had beheld the heavenly wine jugs, he would have been astounded and dismayed, he would have thought that he had lost his mind. But where would poor ʿAlqama see them, when he is probably in a fire whose boiling water (Qur'ān 56:40–55) avails its drinker nothing? What has become of Ibn ʿAbada and his band? He has perished and his wine jug has been broken! Was it not he who said:
>
> As if their wine jug were a gazelle upon a hill;
> draped with linen, its mouth covered;
>
> White, its keeper sets it in the sunlight,
> its neck is wringed with basil boughs,
> its fragrance fills the air.
>
> A mere glance at these heavenly wine jugs is better than a draught of the daughter of the mortal vine or a sip of any saliva to be found in the abode of treachery.[20]

Whatever the benefits of mortal wine, immortal wine is better. Foregoing the latter to indulge in the former is foolhardy:

> If ʿAdī ibn Zayd[21] had been told about these heavenly wines, he

> would have been distracted from wine and the hunt and would have acknowledged that the jugs of his wine and what he obtained from the drinkers of al-Ḥīra and his boon-companions was a trifle, not worth a weed or a rhinestone. . . . Then as for al-Uqayshir al-Asadī,[22] he was afflicted by excoriation of the skin and was wretched until the thronged Day of Resurrection. He said, and perhaps he will repent when his skin is rent:
>
> There destroyed my inheritance
> and whatever wealth I gained
>
> The clinking of small cups
> against the wine jugs' mouths.
>
> What was he and what was his drink? If he had seen with his own eyes those heavenly wine jugs then he would have been certain that he had been seduced by illusion and delighted in delusion. Likewise Iyās ibn al-Aratt,[23] for if he marveled at the wineskins like geese on the riverbank, nevertheless calamity opened the stingiest of fists for him, until it was as if he had never said: "Their wineskins were like geese resting on the river's edge / their necks curved."[24]

Thus for Abū l-ʿAlāʾ mortal wine is both condemned and condemning because it proffers a false promise of immortality: it is, like the earthly abode of which it is the product, ephemeral, deceptive, and treacherous. Al-Maʿarrī defends the Qurʾānic proscription of mortal wine in seemingly Platonic terms: the heavenly wine is a queen who should not mingle with her subjects, a "metaphysical" form of which the terrestrial form is a sorry or deficient imitation:

> In these rivers are vessels in the form of waterfowl and of landfowl: Some are in the shape of cranes, others resemble sparrows (*makākī*)[25] or are in the form of peacocks or ducks; some swim in the current, while others have alighted on the shore. From their mouths flow drinks as delicate as a mirage. . . . All the poets, both ancient and modern, who have described wine would have testified that the types of drink named after places in the ephemeral abode, such as the wine . . . of Ghazza and Bayt Rās and Filisṭīya possessed of centuries . . . that which was produced in the days of Adam and Seth until the time of the mission of the Prophet Muḥammad, of the fast fermented and the slow, are but lowly subjects and this pure

> draught their queen; it is not proper then for her to mingle with them.[26]

Thus the poets' *false* statements concerning mortal, earthly wine are *true* with reference to immortal, heavenly wine. By this stroke of logic the false pagan descriptions of the beverage proscribed by Islam become the appropriate, even necessary, descriptions of the prescribed immortal liquors. So, for example, al-Maʿarrī uses ʿAlqama's line (above, p. 215) to describe the eternal liquor, a line that is remarkably close to the Qur'ānic description, "it causes no throbbing brows, no intoxication" (56:18), of the liquor served to the denizens of the Garden by the immortal youths. Al-Maʿarrī's Islamic Parnassus consists therefore of the realization or actualization of the pagan poetic image. The Qur'ān thus plays the New Testament, as it were, to the Jāhilī poetic Old Testament, at once abrogating and fulfilling it.

In an intentionally ironic way, al-Maʿarrī constructs a spiritual, paradisiac vision by the concretization of the verbal image: the realization of the metaphor and the identification of the two terms of the simile. So for example, whereas the poet Iyās ibn al-Aratt compares the wineskins to geese on a riverbank, and ʿAlqama likens the wine jug to a gazelle (above, pp. 216 and 217), in al-Maʿarrī's description of the Garden there are vessels in the form of waterfowl and crystal ewers in the form of gazelles. Thus the *Seelenvogel,* the image of the immortal soul as a bird,[27] is made to serve at once as both vessel and symbol of immortality. This leads us to surmise that the gazelle, to which the poet's mistress and the women of her tribe are so constantly compared in classical Arabic poetry, has a similar symbolic connotation.

Al-Maʿarrī's irony tends toward satire when he describes Ibn al-Qāriḥ's attendance at a heavenly *majlis* (assembly) in the words of that most libertine of Jāhilī carousers and womanizers, al-Aʿshā:[28]

> Ibn al-Qāriḥ—May God support knowledge by granting him long life!—is with them, as al-Bakrī (al-Aʿshā) said:
>
> I gave them boughs of basil,
> as I reclined,
> and a light wine,
> its strainer moist.
>
> Since it is strong, they don't come to,
> whether after one drink,
> or after two,
> except to cry

"Bring more!"
The one with wine cups,
pearl drops on his ears,
strives for it,
tucking up his shirttails,
diligent.

An oud hears the jingle
of finger cymbals trilled
by a shift-clad slave girl
and responds.[29]

Into the mouth and mind of his self-righteous protagonist, Ibn al-Qāriḥ, al-Maʿarrī also puts the words of the profligate al-Aʿshā:

> Abū ʿUbayda[30] discourses to them upon the battles of the Arabs and the combats of the knights; and al-Aṣmaʿī[31] recites to them the best poetry of every poet. Their souls take delight in this sport, until they cast their vessels into the rivers of nectar. Then the honey flowing against them fills them exquisitely and those vessels clash until a clatter can be heard that would raise the dead. Then the Shaykh (Ibn al-Qāriḥ)—May God beautify the days by prolonging his life!—says, "Alas for the death of al-Aʿshā Maynūn! How often he hastened a trusty mount! How I wish that he had not been turned back by Quraysh when he was headed for the Prophet (May God bless him and give him peace). I was reminded just now, when these vessels clashed together, of what he said in his poem rhymed in *ḥāʾ*:
>
> Many a wind-cooled wine which, when decanted,
> its bubbles burst like blossoms of wild carrot,
>
> Whose fragrance, like the scent of musk, diffuses,
> the *sāqī* pours when someone calls out 'Quick!'
>
> From merchants' wineskins into a
> large black Ḥīran amphora,
>
> So deep it does not care
> if jug and cup dip into it.
> When its wine foams,
> the froth settles, then disappears.

And when the dipping cup clashes with one side,
it reels about and courses to the other.

Then into it the diligent cup is plunged
and from it the drawer draws a draught.

When the jar is empty, we raise our wineskin,
open up its neck vein,
and it bleeds."[32]

Much to Ibn al-Qāriḥ's surprise, al-Aʿshā himself, now a comely and clear-sighted youth (the name al-Aʿshā means night-blind, weak-sighted), appears in the Garden, having obtained salvation through some pious verse he had written late in life. He is, however, forbidden to drink wine in the hereafter and so contents himself with honey and *aqua vitae*.[33] The message is clear: those who indulge in the false promise of immortality in the ephemeral abode will be denied true immortality in the hereafter.

Later, while hunting among the heavenly herds of gazelle, ostrich, and onager with the pre-Islamic Christian poet ʿAdī ibn Zayd, Ibn al-Qāriḥ comes upon Abū Dhuʾayb al-Hudhalī,[34] whose activities in the afterlife are once again the realization of a poetic image:

> My lord the mighty Shaykh (Ibn al-Qāriḥ) and his companion ʿAdī ride on, when suddenly they come upon a man who is milking a she-camel into a vessel of gold. "Who is this man?" they inquire. "Abū Dhuʾayb al-Hudhalī," he replies. They say, "Long life and happiness! May you never be wretched as long as you live! Do not depart![35] Why are you milking when there are entire rivers of milk? This is sheer idiocy!" "There is no harm in it," he replies. "It simply occurred to me just as it occurred to you to go hunting, and I remembered my lines from the prior age:
>
> Indeed a word from you, if you but knew it,
> is bee-gathered honey mixed in the milk
> of she-camels, newly calved, with their young,
>
> Bringing forth their firstborn,
> their parturition recent,
> mixed with the water of mountain streams.

> So God in His power decreed to me this she-camel newly calved with her young, and He it was who guaranteed these delights. So I arose to milk it as usual and I plan to mix in the honey of bees, which in the Garden are the size of stallions." When he has filled his vessel with milk, the Creator—Great is His glory—creates a beehive of gems, whose swarm of bees grazes on the blossoms. Then Abū Dhu'ayb gathers their honey and without a moment's hesitation mixes it with his milk. Then he says, "Won't you have a drink?" So the two of them gulp from his milking vessel gulps of milk which, if they had been divided among the people of hellfire, they too would have obtained eternal life. Then ʿAdī says, "Praise be to God who guided us to this, for we are not ones to be guided aright, unless God guides us. The messengers of our Lord brought the truth and they were summoned to hear that this Garden has been bequeathed to you because of what you have done" (Qur'ān 7:43).[36]

If we now take stock of the imagery that is found repeatedly in the poetry citations that al-Maʿarrī has employed to describe the Garden, we will find a standard group of *topoi* associated with wine: other liquids—honey, pure rain or spring water, milk, the saliva of the beloved; the slave-girl songstress or musician (*qayna*), the young and comely cupbearer (*sāqī*); the wine jars, skins, cups, and ewers that serve as vessels for the wine; spices or perfumes (notably basil) and pearls. It should be remarked that these *topoi* are closely associated in classical Arabic poetry generally, not just in the examples cited by al-Maʿarrī. Turning then to the Qur'ānic descriptions of the Garden, we find a strikingly similar association of images. Perhaps the fullest description is that of sūrat al-Wāqiʿa (sūra of the Resurrection):

> The victors, the victors! Those are the ones who will be brought near to God in gardens of delight—a multitude of the Ancients and very few from the later generations—reclining on woven couches, face to face. Among them circle immortal youths with goblets and pitchers and a cup of spring water that causes neither throbbing brow nor drunkenness. (In it they shall have) whatever fruits they choose and whatever flesh of fowl they shall desire, and wide-eyed houris, like hidden pearls, as recompense for their deeds. . . . The Companions of the Right—O Companions of the Right!—shall be among thornless lote-trees and acacias, their branches serried,

> outstretched shade and waters outpoured, and abundant fruit, never failing nor forbidden, and raised couches. How perfectly we formed (the houris), then made them virgins, affectionate, of like age, for the Companions of the Right. (Qur'ān 56:10–38)

A similar configuration of images is found in sūrat al-Insān (sūra of Man):

> Surely the pious shall drink from a cup whose mixture is camphor, from a spring at which the servants of God drink, making it gush abundantly forth. God . . . has rewarded them for their patience with a garden and silk. In it they shall recline upon couches . . . and there shall be passed around to them vessels of silver and cups of crystal. . . . In it they shall be given to drink from a cup whose mixture is ginger; in it is a fountain that is named Salsabīl. Immortal youths shall circle among them; when you see them, you think them scattered pearls. When you see them you see bliss and a great kingdom. Upon them shall be green silken raiment and brocade; they will be adorned with silver bracelets, and their Lord shall give them to drink a pure draught. (Qur'ān 76:5–21)

And, too, in sūrat al-Muṭaffifīn (sūra of the Stinters):

> Surely the pious shall be in delight, upon couches, gazing. You will know in their faces the radiance of bliss. They will be given to drink of a sealed wine whose seal is musk—so after that let the strivers strive!—and whose mixture is from Tasnīm, a fountain at which do drink those brought near. (Qur'ān 83:22–28)[37]

It is my contention that these two classes of imagery, poetic and Qur'ānic, spring, like the rivers of Paradise, from a single source and that al-Ma'arrī's mingling of them reveals, upon analysis, much about the meaning of both classical Arabic poetry and the Qur'ān.

If the waters of Kawthar confer immortality, then so too must all the other liquid elements that spring from that source. We can then read the occurrences of water, wine, honey, and milk in classical Arabic (especially pre-Islamic) poetry not as merely descriptive, but as symbols of immortality. The incessantly repeated simile likening the saliva of the poet's mistress to wine, honey, and sweet water is no longer a hackneyed commonplace, but a necessary reiteration of the iconography of fertility and immortality.

Likewise we can propose that the images that constantly accompany wine in both poetry and scripture—the cupbearer; the slave girl making music or song; pearls, spices, and perfumes—serve further to convey the message of immortality. It is of some interest here that the same symbols are found in the Dionysiac cult, which was closely associated with the concept of immortality.[38] The similarity—indeed, identity—of the symbols is most striking in Euripides' *Bacchae:*

> The earth flows with milk, flows with wine,
> Flows with nectar of bees;
> The air is thick with a scent of Syrian myrrh. . . .
> 'Sing for joy,
> Praise Dionysus, god of joy!
> Shout like the Phrygians, sing out the tunes you know,
> While the sacred pure-toned flute
> Vibrates the air with holy merriment. . . .'[39]

Even Euripides' description of Dionysus, the god who bears wine and immortality, is strikingly like that of the *sāqī:* "a fellow with golden hair flowing in scented ringlets, the flush of wine in his face and the charm of Aphrodite in his eyes."[40] It is of note, too, that Dionysus is associated with prophecy: "And this god is a prophet; for the Bacchic ecstacy and frenzy contain a strong element of prophecy. When Dionysus enters in power into a human body, he endows the possessed person with power to foretell the future."[41] A second look at sūrat Yūsuf (Sūra of Joseph) in the Qur'ān (12) reveals the presence of this same conglomerate of symbols: the comely—even effeminate—youth, the boy bearing wine to his lord, and prophecy. Further, the association of Bacchus with the Muses/Poetry on the one hand and Delphi/Prophecy on the other suggests the ambiguous identity of those two forms of inspiration and the Prophet Muḥammad's need definitively to cast off the accusations that he was a poet, or one possessed (*majnūn*). One could perhaps speculate that the Qur'ānic proscription of wine was the result, in part, of the necessity of dissociating Muḥammad and his divine inspiration from other pagan cultic forms.

The *sāqī* (cupbearer) is then the bearer of immortality in its liquid form. He is rooted in the same archetypal substratum as Ganymede, Zeus's *sāqī* and *ghulām* (slave boy) in all the sense of that term. Similarly, the Qur'ānic *al-wildān al-mukhalladūn* (immortalized ephebes) are both possessors and purveyors of eternal youth. *Al-wildān al-mukhalladūn* have long been the subject of snickering among the ribald and indignation among the prudish, and rightly so. For although the sexual role of the *sāqī* in pre-Islamic poetry and *al-wildān al-mukhalladūn* in the Qur'ān is not explicitly stated, it is nonetheless inherent in the archetype, and thus eventually and inevitably generated by that archetype.

It is curious to note in the case of Ganymede that in the earlier classical literature he figures as a comely youth whom Zeus desires, albeit on account of his beauty, to serve as his cupbearer. Zeus makes him immortal—Ganymede is literally a *walad mukhallad*—but inherent in the psychology of a middle-aged man's—or god's (and let us remember that in classical Greek times Zeus is no Apollo or Adonis, but a bulky and bearded deity, a father whose own children have reached adulthood)—chasing after beardless youths is a desperate attempt to preserve his own faded youth. It is perhaps inevitable then that Ganymede, the original Etruscan/Latin form of whose name, Catamitus, gives us our "catamite," should in later literature be explicitly depicted as Zeus's minion.[42] A parallel development occurs in Arabic poetry when in the Islamic period—particularly in Abū Nuwās—the discreet *sāqī* of pre-Islamic poetry is sometimes depicted in explicitly erotic terms.[43] What the example of Ganymede tells us is that the reason for the attendance of the immortal ephebes upon the paradisiac carousers—and here both the snickerers and the prudes have missed the point—is that they are symbols of immortality.

This interpretation of the image of the youthful cupbearer as an expression of immortality reveals the mythopoeic underpinning of yet another Qur'ānic passage, that of Yūsuf interpreting the dreams of his fellow prisoners:

> And there entered the prison with him two youths. Said one of them, 'I dreamed that I was pressing grapes (*khamr*).' Said the other, 'I dreamed that I was carrying on my head bread, that birds were eating of. Tell us the interpretation; we see that thou art of the good-doers.'. . . He said, '. . . Fellow prisoners, as for one of you, he shall pour wine for his lord; as for the other, he shall be crucified, and the birds will eat of his head. The matter is decided whereon you enquire.' (Qur'ān 12:36, 41)

Both the interpretations and the dreams are couched in metaphorical (not to say eucharistic) terms: the image of salvation is that of the *sāqī* serving wine to his lord, a terrestrial version of Ganymede and *al-wildān al-mukhalladūn;* the image of perdition is the well-known *topos* of the poetry of blood vengeance: the vultures devouring the unburied corpses of the enemy.[44] Furthermore, in light of Yūsuf's dilemma with his master's wife, we can venture a further interpretation of his fellow prisoners: Inasmuch as wine symbolizes the spirit and bread the flesh, the youth pressing grapes symbolizes loyalty or obedience to his lord or Lord, and hence salvation, whereas the baker and his bread symbolize yielding to carnal desire and thus, perdition.

It should be remarked here that bread and wine as the expression of the body/soul dialectic is a firmly entrenched Mediterranean symbol. In the Bacchic cult it is expressed as the Demeter/Dionysus dialectic. Euripides writes:

> There are two powers, young man, which are supreme in human affairs: first, the goddess Demeter; she is the Earth—call her by what name you will; and she supplies mankind with solid food. Second, Dionysus the son of Semele; the blessing he provides is the counterpart of the blessing of bread; he discovered and bestowed on men the service of drink, the juice that streams from the vine-clusters. . . . Dionysus, himself a god, is poured out in offering to the gods.[45]

This should serve further to remind us then that in Christian doctrine, the dual nature of the eucharist is the expression of the dual nature of Christ—man/bread and god/wine—and it is precisely this dual nature that distinguishes the Christian from the Bacchic myth and cult.[46]

Al-ḥūr al-ʿīn, the fair-skinned, dark-eyed damsels[47] of the Garden along with their poetic counterparts, the *qiyān* (sg. *qayna,* singing slave girls or musicians), are likewise expressions of the immortal soul. Abū l-ʿAlāʾ introduces them in a comic and, at first glance, curious manner:

> Then a gaggle of geese of the Garden passes by, and it is not long before they alight at this very meadow and stop as though awaiting orders. It is in the nature of the fowl of the garden to speak, so he says to them, "What do you want?" "We were inspired to drop into this meadow," they reply, "so that we might sing to those who are drinking here." Then he says, "By the blessing of God Almighty!" Then they shake themselves and become maidens with swelling breasts, trailing the embroidered gowns of the Garden. In their hands are lutes and every sort of musical instrument that might be desired. He is amazed at this, and well he might be—though this is nothing unusual for the power of God—Great is His majesty, mighty is His word. . . . Then (Ibn al-Qāriḥ) says to one of them,

> in order to test them, "sing for me the poem of Abū Umāma (al-Nābigha al-Dhubyānī)[48] . . .
>
> Is there of the people of Mayya someone
> going forth in the evening or at morn, speedy,
> with travel provisions, or without?
>
> in the first heavy mode." Then she played it and sang it in a way that delighted the listener and penetrated his limbs. If an idol graven of stone or a tambourine hewn at the carpenter's shop had heard this voice, it would have danced.[49]

Of note in the context of our argument is the description of music much in the same terms as wine: it delights and causes the limbs to tingle; it brings dumb stone to life. Abū l-ʿAlā''s comic transformation of geese to maidens rests ultimately on the identification of the *qayna* and houri with the *Seelenvogel.* The bird as the symbol of the soul is known to us in forms as divergent as the Holy Spirit and Swan Lake. In Arabic culture it often takes less lyric forms, notably the unavenged soul that takes the form of an owl (*hāma*) and cries for a draught of blood, or, as I have argued in two recent studies, the vultures that feast on the enemy dead in the poetry of blood vengeance.[50] Still, in one case at least it is thoroughly lyrical and combines with a striking intensity the symbols of the immortal soul that we have been discussing here: wine, bird, song, spices, and, conversely, the symbols of death and perdition. I am referring of course to the two closing lines of the *Muʿallaqa* of Imru' al-Qays:

> As if the songbirds of the valley in the early morn
> had had a morning draught of the finest strong spiced wine,
>
> As if the drowned beasts on its far sides at evening
> were wild onions' plucked-out bulbs.[51]

Like the immortal youths, *al-ḥūr al-ʿīn* have given rise to some consternation. This is largely due to the apparently contradictory description of them as being at once *abkār* (virgins) and *urub,* the plural of *arūb,* which means a woman who is affectionate to her husband (Qur'ān 68:36–38). According to al-Ṭabarī's commentary, this passage refers to God's transforming old pussy-eyed, bleary-eyed mortal women into nubile, clear-eyed heavenly consorts for saved mortal men. The point is not so much that they remain virgins in the Garden, but that having borne children and grown old on earth, they have their youth and virginity restored.[52] Ibn Kathīr, in his commentary, provides another interpretation, that the houris have their virginity restored after each encounter[53]—there is no childbirth in the Garden. The implications of this statement are far-reaching and particularly pertinent to understanding why what is illicit on earth becomes licit in the Garden: immorality=immortality. In this world, man is obligated to perpetuate himself by sexual reproduction; this is precisely what is meant by the Islamic prohibition of monkery. Licit sex is that which is sanctioned by marriage for the express purpose of propagation of the species. Illicit sex is that which for social and biological reasons is nonproductive. In the afterlife, however, immortality renders reproduction redundant. This too is the logic behind the Islamic absolute denial of offspring to Allah: paternity and immortality are incompatible. However, that which is illicit on earth because it distracts the mortal from his obligation is unobjectionable in the Garden. The delights of the Garden are thus the immature and carefree—or even, as Freud put it, "perverse, polymorphous"—ones of youth.

The drinking scene then, whether in the pre-Islamic *qaṣīda* of al-Aʿshā or in the Qur'ānic depictions of Paradise, is not descriptive but iconic, consisting of the archetypal symbols of eternal youth and life everlasting. The Olympian deity, the Bacchic celebrant, the bedouin carouser, the saved soul of the true Muslim express their common aspiration in shared symbols: the wine, the spice, the bird, the comely cupbearer, the singing girl. It is not surprising then that the Ṣūfī poets, when attempting to describe the dissolution of the mortal into the immortal, should have chosen to use these same symbols.[54]

Let us examine in more stylistic terms what al-Maʿarrī has done. His text is an interweaving of Qur'ānic paraphrase, poetic quotation, and Qur'ānic quotation, to the extent that the poetic and Qur'ānic almost seem to merge. This constitutes a radical deconstruction of the textual hierarchical barrier that dominates Arabo-Islamic literary construction and perception: the absolute distinction between poetry and the Qur'ān. Typically we find, as for example in Ibn al-Muʿtazz's *Kitāb al-Badīʿ* (Book of the New Style), citations neatly grouped by category. Thus we find under the heading of metaphor (*istiʿāra*) examples from the Qur'ān, the *ḥadīth* of the Prophet, the Companions and other *bulaghā'* (eloquent speakers)—often bedouin, the poetry of the Ancients, and finally, the poetry of the Moderns.[55] In al-Bāqillānī we find the same order in the discussion of *badīʿ* (rhetorical devices): the Qur'ān, the *ḥadīth* of the Prophet, the Companions and other *bulaghā'*, then the poets, starting with Imru' al-Qays and ending with Abū Tammām.[56] The impenetrable barrier of medieval criticism has been replaced in al-Maʿarrī's

Garden by a permeable membrane, as it were, with images like molecules making their way across—or even an undifferentiated plasma.

The conceptual safeguard of this hierarchy is the precept of *Iʿjāz al-Qurʾān,* the inimitability of the Qurʾān, its absolute superiority to all other poetry or prose. Although the precise nature of this *iʿjāz* was not at first clearly defined, by the fourth Islamic century (as in al-Rummānī [d. 384/994], al-Khaṭṭābī [d. 386/996], and al-Bāqillānī [d. 403/1013]) it was taken to be rhetorical or stylistic: the Qurʾān contained figures of speech of a purity and beauty unmatchable by mortal speech, whether poetry or prose.[57] As Von Grunebaum puts it: "It was the contribution of the 10th century to insist on the formal or rhetorical uniqueness of the Koran to such an extent that it became part and parcel of the theological argument for the Book's supernatural character."[58] Or in Van Gelder's words: "as a result of al-Rummānī's and al-Bāqillānī's efforts the dogma of the stylistic superiority of the Koran became an established fact and the study of style (*balāgha* or *badīʿ*) was often justified by, or even equated with, the study of Koranic style."[59]

It is this precept that al-Maʿarrī, at first glance, seems to be making light of.[60] By freely mixing the poetic and the Qurʾānic, he catches the reader off guard. No longer reinforced by the arbitrary isolation and hierarchization, the doctrinal difference between the two is not immediately evident. Al-Aʿshā's carousing scene mingles freely with Qurʾānic paraphrase and even quotation—as when the pre-Islamic Christian poet ʿAdī ibn Zayd spouts the Qurʾān (above, p. 221). In aesthetic—that is, stylistic and rhetorical—terms, the Qurʾānic superiority is nowhere evident in al-Maʿarrī's text. Rather, I would argue that for al-Maʿarrī, *Iʿjāz al-Qurʾān* is an ontological—not rhetorical—quality: the word of God is absolutely true both now and in the hereafter, whereas poetry, as he repeatedly states, is false, mendacious, and deceiving in this world, a fact rendered even more emphatic by poetry's truth in the hereafter—this is analogous to the contrast between earthly and heavenly wine. We should note in passing that al-Maʿarrī's treatment of poetry in the afterlife amounts to a play on the much-disputed literary dictum, *aḥsan al-shiʿr akdhabuhu* (the best poetry is the most mendacious), or is it rather *aḥsan al-shiʿr aṣdaquhu* (the best poetry is the most veracious)?[61] However much of a dilemma this presented to traditional literary criticism, the contradiction is resolved in al-Maʿarrī's Garden: the false mortal image becomes, by the grace of God, the true immortal one—again according to the immorality/immortality dialectic. Thus al-Maʿarrī ultimately makes the Qurʾānic text absolutely distinct from the poetic—not in its images, *topoi,* or tropes, but in its utter veracity, its being above the immorality/immortality dialectic.

NOTES

1. Edward William Lane, *An Arabic-English Lexicon,* 8 vols. (New York: Frederick Ungar Publishing, 1955), s. v. n-q-d.

2. Abū Qāsim al-Ḥasan b. Bishr al-Āmidī, *al-Muwāzana bayn shiʿr Abī Tammām wa-l-Buḥturī,* Aḥmad Ṣaqr, ed., 2 vols. (Cairo: Dār al-Maʿārif, 1961), 1:388 ff., 2.

3. Abū Bakr Muḥammad b. al-Ṭayyib al-Bāqillānī, *Iʿjāz al-Qurʾān,* Aḥmad Ṣaqr, ed. (Cairo: Dār al-Maʿārif, 1963), pp. 219–40. For a translation see Gustave E. von Grunebaum, *A Tenth-Century Document of Arabic Literary Theory and Criticism: The Sections on Poetry of al-Bāqillānī's Iʿjāz al-Qurʾān* (Chicago: University of Chicago Press, n.d.).

4. G. J. H. Van Gelder, *Beyond the Line: Classical Arabic Literary Critics on the Coherence and Unity of the Poem* (Leiden: E. J. Brill, 1982).

5. A thorough descriptive study of the parts of the classical Arabic *qaṣīda* and the motifs proper to them is Renate Jacobi's *Studien zur Poetik der altarabischen Qaside* (Wiesbaden: F. Steiner, 1971).

6. Suzanne Pinckney Stetkevych, "Structuralist Interpretations of pre-Islamic Poetry: Critique and New Directions," *Journal of Near Eastern Studies* 42 (1983): 85–107; "Al-Qaṣīda al-ʿarabīya wa-ṭuqūs al-ʿubūr," *Majallat Majmaʿ al-Lugha al-ʿArabīya bi-Dimashq* 60 (1985): 55–85; "The Rithāʾ of Taʾabbaṭa Sharran: A Study of Blood Vengeance in Early Arabic Poetry," *Journal of Semitic Studies* 31 (1986): 28–45; "Ritual and Sacrificial Elements in the Poetry of Blood-Vengeance: Two Poems by Durayd b. al-Ṣimmah and Muhalhil ibn Rabīʿah," *Journal of Near Eastern Studies* 45 (1986): 31–43. More recently, see Suzanne Pinckney Stetkevych, *The Mute Immortals Speak: Pre-Islamic Poetry and the Poetics of Ritual* (Ithaca, N.Y.: Cornell University Press, 1993) and "Pre-Islamic Panegyric and the Poetics of Redemption," in Suzanne Pinckney Stetkevych, ed., *Reorientations: Arabic and Persian Poetry* (Bloomington, Ind.: Indiana University Press, 1994), pp. 1–57.

7. Qurʾānic translations are based on A. J. Arberry's *The Koran Interpreted* (London: Allen & Unwin, 1955). On these verses and the exegetical controversy surrounding them, see Irfan Shahid's "Another Contribution to Koranic Exegesis: The Sūra of the Poets (XXVI)," *Journal of Arabic Literature* 14 (1985): 1–21. Of particular interest to the discussion at hand is his interpretation of verse 226, "They say what they do not do," as referring to the problem of *taḥaddī/iʿjāz* (Muḥammad's challenge to the poets to produce a Qurʾān-like discourse and their inability to do so), pp. 8–12.

8. Al-Bāqillānī, *Iʿjāz al-Qurʾān,* pp. 8–15, 19–29; von Grunebaum, *A Tenth-Century Document,* Introduction, pp. xiii-xxii; Van Gelder, *Beyond the Line,* pp. 5–9. G. E. von Grunebaum in *The Encyclopaedia of Islam,* 2nd ed., 7 vols. (Leiden: E. J. Brill, 1960–), s. v. Iʿdjāz.

9. Al-Bāqillānī, *Iʿjāz al-Qurʾān,* pp. 8–15; Ibn Rashīq al-Qayrawānī, *al-ʿUmda fī maḥāsin al-shiʿr wa-ādābihi wa-naqdihi,* Muḥammad Muḥyī al-Dīn ʿAbd al-Ḥamīd, ed., 2 vols. (Beirut: Dār al-Jīl, 1972), 1:21.

10. On the relationship of the Qurʾān as text to poetry as antitext, see Jaroslav Stet-

kevych, "Arabic Hermeneutic Terminology: Paradox and the Production of Meaning," *Journal of Near Eastern Studies* 48 (1989): 84–87, and Suzanne Pinckney Stetkevych, "Sarah and the Hyena: Laughter, Menstruation, and the Genesis of a Double-Entendre," *History of Religions* 35(5): 13–41.

11. Ibn Rashīq, *ʿUmda,* 1:30.

12. For an example of the resonance between poetic and Qur'ānic imagery, see my discussion of the abandoned encampment (*aṭlāl*) in S. Stetkevych, "Ṭuqūs al-ʿubūr," pp. 61–65.

13. Ibn Rashīq considers that, in terms of form, the Qur'ān is neither poetry nor prose/oratory: *ʿUmda,* 1:21.

14. Abū l-ʿAlā' al-Maʿarrī, *Risālat al-Ghufrān,* Bint al-Shāṭi' (ʿĀ'isha ʿAbd al-Raḥmān), ed. (Cairo: Dār al-Maʿārif, 7th printing, 1977). On al-Maʿarrī (363–449/973–1058) see Pieter Smoor in *The Encyclopaedia of Islam,* 2nd ed., s. v. al-Maʿarrī.

15. The text of Ibn al-Qāriḥ's Epistle is included in Bint al-Shāṭi''s edition of *Risālat al-Ghufrān,* pp. 21–68.

16. Al-Ṭabarī recounts the following in his commentary on sūrat al-Kawthar: al-Kawthar "is a river in the heavenly Garden whose two banks are of gold and silver; it flows on a bed of pearl and emerald; its water is whiter than milk and sweeter than honey," and again, "its mud is more fragrant than musk," "there come to drink at it birds whose necks are like those of sacrificial camels." Al-Kawthar is also taken to mean simply "plenty, abundance." Abū Jaʿfar Muḥammad b. Jarīr al-Ṭabarī, *Jāmiʿ al-bayān ʿan ta'wīl al-Qur'ān,* 30 vols. (Cairo: Muṣṭafā l-Bābī al-Ḥalabī, 3rd printing, 1968), 30:320–25. It should be remarked here that the material contained in the Qur'ānic commentaries appears to be a major source for al-Maʿarrī's fleshing out of the Qur'ānic and poetic texts.

17. ʿAlqama b. ʿAbada, a pre-Islamic poet of the Christian tribe of Tamīm; see Fuat Sezgin, *Geschichte des arabischen Schrifttums,* 9 vols. (Leiden: E. J. Brill, 1967–), 2:120–22.

18. Al-Maʿarrī puns here on *nār*—both fire and hellfire—thus describing the wine as neither decocted nor infernal.

19. Al-Maʿarrī, *Risālat al-Ghufrān,* pp. 140–43, 153. All translations from *Risālat al-Ghufrān* are my own.

20. Ibid., pp. 145–46.

21. ʿAdī b. Zayd al-ʿIbādī, pre-Islamic poet from the Christian tribe of Tamīm. According to the *Kitāb al-Aghānī* (Book of Songs) he was a court poet and the first Arabic-writing secretary at the Sasanid court at Ctesiphon. See Sezgin, *Geschichte,* 2:178–79.

22. Al-Mughīra b. ʿAbdallāh Abū Muʿriḍ al-Asadī, d. 50/699. He was given the sobriquet al-Uqayshir ("the little peeled one," from *qashara,* to peel), upon which al-Maʿarrī puns, because of his reddish complexion. See ibid., 2:326–27.

23. Iyās b. Khālid al-Ṭā'ī al-Aratt, one of the poets represented in the *Ḥamāsa* of Abū Tammām. See Bint al-Shāṭi''s note in al-Maʿarrī, *Risālat al-Ghufrān,* p. 148.

24. Ibid., pp. 147–48.

25. Al-Maʿarrī puns on *makākī,* at once drinking vessels (plural of *makkāk*) and a kind

of bird (plural of *mukkā'*). Muḥammad b. Mukarram Ibn Manẓūr, *Lisān al-ʿArab* (Beirut: Dār Ṣādir, 1965), s. v., m-k-k.

26. Al-Maʿarrī, *Risālat al-Ghufrān,* pp. 149–50.

27. On the *Seelenvogel* in the Arab world see Ignaz Goldziher, "Der Seelenvogel im islamischen Volksglauben," in *Gesammelte Schriften,* Joseph Desomogyi, ed. (Hildesheim: Georg Olms Verlag, 1970), 4:403–6; Th. Emil Homerin, "Echoes of a Thirsty Owl," *Journal of Near Eastern Studies* 44 (1985): 165–84; S. Stetkevych, "The Rithā' of Ta'abbaṭa Sharran," and *Mute Immortals,* pp. 67–70.

28. Maymūn b. Qays al-Aʿshā, d. 5/625 or 8–9/629–30. A monotheist of Christian outlook. It is said that he was on his way to the Prophet Muḥammad to convert to Islam when he was turned back by the hostile Quraysh. See Sezgin, *Geschichte,* 2:130–32.

29. Al-Maʿarrī, *Risālat al-Ghufrān,* pp. 171–72. A full translation of this poem, with introduction, appears in Michael A. Sells, *Desert Tracings: Six Classic Arabian Odes* (Middletown, Conn.: Wesleyan University Press, 1989), pp. 57–66.

30. Maʿmar b. al-Muthannā Abū ʿUbayda, d. between 207/822 and 213/828. A leading philologist of the Baṣran school who played a major role in the transmission and explication of ancient Arabic poetry. See Sezgin, *Geschichte,* 8:67–71.

31. Abū Saʿīd ʿAbd al-Malik b. Qurayb al-Bāhilī al-Aṣmaʿī, d. 213/828. A great transmitter of poetry and *akhbār* (biographical lore) of the Baṣran school and archrival of Abū ʿUbayda. See ibid., 8:71–76.

32. Al-Maʿarrī, *Risālat al-Ghufrān,* 173–174.

33. Ibid., pp. 180–81.

34. Abū Dhu'ayb al-Hudhalī, a younger contemporary of Muḥammad who converted to Islam along with his tribe in the year 9/630. He is the foremost poet of the only extant tribal anthology (*Dīwān al-Hudhalīyīn*), d. 26/647. See Sezgin, *Geschichte,* 2:255–56.

35. Al-Maʿarrī parodies the oft-repeated plea of the Arabic elegy apostrophizing the dead, "Do not depart (*lā tabʿud*)!" See S. Stetkevych, *Mute Immortals,* pp. 168–71.

36. Al-Maʿarrī, *Risālat al-Ghufrān,* pp. 199–200.

37. Also see Qur'ān 43:71 and 88:14.

38. "Dionysus" article, *Oxford Classical Dictionary,* 2nd ed., N. G. L. Hammond and H. H. Scullard, eds. (Oxford: Clarendon Press, 1970).

39. Euripides, *The Bacchae and Other Plays,* Philip Vellacott, trans. (Baltimore, Md.: Penguin Books, 1954), p. 186.

40. Ibid., p. 188.

41. Ibid., p. 190; Walter F. Otto, *Dionysus: Myth and Cult,* Robert B. Palmer, trans. (Dallas, Tex.: Spring Publications, 1981), pp. 143–51.

42. "Ganymedes" article, *Oxford Classical Dictionary.*

43. See, for example, al-Maʿarrī, *Risālat al-Ghufrān,* pp. 309–10. In the *Dīwān* of Abū Nuwās, see pp. 94, 812, 921, 923. Abū Nuwās, *Dīwān Abī Nuwās bi-riwāyat al-Ṣūlī,* Bahjat ʿAbd al-Ghafūr al-Ḥadīthī, ed. (Baghdad: Dār al-Risāla li-l-Ṭibāʿa, 1980).

44. See S. Stetkevych, "The Rithā' of Ta'abbaṭa Sharran," and "Ritual and Sacrificial Elements."

45. Euripides, *Bacchae,* pp. 189–90.

46. See ibid., p. 182.

47. Although Arab philologists define *ḥūr* (houri), sg. *aḥwar/ḥawrā'*, as having eyes with the black and white sharply contrasted, the constant use of this epithet for nubile maids suggests the Greek *houraios* (in the bloom of youth), especially in the phrase *houraios gamōn* (nubile, marriageable). Lane, *An Arabic-English Lexicon,* and George Liddell, *A Greek-English Lexicon* (Oxford: Clarendon Press, 1940), s. vv.

48. Ziyād b. Muʿāwiya, known as al-Nābigha al-Dhubyānī, court poet first to the Lakhmid and then the Ghassanid pre-Islamic dynasties, d. in or after 602 A.D.; see Sezgin, *Geschichte,* 2:110–13.

49. Al-Maʿarrī, *Risālat al-Ghufrān,* pp. 212–13.

50. See above, note 27.

51. Abū ʿAbdallāh al-Ḥusayn b. Aḥmad al-Zawzanī, *Sharḥ al-Muʿallaqāt al-sabʿ* (Beirut: Dār Ṣādir, 1963), p. 41.

52. Al-Ṭabarī, *Jāmiʿ al-bayān,* 27:184–89.

53. Ismāʿīl b. ʿUmar Ibn Kathīr, *Tafsīr al-Qur'ān al-ʿaẓīm,* 7 vols. (Beirut: Dār al-Andalus, 1966), 6:523–29.

54. See, for example, the *Mīmīya* (Ode in *mīm*) of the mystical poet Ibn al-Fāriḍ (d. 632/1235); Arabic text and translation: A. J. Arberry, *Arabic Poetry: A Primer for Students* (Cambridge: Cambridge University Press, 1965), pp. 126–33.

55. ʿAbdallāh Ibn al-Muʿtazz, *Kitāb al-Badīʿ,* Ignatius Kratchkovsky, ed., Gibb Memorial Series, vol. 10 (London: Luzac & Co., 1935), pp. 3–24.

56. Al-Bāqillānī, *Iʿjāz al-Qur'ān,* pp. 66–70; Von Grunebaum, *Tenth-Century Document,* pp. 1–7.

57. Van Gelder, *Beyond the Line,* pp. 5–6; Von Grunebaum, *Tenth-Century Document,* p. xvii.

58. Ibid., p. xvii.

59. Van Gelder, *Beyond the Line,* p. 6.

60. That al-Maʿarrī had this issue in mind is demonstrated by the *double entendre* of the title of his commentary on the poetry of al-Mutanabbī (a sobriquet that means "the would-be prophet"), sc. *Muʿjiz Aḥmad* (The Miracle of Aḥmad), Aḥmad being both the name of the poet and a variant of the name Muḥammad often applied to the Prophet himself. Furthermore, it is said that al-Maʿarrī attempted to imitate the style of the Qur'ān. See Smoor, "al-Maʿarrī."

61. This issue has been exhaustively treated by J. Christoph Bürgel in his "Die beste Dichtung ist die lügenreichste. Wesen und Bedeutung eines literarischen Streites des arabischen Mittelalters im Lichte komparatistischer Betrachtung," *Oriens* 23 (1974): 7–102.

INDEX